# Capital in the Nineteenth Century

# NBER Series on Long-Term Factors in Economic Development

## A National Bureau of Economic Research Series

EDITED BY CLAUDIA GOLDIN

*Also in the series*

*Claudia Goldin*
UNDERSTANDING THE GENDER GAP:
AN ECONOMIC HISTORY OF AMERICAN
WOMEN (OXFORD UNIVERSITY PRESS,
1990)

*Roderick Floud, Kenneth Wachter,
and Annabel Gregory*
HEIGHT, HEALTH AND HISTORY: NUTRITIONAL
STATUS IN THE UNITED KINGDOM, 1750–1980
(CAMBRIDGE UNIVERSITY PRESS, 1990)

*Robert A. Margo*
RACE AND SCHOOLING IN THE SOUTH, 1880–
1950: AN ECONOMIC HISTORY (UNIVERSITY OF
CHICAGO PRESS, 1990)

*Samuel H. Preston and Michael R. Haines*
FATAL YEARS: CHILD MORTALITY IN LATE
NINETEENTH-CENTURY AMERICA (PRINCETON
UNIVERSITY PRESS, 1991)

*Barry Eichengreen*
GOLDEN FETTERS: THE GOLD STANDARD AND
THE GREAT DEPRESSION, 1919–1939 (OXFORD
UNIVERSITY PRESS, 1992)

*Ronald N. Johnson and
Gary D. Libecap*
THE FEDERAL CIVIL SERVICE SYSTEM AND THE
PROBLEM OF BUREAUCRACY: THE ECONOMICS
AND POLITICS OF INSTITUTIONAL CHANGE
(UNIVERSITY OF CHICAGO PRESS, 1994)

*Naomi R. Lamoreaux*
INSIDER LENDING: BANKS, PERSONAL
CONNECTIONS, AND ECONOMIC DEVELOPMENT
IN INDUSTRIAL NEW ENGLAND (CAMBRIDGE
UNIVERSITY PRESS, 1994)

*Lance E. Davis, Robert E. Gallman,
and Karin Gleiter*
IN PURSUIT OF LEVIATHAN: TECHNOLOGY,
INSTITUTIONS, PRODUCTIVITY, AND PROFITS IN
AMERICAN WHALING, 1816–1906 (UNIVERSITY
OF CHICAGO PRESS, 1997)

*Dora L. Costa*
THE EVOLUTION OF RETIREMENT: AN
AMERICAN ECONOMIC HISTORY, 1880–1990
(UNIVERSITY OF CHICAGO PRESS, 1998)

*Joseph P. Ferrie*
YANKEYS NOW: IMMIGRANTS IN THE
ANTEBELLUM U.S., 1840–1860 (OXFORD
UNIVERSITY PRESS, 1999)

*Robert A. Margo*
WAGES AND LABOR MARKETS IN THE UNITED
STATES, 1820–1860 (UNIVERSITY OF CHICAGO
PRESS, 2000)

*Price V. Fishback and Shawn Everett Kantor*
A PRELUDE TO THE WELFARE STATE: THE ORIGINS
OF WORKERS' COMPENSATION (UNIVERSITY OF
CHICAGO PRESS, 2000)

*Gerardo della Paolera and Alan M. Taylor*
STRAINING AT THE ANCHOR: THE ARGENTINE
CURRENCY BOARD AND THE SEARCH FOR
MACROECONOMIC STABILITY, 1880–1935
(UNIVERSITY OF CHICAGO PRESS, 2001)

*Werner Troesken*
WATER, RACE, AND DISEASE (MIT PRESS, 2004)

*B. Zorina Khan*
THE DEMOCRATIZATION OF INVENTION: PATENTS
AND COPYRIGHTS IN AMERICAN ECONOMIC

DEVELOPMENT, 1790–1920 (CAMBRIDGE
UNIVERSITY PRESS, 2005)

Dora L. Costa and Matthew E. Kahn
HEROES AND COWARDS: THE SOCIAL FACE OF
WAR (PRINCETON UNIVERSITY PRESS, 2008)

Roderick Floud, Robert W. Fogel, Bernard
Harris, and Sok Chul Hong
THE CHANGING BODY: HEALTH, NUTRITION,
AND HUMAN DEVELOPMENT IN THE WESTERN
WORLD SINCE 1700 (CAMBRIDGE UNIVERSITY
PRESS, 2011)

Stanley L. Engerman and Kenneth L. Sokoloff
ECONOMIC DEVELOPMENT IN THE AMERICAS
SINCE 1500: ENDOWMENTS AND INSTITUTIONS
(CAMBRIDGE UNIVERSITY PRESS, 2012)

Robert William Fogel, Enid M. Fogel, Mark
Guglielmo, and Nathaniel Grotte
POLITICAL ARITHMETIC: SIMON KUZNETS AND
THE EMPIRICAL TRADITION IN ECONOMICS
(UNIVERSITY OF CHICAGO PRESS, 2013)

Price Fishback, Jonathan Rose,
and Kenneth Snowden
WELL WORTH SAVING: HOW THE NEW DEAL
SAFEGUARDED HOME OWNERSHIP
(UNIVERSITY OF CHICAGO PRESS, 2013)

Howard Bodenhorn
THE COLOR FACTOR: THE ECONOMICS OF
AFRICAN-AMERICAN WELL-BEING IN THE
NINETEENTH-CENTURY SOUTH (OXFORD
UNIVERSITY PRESS, 2015)

Leah Platt Boustan
COMPETITION IN THE PROMISED LAND:
BLACK MIGRANTS IN NORTHERN
CITIES AND LABOR MARKETS
(PRINCETON UNIVERSITY
PRESS, 2017)

Douglas A. Irwin
CLASHING OVER COMMERCE: A HISTORY OF U.S.
TRADE POLICY (UNIVERSITY OF CHICAGO PRESS,
2017)

# Capital in the Nineteenth Century

ROBERT E. GALLMAN AND
PAUL W. RHODE

THE UNIVERSITY OF CHICAGO PRESS     CHICAGO AND LONDON

The University of Chicago Press, Chicago 60637
The University of Chicago Press, Ltd., London
© 2019 by The University of Chicago
Published 2019
Printed in the United States of America

28 27 26 25 24 23 22 21 20 19    1 2 3 4 5

ISBN-13: 978-0-226-63311-4 (cloth)
ISBN-13: 978-0-226-63325-1 (e-book)
DOI: https://doi.org/10.7208/chicago/9780226633251.001.0001

Library of Congress Cataloging-in-Publication Data

Names: Gallman, Robert E., author. | Rhode, Paul Webb, author.
Title: Capital in the nineteenth century / Robert E. Gallman and Paul W. Rhode.
Other titles: NBER series on long-term factors in economic development.
Description: Chicago ; London : The University of Chicago Press, 2019. |
    Series: NBER series on long-term factors in economic development |
    Includes bibliographical references and index.
Identifiers: LCCN 2019008176 | ISBN 9780226633114 (cloth : alk. paper) |
    ISBN 9780226633251 (e-book)
Subjects: LCSH: United States—Economic conditions—19th century. |
    United States—Economic conditions—19th century—Statistics. | Capital—
    United States—History. | Capital—United States—Statistics. | Gallman, Robert E.
Classification: LCC HC105 .G35 2019 | DDC 332/.041097309034—dc23
LC record available at https://lccn.loc.gov/2019008176

♾ This paper meets the requirements of ANSI/NISO Z39.48–1992 (Permanence of Paper).

# Relation of the Directors to the Work and Publications of the NBER

1. The object of the NBER is to ascertain and present to the economics profession, and to the public more generally, important economic facts and their interpretation in a scientific manner without policy recommendations. The Board of Directors is charged with the responsibility of ensuring that the work of the NBER is carried on in strict conformity with this object.

2. The President shall establish an internal review process to ensure that book manuscripts proposed for publication DO NOT contain policy recommendations. This shall apply both to the proceedings of conferences and to manuscripts by a single author or by one or more co-authors but shall not apply to authors of comments at NBER conferences who are not NBER affiliates.

3. No book manuscript reporting research shall be published by the NBER until the President has sent to each member of the Board a notice that a manuscript is recommended for publication and that in the President's opinion it is suitable for publication in accordance with the above principles of the NBER. Such notification will include a table of contents and an abstract or summary of the manuscript's content, a list of contributors if applicable, and a response form for use by Directors who desire a copy of the manuscript for review. Each manuscript shall contain a summary drawing attention to the nature and treatment of the problem studied and the main conclusions reached.

4. No volume shall be published until forty-five days have elapsed from the above notification of intention to publish it. During this period a copy shall be sent to any Director requesting it, and if any Director objects to publication on the grounds that the manuscript contains policy recommendations, the objection will be presented to the author(s) or editor(s). In case of dispute, all members of the Board shall be notified, and the President shall appoint an ad hoc committee of the Board to decide the matter; thirty days additional shall be granted for this purpose.

5. The President shall present annually to the Board a report describing the internal manuscript review process, any objections made by Directors before publication or by anyone after publication, any disputes about such matters, and how they were handled.

6. Publications of the NBER issued for informational purposes concerning the work of the Bureau, or issued to inform the public of the activities at the Bureau, including but not limited to the NBER Digest and Reporter, shall be consistent with the object stated in paragraph 1. They shall contain a specific disclaimer noting that they have not passed through the review procedures required in this resolution. The Executive Committee of the Board is charged with the review of all such publications from time to time.

7. NBER working papers and manuscripts distributed on the Bureau's web site are not deemed to be publications for the purpose of this resolution, but they shall be consistent with the object stated in paragraph 1. Working papers shall contain a specific disclaimer noting that they have not passed through the review procedures required in this resolution. The NBER's web site shall contain a similar disclaimer. The President shall establish an internal review process to ensure that the working papers and the web site do not contain policy recommendations, and shall report annually to the Board on this process and any concerns raised in connection with it.

8. Unless otherwise determined by the Board or exempted by the terms of paragraphs 6 and 7, a copy of this resolution shall be printed in each NBER publication as described in paragraph 2 above.

# Contents

# Preface

This volume was long in coming. Robert Gallman began his capital stock project more than half a century ago. Its first product was a paper by Gallman and Edward S. Howle titled "Fixed Reproducible Capital in the United States," presented to the 1965 Cliometrics Conference held at Purdue University. (I was delighted recently to discover an original draft of this piece in the papers of Alice Hanson Jones at Columbia University Library.) During his lifetime, Gallman published three important pieces on the American capital stock from the project, and reported on his findings in numerous venues. He wrote up, but did not publish, the material backing his series.

This volume publishes that material. It combines edited text from Gallman's published works, text from his research files, and text that I, Rhode, have written. I have endeavored to convey Gallman's research and thoughts faithfully. I have also tried to be clear about which materials speak with his voice and which speak with mine. Anyone who knew Bob will be able to guess accurately who wrote which text, but I have placed clarifying notes at the front of each chapter specifying the authors. In Gallman's chapters I have revised some of his language, reordered some sections, and added introductory text to improve flow.

I have benefited from discussions over many years with Jeremy Atack, Martha Bailey, Hoyt Bleakley, Peter Coclanis, William Collins, Lee Craig, Paul David, Lance Davis, Richard Easterlin, Stanley Engerman, Alexander Field, Price Fishback, Matthew Gallman, Claudia Goldin, Philip Hoffman, Edward Howle, Alan Olmstead, Debin Ma, William Parker, Jean-Laurent Rosenthal, Elyce Rotella, John Wallis, Thomas Weiss, and Gavin Wright. The result should be treated as "oral tradition," based on a good-faith rendering of my best recollections.

I am especially indebted to Jean-Laurent Rosenthal, Philip Hoffman, and Sabrina De Jaegher for hosting a conference at Caltech in January 2016 to discuss the monograph. I have attempted to bring on board as many of the conference participants' comments and critiques as possible.

A great debt is owed to Shirlene Garner, Gallman's longtime secretary at the University of North Carolina, for her work on the project. I also thank Kristen McGuire, Molly Shapiro, and Hanna Zlotnick for research and editorial assistance. And I am sure that this volume would not have been completed without the contributions of many others.

I wish, finally, to thank Claudia Goldin for her patience and unwavering support, and for locating the wonderful cover art. The Currier and Ives print *Through to the Pacific* displays myriad forms of capital in mid-nineteenth-century America—not only factories, railroads, ships, and harbors, but also houses and land being logged and tilled. The image beautifully captures Gallman's themes.

## CHAPTER ONE

# Robert Gallman's Capital Stock Project

## 1.1. Introduction

Robert Gallman was a builder. In a career spanning five decades, he constructed the best estimates that we have of the US capital stock and national product in the nineteenth century. Extending the work of his mentor Simon Kuznets, Gallman placed our knowledge of the long nineteenth century, a crucial period when the United States achieved modern economic growth and became a global economic leader, on a strong empirical foundation. His rock-solid, well documented, and nearly complete numbers replaced the speculative, underdocumented, and partial estimates previously available (Martin 1939). Gallman's approach was to use the blueprints provided by modern national income accounting, and then to search assiduously in the historical record for the best available statistical materials to use in constructing national product flow and capital stock numbers. His philosophy was plain: to measure twice (or more) and cut once. He then added variations to serve specific purposes, and patched as necessary. Where it was impossible to make estimates on solid foundation, he chose not to build.

Gallman sought to measure the flows of output produced by American factors of production. He was interested in the history of the American

---

This chapter was written by Rhode. Informing this essay are a set of taped interviews that we (Gallman and Rhode) conducted in the months before Gallman's death, as well as countless conversations in classrooms, on the way to seminars, before meetings, at dinners, or on long car trips to conferences.

people, so he focused on factors owned by US citizens rather than on those factors domiciled within the country's borders. (Thus, he typically worked with national product rather than domestic product.) Gallman also sought to measure the American capital stock. As will be noted in the chapters below, he adopted different but related perspectives. One was to see the capital stock as the accumulation saved and invested out of income flows. A second was to view capital as an input into the production process. A third was to use the level and change in the capital stock as proxy measures for long-run economic performance.[1]

One of Gallman's key findings was that structures and improvements to land—rather than machinery—represented the most important components of investment in nineteenth-century America. It is not surprising that construction held special interest for Gallman. He collected old builder's books that documented construction costs, hoping to make detailed comparisons between the United States and Britain over the 1820-to-1880 period in order to contribute to the Habakkuk debate on American and British technologies.[2] His son, Matthew, an important historian in his own right, recalls him as leaving his day job as an economist to engage in home improvement projects on nights and weekends.

E. H. Carr (1961, 17) wrote: "Study the historian before you begin to study the facts." Carr's advice is apt. Gallman's work reflects the activities and interests of his father, who operated a savings and loan to finance housing for working-class families in Passaic, New Jersey, in the 1930s. (Gallman's grandparents were skilled silk workers who migrated from Switzerland.) He was exposed to agriculture by doing chores on a Vermont dairy farm during summers in his youth. Gallman graduated from Cornell (Class of 1948) and began his graduate studies at the University of Pennsylvania. There he worked under Simon Kuznets, the pioneer of national product accounting. Gallman's studies were interrupted by the Korean War, when he served as a military procurement officer in the Washington, DC, area.

With this background, much about Robert Gallman becomes clearer. In the early nineteenth century, investment in structures and land improvement was typically self-financed; farmers cleared the "lower forty" with family labor during the off-season for crop production. As the century advanced, investment in structures was increasingly funded by financial intermediaries including commercial and investment banks, mortgage lenders, insurance companies, and, of course, savings and loans. Part of Gallman's long collaboration with Lance Davis sought to understand this transition.[3]

Gallman's work was not flashy. He did not employ clever theoretical devices, apply advanced statistical techniques, or address burning policy issues. Instead, he engaged in a painstaking effort to build a large statistical structure on a sound empirical foundation. But the implications of his research were revolutionary. His dissertation work on the expansion of value added in commodity production (agriculture, manufacturing, and mining) showed that before the Civil War, economic growth was more rapid and structural change more dramatic than many supposed. His research undergirded the argument of Thomas Cochran and Stanley Engerman that the 1860s were a period of slow growth rather than the breakpoint leading to modern growth, as the Beards asserted. His works showed that American agriculture was productive and progressing, and they helped bolster the revisionist claim that the economic performance of the antebellum South was impressive by world standards (Easterlin 1960; Fogel and Engerman 1974, 247–57). Another early finding was that the manufacturing producer durable flows increased faster than the economy as a whole before 1860, indicating that the investment rate was rising. Gallman also noted that the share of gross investment in GNP was relatively high as early as the mid-1830s.[4] The US experience contrasted with that of Britain, where the rate of capital formation reached high levels "only very late in the process of industrialization" (Davis and Gallman 1973, 442; Deane and Cole 1962). These discoveries about product flows led him to begin estimating the US capital stock. His work was always presented in carefully crafted prose that, apart from select passages reflecting his love of literature, was not ornate.

Gallman did not pursue controversy in his scholarship, but he also did not flee conflict when it arose. As one example, he took issue with Edward Pessen's characterization of the Jacksonian period. Pessen (1977, 137) argued that the phrase "the age of the common man" was a fraud because "wealth in early 19th-century America was unevenly distributed and becoming more so" over time. Gallman (1978, 1981) accepted the findings of Lee Soltow (1975) that the antebellum era was a period of great inequality of wealth—most obviously between enslaved African-Americans and their white masters—but with no demonstrable trend toward greater inequality. Such wealth inequality was in part a function of the age structure of the American population, specifically the high fraction who were young. While most young white males did not own property, most would do so at some point in their lives. Gallman (1978, 190) also noted that in 1850, even low-income Americans enjoyed higher consumption standards than most humans who had ever lived.

Gallman was sympathetic to the perspective that GNP and GDP were concepts defined for a particular time and place (Coyle 2014; Fogel 1999, Philpsen 2015). The national income accounts were not universals, but rather were measures of performance appropriate to specific historical contexts. It is not surprising that he chose to focus on the market-oriented economies of the "long nineteenth century" (Gallman's dating of this period is elastic; it begins as early as 1774 and ends as late as 1909). He was impressed and intrigued that in the mid-nineteenth century, Ezra Seaman (1852) produced national income estimates similar to those that came from a modern framework. He respected the earlier statistical work of Samuel Blodget (1806, 1810), Timothy Pitkin (1835), and George Tucker (1843). Gallman was concerned about the proper valuation of household production, especially of women's unpaid household labor (see Gallman 1966, 35, 74–76; Goldin 1990, 226). He felt that it made sense to measure performance in the antebellum South by treating enslaved African-Americans as members of the population rather than as components of the capital stock or as intermediate inputs (equivalent to livestock) in the production of output for the free population. As a consequence, Gallman (2000, 18) always treated slaves as people, not property.[5]

Because of his training under Kuznets, Gallman had a different approach to price indexes than is common today. On the one hand, he recognized the great importance of price indexes in creating sensible accounts. He held that his real capital stock numbers were only as good as the indexes of Dorothy Brady (1966) that he used to adjust the nominal figures.[6] He further believed that introduction of "new goods" represented one of the most important but hard-to-measure ways in which the standard of living changed.

On the other hand, Gallman did not accept the now-standard theoretical approaches—based on utility or production functions—to assess or correct the biases of fixed-weight Laspayres or Paasche indexes. He did not use chain-linked Ideal indexes, and he eschewed double deflation of value added.[7] Following Kuznets, he argued that index number problems were akin to the standard difficulties of interpreting the past:

> For historians, this kind of problem is familiar, and is perhaps no longer perceived as a problem. Histories written by historians of the late eighteenth century differ from those written by historians of the late twentieth century, and the reason is not simply that they made use of different bodies of evidence or different techniques. The two sets of historians have written from two different

historical contexts. The capital stock is an evaluative concept and evaluations depend upon the circumstances—cultural, intellectual, social, economic—in which they are made. The construction of a capital stock series based on, e.g., prices of 1860, means the construction of a series that appraises events in the context of the technology and prices—formed by cultural, intellectual, social, economic conditions—of 1860. It should not be a cause of either surprise or frustration that a series based on, say, 1800 or 1900 or 1990 would yield somewhat different results. Indeed, the contrasts may prove illuminating.[8]

Changes in an index based on 1860 prices showed how conditions would look from the perspective of someone living in 1860. Changes in an index based in 1900 prices would do the same from the perspective of someone living then. Each was "true" from its point of view—which takes quite a postmodern cultural perspective.

I do not know precisely why Gallman held these views. It may be that he did not believe that production or consumption functions were fixed over time, or that he thought creating a chain-weight index was not worth the trouble.[9] The distortions caused by substitution were small compared with the other issues involved in measuring the aggregate capital stock. For the most important historical change in the early period—from household to market production—price indexes were not illuminating.

Reflecting his desire to look at economic development from different perspectives, Gallman created alternative series. As we will see, he defined and calculated conventional income and capital stock numbers to link with the twentieth-century US Department of Commerce accounts. They reveal growth in the categories that his contemporaries considered important. But he came to see that the conventional definitions of income and capital were inadequate. He went on to define and create broader related measures of income and capital, including unconventional or nonmarket activities of importance to nineteenth-century participants in the growth process. A key investment activity of this form was the breaking and clearing of land to make it suitable for agricultural production. Economic performance could appear different if one was looking backward or looking forward.

Gallman was aware of the Cambridge Capital Controversy swirling around the economic profession when he was first constructing his capital stock estimates. The papers in his office included literature on this debate, specifically on problems of defining the aggregate capital stock. But the controversy, especially the debate over the validity of specifying an aggregate production function, did not affect his scholarly enterprise. The total capital stock, in his view, had an obvious meaning to participants in the economic growth process. The empirical difficulties of assembling, refining, and "testing" the historical data outweighed the theoretical problems generated by hypothetical examples of what was called "reswitching."[10] He was keenly aware of differences among types of capital and of differences in the methods used to compute their values.

One can learn from Gallman's silences as well, from his general practice of saying only good things about others. He did not appreciate speculative efforts to construct macrodata or to model the aggregate economy. For example, Gallman said of Raymond Goldsmith's (1952) estimates of the wealth stock in the pre-1900 period that at least Goldsmith provided a full discussion of how his numbers were constructed, so one could easily judge how reliable they were. He did, however, express more confidence in Goldsmith's twentieth-century numbers.

Gallman trusted the evidence about economic performance presented by the past, and respected the opinions and measurements of past authorities. He relied on published census returns, but expressed skepticism about the accuracy of the micro-level census data.[11] Gallman quoted Kuznets likening the census to the lead character in Swift's *Gulliver's Travels*. However handsome Gulliver was at normal scale, when tied down and examined by the Lilliputians, his pores appeared as giant imperfections. Similarly, the individual records in the manuscript census contained many inconsistencies and gaps in coverage that were smoothed out at a larger scale.

## 1.2. The Long Build

Gallman's capital stock project spanned several decades. Starting in the mid-1960s, he worked with his student Edward S. Howle to estimate the stock by two-digit sector and by category (structure, equipment, inventories, and so on). This work went on hiatus when Howle left academia in the mid-1970s. Gallman restarted the project in the early 1980s. In the interim, he worked with Lance Davis to interpret the findings about the growth of the capital stock and to relate the process of capital accumulation to American financial development.[12]

Table 1.1 lays out a detailed chronology of Gallman's contributions estimating capital stock and national product statistics. Although he presented

TABLE 1.1 **Development, use, and refinement of Robert E. Gallman's national product and capital stock estimates**

Gross national product$_t$ = consumption$_t$ + gross_investment$_t$ +
  government spending$_t$ + net_exports$_t$

Gross investment$_t$ = manufactured durables$_t$ + construction$_t$ + changes in inventories$_t$
Consumption$_t$ = perishables$_t$ + semidurables$_t$ + consumer durables$_t$ + services$_t$
Capital$_{t+1}$ = capital$_{t+1}$ + net investment$_t$ = capital$_{t+1}$ + gross investment$_t$ – depreciation$_t$

**Estimation of commodity production**

Robert E. Gallman, "Commodity Output, 1839–1899," in William N. Parker, ed., *Trends in the American Economy in the Nineteenth Century*, Studies in Income and Wealth, Vol. 24 (Princeton, NJ: Princeton University Press, 1960), 13–67.

**Appraisal of existing estimates and refinement of benchmarks**

Robert E. Gallman, "Estimates of American National Product Made before the Civil War," in *Essays in the Quantitative Study of Economic Growth, Presented to Simon Kuznets on the Occasion of his Sixtieth Birthday*, special issue, *Economic Development and Cultural Change* (April 1961): 392–412.

**Estimation of gross national product and components in current and 1860 dollars**

Robert E. Gallman, "Gross National Product in the United States, 1834–1909," in Dorothy S. Brady, ed., *Output, Employment, and Productivity in the United States after 1800*, Studies in Income and Wealth, Vol. 30 (New York: Columbia University Press, 1966), 3–76. Gallman makes additions based on the work of Martin Primack, Albert Fishlow, and Jerome Cranmer.

**Addition of decadal average inventory changes**

Robert E. Gallman, "The Social Distribution of Wealth in the United States of America," *Third International Conference of Economic History* (Paris: Mouton, 1965), 313–24.

**Creation of decadal census-based capital stock estimates, including consumer durables**

Robert E. Gallman and Edward S. Howle, *The Structure of U.S. Wealth in the 19th Century.*

**Addition of unconventional investment and analysis of structural change**

Robert E. Gallman and Edward S. Howle, "Trends in the Structure of the American Economy since 1840," in Robert W. Fogel and Stanley L. Engerman, eds., *The Reinterpretation of American Economic History* (New York: Harper & Row, 1971), 25–37. GNP variant I captures the NBER concept, and GNP variant II includes "the value of improvements to farmlands made with farm construction materials and value added by home manufacturing."

**Incorporation of depreciation and unconventional investment**

Lance E. Davis and Robert E. Gallman, "The Share of Saving and Investment in Gross National Product during the 19th Century, United States of America," in F. C. Lane, ed., *Fourth International Conference of Economic History, Bloomington, 1968* (Mouton, 1973), 437–66.

**Improvement of decadal service sector estimates**

Robert E. Gallman and Thomas Weiss, "The Service Industries in the Nineteenth Century," in Victor R. Fuchs, ed., *Production and Productivity in the Service Industries*, Studies in Income and Wealth, Vol. 34 (New York: Columbia University Press, 1969), 287–381.

**Calculation of net national product and incorporation of service sector estimates into decadal product**

Robert E. Gallman, "The Pace and Pattern of American Economic Growth" in Lance E. Davis et al., *American Economic Growth: An Economist's History of the United States* (New York: Harper & Row, 1972), 15–60.

*continues*

TABLE I.I *(continued)*

**Improvement of agricultural product and investment (inventory and nonconventional activities) estimates**

> Robert E. Gallman, "A Note of the Patent Office Estimates, 1841–1848," *Journal of Economic History* (June 1963): 185–95.
>
> Robert E. Gallman, "Changes in Total Agricultural Factor Productivity in the Nineteenth Century," *Agricultural History* 46, no. 1 (Jan. 1972): 191–209.
>
> Robert E. Gallman, "The Agricultural Sector and the Pace of Economic Growth: U.S. Experience in the 19th Century," in David C. Klingaman and Richard K. Vedder, eds., *Essays in 19th Century Economic History* (Athens: Ohio University Press, 1975), 35–76.

**Use of data to critique conjectural estimate**

> Robert E. Gallman, "The Statistical Approach: Fundamental Concepts as Applied to History," in George Rogers Taylor and Lucius F. Ellsworth, eds., *Approaches to American Economic History* (Charlottesville: University Press of Virginia, 1971), 63–86.

**Analysis of the rise of the net capital formation rate**

> Lance E. Davis and Robert E. Gallman, "Capital Formation in the United States during the Nineteenth Century," in Peter Mathias and M. M. Postan, eds., *Cambridge Economic History of Europe Vol. VII: The Industrial Economies, Capital, Labour, and Enterprise. Part 2, The United States, Japan, and Russia* (Cambridge: Cambridge University Press, 1978), 1–69.

**Exploration of improvements in construction estimates, and use of producer durable flows to estimate stocks**

> Robert E. Gallman, "Investment Flows and Capital Stocks: U.S. Experience in the Nineteenth Century," in Peter Kilby, ed., *Quantity and Quiddity: Essays in U.S. Economic History* (Middleton, CT: Wesleyan University Press, 1987), 214–54.

**Improvement of inventory estimates**

> Robert E. Gallman, "The United States Capital Stock in the Nineteenth Century," in Stanley L. Engerman and Robert E. Gallman, eds., *Long-Term Factors in American Economic Growth*, Studies in Income and Wealth, Vol. 51 (Chicago: University of Chicago Press, 1986), 165–213.

**Push of capital stock estimates back to colonial period**

> Robert E. Gallman, "American Economic Growth before the Civil War: The Testimony of the Capital Stock Estimates," in Robert E. Gallman and John Joseph Wallis, eds., *American Economic Growth and Standards of Living before the Civil War* (Chicago: University of Chicago Press, 1992), 79–115.

**Examination of forces driving nineteenth-century US economic growth and capital accumulation**

> Stanley L. Engerman and Robert E. Gallman, "U.S. Economic Growth, 1790–1860," *Research in Economic History* 8 (1983): 1–46.
>
> Lance E. Davis and Robert E. Gallman, "Savings, Investment, and Economic Growth: The United States in the 19th Century," in John James and Mark Thomas, eds., *Capitalism in Context* (Chicago: University of Chicago Press, 1994), 202–29.

**Incorporation of revisions**

> Robert E. Gallman, "Economic Growth and Structural Change in the Long Nineteenth Century," in Stanley Engerman and Robert E. Gallman, eds., *Cambridge Economic History of the United States*, Vol. 2 (Cambridge: Cambridge University Press, 2000), 1–56.
>
> Lance E. Davis and Robert E. Gallman, *Evolving Financial Markets and International Capital Flows* (Cambridge: Cambridge University Press, 2001).

variants of his estimates, he avoided a range of figures and just gave his best estimate. He sought to provide a single number for each well-defined concept. He refined and corrected the numbers as new data became available and when errors surfaced. He typically began the estimation process by using the census data to create solid decadal benchmarks. He made extensive efforts to ensure consistency and to "test" his series, comparing them against one another and against external evidence. For the flow estimates, he also used available statistics to construct annual series running through the benchmarks. The goal was to remove the effects of short-run fluctuation in long-run comparisons.

Gallman's achievement is all the more impressive given that he was working without computers or spreadsheet software. His accounts were kept on paper, and the tabulations were done on a calculator or adding machine. (After the late 1980s, Gallman had a desktop computer, a technology that he disliked.) His choices have consequences. He left us with a dauntingly large paper trail. It reveals small corrections or revisions made in some parts but not changed everywhere, although such cases are rare. Where he reported rates or ratios of variables over intervals of several years, they are typically ratios of sums, rather than averages of year-by-year rates.[13] He reported numbers to the same number of places after the decimal, not to the same number of significant digits. When he reported annual growth rates, they are typically compounded annually rather than continuously. The growth rates reported below have been standardized as continuously compounded rates of change calculated to three significant digits. Gallman almost always reported his numbers in tables, and rarely used graphs or figures. He performed numerous consistency tests, comparing one set of estimates with others, but did not use formal statistical tests. He knew, without explicitly saying so, that every number reported came with error bounds.

## 1.3. Contents of This Volume

This volume brings together Gallman's work estimating the US capital stock over the long nineteenth century, from 1774 to 1900. Chapter 2 introduces the decadal census-style (point-in-time) estimates that form this volume's empirical core. One theme motivating Gallman's investigation into the capital stock is that information about wealth during this period is more readily available and more comprehensive than evidence about income. The capital stock, when measured at fixed prices, is less volatile than income. An examination of the levels and changes in wealth provides valuable clues about economic performance.

Chapter 3 reproduces Gallman's definitive analysis of the data for the 1840–1900 period. These numbers link well to statistics reported in chapter 2. Chapter 4 pushes the investigation back to 1774, the eve of US independence. It introduces his estimates for the late colonial and early national periods; and it discusses the key role of investments in land clearing and breaking, an unconventional form of capital formation.

Chapter 5 presents and analyzes his annual estimates of national product over the 1834–1909 period. These series, reported as decadal averages, underlie much of what we know about American growth in the mid-nineteenth century. Gallman circulated versions of the annual series widely, but did not publish the details. This chapter documents the construction of the national product series, corrects minor errors, and compares Gallman's series with alternative estimates. The chapter also explains why Gallman considered his annual series to be unsuitable for business-cycle analysis.

Chapter 6 uses Gallman's annual flow data to generate capital stock estimates using perpetual inventory methods. The construction involves cumulating the depreciation-adjusted value of annual flows of real investments in manufactured producer durables and structures to derive alternative estimates of the capital stock. He considered these series useful for testing the census-style estimates for consistency and content. The investigation also revealed how depreciation affected the level and growth of the capital stock.

Chapters 7 to 12 present the detailed construction of the capital stock for individual sectors. Chapter 13 introduces Gallman's estimates of consumer durable expenditures, which are largely based on the annual flow data. Chapter 14 lays out his estimation procedures for capital in the colonial and early national period. These chapters have value for scholars beyond providing the supporting material for the aggregate estimates. They provide research leads, sources, and methods from one of the preeminent students of American economic history. Further, these chapters display Gallman's deep knowledge about the structure of the economy, and his considered judgments about available statistical sources. They supply essential materials for those who want to create better estimates, an endeavor that Gallman would have fully appreciated. The chapters on agriculture, manufacturing, and mining are especially rich.

## 1.4. Gallman's Major Findings

The American capital stock expanded with extraordinary speed over the long nineteenth century. As Gallman's data in table 1.2 show, the real US capital stock increased by a multiplicative factor of 276 between 1774 and 1900. The capital stock grew faster than total output (GNP), which expanded by a factor of 118 over this period, and faster than population, which expanded by a factor of 32. Gallman observed that demand for capital was increasing so rapidly that the risk of investing at the "wrong time" or in the "wrong place" was greatly reduced. One did not build ahead of demand for long. Most American capital was quite young and embodied current technology.

Gallman's numbers reveal that while GNP grew at a relatively steady rate over the long nineteenth century, its growth path was not "balanced" in the way that macro-growth economists assume today. Kaldor's (1961) famous "stylized facts" did not apply; the capital-to-output ratio and saving rate were not constants.[14] Over the nineteenth century, as the work of Abramovitz and David (1973a, 1973b) indicates, the United States was traversing to a new more capital-intensive equilibrium growth path.

TABLE 1.2  **Real capital and GNP, 1774–1900**

|        | National capital (in millions of 1860 dollars) | GNP (in millions of 1860 dollars) | GNP per capita (in 1860 dollars) |
|--------|-----------------------------------------------|-----------------------------------|----------------------------------|
| 1774   | 185    | 149    | 63.3   |
| 1799   | 566    | 360    | 68.0   |
| 1805   | 830    | 489    | 73.6   |
| 1815   | 1,057  | 641    | 75.6   |
| 1840   | 2,798  | 1,610  | 96.5   |
| 1850   | 4,621  | 2,628  | 116.1  |
| 1860   | 8,974  | 4,226  | 135.9  |
| 1870   | 10,889 | 5,547  | 142.0  |
| 1880   | 16,939 | 8,711  | 178.9  |
| 1890   | 34,525 | 12,915 | 211.3  |
| 1900   | 51,121 | 17,546 | 236.6  |

Notes: Capital and GNP are conventional constant (1860) price concepts, and include change in inventories. The conventional concept excludes the value of land improvements other than farm buildings. Dating for GNP, 1799 is 1800, 1805 is 1807, 1815 is an average of 1810 and 1820, 1840 is 1834–43, 1850 is 1844–53, 1860 is 1859, 1870 is 1869, 1880 is 1874–83, 1890 is 1884–93, and 1900 is 1894–1903.

Source: Capital is from tables 2.1 and 2.2; GNP and GNP per capita are from Gallman 2000, 7, 22.

TABLE 1.3  **Gross capital formation as percentage shares of gross investment in GNP**

|  | Conventional gross I/GNP valued in 1860 prices | Conventional gross I/GNP valued in current prices | Unconventional gross I/GNP valued in 1860 prices |
|---|---|---|---|
| 1834–43 | 12 | — | 19 |
| 1839–48 | 14 | 14 | 17 |
| 1844–53 | 16 | 16 | 18 |
| 1849–58 | 17 | 17 | 20 |
| 1869–78 | 24 | 19 | 26 |
| 1874–83 | 24 | 19 | 25 |
| 1879–88 | 25 | 21 | 26 |
| 1884–93 | 27 | 23 | 28 |
| 1889–98 | 29 | 23 | 30 |
| 1894–1903 | 28 | 21 | 29 |
| 1899–1908 | 29 | 22 | 29 |

Note: Unconventional capital adds investment flows for land formation to the conventional capital; both the numerator and denominator include changes in inventories. The unconventional income excludes home manufactures, due to the absence of constant price data. See also table 5.7.
Source: Gallman 2000, 39.

Gallman's numbers show that the US capital-to-output ratio more than doubled over the long nineteenth century. Using the conventional constant-price series, the capital-to-output ratio in 1900 was 2.34 times its 1774 value. Focusing on the period when the data are stronger, the 1900 ratio was 1.76 times its 1840 value. The increase in the capital-to-output ratio occurred in virtually every sector.

The share of output devoted to capital formation also soared, driving the rapid growth of the American capital stock. Table 1.3 displays Gallman's series on the rate of gross capital formation.[15] One of Gallman's striking initial findings was how high the rate was by the late 1830s. By the conventional constant-price measure, the United States was saving and investing 12 percent of output between 1834 and 1843; by the unconventional measures, the ratio was 19 percent. From these high levels, the rate of capital formation climbed higher over the nineteenth century.

According to the conventional constant-price series, the rate of capital formation more than doubled over the 1840–1900 period. The rise is slightly less pronounced if one examines the conventional current-price series; allowing for price changes lowers the rates at the end because the relative price of capital goods fell. The rise is also moderated in the unconventional constant-price series; adding investments in land clearing pushes up the rates at the beginning. The capital formation rate increases even in the new series. In an important way, the new series serves as robustness checks, showing that patterns detected in data series constructed from a twentieth-century viewpoint are present in series constructed from a nineteenth-century perspective. The available evidence, moreover, indicates that the capital formation rate in the 1799–1815 period could not have been as high as it was in the late 1830s and early 1840s, when the data in table 1.2 begin. The large rise in the saving rate was real. Gallman tended to use the concepts "saving rate" and "investment rate" interchangeably. This is appropriate for nineteenth-century America, because government expenditures were typically close to tax and tariff receipts, and net exports were a small share of income. In addition, at least in the early periods, the savers and investors were often the same people.

In a straightforward accounting sense, the rising capital-to-output ratio was not due to the "process of industrialization," at least as narrowly defined. Gallman and Howle (1971, 31–32) showed that manufacturing was less capital-intensive than agriculture, so that the rising share of the manufacturing sector in economic activity actually lowered the capital-to-output ratio of the overall economy. He performed several shift-share analyses to gauge the effects of the sectoral reallocation. He argued that by broadening one's perspective to include the spread of the railroad and the growth of urban housing, one could link the process of industrial development with the increasing capital intensity of the American economy.

Including the forces that caused the price of capital goods to fall relative to consumer goods over the second half of the nineteenth century provides another link between industrial advance and the rise in the economy-wide capital-to-output ratio. Gallman showed that over the second half of the nineteenth century, the falling price of capital goods relative to the price of all output, and especially the sharply falling price of equipment, had important consequences for the rate and distribution of capital formation. But to invoke the "age of the machine" misses much of the picture of nineteenth-century American economic growth. The share of structures in the US capital stock was three to four times larger than that of equipment in current price terms (see panel A of figure 1.1). Equipment's share did rise over time, especially if one examines the constant 1860 price series which adjusted for their declining relative price (see Panel B of figure 1.1). But, as Gallman showed, by either constant or current price measures, structures always made up the largest share of the capital stock.[16]

Much of the investment activity in the long nineteenth century was mundane and did not involve sophisticated new machines or technologies.

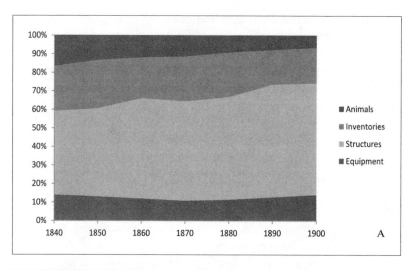

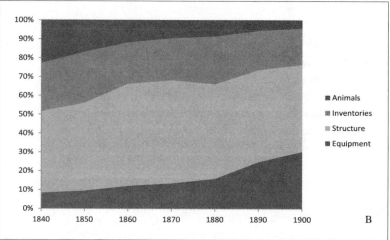

FIGURE 1.1 Shares of conventionally defined domestic capital, 1840–1900: (a) current prices; (b) constant price. Source: table 2.1.

Keeping cattle over the winter to work and breed during the following year, rather than slaughtering and consuming them, is a prototypical example. Clearing forests to create farmland by using simple tools such as axes, wedges, and small amounts of animal power, and breaking the prairie soils with ox-drawn plows are other examples. The importance of these latter activities in the first part of the nineteenth century was so great that

Gallman created an alternative capital stock series including the value of farm improvements. About one-quarter of all capital formation between 1799 and 1840 was in the form of land clearing and breaking. Gallman found that the value of land improvements (which included clearing and breaking, fencing, and irrigation, but excluded buildings) represented about one-eighth (12.2 percent) of the total US reproducible capital stock in 1900. In 1840 the figure was nearly one-third.[17]

Mechanization is often argued to be the most important change in American agriculture after 1840. Investment in equipment did increase at a faster rate (4.8 percent per annum) than did land improvement (2.3 percent) between 1840 and 1900. But in terms of absolute values and their changes, land improvements still predominated. The total value of investment in land improvements between 1840 and 1900 was over four times that in equipment. In 1900, the value of land improvements represented more than half (54 percent) of all reproducible capital in the agricultural sector, whereas equipment made up less than 10 percent.

Much of this investment, especially for the do-it-yourself land improvement projects, was produced domestically; most was self-financed. Only a small share of capital goods was imported. Gallman (1966, 17) noted that the largest category of imported capital goods in the late antebellum period was for saddles and harnesses. A small fraction of investments, principally for railroad bonds, was financed in foreign (mainly London) markets. But, due to both domestic accumulation and improved international financial integration, real interest rates fell over the nineteenth century (Davis and Gallman 1994, 211). Capital accumulated as self-financed, do-it-yourself land improvement or housing projects had different effects on income and wealth inequality than are conventionally considered (for example, by Piketty 2014). In the areas dominated by family farms and small businesses, there was widespread participation in the process of economic growth. In this way, the United States and other settler economies present a contrast to Europe that is worth exploring much more fully.

Durable goods did not flow only onto farms and factories, but into households as well. Many kinds of capital equipment, such as sewing machines, were initially producer durables, but once they were made smaller and less expensive, they were sold to consumers and used in domestic production. Gallman and Howle (1971, 33) found that the share of durables in consumption spending "rose strongly between the pre-Civil War period and the third and fourth decades" of the twentieth century. The share (measured both in current and constant dollar terms) doubled from

5 percent in the 1839–58 period to 10 percent in the 1919–38 period, and then remained constant through the 1939–53 period. Such growth refutes a commonly held view that nothing happened until the consumer durables revolution of the 1920s.

Gallman found that the onset of modern economic growth preceded the American Civil War (1861–65) by several decades. His annual data show that per capita output grew at a high, sustained rate from the 1830s at the latest. Available (admittedly weaker) evidence indicates that economic growth was slower before this period. The 1860s saw low growth of income and the capital stock. The post-reconstruction period witnessed more rapid income growth and capital accumulation than before.

From a growth accounting approach, Gallman highlighted a contrast between the nineteenth and twentieth centuries. In the first half of the twentieth century, as is well known from the work of Abramovitz (1956), Denison (1962), and Solow (1957), capital deepening—the rise of the capital-labor ratio—explained only a small share of per capita income growth. Most such growth came from the residual, or what came to be redefined as total factor productivity. Using his conventional capital stock estimates, Gallman showed that, during the mid- and late-nineteenth century, capital formation was a potent force in explaining per capita income growth. (The conventional estimates allow for more consistent comparisons between the nineteenth and twentieth centuries.) But Gallman being Gallman, he did not stop there. He returned to the issue using his broader unconventional capital stock estimates. These numbers start higher than the conventional estimates, and grow more slowly. In this growth accounting exercise, the contribution of capital formation is somewhat diminished, while that of total factor productivity is enhanced. This result is eminently sensible. It adds a nice twist: it is only by fully accounting for the mundane old types of capital that the real contributions of new innovations come to light. The revised calculations do show that the capital formation was an unusually important source of income growth in the mid- and late-nineteenth century.

## 1.5. Conclusion

Gallman was a builder. What's more, he was an architect and artisan. A problem with undertaking a project as large as Gallman envisioned is that it becomes difficult to stop. It is easier to take a pause than to decide the work is finally done. Gallman had plans and preliminary material to do much more, adding greater geographic details, extending the current price estimates and making closer connections between the different methods based on stocks and flows.

As the material in this volume reveals, Gallman built a structure of enormous value. He did so with care, knowledge, and insight. He left detailed records about how he proceeded, the materials he used, and the judgments he made. It is all there for those who follow, those who wish to use the data on capital and income, and those who wish to start the construction process anew.[18]

# Gallman's Core Capital Stock Data

## 2.1. Introduction

G allman's core data on the capital stock appear in tables 2.1 and 2.2. The tables present his current-price series, the constant-price (in 1860 dollars) series, and the implicit price deflators that link the two capital stock series.

Table 2.1 summarizes the census-style (point-in-time) estimates of the capital stock by two-digit industrial sector for the 1840–1900 period. They are subdivided into types of capital: equipment, structures, inventories, land improvements, and net foreign claims. They refer to the stock on 1 June of the census year. The principal, though not only, source was the federal census. The US Census Office collected and published reasonably consistent national data on the capital stock for manufactures on a decadal basis from 1840 on, for agriculture from 1850 on, for the mineral industries from 1870 on, and for transportation business in 1880 and 1890, among other economic activities. The availability of the census data provided a powerful impetus to build an estimation framework focused on years ending in nine or zero. Information for activities not covered by the census was to be fit into this framework.

The census years occurred in different phases of the business cycle and did not represent "natural" breakpoints for economic analysis. (Such concerns matter more for annual product flows than for the capital stock, which was accumulated over longer periods.) Gallman's core series began in 1840. This was the first federal census that he felt covered economic activity in a reasonably comprehensive and accurate manner. He

This chapter was written by Rhode.

TABLE 2.1 **Census-style estimates of US capital stock measured in current and 1860 prices, 1840–1900, in millions of dollars**

Panel A. Current prices

| | 1840 | 1850 | 1860 | 1870 | 1880 | 1890 | 1900 |
|---|---|---|---|---|---|---|---|
| **Agriculture** | | | | | | | |
| Buildings | 415 | 599 | 1,277 | 1,949 | 2,115 | 2,760 | 3,560 |
| Equipment | 119 | 152 | 246 | 337 | 407 | 494 | 750 |
| Animals | 445 | 587 | 1,074 | 1,666 | 1,844 | 2,716 | 3,068 |
| Clearing and breaking land | 1,048 | 1,484 | 2,600 | 3,118 | 3,409 | 3,955 | 4,232 |
| Fences | 318 | 432 | 719 | 957 | 1,149 | 1,596 | 2,589 |
| Drainage and irrigation | | < 0.5 | 1 | 7 | 23 | 58 | 120 |
| Irrigation for rice | 5 | 9 | 10 | 4 | 5 | 5 | 10 |
| **Mining** | | | | | | | |
| Improvements | 3 | 5 | 16 | 53 | 145 | 265 | 412 |
| Equipment | 2 | 3 | 9 | 26 | 48 | 86 | 146 |
| **Manufacturing** | | | | | | | |
| Improvements | 75 | 130 | 238 | 536 | 706 | 1,493 | 2,150 |
| Equipment | 70 | 124 | 232 | 536 | 737 | 1,584 | 2,543 |
| **Nonfarm Residences** | 373 | 724 | 1,833 | 2,518 | 4,063 | 9,374 | 11,723 |
| **Trade** | | | | | | | |
| Improvements | 68 | 133 | 336 | 461 | 744 | 1,717 | 2,147 |
| Equipment | 65 | 126 | 319 | 439 | 708 | 1,633 | 2,043 |
| **Shipping** | | | | | | | |
| Improvements | 20 | 28 | 37 | 28 | 27 | 39 | 60 |
| Vessels | 118 | 158 | 210 | 158 | 156 | 221 | 343 |
| **Canals and river improvements** | 110 | 151 | 184 | 168 | 173 | 171 | 211 |
| **Railroads** | | | | | | | |
| Improvements | 61 | 155 | 666 | 1,610 | 2,254 | 3,925 | 4,607 |
| Equipment | 4 | 15 | 74 | 86 | 204 | 337 | 376 |
| **Street railways** | | | | | | | |
| Improvements | | 2 | 8 | 23 | 78 | 210 | 867 |
| Equipment | | 1 | 2 | 6 | 12 | 42 | 207 |
| **Pullman and express cars** | | | | 13 | 31 | 52 | 58 |
| **Telephone** | | | | | | | |
| Improvements | | | | | 3 | 17 | 91 |
| Equipment | | | | | 3 | 18 | 107 |
| **Telegraph** | | | | | | | |
| Improvements | | < 0.5 | 2 | 7 | 13 | 34 | 44 |
| Equipment | | < 0.5 | < 0.5 | 1 | 1 | 3 | 3 |
| **Electric light and power** | | | | | | 41 | 251 |
| **Pipelines** | | | | | | | |
| Improvements | | | | | 10 | 42 | 141 |
| Equipment | | | | | 1 | 2 | 8 |
| **Churches** | 50 | 87 | 171 | 355 | 520 | 679 | 1,040 |
| **Government buildings** | 8 | 10 | 16 | 22 | 46 | 92 | 124 |
| **Schools** | 37 | 69 | 114 | 179 | 281 | 471 | 785 |
| **Inventories** | 655 | 1,150 | 2,000 | 3,568 | 4,836 | 6,583 | 8,978 |
| **Net international assets** | −176 | −63 | −124 | −1,035 | −1,084 | −1,735 | −819 |
| | | | | | | | |
| **Domestic capital variant A** | 4,069 | 6,334 | 12,394 | 18,831 | 24,752 | 40,715 | 53,784 |
| **Domestic capital variant Ā** | 3,746 | 5,893 | 11,664 | 17,863 | 23,575 | 39,056 | 51,065 |
| **Domestic capital variant B** | 2,698 | 4,409 | 9,064 | 14,745 | 20,166 | 35,101 | 46,833 |

*continues*

TABLE 2.1 (*continued*)

Panel A. Current prices

| | | | | | | | |
|---|---|---|---|---|---|---|---|
| **National capital variant A** | 3,893 | 6,271 | 12,270 | 17,796 | 23,668 | 38,980 | 52,965 |
| **National capital variant Ā** | 3,570 | 5,830 | 11,540 | 16,828 | 22,491 | 37,321 | 50,246 |
| **National capital variant B** | 2,522 | 4,346 | 8,940 | 13,710 | 19,082 | 33,366 | 46,014 |

Panel B. Constant 1860 prices

| | 1840 | 1850 | 1860 | 1870 | 1880 | 1890 | 1900 |
|---|---|---|---|---|---|---|---|
| **Agriculture** | | | | | | | |
| Buildings | 437 | 624 | 1,277 | 1,523 | 1,627 | 2,044 | 2,697 |
| Equipment | 78 | 115 | 246 | 288 | 485 | 772 | 1,364 |
| Animals | 676 | 791 | 1,074 | 1,111 | 1,545 | 2,055 | 2,220 |
| Clearing and breaking land | 1,424 | 1,861 | 2,600 | 2,817 | 3,797 | 4,338 | 4,740 |
| Fences | 424 | 526 | 719 | 775 | 1,143 | 1,461 | 2,421 |
| Drainage and irrigation | | 1 | 1 | 5 | 18 | 48 | 89 |
| Irrigation for rice | 7 | 12 | 10 | 5 | 6 | 5 | 11 |
| **Mining** | | | | | | | |
| Improvements | 2 | 4 | 16 | 42 | 106 | 223 | 412 |
| Equipment | 2 | 3 | 9 | 25 | 58 | 115 | 271 |
| **Manufacturing** | | | | | | | |
| Improvements | 70 | 120 | 238 | 596 | 619 | 1,641 | 2,416 |
| Equipment | 48 | 90 | 232 | 510 | 970 | 4,950 | 9,082 |
| **Nonfarm Residences Trade** | 393 | 754 | 1,833 | 1,967 | 3,125 | 6,944 | 8,881 |
| Improvements | 65 | 125 | 336 | 485 | 653 | 1,887 | 2,412 |
| Equipment | 46 | 92 | 319 | 375 | 722 | 1,899 | 2,761 |
| **Shipping** | | | | | | | |
| Improvements | 19 | 26 | 37 | 31 | 24 | 42 | 67 |
| Vessels | 69 | 126 | 210 | 188 | 205 | 388 | 673 |
| **Canals and river improvements** | 139 | 182 | 217 | 190 | 190 | 181 | 201 |
| **Railroads** | | | | | | | |
| Improvements | 61 | 176 | 666 | 1,064 | 1,925 | 3,648 | 4,227 |
| Equipment | 5 | 17 | 74 | 139 | 334 | 688 | 875 |
| **Street railways** | | | | | | | |
| Improvements | | 3 | 9 | 20 | 59 | 181 | 794 |
| Equipment | | 1 | 2 | 7 | 19 | 76 | 445 |
| **Pullman and express cars** | | | | 22 | 51 | 106 | 135 |
| **Telephone** | | | | | | | |
| Improvements | | | | | 3 | 14 | 79 |
| Equipment | | | | | 3 | 18 | 112 |
| **Telegraph** | | | | | | | |
| Improvements | | <0.5 | 2 | 5 | 10 | 29 | 39 |
| Equipment | | <0.5 | <0.5 | 1 | 1 | 3 | 3 |
| **Electric light and power** | | | | | | 41 | 235 |
| **Pipelines** | | | | | | | |
| Improvements | | | | | 8 | 33 | 106 |
| Equipment | | | | | 1 | 3 | 25 |
| **Churches** | 53 | 91 | 171 | 277 | 400 | 503 | 788 |
| **Government buildings** | 8 | 9 | 16 | 21 | 44 | 94 | 111 |
| **Schools** | 39 | 72 | 114 | 140 | 216 | 349 | 595 |

TABLE 2.1 *(continued)*

Panel B. Constant 1860 prices

| | | | | | | | |
|---|---|---|---|---|---|---|---|
| **Inventories** | 763 | 1,270 | 2,000 | 2,575 | 4,530 | 7,570 | 10,026 |
| **Net international assets** | −175 | −70 | −124 | −713 | −1,004 | −1,972 | −931 |
| **Domestic capital variant A** | 4,828 | 7,091 | 12,428 | 15,204 | 22,907 | 42,349 | 59,313 |
| **Domestic capital variant Ā** | 4,397 | 6,552 | 11,698 | 14,419 | 21,740 | 40,835 | 56,792 |
| **Domestic capital variant B** | 2,973 | 4,691 | 9,098 | 11,602 | 17,943 | 36,467 | 52,052 |
| **National capital variant A** | 4,653 | 7,021 | 12,304 | 14,491 | 21,903 | 40,377 | 58,382 |
| **National capital variant Ā** | 4,222 | 6,482 | 11,574 | 13,706 | 20,736 | 38,863 | 55,861 |
| **National capital variant B** | 2,798 | 4,621 | 8,974 | 10,889 | 16,939 | 34,525 | 51,121 |

Panel C. Price indexes

| **Price index numbers** | 1840 | 1850 | 1860 | 1870 | 1880 | 1890 | 1900 |
|---|---|---|---|---|---|---|---|
| **Agriculture** | | | | | | | |
| Buildings | 95 | 96 | 100 | 128 | 130 | 135 | 132 |
| Equipment | 152 | 132 | 100 | 117 | 84 | 64 | 55 |
| Animals | 66 | 74 | 100 | 150 | 119 | 132 | 138 |
| Clearing and breaking land | 74 | 80 | 100 | 111 | 90 | 91 | 89 |
| Fences | 75 | 82 | 100 | 123 | 101 | 109 | 107 |
| **Mining** | | | | | | | |
| Improvements | 95 | 113 | 100 | 127 | 137 | 119 | 100 |
| Equipment | 103 | 105 | 100 | 102 | 83 | 75 | 54 |
| **Manufacturing** | | | | | | | |
| Improvements | 107 | 108 | 100 | 90 | 114 | 91 | 89 |
| Equipment | 145 | 138 | 100 | 105 | 76 | 32 | 28 |
| **Nonfarm residences trade** | 95 | 96 | 100 | 128 | 130 | 135 | 132 |
| Improvements | 105 | 106 | 100 | 95 | 114 | 91 | 89 |
| Equipment | 140 | 137 | 100 | 117 | 98 | 86 | 74 |
| **Shipping** | | | | | | | |
| Improvements | 107 | 108 | 100 | 90 | 114 | 91 | 89 |
| Equipment | 170 | 126 | 100 | 84 | 76 | 57 | 51 |
| **Railroads** | | | | | | | |
| Improvements | 100 | 88 | 100 | 151 | 117 | 108 | 109 |
| Equipment | 79 | 84 | 100 | 62 | 61 | 49 | 43 |
| **Pullman and express cars** | | | | 62 | 61 | 49 | 43 |
| **Telephone** | | | | | | | |
| Improvements | | | | | 126 | 118 | 115 |
| Equipment | | | | | 100 | 100 | 96 |
| **Telegraph** | | | | | | | |
| Improvements | | 92 | 100 | 144 | 126 | 118 | 115 |
| Equipment | | 122 | 100 | 133 | 100 | 100 | 96 |
| **Churches and schools** | 95 | 96 | 100 | 128 | 130 | 135 | 132 |
| **Inventories** | 87 | 91 | 100 | 139 | 107 | 87 | 90 |

Source: See text.

did consider his 1840 numbers weaker than most of the others; the census of agriculture had not yet begun to report data on the capital stock and land values. He also judged the 1870 numbers less solid—due to disruptions during the American Civil War, price volatility, and census under-enumeration—and suspected that the 1880 numbers might be low. (Gallman 1986, 191–93). Gallman's estimation process ended in 1900 when other series became available. Indeed, he originally intended to link up his estimates with the Goldsmith series that start in 1900.

Gallman described the relationship of his estimates to the previous literature as follows:

> There is no published capital stock series that covers all of the years and provides all of the details that the new series does. . . . Goldsmith's series (1952) lacks data for 1840, 1860, and 1870 and is not available in as much detail . . . Kuznets's (1946) estimates . . . contain no components for the period before 1880 and no estimates at all of inventories or the foreign sector. Kendrick's figures (which depend upon the work of Ulmer, Tostlebe, Creamer, Borenstein, Dobrovolsky, Barger and others, gathered together in Kuznets, 1961), do not cover all sectors of the economy and do not run back of 1869. As they appear in Kendrick's book, they are also only available in constant prices." [All of these studies were completed before the early 1960s; since then,] "work has come forward that provides a firmer basis for estimates than was previously available.[1]

Table 2.2 presents census-style estimates for the 1774 to 1815 period. Gallman used data from Alice Hanson Jones, Samuel Blodget Jr., and the federal tax records in constructing capital stock estimates for the period before 1840. The figures, which were subdivided by types of capital, were constructed to be comparable to the 1840–1900 series; data to make sectoral divisions were less complete.

In tables 2.1 and 2.2, Gallman presents both "domestic capital" series, covering the stock within the boundaries of the United States, and "national capital" series, covering the stock owned by US nationals. The two differ modestly over the nineteenth century, as indicated by the small magnitude of the "net international assets" series.[2]

Gallman sought to estimate the value of the capital stock in a consistent, forward-looking way. He wanted numbers net of depreciation and independent of backward-looking book (accounting) evaluations. He preferred measures such as market value or reproduction costs. Scholars in economic history often repeat Gallman's summary judgment that the eval-

TABLE 2.2 **Census-style estimates of US capital stock, measured in current and 1860 prices, 1744–1815, in millions of dollars**

|  | 1774 | 1799 | 1805 | 1815 |
|---|---|---|---|---|
| **Measured in current prices** | | | | |
| Structures | 67 | 227 | 352 | 697 |
| Animals | 42 | 120 | 160 | 354 |
| Clearing and breaking land | 113 | 380 | 381 | 401 |
| Shipping | 8 | 49 | 80 | 127 |
| Other equipment | 15 | 46 | 65 | 88 |
| Inventories | 39 | 240 | 336 | 443 |
| Net international assets | −22 | −64 | −57 | −55 |
| Domestic capital variant Ā | 284 | 1,062 | 1,374 | 2,110 |
| Domestic capital variant B | 171 | 682 | 993 | 1,709 |
| National capital variant Ā | 262 | 998 | 1,317 | 2,055 |
| National capital variant B | 149 | 618 | 936 | 1,654 |
| **Measured in 1860 prices** | | | | |
| Structures | 84 | 206 | 349 | 450 |
| Animals | 52 | 139 | 167 | 241 |
| Clearing and breaking land | 269 | 479 | 526 | 611 |
| Shipping | 8 | 33 | 46 | 51 |
| Other equipment | 9 | 20 | 29 | 30 |
| Inventories | 59 | 215 | 276 | 315 |
| Net international assets | −27 | −47 | −37 | −30 |
| Domestic capital variant Ā | 481 | 1,092 | 1,393 | 1,698 |
| Domestic capital variant B | 212 | 613 | 867 | 1,087 |
| National capital variant Ā | 454 | 1,045 | 1,356 | 1,668 |
| National capital variant B | 185 | 566 | 830 | 1,057 |
| **Price index numbers** | | | | |
| Structures | 80 | 110 | 101 | 155 |
| Animals | 81 | 87 | 96 | 147 |
| Clearing and breaking land | 42 | 79 | 72 | 66 |
| Other equipment | 161 | 225 | 224 | 289 |

Source: See text.

uations in the census of agriculture and manufactures reflected the depreciated stock valued at market prices. The discussion in the estimating chapters below reveal that Gallman treated this judgment as less than definitive.

Due to problems of data availability, Gallman at times constructed components of the stock estimates by applying perpetual inventory methods to flow data. That is, he combined data on the annual flows of investment with assumptions about depreciation rates to create estimates of the cumulated total of the capital in place. The bulk of this volume details how he made his estimates, documents the data sources and definitions, justifies his interpretations and assumptions, explains the adjustments and corrections that he made, and provides a battery of consistency tests.

The statistics in table 2.1 and table 2.2 are related to the data reported in chapters 3 and 4 respectively. To avoid confusion, it is helpful to label the variants of the capital stock that Gallman used. Chapter 3 introduces a conventional measure of the capital stock and an unconventional measure including resources devoted to land breaking and clearing, fencing, irrigation, and drainage.[3] Gallman labeled the broad nonconventional measure variant A, and the conventional measure variant B.

Chapter 4 pushes the capital stock series back to 1774. Data limitations led to the use of a somewhat less comprehensive unconventional measure. The estimates in chapter 4 for land improvements included only the resources devoted to land breaking and clearing and not those devoted to fencing, irrigation, and drainage. It will be helpful to label this more narrow unconventional concept as variant Ā.

Table 2.1, covering the period from 1840 on, allows the calculation of all three variants. Table 2.2, covering the period before 1840, includes the components needed to calculate variant B and variant Ā, but not variant A. Variant A includes all the rows; variant Ā drops the rows for fencing and irrigation/drainage; variant B also drops the row for land clearing and breaking and has none of the numbers on land improvements. The differences between variants A and Ā are small but nontrivial in the periods when both can be computed. In 1850, national capital variant A exceeded variant Ā by 7.0 percent in current prices and by 7.7 percent in 1860 prices. Gallman typically used variant Ā as well as variant B in his longer-run analysis.[4] The concepts for improvements parallel those for capital.

The following notation (in which the prefixes are suppressed) clarifies matters:

Capital variant B = conventionally defined reproducible capital

Capital variant Ā = capital variant B + land clearing and breaking

Capital variant A = capital variant Ā + fencing + irrigation and drainage

Improvements variant B = structures (including farm buildings)

Improvements variant Ā = improvements variant B + land clearing and breaking

Improvements variant A = improvements variant Ā + fencing + irrigation and drainage

Chapter 3 (especially table 3.1) provides a broad overview of the different sources and methods used for the core 1840–1900 period. Chapters 4 and 14 explain the construction of estimates for the colonial and early national periods. Chapter 5 introduces Gallman's annual product data. Chapter 6 compares capital stock estimates made from the perpetual inventory methods applied to annual product flows with those created from census data. Chapters 7 to 12 describe in detail Gallman's estimation methods sector-by-sector. Chapter 13 covers consumer durables. Table 2.3 offers a concordance between the rows in table 2.1 and the tables in chapters 7 through 12.

Several issues merit note:

(1) Canal and river improvements and street railroad improvements in 1860 have different values in constant and current prices. This is odd because the current year is the same as the base year of the constant price series. The discrepancies are a result of accumulating depreciated capital of different vintages. These discrepancies create very small differences (on the order of 0.25 percent in the domestic capital variant A series) between the current and constant valuations of the total capital in 1860. In that year, the two concepts should by definition be identical. No attempt has been made to fix this minor problem.

(2) A similar issue exists for consumer durables.

(3) Electric light and power are defined in 1890 prices rather than 1860 prices. This is a new goods problem without apparent solution, given the lack of useable 1860 prices. This sector first appeared in Gallman's numbers in 1890. (Pipelines and telephones had entered in 1880; Pullman and express cars in 1870; street railways and telegraphs in 1850.) To gauge the magnitude of the new goods problem, note that in 1900, sectors entering after 1840 constituted 3.7 percent of the domestic capital variant A series evaluated at 1860 prices, and 3.5 percent evaluated at current prices. The subset of sectors entering after 1860 constituted 1.5 percent of the total by either measure.

(4) Gallman's estimates did not cover the value of roads, waterworks, or standing timber. See Gallman 1986, 183, 209.

(5) There are a number of small discrepancies. Net international assets is –176 in the 1840 current value cell, but –178 in the backing material. Gallman's price index for trade improvements in 1870 is 95, and not 90, which appears to be more consistent.

TABLE 2.3 **Concordance between table 12.1 and source tables in chapters 7–12**

| Sector | Source tables | | | |
|---|---|---|---|---|
| | Current prices | 1860 prices | Capital variant | Capital type |
| **Agriculture** | | | | |
| Buildings | 7.2 | 7.2 | B | Structures |
| Equipment | 7.2 | 7.2 | B | Equipment |
| Animals | 7.3 | 7.3 | B | Inventories |
| Clearing and breaking land | 7.7 | 7.7 | Ā | Improvements |
| Fences | 7.8 | 7.8 | A | Improvements |
| Drainage and irrigation | 7.11 | 7.11 | A | Improvements |
| Irrigation for rice | 7.11 | 7.11 | A | Improvements |
| **Mining** | | | | |
| Improvements | 8.5 | 8.5 | B | Structures |
| Equipment | 8.5 | 8.5 | B | Equipment |
| **Manufacturing** | | | | |
| Improvements | 8.9 | 8.9 | B | Structures |
| Equipment | 8.9 | 8.9 | B | Equipment |
| **Nonfarm Residences** | 9.11 | 9.11 | B | Structures |
| **Trade** | | | | |
| Improvements | 9.11 | 9.11 | B | Structures |
| Equipment | 9.10 | 9.10 | B | Equipment |
| **Shipping** | | | | |
| Improvements | 10.1 | 10.1 | B | Structures |
| Vessels | 10.1 | 10.1 | B | Equipment |
| **Canals and river improvements** | 10.4 | 10.4 | B | Structures |
| **Railroads** | | | | |
| Improvements | 10.9 | 10.9 | B | Structures |
| Equipment | 10.9 | 10.9 | B | Equipment |
| **Street railways** | | | | |
| Improvements | 10.11 | 10.11 | B | Structures |
| Equipment | 10.12 | 10.12 | B | Equipment |
| **Pullman and express cars** | 10.13 | 10.13 | B | Equipment |
| **Telephone** | | | | |
| Improvements | 11.1 | 11.11 | B | Structures |
| Equipment | 11.1 | 11.11 | B | Equipment |
| **Telegraph** | | | | |
| Improvements | 11.7 | 11.7 | B | Structures |
| Equipment | 11.7 | 11.7 | B | Equipment |
| **Electric light and power** | 11.12 | 11.12 | B | Structures |
| **Pipelines** | | | | |
| Improvements | 10.14 | 10.14 | B | Structures |
| Equipment | 10.14 | 10.14 | B | Equipment |
| **Churches** | 9.12 | 9.12 | B | Structures |
| **Government buildings** | 9.12 | 9.12 | B | Structures |
| **Schools** | 9.12 | 9.12 | B | Structures |
| **Inventories** | 12.5 | 12.5 | B | Inventories |
| **Net international assets** | 12.6 | 12.6 | B | International |

Source: See text.

## 2.3. Wealth Estimates

The backing materials also document the sources for Gallman's wealth estimates. The estimates are available only in current-price terms and begin in 1850 (when the census began to report value of farm land). Gallman defined national wealth to include the reproducible capital, the value of land, and net international assets. He defined domestic wealth to include reproducible capital and the value of land. Thus,

National wealth = capital + value of land + net international assets;

domestic wealth = capital + value of land.

Both wealth concepts exclude paper claims, consumer durables, and human capital, even in the form of property rights to slaves. (Gallman 1986, 166).[5]

Gallman also in places uses the term "real estate." Real estate includes the value of land, structures, and other improvements to land.

Table 2.4 pulls the data together. It presents Gallman's variant A and variant B capital stock estimates in current and constant (1860) price terms. It shows the domestic and national capital series (the difference is the international sector). It also relates the current-price capital stock to wealth, for the 1850 to 1900 period. Wealth equals the value of the capital stock plus the value of land. (The absence of land values, specifically for raw farm land in 1840, prevents the calculation of wealth in that year.) Conventional reproducible national capital (variant B) grew faster than national wealth as a whole over the 1850–1900 period, whereas nonconventional national capital (variant A) grew more slowly.

Gallman did not separately publish the land value estimates that entered in his wealth concept. The backing materials include information about the value of land by sector. Table 2.5 collects the numbers from across the chapters. The results are of independent interest. The share of land in national wealth rose from 20.5 percent in 1850 to 27.6 percent by 1900. The direction of this change may come as a surprise, considering the declining share of agriculture in the American economy. Several points merit mention. First, the calculations consider "raw" land (subtracting structures and improvements). Second, land was an important input in housing as well as agriculture. Farmland made up less than one-half of land value in 1850, and considerably less than one-third by 1900. In 1890 and 1900, the value of

TABLE 2.4 **Wealth and capital stock estimates, measured in current and 1860 prices, 1840–1900, in millions of dollars**

| | 1840 | 1850 | 1860 | 1870 | 1880 | 1890 | 1900 |
|---|---|---|---|---|---|---|---|
| **Measured in current prices** | | | | | | | |
| Domestic wealth | — | 7,953 | 16,515 | 25,242 | 33,382 | 56,657 | 73,936 |
| National wealth | — | 7,890 | 16,391 | 24,207 | 32,198 | 54,922 | 73,117 |
| Domestic capital variant A | 4,069 | 6,334 | 12,394 | 18,831 | 24,752 | 40,715 | 53,784 |
| National capital- variant A | 3,893 | 6,271 | 12,270 | 17,796 | 23,668 | 38,980 | 52,965 |
| Improvements, variant A | 2,591 | 4,018 | 8,228 | 11,995 | 15,764 | 26,944 | 35,154 |
| Equipment[c] | 378 | 579 | 1,092 | 1,601 | 2,307 | 4,510 | 6,832 |
| Inventories[ac] | 1,100 | 1,737 | 3,074 | 5,234 | 6,680 | 9,299 | 12,046 |
| International sector[bc] | −176 | −63 | −124 | −1,035 | −1,084 | −1,735 | −819 |
| Domestic capital variant B | 2,698 | 4,409 | 9,064 | 14,745 | 20,166 | 35,101 | 46,833 |
| National capital variant B | 2,522 | 4,346 | 8,940 | 13,710 | 19,082 | 33,366 | 46,014 |
| Improvements, variant B | 1,220 | 2,093 | 4,898 | 7,909 | 11,178 | 21,330 | 28,203 |
| **Measured in 1860 prices** | | | | | | | |
| Domestic capital variant A | 4,828 | 7,091 | 12,428 | 15,204 | 22,907 | 42,349 | 59,313 |
| National capital- variant A | 4,653 | 7,021 | 12,304 | 14,491 | 21,903 | 40,377 | 58,382 |
| Improvements, variant A | 3,141 | 4,586 | 8,262 | 9,963 | 13,983 | 23,706 | 31,321 |
| Equipment[c] | 248 | 444 | 1,092 | 1,554 | 2,848 | 9,056 | 15,978 |
| Inventories[ac] | 1,439 | 2,061 | 3,074 | 3,686 | 6,075 | 9,625 | 12,246 |
| International sector[bc] | −175 | −70 | −124 | −713 | −1,004 | −1,972 | −931 |
| Domestic capital variant B | 2,973 | 4,691 | 9,098 | 11,602 | 17,943 | 36,467 | 52,052 |
| National capital variant B | 2,798 | 4,621 | 8,974 | 10,889 | 16,939 | 34,525 | 51,121 |
| Improvements, variant B | 1,286 | 2,186 | 4,932 | 6,361 | 9,019 | 17,854 | 24,060 |

Notes:
[a] Excluding inventories of monetary metals
[b] Including inventories of monetary metals
[c] Same in variants A and B.
This table corrects an error in the 1880 national wealth variant A figure. To be consistent with underlying data, it uses 32.32 instead of 32.22, which appeared in Gallman 1986, 204. The sources of the small difference between the current and constant value series in 1860 are discrepancies in the evaluation of canal and river improvements and of street railroad capital.
Sources: See text.

land in the nonfarm residential real estate sector exceeded that in agriculture.[6] Third, these land figures exclude structures and other improvements. If the value of other improvements is included, the value of land in agriculture exceeded that in the nonagricultural residential sector. But if the value of structures is then added, the value of real estate in the nonagricultural residential sector exceeded that in agriculture.

Gallman's figures can be compared with those of Raymond Goldsmith (1952), who built his pre-1900 wealth estimates from the federal census. Goldsmith questioned the consistency of its valuation method, which included original cost, book value, and market value / reproduction cost basis approaches. Goldsmith (1952, 264) thought the margin of error in his

TABLE 2.5  **Value of land at current prices, 1840–1900, in millions of dollars**

| | 1840 | 1850 | 1860 | 1870 | 1880 | 1890 | 1900 |
|---|---|---|---|---|---|---|---|
| **Panel A. Total value** | | | | | | | |
| Total land | — | 1,619 | 4,121 | 6,411 | 8,530 | 15,942 | 20,152 |
| Raw farmland | — | 748 | 2,039 | 3,226 | 3,496 | 4,905 | 6,104 |
| Mineral land | 9 | 21 | 67 | 203 | 457 | 818 | 1,271 |
| Manufacturing land | 86 | 143 | 250 | 536 | 671 | 1,318 | 1,522 |
| Non-ag residential land | 212 | 413 | 1,045 | 1,435 | 2,315 | 5,342 | 6,681 |
| Trade land | 127 | 246 | 623 | 857 | 1,382 | 3,188 | 3,988 |
| Shipping land | 27 | 36 | 48 | 36 | 35 | 50 | 78 |
| Railroad land | 4 | 11 | 47 | 113 | 158 | 275 | 323 |
| Street RR land | | 1 | 2 | 5 | 15 | 41 | 157 |
| Telephone land | | | | | | 1 | 8 |
| Electric light & power land | | | | | | 2 | 12 |
| Pipeline land | | | | | 1 | 2 | 8 |
| | | | | | | | |
| **Panel B. Value of real estate** | | | | | | | |
| Agricultural real estate | — | 3,272 | 6,646 | 9,261 | 10,197 | 13,279 | 16,615 |
| Agricultural buildings | 415 | 599 | 1,277 | 1,949 | 2,115 | 2,760 | 3,560 |
| Other ag improvements | 1,371 | 1,925 | 3,330 | 4,086 | 4,586 | 5,614 | 6,951 |
| "Raw" farmland | — | 748 | 2,039 | 3,226 | 3,496 | 4,905 | 6,104 |
| | | | | | | | |
| Non-ag residential real estate | 585 | 1,137 | 2,878 | 3,953 | 6,378 | 14,716 | 18,404 |
| Non-ag residences | 373 | 724 | 1,833 | 2,518 | 4,063 | 9,374 | 11,723 |
| Non-ag residential land | 212 | 413 | 1,045 | 1,435 | 2,315 | 5,342 | 6,681 |
| | | | | | | | |
| Trade real estate | 195 | 379 | 959 | 1,318 | 2,126 | 4,905 | 6,135 |
| Trade improvements | 68 | 133 | 336 | 461 | 744 | 1,717 | 2,147 |
| Land used for trade | 127 | 246 | 623 | 857 | 1,382 | 3,188 | 3,988 |
| | | | | | | | |
| **Panel C. Value per acre** | | | | | | | |
| "Raw" farmland, | | | | | | | |
| dollars/acre | — | 2.55 | 5.01 | 7.91 | 6.55 | 7.87 | 7.26 |
| | | | | | | | |
| **Panel D. Percentage share of wealth** | | | | | | | |
| Total land relative to | | | | | | | |
| domestic wealth | — | 20.4 | 25 | 25.4 | 25.6 | 28.1 | 27.3 |
| national wealth | — | 20.5 | 25.1 | 26.4 | 26.4 | 29 | 27.6 |
| Nonagricultural residential real estate relative to | | | | | | | |
| domestic wealth | — | 14.3 | 17.4 | 15.7 | 19.1 | 26 | 24.9 |
| national wealth | — | 14.4 | 17.6 | 16.3 | 19.8 | 26.8 | 25.2 |

Note: The value of "raw" farmland is computed as the value of farms minus the value of buildings, land clearing and breaking, fences, irrigation, and drainage.
Source: See text.

TABLE 2.6 **Comparison of Gallman and Goldsmith, in billions of current dollars**

|                                          | 1850 | 1880 | 1890 | 1900 |
|------------------------------------------|------|------|------|------|
| Gallman national capital,variant B       | 4.4  | 19.0 | 33.4 | 46.0 |
| Goldsmith reproducible tangible assets   | 4.2  | 23.5 | 41.7 | 57.8 |

Source: Goldsmith 1952, 306; derived from column 2 minus column 17.

TABLE 2.7 **Current-value capital-to-output and wealth-to-output ratios, 1840–1900**

|                      | 1840 | 1850 | 1860 | 1870 | 1880 | 1890 | 1900 |
|----------------------|------|------|------|------|------|------|------|
| National wealth/GNP  | —    | 2.98 | 3.88 | —    | 3.31 | 4.38 | 4.48 |
| Domestic wealth/GNP  | —    | 3.00 | 3.91 | —    | 3.42 | 4.52 | 4.53 |
| National capital/GNP | 2.16 | 2.37 | 2.90 | —    | 2.44 | 3.11 | 3.24 |
| Domestic capital/GNP | 2.26 | 2.39 | 2.93 | —    | 2.54 | 3.25 | 3.29 |

Notes: Wealth and capital stock are current-value variant A series. Wealth is capital plus land.
Source: Current-price GNP from Gallman 2000, table 1.6. 1840 GNP is the average of 1834–43; 1850 is 1844–53;
1860 is 1859; 1880 is 1874–83; 1890 is 1884–93; and 1900 is 1894–1903.

estimates was "hardly less than 10 to 20 percent at any date"; the margin became worse the further he pushed his estimates back in time. Goldsmith continued: "It is not certain that comparability is impaired by as much as the size of the margin may imply because the error probably tends in the same direction for most if not all benchmarks." Comparisons within the dataset may not suffer, but comparisons with other sources of data certainly do. Table 2.6 compares Gallman's current-value national capital variant B numbers with Goldsmith's (1952, 308) reproducible tangible assets figures (excluding consumer durables). Gallman's estimates are slightly higher than Goldsmith's in 1850, but are much lower by the end of the nineteenth century (see also table 3.4).

Table 2.7 reports that capital-to-GNP ratios calculated from Gallman's current-price estimates yield numbers for the second half of the nineteenth century ranging between about 2.4 and 3.3.[7] The analogous wealth-to-GNP ratios range between about 3.0 and 4.5. The ratios rise over the period, with an interruption in the decades right after 1860. The temporary fall is possibly due to Civil War–era destruction (Goldin and Lewis 1975). These capital-to-output ratios differ slightly from those in Gallman (1986) principally due to the use of different GNP numbers in the denominator. Gallman (1986, 192) also reports lower ratios in 1880 than in 1860.[8] This picture contrasts with the smooth rise over this period appearing in Piketty and Zucman (2015).

TABLE 2.8 **Price Indexes for GDP and capital, 1840–1900**

|  | 1840 | 1850 | 1860 | 1870 | 1880 | 1890 | 1900 |
|---|---|---|---|---|---|---|---|
| GDP deflator | 94 | 93 | 100 | 131 | 106 | 96 | 92 |
| Domestic capital, variant A | 91 | 92 | 100 | 125 | 109 | 106 | 105 |
| Improvements, variant A/B | 74 | 80 | 100 | 114 | 92 | 95 | 93 |
| Improvements, variant B | 97 | 96 | 100 | 127 | 126 | 125 | 123 |
| Equipment | 145 | 130 | 100 | 104 | 83 | 61 | 53 |
| Inventories | 80 | 85 | 100 | 143 | 111 | 103 | 107 |

Note: Telegraph equipment is excluded because price information is not available for 1840. Improvements, variant A/B, are the components included in variant A that are not included in variant B.

Sources: GDP deflator from Carter et al. 2006, Ca13. Capital price indexes, table 2.1. $Pt_{,C} = Sum(Pt_{,c}C * K_{1860,c} / Sum[K_{1860, c}C])$.

The change in the capital-to-output ratio in current prices is driven in part by prices and in part by quantities. The evidence on price movements in table 2.8 helps to sort out the effects. The series have other important implications of note. The table presents information of the GDP deflator from 1840 to 1900, using a base of 1860 = 100. It also presents price series for types on capital based on the price indexes in table 2.1 weighed by the stock of capital in 1860. As an example, the equipment price series is derived by multiplying the individual equipment components in 1860 by the price indexes for each specific year, summing the total, and then dividing by the 1860 sum. What the series show is that the price of capital rose in the 1860s, but slightly more slowly than the GDP deflator. In the 1870s, the price of capital fell, but more slowly than the GDP deflator. Overall the relative price of capital increased between 1860 and 1880; consequently, the fall of the current-price capital-to-output ratio over that period is not simply a nominal phenomenon.

One other notable feature of the price data is the contrasting movement of the price of improvements and equipment. The price of improvements rose between 1840 and 1900 relative to the GDP deflator. This is true for the improvements included in variant B and those included in variant A exclusively. The price of equipment fell sharply relative to the GDP deflator (see also Brady 1966). Moreover, the price of equipment declined continuously, relative to the price of improvements included in variant B, which as a shorthand term we can call structures. The price ratio of equipment to structures in 1900 was less than three-tenths (28.8 percent) of what it was in 1840. Over the same period, the quantity ratio of equipment to structures (where quantities are measured by the stocks in fixed 1860 prices) increased almost 3.5 times. The changes in relative quantities reflected both substitution within specific sectors to higher equipment-to-structure ratios, and the more rapid expansion of sectors (such as manufacturing and trade) characterized by high equipment-to-structure ratios.[9] Gallman was always quick to point out the greater importance of structures relative to equipment in the US capital stock during the nineteenth century. But these price and quantity movements give life to the image of the period as the "age of the machine." That was what was new and different.

## 2.6. Conclusion

This chapter has laid out Gallman's main capital stock tables. Chapters 7 through 14 will describe the derivation of Gallman's estimates in detail. Chapters 3 and 4 reproduce Gallman's interpretations of the main results from the series, for the core 1840–1900 period and the 1774–1980 period, respectively.

## CHAPTER THREE

# The United States Capital Stock, 1840–1900

## 3.1. Introduction

There are at least four scholarly uses for aggregate capital stock series. First, they can be used in place of national product series—or in addition to national product series—to describe the scale, structure, and growth of the economy. There is no reason why, over short or even intermediate periods, the capital stock should grow at exactly the pace of the national product, but over the long run there should be a considerable degree of similarity. For this reason, capital stock series have sometimes been used as proxies for national product series in the measurement of long-term growth (Jones 1980). But one could easily make a case for the use of such series as independent indexes of growth, not simply as proxies for national product. Looked at and measured in one way, the capital stock of a given year describes the accumulated savings of the past; looked at and measured in a different way, it is a vision of future production. Either way, we have a picture of the economy that is different from the one provided by the national product, and one that is analytically useful.

Second, capital stock series have appeared as arguments in consumption functions and, thereby, in the analysis of the level of economic activity, cyclical variations, and economic growth. Land and consumers' durables are helpful additions to capital in these uses, as are paper claims.

Gallman published the substance of this chapter as Gallman 1986; Rhode reordered and revised the text to enhance its fit and flow in this volume. Rhode recalculated the growth rates on a continuously compounded basis, creating slight differences from the numbers appearing in Gallman 1986.

Third, the capital stock is a consequence of savings and investment decisions, with which are tied up choices of technique. The level and structure of the capital stock emerge out of these decisions, and capital stock series are used in studying them.

Fourth and finally, capital stock series are used in the analysis of production relationships and the sources of economic growth. In this chapter, the capital stock series are put chiefly to the first use and, to a limited extent, to the third and fourth.

This chapter describes and analyzes the estimates of the value of the US fixed capital stock, in current prices and in 1860 prices, at decade intervals from 1840 to 1900. The series contain estimates of the value of land, except agricultural land in 1840. The chapter will use the term "national wealth" to refer to the value of reproducible capital, land, stocks of monetary metals, and net claims on foreigners. "Domestic wealth" will mean the value of reproducible capital and land. Notice that paper claims are excluded from both of these aggregates, as are consumers' durables and human capital. The terms "national capital" and "domestic capital" refer to national wealth and domestic wealth respectively, minus the value of land. The concepts referred to here as "wealth" and "capital" are sometimes called by others "capital" and "reproducible capital" respectively.

Section 3.2 details the types of estimating procedures and tests adopted and their general results, the identity and character of the principal sources used, and the theoretical concepts that guided the work. Section 3.3 is concerned with the theoretical and quantitative relationships between the refined Gallman estimates and those already in the field: the Goldsmith and Kuznets series, as well as the original Gallman-Howle figures (Kuznets 1946; Goldsmith 1952; Gallman and Howle 1965; Gallman 1965). Section 3.4 considers the ways in which the refined Gallman series illuminate the nature of the nineteenth-century US economy and the course of US economic development.

## 3.2. Methods of Estimating the Capital Stock

Capital stock estimates can be made in two ways: they can be cumulated from annual investment flow data (Raymond Goldsmith's [1956] perpetual inventory method) or they can be assembled from censuses of the capital stock. If census and annual flow data were perfectly accurate, if the identical concepts were embodied in each, and if appropriate estimating procedures were used, then perpetual inventory and census procedures would yield the same results. In fact, they rarely do, though given the rich opportunities for discrepancies to arise, it is surprising how narrow the margins of difference often are.

The choice between the two techniques turns on the types and quality of data available. From 1850 through 1900 there were six reasonably comprehensive federal censuses of wealth, while for 1805 and 1840 we have census-style estimates constructed by able and informed contemporaries— Samuel Blodget (1806) and Ezra Seaman (1852)—chiefly from federal census, taxation, and trade data. Investment flow data, from which perpetual inventory estimates might be made, are less generally available. But researchers have subsequently produced additional data that offer opportunities for estimates superior to those derivable from nineteenth-century census-style data. The best were assembled in the extraordinarily well conceived and careful work of Albert Fishlow (1965, 1966) on the railroads. The estimates use Fishlow as the bases for the railroad series; Cranmer (1960) and Segal (1961) for canals; North (1960) and Simon (1960) for the international sector; and Ulmer (1960) for telephones and for electric light and power. Perpetual inventory methods were used to create figures for the telegraph industry and for consumers' durables. No doubt other sectoral estimates could be constructed, with profit, from flow data, although one doubts that the remaining opportunities are quantitatively important. The estimates described in this chapter are chiefly (and by necessity) drawn from census-style data (see table 3.1).

There are also some aggregate flow data which, while not very helpful in the derivation of sectoral estimates, proved useful in the construction of aggregate perpetual inventory estimates of manufactured producers' durables and structures—estimates that we have used for checking the census-style figures and for constructing annual capital stock series.

### 3.2.1. Valuation of Capital

In principle, capital stocks might be valued in any number of ways.[1] In practice, there are only three ways of any importance, two of which exist in two variants. (This refers to current price estimates; constant price estimates are discussed below.) Capital can be valued at acquisition cost (which is also referred to as "book value"), at reproduction cost, and at market value.[2]

Acquisition cost corresponds to the notion, expressed above, of the capital stock as piled-up savings. The great difficulty posed by such

TABLE 3.1 **Estimation methods, valuation bases, and principal sources of national capital stock estimates, measured in current prices, 1840–1900**

| | Estimation methods[a] | | Valuation bases[b] | | | Principal sources[cd] | |
|---|---|---|---|---|---|---|---|
| | Perpetual inventory | Census | Book value | Reproduction cost | Market price | Census | Other |
| **A. By sectors** | | | | | | | |
| Agriculture | | x | | | x | x | x |
| Mining | | x | | | x | x | |
| Manufacturing | | x | | | x | x | |
| Nonfarm residences | | x | | | | | |
| Shipping | | x | | | x | x | x |
| Canals and river improvements | x | | x | | | x | x |
| Railroads | x | | | x | | | x |
| Street railroads | | x | x | | | x | |
| Pullman and express cars | | x | | x | | x | |
| Telephone | x | | | x | | | x |
| Telegraph | x | | | x | | | x |
| Electric light and power | x | | | x | | | x |
| Pipelines | | x | x | | | | x |
| Churches | | x | | | x | x | x |
| Government buildings | x | x | x | | | | x |
| Schools | | x | | | x | | x |
| Inventories (excluding animals) | x | | | | x | x | x |
| International sector | x | x | x[e] | | | | x |
| **B. Percentages** | | | | | | | |
| 1840 | 19 | 81 | 3 | 38 | 59 | 20 | 80 |
| 1850 | 23 | 77 | 2 | 34 | 64 | 50 | 50 |
| 1860 | 23 | 77 | 2 | 33 | 65 | 50 | 50 |
| 1870 | 27 | 73 | 1 | 27 | 72 | 50 | 50 |
| 1880 | 29 | 71 | 1 | 30 | 69 | 55 | 45 |
| 1890 | 26 | 74 | 1 | 26 | 73 | 60 | 40 |
| 1900 | 27 | 73 | 3 | 26 | 72 | 60 | 40 |

Notes:
[a]"Perpetual inventory" is used here to refer to any and all cases in which estimates were derived from flow data; "census" means any and all cases in which estimates were derived from stock data.
[b]There remain some doubts concerning valuation bases (see text). In particular, a number of the estimates identified as expressed in market prices may in fact refer to net reproduction cost.
[c]Both columns are checked (panel A) in cases in which the census was the principal source in certain years but not in others, and in those cases in which the census and some other source were about equally important in all years.
[d]The percentages in panel B are rough estimates of the relative importance of census and noncensus sources.
[e]Less bad debts.
Sources: See text.

estimates is that the capital stock of each year is valued in the prices of many different years, so that no meaningful comparisons (at least none that comes to mind) can be made. This difficulty can be overcome by adjusting the data by means of a general price index—a consumer price index would be best—so that all elements of the capital stock of a given year are expressed in the prices of that year. A capital stock so valued retains the sense of acquisition cost: the valuation expresses the capital stock in terms of forgone consumption. The forgone consumption consists of the consumption goods given up in the year of investment, expressed in the prices of the year to which the capital stock estimate refers. Unambiguous comparisons can thus be drawn—with the national product of the same year, for example.

The capital stock may also be valued at reproduction cost. Each item is valued at the cost of the resources that would be required to replicate it in the year to which the capital stock estimate refers, given the factor prices and techniques of production of that year. The capital stock thus has the sense of congealed productive resources, valued consistently, so that a summation has a precise meaning. Such estimates are well adapted to the study of production relationships. They avoid, in some measure, the circularity problem implicit in market value estimates. Compared to acquisition cost estimates, they express the capital stock in terms of current productive resources rather than historical forgone consumption.

The third system values the capital stock in market prices; that is, each item of capital is appraised at the price it would bring in the current market. The market value of a piece of capital is presumably a function of its productivity, its expected life, and the going rate of interest. The capital stock, so valued, expresses the income that capital is expected to earn, discounted back to the year to which the estimate refers. Such a measure would be useful in consumption function applications, as well as in describing the scale and structure of the economy.

Book and reproduction cost measures differ, theoretically, in that the former measures the capital stock in terms of what was given up to obtain it, while the latter measures the capital stock in terms of what would have to be given up in the current year to reproduce it. In an unchanging economy in equilibrium, these measures would be identical. In an economy in which there were no changes except in the price level, they could be made identical by means of the deflation adjustment described above. In the absence of this adjustment, book value would exceed reproduction cost whenever the price level was falling, and vice versa. Changes in relative prices could lead to the divergence of the two measures, even after adjustment. Thus, if the prices of capital goods fell relative to the prices of consumption goods, adjusted book value measures would exceed reproduction cost, and vice versa. (All of the above analysis rests on the assumption that the market price of new capital goods equals the reproduction cost of these goods. If that is not the case, matters become more complicated, as will appear.)

In fact, we know that neither the price indexes of consumption goods nor those of capital goods exhibited a very pronounced trend between 1820 and 1860, though the latter fell slightly as compared with the former (see Brady 1964; US Bureau of the Census 1960, series E-1, E-7, E-8). Between 1859 and 1869–78, the price index of consumption goods rose dramatically while the price index of capital goods did not (Gallman 1966). The two indexes then fell pronouncedly until nearly the end of the nineteenth century, the latter declining the more markedly. Thus, for the dates of concern here, book value (adjusted and unadjusted) probably exceeded reproduction cost modestly, in 1840–60 and, more markedly, in 1880–1900, adjusted book value also probably exceeded reproduction cost in 1870.

Book value measures look to the past (what was given up to obtain capital) while market values look to the future (earnings potential). In an unchanging economy in equilibrium, and with perfect knowledge, book value and market value would differ only in that the former treats each piece of capital as though it were new, while the latter does not. Even in an unchanging economy, fixed capital would gradually wear out. Therefore, old fixed capital would sell for less than new fixed capital, and a capital stock expressed in market values would be smaller than one expressed in book values. The disparity could easily be removed by deducting capital consumption from the book value measures, producing estimates of net book value.

The effects of changing prices (levels and relative prices) on the relative magnitudes of net book and market values are presumably much the same as the effects of changing prices on the relative magnitudes of book and reproduction cost values (see above). Once we drop the assumption of perfect knowledge, other opportunities for divergence between capital stock estimates based on these two concepts emerge. Specifically, deviations between the expected life of individual pieces of fixed capital (on which capital consumption allowances rest) and their actual life may arise. These deviations may prove in practice not to be serious, in view of the opportunity for errors of opposite direction to offset in the aggregate, though a general change in the rate of innovation could produce an uncompensated deviation.[3] Changes in the interest rate produce systematic shifts in the relative values of assets of differing life expectation in the market, but they do not influence aggregate net book values. Actual changes in the interest rate over the last sixty years of the nineteenth century seem likely to have raised market values above net book values from 1870 onward; but not by much, except perhaps for the year 1900 (Gallman 1987).

Once allowance is made for capital consumption, reproduction cost (that is, net reproduction cost) ought to be similar to market value. Indeed, if the economy were in equilibrium—such that the market price of new capital equaled its reproduction cost[4]—and if capital consumption allowances followed the pattern implicit in the structure of the sales prices of capital goods of differing vintage, then market value and net reproduction cost would be identical. In fact, however, these conditions are not met. Market prices deviate from the value of resources used up in production (there are profits or losses), and capital consumption allowances fail to reflect precisely the structure of prices of capital of differing age. Thus, divergences arise between market value and net reproduction cost—divergences of a type discussed previously in connection with book and market values.

Finally, it should be said that the deviations among net book value, net reproduction cost, and market value are least marked for items recently produced; in equilibrium, there is no deviation at all for new goods. The faster a capital stock grows, ceteris paribus, the lower the average age of capital and the narrower the differences among book value, reproduction cost, and market value. As will appear, the US capital stock grew at an extraordinarily rapid pace in the nineteenth century. Thus, the application of the three concepts might produce net valuations that differed little from one concept to the next. The market value and reproduction cost of inventories also will normally differ little. Thus, the more important inventories are in the total capital stock, the smaller the disparity between aggregate reproduction cost and aggregate market value, ceteris paribus. Inventories were in fact an important element of the nineteenth-century capital stock, partly because agriculture bulked large in the economy and agriculture held large inventories (e.g., of animals).

If data were readily available and estimates costlessly made, it would be desirable to have sets of capital stock estimates based on acquisition costs, reproduction costs, and market values. Comparisons among the estimates would have interesting analytical uses (e.g., Tobin's $q$). Unfortunately, these conditions do not obtain. Data are less than abundant and less than perfect; the assembly of estimates is not costless.

The data that have been most abundant have been acquisition cost data, since firms maintain records of sales and purchases and keep books on their capital stock. Given good price data, evidence on purchases and sales can also be converted into perpetual inventory reproduction cost estimates, although the procedure is not problem-free. Market values and census-type figures on reproduction cost are much harder to obtain. Few elements of the capital stock (apart from goods held in inventory) are sold in any given year. If the capital stock is to be valued at market prices, imputations must be drawn from recorded prices in markets that may be very thin (see also Kuznets 1938).

Estimating reproduction cost is even more difficult, since it sometimes requires that one work out the cost, in a given year, of producing a good that in fact was not produced in that year. These are familiar points. But we should not lose sight of the fact that market and reproduction costs are constantly being estimated, and that there are experts who spend their lives at these tasks—experts hired by insurance companies, the loan departments of banks, and various tax offices. Indeed, anyone who owns a home has a fair idea of what it would bring on the market, or what it would take to rebuild it, despite the gyrations of the real estate market.

In the nineteenth century, book value data were much less common than they are today. Until late in the century, most firms charged off capital purchases on current accounts. Thus, there were few books to refer to when the census taker came around. Perhaps equally important, businessmen did not think in terms of book value. It was more natural for them to appraise plant and equipment in terms of what it would take to replace it should it all burn down, or what it might sell for. This was even more clearly the case for farmers and householders viewing their property. These notions of value seem to have influenced the designers of census questions. While the questions are by no means always crystal clear, they seem to refer most often to market value or net reproduction cost. (The two concepts are not always clearly distinguished.) There is little doubt—especially for the first three or four census dates—that book value was only rarely sought by census takers, though how rarely is a matter on which there is not full agreement. Gallman and Howle (1965) concluded that most of the census returns they used were expressed in market values or net reproduction costs (see table 3.1). But this position stands in opposition to very good authority; Kuznets (1946) and Creamer, Dobrovolsky, and Borenstein (1960), for example, believe that the manufacturing censuses for 1880, 1890, and 1900 returned book value.

The distinctions among book value, market value, and reproduction cost may not have great practical significance in any case, so far as the nineteenth-century capital stock is concerned.[5] This is especially true in view of the wide margins for error that must be assigned to the estimates. More important is whether the census measurements of fixed capital are net or gross. There exists a test that does not rely on the interpretation of nineteenth-century language. One can check the census data (land improvements and manufactured producers' durables, separately) against perpetual inventory estimates based on reproduction cost.

As the story of these tests has been told elsewhere (Davis and Gallman 1973; Gallman 1987; and chapter 6 in this volume), only a brief summary is offered here. The net reproduction cost estimates check quite closely with the census aggregates before the Civil War, suggesting that the latter are indeed net valuations. There is also some support for the notion that the census valuations refer to reproduction cost and that they are accurate. The postbellum fit is poorer, but the evidence for the belief that the census figures are net is strong: the perpetual inventory figures typically exceed the census figures.

Our estimates of agricultural land improvements (clearing, breaking, fencing, draining, irrigating) depend chiefly on census physical stock data (e.g., acres of improved land) and various coefficients developed from the work of Martin Primack (1962). Given the form of the data, we were restricted to the construction of reproduction cost figures. Fishlow's (1965, 1966) estimates of railroad investment also rest on physical data, as do our estimates for the telegraph industry. In these cases, however, the form of the data left open the possibility of constructing book value series. In order to maintain consistency with most of the rest of the work—and because we believed they would prove more useful—we chose to produce reproduction cost estimates instead.

The capital stock figures, thus, consist chiefly of net reproduction cost or market value estimates, as table 3.1 indicates. The assignment of items to the reproduction cost category in table 3.1 is sure, but the same cannot be said of the estimates referred to as "market value." For a number of these, the valuation may in fact refer to net reproduction cost. The practical distinctions between these two types of measures on the dates to which the capital stock estimates refer, however, are unlikely to be very important, for the reasons given earlier in this section.

All of the data—including the federal census data—underwent considerable processing and testing during the construction of the estimates.

The estimating and testing notes are included in chapters 7–12 in this volume. Some general statements of appraisal can be ventured, however.

The evidence is considerably weaker for 1840 and 1870 than for the other census dates. The 1840 census provided much less information on wealth than did the censuses in subsequent years (though with respect to the trade sector, it was unusually helpful). Also, prices fell dramatically across that census year, which means that it is very important to date the available evidence correctly. We cannot be absolutely sure that we have done so. The census dragged on for an inordinate length of time, so that the dating of census magnitudes is problematic. We also were obliged to depend heavily on the work of Ezra Seaman (1852), who was not always entirely clear about his valuation base. The 1870 census came at a difficult time, and it is widely believed that Southern wealth was badly returned (Ransom and Sutch 1975). Nonetheless, it must be said that the results of the perpetual inventory tests for these two dates do not impugn the stock estimates. The test is particularly difficult to run for 1840 and 1870, and the results must be regarded as particularly chancy. Still, it is moderately reassuring that the stock and flow estimates are about as consistent at these dates as at any others in our series.[6]

The test for 1880 is less successful. It suggests that our stock estimates at that date—for both equipment and improvements—may be too low. These are matters to which we will return below. It is perhaps sufficient to say here that the capital stock figures are much more likely to tell an accurate story of the long-term rate of growth and structural changes of the capital stock than of the decade-to-decade changes, and this is particularly true after 1860.

### 3.2.2. Constant Price Series

The best capital stock deflators available are to be found among the price index numbers assembled by Dorothy Brady (1966) to deflate components of the GNP. The Brady indexes are the best for several reasons: they are true price index numbers of capital goods (including structures), they are available in considerable detail, they were constructed with careful regard to their theoretical meaning, and their theoretical meaning makes them reasonably apt deflators for capital stock series valued in terms of reproduction cost or market value (see also Brady 1964). They are not perfect, but, in the absence of price data for old capital, they are as close to perfection as can be had. They are linked price indexes describing, in principle, the movement of the prices of capital goods of unchanging quality. If the economy were in equilibrium in all the relevant years, such that market prices and reproduction costs of new goods were identical, and if the prices of new and old goods moved closely together over time (i.e., if the interest rate was the same at each relevant date and the rate of obsolescence was unchanging), then deflation of capital stock estimates valued in market prices or net reproduction costs would yield a constant price series expressed in net reproduction costs. That is, it would produce a series in which each element measured the net reproduction cost of the capital stock, given the factor prices and techniques of producing capital goods of the base year. These conditions were surely not met: the interest rate changed, affecting the relative magnitudes of market value and reproduction cost. Nonetheless, the constant price capital stock series approximates more nearly to a reproduction cost series than it does to any other coherent concept.

While the Brady indexes were the chief deflators we used, other price data figure in important ways in the construction of the constant price capital stock series. Some important components of the capital stock were built up by placing values on counts of capital goods, described in physical terms. In these cases—improvements to agricultural land (structures apart), railroads, the telegraph, farm animal inventories, crop inventories—constant price estimates could be made directly from the evidence on physical counts and base year prices, and we could be sure that the series so constructed were true reproduction cost series, or very close thereto. Inventories of manufactured goods and imports were deflated with price indexes germane to the types of products incorporated in these inventories, drawn from sources other than the Brady papers (Gallman 1960; US Bureau of the Census 1960, series U-34, E-1, E-70).

The Brady indexes refer to the census years (beginning on 1 June of the years ending in nine and ending on 31 May of the years ending in zero) before the Civil War, and to calendar years ending in nine after the Civil War. The current-year capital stock valuations to which the Brady indexes apply refer to 1 June of the years ending in zero. The Brady indexes are adjusted on the basis of other available price data to make them conform to the appropriate dates. Gaps in the coverage of the Brady indexes were filled similarly.

### 3.2.3. Original and Refined Capital Stock Series Compared

The series presented here are refinements completed by Gallman to estimates made in collaboration with Edward Howle in the mid-1960s. The original Gallman-Howle estimates of the value of property employed in agriculture extract from the value of agricultural land and list separately the value of agricultural structures. These estimates treat all other agricultural improvements as part of the value of land. This accounting approach brought the estimates into conceptual alignment with the twentieth-century estimates.[7]

The refined Gallman figures include two sets of estimates, variants A and B. Variant A treats all improvements to farmland as capital. Variant B excludes land improvement other than structures. Variant B captures a conventional definition of reproducible capital, and is conceptually close to the original Gallman-Howle series. The two capital stock variants correspond to two variants of the GNP series appearing in Gallman (1966). The variant A capital stock estimates correspond conceptually, with the GNP II series that includes investment flows devoted to land clearing. The variant B capital stock estimates corresponds conceptually, with the GNP I series that excludes investment flows devoted to land clearing. For purposes of analyzing nineteenth-century developments (when land clearing was important), the GNP II series is certainly more appropriate than the GNP I series; similarly, the broader capital stock series (variant A) would be superior for these purposes to the narrower series (variant B), which reflects twentieth-century conventions.

The difference between variants A and B is the reproduction cost of clearing and breaking farmland, fencing it, and draining and irrigating it. The estimates of the value of land improvement are based on the work of Martin Primack (1962). The value of fences was taken net of capital consumption. Capital retirements were deducted from the other items, but no allowance was made for capital consumption, on the ground that normal maintenance would prevent physical deterioration of these improvements. Clearly some deduction in value should have been made to account for the deterioration of improvements on land withdrawn from production but not yet returned, for census purposes, as unimproved (i.e., land retired from cultivation), but no system for making this type of adjustment could be devised. The improvements estimates are therefore almost certainly overstated, as compared with the values recorded for other elements of the capital stock.

Farm improvements (exclusive of structures) constituted a very large part of the capital stock, but a part that declined in relative importance as time passed. Thus roughly 60 percent of the agricultural capital stock consisted of these improvements in the years 1840 and 1850—a fraction

TABLE 3.2 **Ratios of the value of farm improvements (exclusive of structures) to the value of US farm capital and the value of US domestic capital, measured in current and constant prices, 1840–1900**

|  |  | 1840 | 1850 | 1860 | 1870 | 1880 | 1890 | 1900 |
|---|---|---|---|---|---|---|---|---|
| Relative to farm capital | Current prices | 0.58 | 0.59 | 0.56 | 0.51 | 0.51 | 0.48 | 0.49 |
|  | 1860 prices | 0.61 | 0.61 | 0.56 | 0.55 | 0.58 | 0.55 | 0.54 |
| Relative to domestic capital | Current prices | 0.34 | 0.3 | 0.27 | 0.22 | 0.18 | 0.14 | 0.13 |
|  | 1860 prices | 0.38 | 0.34 | 0.27 | 0.24 | 0.22 | 0.14 | 0.12 |

Note: The denominators include farm improvements.
Source: See text.

that fell to less than 50 percent, in current prices, in 1900, and something over 50 percent, in constant prices. The fraction of total domestic capital accounted for by these improvements fell from between 35 and 40 percent in 1840 to just over 10 percent in 1900 (see table 3.2). It should be clear, then, that the refined Gallman variant A series, which is inclusive of improvements, is substantially larger than the original Gallman-Howle capital stock series, and exhibits a substantially lower rate of growth.

On balance, the other revisions made in the constant price series are not of overwhelming quantitative significance. In no year do they amount to more than 10 percent of the value of the domestic capital stock, but they are far from negligible. The adjustment for 1840 is in an upward direction, and those for the 1870–1900 period in a downward direction.

The original Gallman-Howle series, expressed in constant prices, was never published, but a set of index numbers based on it appeared in *American Economic Growth: An Economist's History of the United States* (Davis et al. 1972, 34). These index numbers provide the best bases for comparing the original Gallman-Howle series with the refined Gallman series.[8]

The comparisons can be made with data in table 3.3, which show that both variants of refined series describe lower long-term rates of growth than do the original (panels A and C). The disparities are wider when the refined series, inclusive of all farmland improvements (variant A in table 3.3), is compared with the original series. That is reasonable enough, in view of the conceptual difference between the two series and the well-known fact that the agricultural sector grew at a slower pace over the last six decades of the century than did the rest of the economy.

TABLE 3.3  Comparisons of the refined Gallman and original Gallman-Howle national capital stock series, measured in 1860 prices, 1840–1900

**A. Index numbers on the base 1860 = 100**

|   |   | 1840 | 1850 | 1860 | 1870 | 1880 | 1890 | 1900 |
|---|---|------|------|------|------|------|------|------|
| 1 | Refined series, variant A[a] | 38 | 57 | 100 | 118 | 178 | 328 | 475 |
| 2 | Refined series, variant B[b] | 31 | 51 | 100 | 121 | 189 | 385 | 570 |
| 3 | Original series | 28 | 51 | 100 | 143 | 220 | 437 | 656 |

**B. Annual rates of growth, short intervals (%)**

|   |   | 1840–50 | 1850–60 | 1860–70 | 1870–80 | 1880–90 | 1890–1900 |
|---|---|---------|---------|---------|---------|---------|-----------|
| 1 | Refined series, variant A[a] | 4.12 | 5.61 | 1.66 | 4.11 | 6.12 | 3.69 |
| 2 | Refined series, variant B[b] | 5.01 | 6.61 | 1.96 | 4.40 | 7.12 | 3.92 |
| 3 | Original series | 5.93 | 6.79 | 3.61 | 4.27 | 6.86 | 4.07 |

**C. Annual rates of growth, long intervals (%)**

|   |   | 1840–1900 | 1850–1900 | 1860–1900 | 1870–1900 | 1880–1900 |
|---|---|-----------|-----------|-----------|-----------|-----------|
| 1 | Refined series, variant A[a] | 4.22 | 4.24 | 3.89 | 4.64 | 4.90 |
| 2 | Refined series, variant B[b] | 4.84 | 4.81 | 4.35 | 5.15 | 5.52 |
| 3 | Original series | 5.26 | 5.12 | 4.70 | 5.07 | 5.47 |

Notes: [a]Includes all improvements to farmland. [b]Excludes all improvements to farmland except structures.
Sources: Refined series, see text. Original series derived from data in Davis et al. 1972, 34.

But even when the conceptual difference is removed—when the variant B series is substituted for the variant A series—the refined estimates exhibit somewhat lower long-term rates of growth than do the original estimates. The margins are not great, however: less than one-half of a percentage point in every case. The data on the decadal rates of growth show, moreover, that in only two decades, 1840–50 and 1860–70, are the disparities in growth rates at all wide (panel B). These are the decadal growth rates that are affected by the major estimating changes described at the top of this section. It should also be pointed out that the refined and original series exhibit the same patterns of change over time, the rate of growth rising from 1840–50 to 1850–60, falling to 1860–70, rising again to 1870–80 and 1880–90, and finally falling to 1890–1900.

On the whole, the refined series differ from the original in important respects, but once allowance is made for differences in concept and coverage, they appear to tell roughly the same story with respect to the rate of growth of the capital stock.

Two preexisting sets of comprehensive capital stock estimates cover a substantial part of the nineteenth century: Simon Kuznets's (1946) series, reported in *National Product since 1869*, which cover the years 1880, 1890, and 1900; and Raymond Goldsmith's (1952) revisions to the Kuznets figures and extension of them to 1850. There were also many sectoral estimates, deriving from a major program at the NBER in which Creamer, Dobrovolsky, and Borenstein (1960); Ulmer (1960); Grebler, et al. (1956); and Tostlebe (1957) participated (see also Kuznets 1961 and Kendrick 1961).

Kuznets's (1946) *National Product since 1869* provided the framework for this analysis. The volume contains very detailed estimates, together with full descriptions of estimating procedures. The idea was to modify Kuznets's estimates in light of the work that had come forward since *National Product since 1869* was published, and to extend the estimates to the years 1840, 1850, 1860, and 1870. The Goldsmith (1952) estimates for 1850, while available in less detail, were to serve as an antebellum benchmark.

Table 3.4 compares the refined Gallman series with the Kuznets and Goldsmith estimates. It will be seen that in the cases of fixed reproducible capital in farming, street railroads, shipping, canals, river improvements, and pipelines and in the cases of inventories of farm livestock and monetary metals, the differences are slight. (In the cases of street railroads and pipelines, there are no differences at all.) For the rest, there are substantial differences. As they relate to the Kuznets and Gallman estimates,

TABLE 3.4 **Ratios of the Goldsmith (1850, and elsewhere where indicated) and Kuznets (1880–1900) capital stock estimates, measured in current prices, to the refined Gallman estimates**

|   |   | 1850 | 1880 | 1890 | 1900 |
|---|---|---|---|---|---|
| **A. Fixed reproducible capital** | | | | | |
| 1 | Agriculture, variant B[a] | 1.07 | 0.97 | 0.97 | 1.00 |
| 2 | Mining | | 1.21 | 1.15 | 1.32 |
| 3 | Manufacturing | | 0.72 | 0.8 | 0.85 |
| 4 | Other industrial (trade) | | 1.56 | 1.27 | 1.28 |
| 5 | Nonfarm residences | | | | |
|   | Goldsmith | 1.10 | 1.20 | 1.15 | 1.28 |
|   | Kuznets | | 0.83 | 0.72 | 0.81 |
| 6 | Steam railroads | | 1.54 | 1.56 | 1.71 |
| 7 | Street railroads | | 1.37 | 1.38 | 1.32 |
| 8 | Pullman cars | | 1.32 | 1.37 | 1.57 |
| 9 | Telephones | | 2.81 | 1.98 | 1.95 |
| 10 | Shipping, canals, and river improvements | | 0.85 | 0.92 | 0.95 |
| 11 | Electric light and power | | | 1.63 | 1.42 |
| 12 | Waterworks[b] | | | | |
| 13 | Irrigation | | 1 | 1 | 0.78 |
| 14 | Pipelines | | 1 | 1 | 1 |
| **B. Inventories (Goldsmith)** | | | | | |
| 1 | Farm livestock | 0.92 | 1.05 | 0.96 | 1.06 |
| 2 | Monetary metals | 1 | 1.2 | 1 | 1 |
| 3 | Net international debits | 1.36 | 0.69 | 0.97 | 1.12 |
| 4 | Other inventories | 0.52 | 0.96 | 1.06 | 0.94 |
| **C. Totals** | | | | | |
| 1 | Fixed reproducible capital (Kuznets)[a] | | 1.10 | 1.04 | 1.11 |
| 2 | National capital (Goldsmith) | 0.89 | 1.17 | 1.16 | 1.2 |

Notes:
[a] Excluding farmland improvements, other than structures.
[b] Not estimated by Gallman.
Sources: Goldsmith 1952; Kuznets 1946.

they tend to cancel out, so that the values of aggregate fixed reproducible capital fall within 11 percent of each other in each year, the Kuznets figures being the higher. The net gaps between the Goldsmith and the Gallman estimates are wider, and they also run in opposite directions in 1850 and the later years. Thus, the Goldsmith series describes a substantially higher rate of growth across the nineteenth century than does the refined Gallman series, even when differences of concept and coverage are eliminated.[9]

The differences between the refined Gallman estimates and those of Goldsmith and Kuznets were due in part to newly available evidence, to different interpretations of the evidence, and to the use here and there of different concepts. Examples of new data based on later research by other scholars include the estimates relating to agriculture, the "other industrial" (or "trade") sector, nonfarm residences, steam railroads, telephones, canals and river improvements, electric power and light, irrigation, tax-exempt property, and international claims. Examples of new data based on research by Gallman and Howle include the estimates for inventories and the telegraph. Examples of different interpretations of existing evidence include the estimates for mining and manufacturing. (It appears that rented real estate was inadvertently left out of Kuznets's manufacturing estimates.) Examples of the use of different concepts include steam railroads and the telegraph, where estimates of net reproduction cost were substituted for book value.

In summary, then, the refined Gallman capital stock estimates are net of capital retirements and net of capital consumption. While a few of the components (current prices) are expressed in book values, most are in market prices or in net reproduction costs. Conceptually, the refined series differ importantly from the original; substantively, somewhat less. The substantive differences between the refined Gallman series and the Goldsmith and Kuznets nineteenth-century series are wide enough that one might anticipate that accounts of economic structure and change based on the refined series would offer an element of novelty.

## 3.4. Capital and Economic Growth

### 3.4.1. Rates of Growth

How did the growth experience of the US economy between 1840 and 1900 compare with growth at other times or in other places? It is difficult to make meaningful direct comparisons of this type, but a fairly obvious indirect one can be made. We know that the US real national product increased between the 1830s and 1900 at an exceptionally high rate (Gallman 1966; Davis et al. 1972, ch. 2). Unless the rates of change of capital stocks and national products diverged widely—which is highly improbable—the US capital stock must also have grown rapidly. That means that the US capital stock was probably relatively young, with a high proportion of the stock embodying best-practice techniques (Gallman 1978).

In fact, the data in table 3.5 show that the capital stock actually grew faster than the national product, in both current and constant prices, in both variants, over long periods and over most of the short periods identified in the table. That fact has a rather important set of implications. But before considering them, it will pay us to look at other aspects of the evidence in the table.

Rates of change of both variants A and B of the capital stock are contained in table 3.5. It will be observed that the rates of change of the variant B series are always at least as large as the rates of change of the variant A series, and usually larger. One should recall that the variant A series includes investment in agricultural land clearing, fencing, and the construction of drainage and irrigation ditches, while the variant B series does not. The variant A series grew more slowly because this component of the capital stock increased at a below average pace. This in turn was a consequence both of the fact that the value of improvements of this type (measured in reproduction costs) constituted a declining fraction of the value of the agricultural capital stock (in both current and constant prices) and of the fact that the agricultural sector—including the capital stock thereof—grew more slowly than the rest of the economy. The former development reflected both a slowing in the rate (percentage) at which agricultural land was being added to the stock, and in the continued high rates of increase of the stocks of agricultural structures and equipment, particularly the latter. Agriculture was becoming more highly mechanized.

A second feature of table 3.5 worth remarking is that the rates of growth recorded therein exhibit, on the whole, a downward long-term movement. This is true of both of the GNP series, in current and constant prices; both of the capital series, in current prices; and the variant B series, in constant prices. The variant A series, in constant prices, is only a moderate exception. It exhibits lower rates of growth for the periods 1860–1900 and 1870–1900 than for 1840–60, which makes it consistent with the variant B and GNP series. But if the period is broken into three equal lengths, the variant A series shows equal rates of growth for 1840–60 and 1880–1900, the rate for the period 1860–80 being considerably lower. This is the one bit of evidence running against a conclusion of general retardation in rates of growth across the latter part of the nineteenth century. The exception is not a very important one, however, in view of the reservations expressed above concerning the 1880 capital stock figure. If the estimate for that date is indeed biased downward, then an appropriate adjustment would remove this one exception to the general finding of retardation in the rates of growth of the GNP and the capital stock, a development begun in the nineteenth century and continued in the twentieth.

A third piece of information emerging from table 3.5 is that the decade-to-decade variations in the rates of growth of the GNP and the capital stock are reasonably consistent. Thus, the long-swing boom of the 1850s

TABLE 3.5 **Annual rates of growth of the national capital stock and GNP, 1840–1900**

| | Variant A[a] | | Variant B[a] | |
|---|---|---|---|---|
| | Capital stock | GNP[b] | Capital stock | GNP |
| **A. Measured in current prices** | | | | |
| Long-term | | | | |
| 1840–1900 | 4.35% | 3.86% | 4.84% | 3.96% |
| Intermediate | | | | |
| 1840–60 | 5.74 | 4.81 | 6.33 | 4.98 |
| 1860–1900 | 3.66 | 3.38 | 4.10 | 3.44 |
| 1870–1900 | 3.64 | (2.09)[c] | 4.04 | (2.12)[c] |
| 1860–80 | 3.31 | 4.16 | 3.79 | 4.24 |
| 1880–1900 | 4.00 | 2.61 | 4.40 | 2.64 |
| Short-term | | | | |
| 1840–50 | 4.77 | 3.73 | 5.46 | 4.10 |
| 1850–60 | 6.71 | 5.89 | 7.20 | 5.86 |
| 1860–70 | 3.72 | (4.39)[d] | 4.28 | (4.38)[d] |
| 1870–80 | 2.90 | (3.67)[e] | 3.31 | (3.98)[e] |
| 1880–90 | 4.94 | 2.49 | 5.59 | 2.54 |
| 1890–1900 | 3.07 | 2.74 | 3.21 | 2.75 |
| **B. Measured in 1860 prices** | | | | |
| Long-term | | | | |
| 1840–1900 | 4.22% | 3.86% | 4.84% | 3.98% |
| Intermediate | | | | |
| 1840–60 | 4.86 | 4.39 | 5.82 | 4.64 |
| 1860–1900 | 3.89 | 3.59 | 4.35 | 3.64 |
| 1870–1900 | 4.64 | (2.85)[c] | 5.52 | (2.89)[c] |
| 1860–80 | 2.88 | 3.61 | 3.1 | 3.68 |
| 1880–1900 | 4.86 | 3.57 | 5.52 | 3.61 |
| Short-term | | | | |
| 1840–50 | 4.12 | 3.56 | 5.01 | 4.04 |
| 1850–60 | 5.61 | 5.22 | 6.63 | 5.20 |
| 1860–70 | 1.66 | (3.03)[d] | 1.96 | (3.07)[d] |
| 1870–80 | 4.11 | (5.28)[e] | 4.40 | (5.44)[e] |

*continues*

TABLE 3.5 **(continued)**

| | Variant A[a] | | Variant B[a] | |
|---|---|---|---|---|
| | Capital stock | GNP[b] | Capital stock | GNP |
| 1880–90 | 6.12 | 4.05 | 7.12 | 4.13 |
| 1890–1900 | 3.69 | 3.07 | 3.92 | 3.09 |
| **C. Implicit price index** | | | | |
| 1840 | 84 | 97(94)[g] | 90 | 99(94)[g] |
| 1850 | 89 | 91(95)[g] | 94 | 91(96)[g] |
| 1860 | 100 | 100 | 100 | 100 |
| 1870 | 123 | (123)[h] | 126 | (123)[h] |
| 1880 | 108 | 113 | 113 | 115 |
| 1890 | 97 | 97 | 97 | 97 |
| 1900 | 91 | 94 | 90 | 94 |

Notes:

[a] The variant A measures include improvements to agricultural land; the variant B measures exclude all such improvements other than structures.

[b] The dates to which the GNP estimates refer differ slightly from the dates in the stub:

| Stub | GNP estimates |
|---|---|
| 1840 | 1839 |
| 1850 | 1849 |
| 1860 | 1859 |
| 1870 | Mean of 1869–78 |
| 1880 | Mean of 1874–83 |
| 1890 | Mean of 1884–93 |
| 1900 | Mean of 1894–1903 |

[c] These rates of growth were computed from data for 1869–78 and 1894–1903 (means of annual data), and thus refer to the period 1873.5–1898.5.

[d] These rates of growth were computed from data for 1859 and 1869–79 (mean of annual data), and thus refer to the period 1859–73.5.

[e] These rates of growth were computed from data for 1869–78 and 1874–83 (means of annual data), and thus refer to the period 1873.5–78.5.

[f] The dates to which the GNP estimates refer differ slightly from the dates in the stub:

| Stub | GNP Estimates |
|---|---|
| 1840 | Mean of 1834–43 |
| 1850 | Mean of 1844–53 |
| 1860 | 1859 |

For the rest, see note b above.

[g] The implicit price indexes were computed from annual current price data (1839, 1849) and decade average constant price data (1834–43, 1844–53); see notes b and f above. The index numbers in parentheses were computed from annual data above (1839, 1849).

[h] Refers to the period 1869–78.

Sources:

(1) See text.

(2) GNP estimates: Variant B, Gallman 1966, 26, table A-1 (See note b below). Variant A computed from Gallman 1966, pp. 26 and 35, tables A-1 and A-4, variant I, and the implicit price index of improvements to farmland (exclusive of structures) computed from data underlying the appendix. GNP A is defined as conventional GNP plus the value of improvements to farmland (table A4 in Gallman 1966). The numbers in the table assume that average annual improvements, 1849–58, were equal to improvements in 1859. Constant price improvements (table A4 in Gallman 1966) were converted to current prices by means of the price index of agricultural land improvements, exclusive of structures, implicit in the data underlying the appendix. The numbers in the table assumed that the value of improvements (current and constant prices) in 1839 and 1849 were equal to the mean values in 1834–43 and 1844–54 respectively.

clearly emerges from the record provided by table 3.5, rates of growth rising above the levels attained in the 1840s (with the exception of the current price GNP variant B series), while the rates of change of all series drop sharply in the Civil War decade, 1860–70.[10] Between 1870 and 1880 the rates of change of the current price series continue to fall, reflecting the price deflation of the period, while the rates of change of the real series all rise. All of these variations are reassuring. They correspond to what one might have expected, from a knowledge of the qualitative history of the period and of quantitative studies of a micro variety. It is also reasonable to expect the rates of change of the GNP and capital stock series to move together as they do. These features of table 3.5 thus enhance one's confidence in the capital stock series, but necessarily offer no new insights into the period.

The consistency in the movements of the rates of change of the two sets of series ends with 1880. Thereafter, the rate of growth of the GNP series, expressed in constant prices, falls persistently, while the rate of growth of the current price series falls and then rises. The rates of change of the current and constant price stock series follow neither of these patterns, rising between 1880 and 1890 and falling between 1890 and 1900. Thus, the variations in the rates of growth of the GNP and capital stock series diverge across the last two decades of the century. Once again, if the capital stock estimate for 1880 is indeed too low, adjusting it might bring the patterns of change of the two series more nearly into line.

### 3.4.2. Sources of Growth

How do the revised Gallman capital stock series (in table 3.5) affect our understanding of the sources of economic growth? Davis et al. (1972) and Gallman (1980) had performed standard growth accounting analysis on the basis of the original Gallman-Howle capital series. Table 3.6 compares the results from reworking the analysis using the refined series, together with the original figures. The revisions leave everything unchanged from the earlier set of calculations, with the following exceptions: in the new calculations based on the variant B series, the contributions of the capital stock and productivity are recomputed; in the new calculations based on the variant A series, the contributions of capital, productivity, and land are recomputed. The variant B series is conceptually identical to the original Gallman-Howle series. It was therefore possible to substitute it into the calculations without changing anything else, except for the contribution of productivity change to economic growth. Because productivity change is taken as a residual, the introduction of a new capital stock series necessarily produces changes in the productivity figures. The variant A series differs conceptually from the original Gallman-Howle series, incorporating elements of value attributed to land in the Gallman-Howle framework. Substituting variant A into the calculations therefore required reestimating the land supply and the system of weights to be attached to the rates of change of capital and land. The details of these calculations are given in the notes to table 3.6. Note that the labor input is the size of labor force, without accounting for human capital or hours worked. The land input is restricted to agricultural land.

Table 3.6 is organized as a set of "sources of growth" calculations of the type made popular by Edward Denison. Panel A shows the contribution of each factor of production and productivity change to the rate of growth of real net national product and real net national product per capita. Panel B displays these figures in the form of percentile distributions.

The calculations based on the original series invited the conclusion that nineteenth-century growth could be attributed chiefly to increases in the supply of factors of production, in contradistinction to that of the twentieth century, in which productivity change was the leading source of growth. The refined capital stock series do not oblige us to change this view dramatically. But they do argue for the assignment of a somewhat larger importance to nineteenth-century productivity change than recent custom has accorded it. In particular, use of the variant A series leads to the conclusion that productivity change accounted for almost six-tenths of the growth of per capita NNP in the nineteenth century. This is lower than the figure recorded for the twentieth century (almost eight-tenths), but is by no means low. The term "productivity" covers the influences of a multitude of forces operating on output. Perhaps a more meaningful way to put the conclusion is to say that the calculations in table 3.6 (variant A) assign to the factor inputs, narrowly defined, responsibility for only a little more than two-fifths of the increase in per capita real national product across the last six decades of the nineteenth century. The role of other forces, therefore, cannot be regarded as small.

### 3.4.3. Capital-to-Output Ratios

The capital stock increased faster than the national product, according to the data in table 3.5. This means that the capital-to-output ratio was rising; the economy was engaged in capital deepening. Table 3.7 is organized

TABLE 3.6 **Contributions of factor inputs and productivity to the growth of net national product, total and per capita, 1840–1960**

|  |  | 1840–1900 | | | 1900–60 |
|---|---|---|---|---|---|
|  |  | Original | Refined | | |
|  |  |  | Variant A | Variant B | Original |
| **A. Average annual rates of growth** | | | | | |
| I. Net national product, total | | | | | |
| 1 | Labor force | 1.88% | 1.88% | 1.88% | 1.09% |
| 2 | Land supply | 0.38 | 0.13 | 0.38 | 0.08 |
| 3 | Capital stock | 1.03 | 1.12 | 0.94 | 0.58 |
| 4 | Productivity | 0.69 | 0.85 | 0.78 | 1.38 |
| 5 | Totals | 3.98 | 3.98 | 3.98 | 3.12 |
| II. Net national product per capita | | | | | |
| 1 | Labor force | 0.17% | 0.17% | 0.17% | 0.11% |
| 2 | Land supply | 0.05 | 0.02 | 0.05 | -0.01 |
| 3 | Capital stock | 0.55 | 0.42 | 0.46 | 0.28 |
| 4 | Productivity | 0.69 | 0.85 | 0.78 | 1.31 |
| 5 | Totals | 1.46 | 1.46 | 1.46 | 1.69 |
| **B. Percentage distributions** | | | | | |
| I. Net national product, total | | | | | |
| 1 | Labor force | 47.2% | 47.2% | 47.2% | 34.8% |
| 2 | Land supply | 9.6 | 3.3 | 9.6 | 2.5 |
| 3 | Capital stock | 25.9 | 28.1 | 23.6 | 18.6 |
| 4 | Productivity | 17.3 | 21.4 | 19.6 | 44.1 |
| 5 | Totals | 100 | 100 | 100 | 100 |
| II. Net national product per capita | | | | | |
| 1 | Labor force | 11.6% | 11.6% | 11.6% | 6.7% |
| 2 | Land supply | 3.6 | 1.6 | 3.6 | -0.6 |
| 3 | Capital stock | 37.5 | 28.6 | 31.5 | 16.4 |
| 4 | Productivity | 47.3 | 58.2 | 53.3 | 77.5 |
| 5 | Totals | 100 | 100 | 100 | 100 |

Sources: All of these figures, except the ones labeled "Land supply, variant A," "Capital stock, variants A and B," and "Productivity, variants A and B" were taken from Davis et al. 1972, table 2.12, and Gallman 1980, tables 1 and 2, or were computed from these tables or their underlying data. The productivity figures in panel A were taken as residuals. The data in panel A labeled "Capital stock, variants A and B" were derived by weighting rates of change with appropriate income share weights. The rates of change were taken from table 3.5, above (in the case of panel A, part D) or were computed by subtracting the rate of change of population from the rate of change in table 3.5 (in the case of panel A, part II). The income share weight for the variant B series (0.19) was taken from the notes to table 2.12 of Davis et al. 1972. The income share weight for the variant A capital series (0.26) was computed by raising the variant B weight in the same proportion as the variant A capital stock figure (current prices) exceeds the variant B figure, in 1860. The average annual rate of change of the variant A land supply figure was computed from US Bureau of the Census 1960, series K-2, 1850–1900. The income share weight (0.06) was computed by subtracting the capital stock weight (0.26) from the sum of the land and capital stock weights (0.32) employed for the variant B calculations.

to describe this process. The data leave something to be desired because, for the period before the Civil War, some of the ratios depend upon data referring to individual years. The ratios, therefore, are influenced by events peculiar to these years and may not be fully representative of the period 1840–60. The postbellum estimates are less susceptible to this

TABLE 3.7  **Capital-to-output ratios, measured in current and 1860 prices, 1840–1900**

| Year | Variant A | Variant B | Inventories | Farm improvements[b] | Other improvements | Equipment |
|------|-----------|-----------|-------------|----------------------|--------------------|-----------|
| | | | | Numerators[a] | | |
| **A. Measured in current prices** | | | | | | |
| 1840 | 2.37 | 1.63 | 0.67 | 0.84 | 0.74 | 0.23 |
| 1850 | 2.64 | 1.87 | 0.73 | 0.81 | 0.88 | 0.24 |
| 1860 | 2.86 | 2.14 | 0.72 | 0.78 | 1.14 | 0.25 |
| 1875 | 2.58 | 2.08 | 0.74 | 0.54 | 1.19 | 0.24 |
| 1880 | 2.45 | 2.00 | 0.69 | 0.48 | 1.16 | 0.24 |
| 1890 | 3.14 | 2.71 | 0.75 | 0.45 | 1.72 | 0.36 |
| 1900 | 3.25 | 2.84 | 0.74 | 0.43 | 1.73 | 0.40 |
| **B. Measured in 1860 prices** | | | | | | |
| 1840 | 2.75 | 1.79 | 0.85 | 1.10 | 0.76 | 0.15 |
| 1850 | 2.69 | 1.82 | 0.79 | 0.92 | 0.84 | 0.17 |
| 1860 | 2.92 | 2.19 | 0.73 | 0.79 | 1.17 | 0.26 |
| 1875 | 2.78 | 2.17 | 0.75 | 0.65 | 1.18 | 0.34 |
| 1880 | 2.57 | 2.02 | 0.71 | 0.58 | 1.06 | 0.33 |
| 1890 | 3.16 | 2.72 | 0.75 | 0.46 | 1.40 | 0.70 |
| 1900 | 3.36 | 2.95 | 0.70 | 0.42 | 1.38 | 0.91 |

Notes: [a]All the denominators, except for those for column 2, are GNP, variant A (see table 3.5); the denominators for column 2 are GNP, variant B. [b]Exclusive of structures.
Sources: See the source notes to table 3.5.

criticism because the national product data are decade averages, centered roughly on the years to which the capital stock figures refer (see the notes to table 3.7). One should remember also that the estimates are not equally reliable; those for 1840, 1870, and 1880 rest on capital stock data that are probably less strong than the data for the other years. Differences in ratios between one year and the next should not be given undue importance. It is the general drift of the ratios that should be the focus of our interest.

The aggregate capital-to-output ratios (first two columns of table 3.7) do in fact rise over time, and this is true of both the variant A and the variant B series in current and constant prices. The variant A ratios are much larger than the variant B ratios, indicating the great quantitative significance of the component of capital consisting of farmland clearing, fencing, and so on (see also the fourth column), components included in variant A but not variant B. The variant A ratios also rise less rapidly than the variant B ratios, reflecting the declining relative importance of these forms of agricultural land improvement. But both series, in current and constant prices, exhibit a fairly marked increase; or perhaps it would be best to speak of two increases. All of the series show some rise before the

Civil War, a decline to the first two postbellum dates for which we have ratios, and then a more pronounced increase to the end of the nineteenth century.

The last four columns of table 3.7 show that the increase of the aggregate capital-to-output ratio reflects exclusively developments with respect to equipment and improvements, other than agricultural land improvements. In current prices, inventories increased about as fast as did the national product, the inventory-to-output ratio changing little. In constant prices it actually declined moderately. The ratio of farm improvements to national product fell quite dramatically, especially in constant prices. On the other hand, the ratios of "other improvements" and of machinery and equipment to output rose vigorously, the latter particularly in the constant price variant; the relative prices of machinery and equipment were falling dramatically. By the end of the nineteenth century, the structure of the capital stock had changed strikingly. Whereas in 1840 farm improvements were the most important components of capital, accounting for over two-thirds of the value of the stock in constant prices, by 1900 their share had fallen to about a third. Machinery and equipment, composing barely 5 percent of the stock (constant prices) in 1840, were over 25 percent of the stock in 1900. Accompanying the capital deepening there was, then, a substantial reshaping of the stock, with new forms of capital rising to prominence.

The last four columns of table 3.7 also throw some light on the nature of the decline in the capital-to-output ratio between 1860 and 1875. Changes in the ratios of inventories, equipment, and "other improvements" to output clearly are not responsible. The first rose moderately, in both current and constant prices, whereas the other two either changed very little (equipment, in current prices), or rose vigorously (equipment, in constant prices; "other improvements," in current prices). But the ratio of "farm improvements" to GNP declined very sharply (especially in current prices) and played a major role in the observed capital shallowing for the economy as a whole. This development may reflect the effects of the Civil War. In the South, some improved land was allowed to return to nature during the war, while in the North the pace at which land was improved slackened for lack of labor. One would think that the effects of the Civil War on improved land would have been largely removed by 1875, but it may be that the value of improvements had not yet attained the level it would have reached had there been no war.

A second factor also bears on the change in the aggregate capital-to-output ratio between 1860 and 1875. Bear in mind that the numerator of

TABLE 3.8  **Capital-to-output ratios, 1860 and 1875**

|                              | 1860 | 1875 |
| ---------------------------- | ---- | ---- |
| **Measured in current prices** |      |      |
| Sum                          | 2.86 | 2.71 |
| Column 1                     | 2.86 | 2.59 |
| **Measured in 1860 prices**  |      |      |
| Sum                          | 2.95 | 2.92 |
| Column 1                     | 2.92 | 2.78 |

Source: See text.

the ratio is the national capital stock, an aggregate (variant A) composed of the four components discussed above—inventories, equipment, farm improvements, and other improvements—plus net claims on foreigners. The latter is represented only indirectly in table 3.7; that is, there is no column containing estimates of "net claims"-to-output ratios, paralleling the last four columns. The reason is that net claims represented a negative value in all the years of table 3.7, a relatively small one in most of them. Between 1860 and 1875, however, the size of this variable increased, going from a small negative value in 1860 to a very large one in 1875. This was also probably a consequence of the Civil War, which increased the volume of negotiable American debt, altered the disposition of American savings, and changed the American balance of trade. In any case, this phenomenon also played a role in the decline of the capital-to-output ratio between 1860 and 1875 (Williamson 1974).

An indication of the importance of the impacts of the Civil War is easily obtained. The sum of the ratios in the last four columns of table 3.7 in each year approximates the variant A ratio of domestic capital to GNP. The difference between this sum and the value in the first column measures the effect of net claims on foreigners on the national capital-to-output ratio. The sums and the entries from column 1 for 1860 and 1875 are as shown in table 3.8. The sums are almost identical with the first column values in 1860, but larger than the first column values in 1875. More to the point, the sums drop slightly between the two years in constant prices, while they fall more dramatically in current prices. The decline in the aggregate national capital-to-output ratio, then, reflects both changes in the international circumstances of the United States and changes in the agricultural sector, both sets of changes probably being legacies of the Civil War.

### 3.4.4. Capital-to-Output Ratios by Industry

Table 3.9 gathers together data at the industrial sectoral level, with the object of seeing how pervasive the trend toward higher capital-to-output ratios was. The evidence in Table 3.9 should be approached with great caution. All of the sectoral output data (value added) are discrete, being distributed at ten-year intervals from 1840 to 1900. Ratios measured from such data are likely to be unstable, particularly when computed for narrow industrial sectors. Furthermore, since it is not possible to distribute all inventories accurately among industrial sectors, they are left out of account here. The ratios measure only fixed capital. The variations among these sectoral ratios in table 3.9 may not accurately represent sectoral variations in more comprehensively defined capital-to-output ratios. In particular, the ratios in table 3.9 probably understate the relative degree to which the "commerce" sector held capital. Additionally, the agricultural value-added data underlying lines 1(a and b) and 8(a and b) should have been adjusted to conform precisely to the variant A and B concepts.

TABLE 3.9  **Sectoral depreciable capital-to-value-added ratios, measured in current and 1860 prices, 1840–1900**

**Panel A. Depreciable capital-to-value-added Ratios**

|   |   | 1840 | 1850 | 1860 | 1870 | 1880 | 1890 | 1900 |
|---|---|---|---|---|---|---|---|---|
|   | **Measured in current prices** | | | | | | | |
| 1 | Agriculture | | | | | | | |
| a | Variant A | 3.23 | 3.25 | 2.51 | 2.73 | 3.21 | 3.31 | 3.31 |
| b | Variant B | 0.75 | 0.91 | 1.02 | 0.90 | 0.97 | 1.18 | 1.27 |
| 2 | Mining, manufacturing, and hand trades | 0.53 | 0.52 | 0.53 | 0.61 | 0.72 | 0.80 | 0.88 |
| 3 | All other private business (excl. residences) | 0.90 | 1.08 | 1.31 | 1.21 | 1.29 | 1.45 | 1.46 |
| a | Transportation and public utilities | 2.85 | 4.95 | 4.57 | 4.27 | 4.27 | 3.99 | 4.15 |
| b | Commerce and all other private business | 0.35 | 0.42 | 0.57 | 0.45 | 0.53 | 0.73 | 0.68 |
| 4 | Government and education | 1.36 | 1.76 | 1.32 | 1.27 | 1.70 | 1.45 | 1.82 |
| 5 | Farm and nonfarm residences | 4.75 | 5.33 | 7.87 | 6.28 | 8.86 | 11.3 | 10.99 |
| 6 | Weighted averages, lines 1–4 | | | | | | | |

*continues*

TABLE 3.9 *(continued)*

**Panel A. Depreciable capital-to-value-added Ratios**

|   |   | 1840 | 1850 | 1860 | 1870 | 1880 | 1890 | 1900 |
|---|---|------|------|------|------|------|------|------|
| a | Fixed (1860) v.a. weights, variant A | 1.47 | 1.86 | 1.87 | 1.56 | 1.70 | 1.93 | 1.99 |
| b | Fixed (1860) v.a. weights, variant B | 0.74 | 0.97 | 1.03 | 0.94 | 1.03 | 1.16 | 1.22 |
| c | Fixed K/O weights, variant A | 2.10 | 1.82 | 1.87 | 1.82 | 1.77 | 1.54 | 1.52 |
| d | Fixed K/O weights, variant B | 1.10 | 0.95 | 1.03 | 1.02 | 1.07 | 1.07 | 1.07 |
| 7 | Weighted averages, lines 1–5 | | | | | | | |
| a | Fixed (1860) v.a. weights, variant A | 1.77 | 2.17 | 2.41 | 1.98 | 2.34 | 2.77 | 2.80 |
| b | Fixed (1860) v.a. weights, variant B | 1.10 | 1.35 | 1.63 | 1.42 | 1.72 | 2.06 | 2.09 |
| c | Fixed K/O weights, variant A | 2.69 | 2.48 | 2.41 | 2.36 | 2.23 | 1.96 | 1.93 |
| d | Fixed K/O weights, variant B | 1.77 | 1.70 | 1.63 | 1.62 | 1.61 | 1.54 | 1.53 |
| | **Measured in 1860 prices** | | | | | | | |
| 8 | Agriculture | | | | | | | |
| a | Variant A | 3.01 | 3.19 | 3.27 | 3.18 | 2.76 | 2.72 | 2.90 |
| b | Variant B | 0.65 | 0.75 | 1.02 | 1.05 | 0.81 | 0.87 | 1.04 |
| 9 | Mining and manufacturing | 0.63 | 0.43 | 0.55 | 0.99 | 0.83 | 1.54 | 1.79 |

**Panel B. Weights**

|   | Lines 6a + 6b | Lines 7a + 7b |
|---|------|------|
| Agriculture | 0.38 | 0.35 |
| Mining, etc. | 0.24 | 0.22 |
| Transportation, etc. | 0.07 | 0.06 |
| Commerce, etc. | 0.29 | 0.26 |
| Government, etc. | 0.02 | 0.02 |
| Residences | | 0.09 |

**Panel C. Shares**

|   | 1840 | 1850 | 1860 | 1870 | 1880 | 1890 | 1900 |
|---|------|------|------|------|------|------|------|
| **Lines 6c and 6d** | | | | | | | |
| Agriculture | 0.45 | 0.39 | 0.38 | 0.36 | 0.31 | 0.21 | 0.20 |
| Manufacturing, etc. | 0.19 | 0.25 | 0.24 | 0.24 | 0.27 | 0.32 | 0.33 |
| Transportation, etc. | 0.08 | 0.05 | 0.07 | 0.07 | 0.09 | 0.10 | 0.10 |
| Commerce, etc. | 0.26 | 0.29 | 0.29 | 0.31 | 0.31 | 0.34 | 0.34 |
| Government, etc. | 0.02 | 0.02 | 0.02 | 0.02 | 0.02 | 0.03 | 0.03 |

TABLE 3.9 *(continued)*

**Panel C. Shares**

|  | 1840 | 1850 | 1860 | 1870 | 1880 | 1890 | 1900 |
|---|---|---|---|---|---|---|---|
| **Lines 7c and 7d** | | | | | | | |
| Agriculture | 0.41 | 0.35 | 0.35 | 0.33 | 0.28 | 0.19 | 0.18 |
| Manufacturing, etc. | 0.17 | 0.22 | 0.22 | 0.24 | 0.25 | 0.30 | 0.31 |
| Transportation, etc. | 0.07 | 0.04 | 0.06 | 0.06 | 0.08 | 0.09 | 0.09 |
| Commerce, etc. | 0.23 | 0.26 | 0.26 | 0.26 | 0.29 | 0.32 | 0.32 |
| Government, etc. | 0.02 | 0.02 | 0.02 | 0.02 | 0.02 | 0.03 | 0.03 |
| Residences | 0.10 | 0.11 | 0.09 | 0.09 | 0.08 | 0.07 | 0.07 |

Notes: v.a. = value added; K/O = capital-to-output ratio.
Sources:
Panel A. The value-added data are from Gallman 1960 and Gallman and Weiss 1969. The same agricultural value-added series were used to compute the ratios in lines 1a and 1b. (That is, no adjustments were made to bring them into closer conformity with the variant A and B concepts.) The same is true of lines 8a and 8b. Value added by construction (variant A) was included in the data from which lines 3a and 3b were computed. The numerators of the ratios of line 5 include the value of all farm buildings. The mining and manufacturing ratios, in current prices, are as follows: 1840, 0.60; 1850, 0.56; 1860, 0.58; 1870, 0.66; 1880, 0.77; 1890, 0.85; 1900, 0.95. Lines 6a, 6b, 7a, and 7b were computed by weighting the capital-to-output ratios in the body of the table by the shares of the sectors in the total value added of all sectors taken together. The weights are from panel B.
  Lines 6c, 6d, 7c, and 7d were computed by multiplying the 1860 capital-to-output ratios in the body of the table by annual sectoral shares in total value added. The shares are from panel C.
  The ratios of the sum of the value-added measures to GNP, variant A, are as follows: 1839, 1.03; 1849, 1.03; 1859, 0.98; 1869, 1.03; 1879, 104; 1889, 1.17; 1899, 1.16. Correcting the value-added and GNP estimates to put them both on the same basis, with respect to the treatment of farm improvements (variant A concept) and the international sector (i.e., leaving changes in claims against foreigners out of both sets of measures), and deducting from the value-added series those elements that are most likely to involve double counting (value added by steam railroads, public utilities, banks, fire and marine insurance, lawyers and engineers, "all other" professionals, and the independent hand trades), the ratios become thus: 1839, 1.05; 1849, 0.94; 1859, 0.96; 1869, 0.92; 1879, 0.93; 1889, 1.00; 1899, 1.00. The reconciliation between the two series is by no means perfect; the upward movement of the ratio from 1879 to 1889 is more than negligible. Nonetheless, the long-term trend is much reduced in the second tabulation, as compared with the first, and the variations from one year to the next are not large, in the context of the observed annual changes in GNP.

But these and other readily imagined adjustments were not made, as they are quite unlikely to alter the general results emerging from table 3.9 in any case.

Finally, it should be said that the sectoral value-added data have never been fully reconciled with the GNP data forming the bases of tables 3.5 and 3.7. When obvious conceptual or measurement differences between the two are eliminated (differences pertaining to the handling of the international sector and farm improvements), the sum of the value-added series exceeds the value of the GNP series in all years but one, the margin between the two widening over time. That is a reasonable result, in a general way. The aggregated value-added series are less net than the GNP series, the value of intermediate services being double-counted in the former but not in the latter. One would suppose that such duplication probably increased in relative importance as time passed. The value-added and GNP series, then, may be fully reconcilable. But since the former exhibits a higher rate of growth than the latter (due to the double-counting of intermediate services in the former), it follows that capital-to-output ratios computed from the former will show less tendency to rise over time than will capital-to-output ratios computed from the latter. That must be borne in mind when tables 3.7 and 3.9 are compared.

The analysis begins with three sectors: agriculture; mining, manufacturing, and hand trades; all other private business. The estimates for these sectors are relatively strong (that is, compared with the estimates on which the other ratios in table 3.9 depend), the capital and value-added estimates are independent in each case, and the sectors are sufficiently broad so that one can hope for a modicum of stability in the ratios.

All of the series, except for agriculture, variant A, show quite pronounced upward movements over time. The variant A series shows no very clear trend, in either current or constant prices. The variant B series and the ratios for the "all other private business" sector rise strongly before the Civil War, flatten out between 1860 and 1880, and then rise again strongly, while the "mining, manufacturing, and hand trades" sector exhibits a ratio that neither rises nor falls before the Civil War, but increases strongly from 1860 to 1900 in both current and constant prices. It would be fair to say, then, that the upward movement of the national capital-to-output ratio (table 3.7) represents a fairly pervasive movement, affecting the chief industrial sectors.

These conclusions are moderated only slightly if we look within the "all other private business" sector and observe the ratios for its two dissimilar components, "transportation and public utilities" and "commerce and all other private business." The ratios for the former are fairly volatile but show no long-term trend. That is not the case for the latter, the ratios for which move strongly upward to 1860, show no trend for the next twenty years, but rise pronouncedly again across the last twenty years.

The ratios for the remaining two sectors, government and education, and farm and nonfarm residences, also rise strongly and quite persistently, but there are reasons to place less emphasis on these data. The first sector is a very small one, and the capital stock data, with respect to government, refer only to buildings, while the education capital data include land as well as capital. Thus the evidence is not entirely apposite.

There are even more serious problems with respect to the residential

sector. The denominator of the ratio includes the shelter value of all residences, farm and nonfarm. Since the capital stock series do not distinguish farm residences, all farm buildings are included in the numerator,
which means that all of the ratios for this sector are biased upward. Furthermore, the denominator was initially estimated on the basis of capital
stock data (see Gallman and Weiss 1969), although not the capital stock
data appearing in the numerators of these ratios. Thus, the ratios cannot be taken very seriously. They are included for the sake of completeness and because the data do figure, in another form, in table 3.7, and the
reader is therefore entitled to know something about them.

Whether or not the estimating procedures were proper (for the purpose of measuring the capital-to-output ratio), the relationships obtained
between value added and the capital stock of the "residences" sector are
plausible. Reversing the ratios and adding land to residential capital, we
have estimates of the rate of return (gross) to residential property. The
computed rate follows fairly closely the pattern of the interest rate (at
least from 1860 onward), a result which might have been anticipated on
theoretical grounds. Thus, at least the value-added and capital stock data
for this sector seem consistent.

The point draws attention to a factor that figured in the upward drift of
all the capital-to-output ratios. The interest rate was falling through most
of the postbellum period. This was certainly true of the nominal rate, and
probably true of the real rate as well (see Davis and Gallman 1978). This
development affected the capital-to-output ratio, as measured here, in
two ways. First, a declining interest rate, ceteris paribus, leads to a rise in
the market value of the existing capital stock. (Bear in mind that many of
the capital values underlying table 3.9 are market values.) The increase
in market value, ceteris paribus, induces investment, since market price
exceeds reproduction cost. A falling interest rate, then, produces a temporary rise in the capital-to-output ratio, reflecting nominal changes only;
but in the long run it produces an increase based on real phenomena:
capital deepening. The actual interest rate reductions of the postbellum
period were sufficiently gradual that we may suppose that the increases in
the ratios described in tables 3.7 and 3.9 rest chiefly on real, not nominal,
developments.

The capital-to-output ratios in table 3.9 differ widely from one sector
to the next. In some measure this reflects no more than the fact that the
data exclude certain types of capital. But that is certainly not all there is to
it. The residential and transportation and public utilities sectors were, in

fact, more capital intensive than were the secondary sectors, for example. Since the structure of the economy was changing in important ways, the level of the aggregate capital-to-output ratio may have been influenced by the shifting relative importance of the various sectors. Lines 6(a–d) and 7(a–d) were computed to help settle that issue. The lines contain various weighted average capital-to-output ratios, sets of calculations appearing for variant A and B estimates, and for both all sectors except the questionable "residences" sector. In one set of calculations, 6(a and b) and 7(a and b), sectoral valueadded weights were held constant and sectoral capital-to-output ratios were allowed to vary over time. In the other, 6(c and d) and 7(c and d), capital-to-output ratios were held constant while value-added weights were allowed to change over time. The first set of calculations shows the effects of rising sectoral ratios on the aggregate ratio, no allowance being made for the effects of structural changes. In the second set, only structural changes influence the weighted averages.

The calculations show that the structural changes of the economy either produced no direct net long-term effect on the aggregate ratio, as in line 6d, or else reduced the ratio. The entire increase in the aggregate ratio was occasioned by developments within sectors. The explanation lies in the nature of the structural change that took place. The two sectors that exhibited the most pronounced alterations in their relative importance were agriculture and industry (mining, manufacturing, and hand trades), the former experiencing a pronounced loss in its share in aggregate value added, the latter a pronounced gain. The former had a high depreciable capital-to-output ratio (especially in the variant A form), the latter a very low one. The clear tendency of the exchange in degrees of relative importance of the two sectors was to force down the overall capital-to-output ratio. Two less pronounced compositional shifts in aggregate value added had the same effect. The "residences" sector, with a very high capital-to-output ratio, experienced a moderate loss in relative importance, while the "commerce, etc." sector, with a low ratio, gained in relative importance.[11] The one structural change that worked against the downward movement of the overall ratio was the growing relative size of the transportation and public utilities sector, with its exceptionally large capital-to-output ratio. All of these structural developments were interrelated: all were part of the general process of modernization, which consisted of the transfer of economic activities into the orbit of the market, increasing specialization and trade, and the movement of information and goods over longer distances and at faster rates.

While these structural changes had no pronounced direct effect on the depreciable capital-to-output ratio, they did influence the means by which the capital stock was assembled.[12] In the antebellum years, almost half of the depreciable capital stock (constant prices) consisted of agricultural land improvements, many created by family labor, by labor attached to the plantation on which they were constructed, or by other local sources of labor. These works were typically carried out in the off-season—the spaces in the agricultural year when there were no pressing tasks, such as planting or harvesting, associated with the growing crops. Little external finance was required to carry them out. But the structural changes of modernization brought to the fore industries, forms of capital, and organizational scales of operation that enhanced the roles of markets and of external finance in the provision of capital. Thus, the relative stability in the weighted averages of lines 6c, 6d, 7c, and 7d mask important developments with respect to American capital formation and finance.

The capital-to-output ratio can rise if the rate of growth of output falls without a compensating fall in the net investment proportion, if the net investment proportion (net investment to output) rises without a compensating increase in the rate of growth of output, or if some combination of these developments occurs.[13] The data of table 3.5 show that the rate of growth of output—GNP—did, in fact, decline during the nineteenth century. But what happened to the net investment proportion? Table 3.10 is organized to answer this question.

There are two ways of measuring the US investment proportion during the last six decades of the nineteenth century. Net investment can be measured across each decade after 1840 as the increment in the capital stock between the terminal dates of the decade. It can then be combined with estimates of the value of flows of commodities and services to consumers (1839–48, 1849–58, etc., in Gallman 1960, 27) to form estimates of net product (table 3.10, cols. 1, 2, and 4). This procedure does not result in useful estimates if current price stock data are employed; thus the estimates in table 3.10 all rest on constant price data. It should be said, however, that even the constant price estimates leave something to be desired, in view of the moderately ambiguous conceptual character of the stock estimates.

In the second procedure, net investment flows are estimated by subtracting from gross investment flows (Gallman 1960, 34) the value of capital consumption (table 3.10, col. 5). The latter can be estimated from the capital stock data, given estimates of the average age and useful life of the

TABLE 3.10  **Capital formation proportions, measured in 1860 prices, 1839–48 through 1889–98**

| Percentage | (1) | (2) | (3) | (4) | (5) | (6) | (7) |
|---|---|---|---|---|---|---|---|
| | National Capital | | | Depreciable Capital | | | |
| | Variant A | Variant B | | Variant B | | | |
| | Net | Net | Gross | Net I | Net II | Gross I | Gross II |
| 1839–48 | 12.1 | 9.6 | 14.3 | 6.0 | 5.6 | 11.1 | 10.6 |
| 1849–58 | 15.7 | 13.3 | 18.8 | 10.7 | 8.8 | 16.5 | 14.8 |
| 1869–78 | 12.8 | 10.7 | 18.4 | 7.3 | 15.4 | 15.5 | 22.3 |
| 1879–88 | 18.3 | 17.5 | 25.9 | 15.4 | 13.4 | 24.1 | 22.6 |
| 1889–98 | 14.8 | 13.8 | 26.4 | 11.1 | 15.7 | 24.5 | 27.9 |
| 1839–58 | 14.4 | 12.0 | 17.4 | 9.0 | 7.3 | 14.8 | 13.1 |
| 1869–98 | 15.6 | 14.5 | 25.1 | 11.9 | 14.3 | 23.0 | 25.0 |

Notes and sources:

The entries are a ratio × 100 where the denominator of each ratio is the sum of the numerator plus the value of flows to consumers, prices of 1860 from Gallman 1960, p. 27, column 5. The numerators are as follows:

Column 1: Increment to the national capital stock, variant A, 1860 prices, 1840–50, 1850–60, etc.

Column 2: Increment to the national capital stock, variant B, 1860 prices, 1840–50, 1850–60, etc.

Column 3: The numerators from column 2 plus capital consumption, the latter estimated at 10 percent of the value of machinery and equipment and 4 percent of the value of improvements (exclusive of farmland clearing, etc.). These estimates approximate straight-line capital consumption on the assumptions that machinery and equipment had a useful life of fifteen years and that the stock was on average five years old, and that improvements had a useful life of forty years and that the stock was on average fifteen years old.

Column 4: Increment to the depreciable capital stock (machinery, equipment, and improvements), exclusive of farmland clearing, etc.

Column 5: The numerators of column 7 minus the capital consumption allowances underlying column 3.

Column 6: The numerators of column 4 plus the capital consumption allowances underlying column 3.

Column 7: Gallman 1960, p. 34, column 1 plus column 2.

various components of the depreciable capital stock. The flow data are of such a character that investment proportions can be estimated for depreciable capital. Given estimates of capital consumption, it is also possible to generate gross investment shares, in which the measurement of gross investment depends exclusively on stock data (table 3.10, col. 3, 6). Of course, gross share estimates can also be made directly from the flow data (table 3.10, col. 7). Since the stock and flow data are not fully consistent, we have chosen to make estimates of investment proportions based on both sets of data, so that the fuller range of results obtainable from the data is exhibited.

All of the columns of table 3.10 devoted to the net proportion show it drifting upward over time. The movement is not uniformly persistent: the ratio actually falls between 1849–58 and 1869–78, as well as between 1879–88 and 1889–98, in the series depending exclusively on the stock estimates. This is not, however, altogether unexpected. As previously indicated, the 1880 stock estimate may be too low. Adjusting it upward appropriately might eliminate the first decline, although not the second. In any case, it would be expecting too much to hope to establish the timing of the upward movement of the proportion exactly with data of this type. More important is the fact of the long-term upward movement, a fact that emerges clearly in the data in the last two lines of table 3.10—more clearly from the flow data (col. 5) than from the stock data (cols. 1, 2, 4), however, and from the measures incorporating a narrow definition of capital (cols. 2 and particularly 4) more than from the ones based on a broad definition (col. 1).[14]

The increase in the net investment proportion required an even more pronounced increase in the gross investment proportion (cols. 3, 6, and 7). We do not need to go far to seek the explanation: the rising depreciable capital-to-output ratio meant that, ceteris paribus, the share of capital consumption in national product was rising. But in fact, other things were not equal: the structure of the depreciable capital stock was changing, the shorter-lived machinery and equipment increasing in importance relative to the longer-lived improvements. This structural change increased the share of national product accounted for by capital consumption.

These two developments meant that the share of GNP (based on the concept adopted in Gallman 1960) accounted for by gross investment more than doubled between the 1840s and the 1890s. One must further remember that the forms of investment and their relationships with the market were changing. The requirements for a rich and well-articulated system of intermediation were expanding (Davis and Gallman 1973, 2001).

## 3.4. Concluding Comparisons

To say that US capital stock increased rapidly or slowly between 1840 and 1900 is to make a comparative statement. It is to say that the stock increased rapidly or slowly compared to other times—earlier or later—or to other places. So far as earlier times are concerned, Alice Jones's (1980) wealth data for 1774 and the Gallman figures for the early part of the nineteenth century would provide bases for a relevant comparison. The exercise is done in chapter 4.

Here we make comparisons with subsequent times. Raymond Goldsmith's (1982) extension of his estimates to 1980 provides us with data

covering virtually the entire twentieth century. In concept, the refined Gallman variant B estimates are virtually identical to Goldsmith's twentieth-
century series.[15] Where the two overlap—at 1900—they are also substantively quite similar. Where differences of detail appear, aggregating up to
the next relevant level virtually removes them. For example, the estimates
of agricultural structures and equipment differ, in the two series, in 1900, but
the sums of the two—agricultural fixed capital—are virtually identical. The
same is true with respect to nonfarm residential land and nonfarm residential structures.[16] Thus the two series link together reasonably well, providing
coverage for a period of 140 years, the link being particularly good for "domestic wealth." Here, however, Goldsmith's domestic capital series will be
compared with the Gallman national capital series. For present purposes,
the consequences of the conceptual and substantive differences between the
series are trivial.

According to Goldsmith, domestic capital (reproducible tangible assets, narrow definition), in current prices, increased at an average annual
rate of 5.79 percent between 1901 and 1929, 5.00 percent between 1930
and 1953, and 8.20 percent between 1954 and 1980. These are, on the
whole, higher rates of change than are exhibited by the refined Gallman
series over similarly extended periods (see table 3.5). This is true whether
one looks at the variant A (which, recall, includes the value of improvements to farmland) or the variant B series (which excludes them). The
explanation lies in the price history of the two centuries. While prices rose
and fell dramatically in both the nineteenth and twentieth centuries, the
longterm drift in the former period was neither powerfully upward nor
powerfully downward. That is not true of the twentieth century, however.
Prices moved strongly upward, on average, between 1901 and 1929, 1930
and 1953, and 1953 and 1980.

The more relevant comparison uses the constant price series. Thus, deflating on the base 1929, Goldsmith's real capital stock increased at rates of
only 3.60 percent between 1901 and 1929, 1.68 percent between 1930 and
1953 and 3.60 percent between 1954 and 1980. Thus, in each of the three
periods, growth was lower than most of the rates exhibited in table 3.5.[17]
Over the full sweep of the years 1900 through 1980, the current price series rose 6.36 percent per year, on average, while the constant price series increased only 2.80 percent, the former substantially higher and the
latter substantially lower than the long-term nineteenth-century rates (see
table 3.5). Comparing the experiences of the two centuries, then, we find
marked retardation of the rate of growth of the real magnitudes, just as had

been previously discovered with respect to the real national product (Gallman 1966).

By the standard of twentieth-century experience, the capital stock grew rapidly between 1840 and 1900. The evidence in the next chapter will show that it also grew rapidly by the standard of what had gone before.

# Capital and American Economic Growth, 1774–1980

## 4.1. Introduction

This chapter greatly expands the temporal scope of our analysis of the capital stock in the nineteenth century. It links the decadal data from the 1840–1900 period to comparable aggregate series for the twentieth century and, more ambitiously, pushes back estimates to 1774. The United States achieved "modern economic growth"—that is, a high sustained rate of annual per capita income increase—during the period between 1774 and 1860. Changes in the capital stock provide clues into the timing and nature of this transformation.

A virtue of a capital stock series as an indicator of growth is that the short-term movements of such a series are likely to be much less violent than, for example, the short-term movements of a true income series. If estimates are available only at intermittent years, the rates of growth computed from the former are much less likely to be influenced by transient phenomena than are the rates of growth of the latter. As we will see, the capital stock evidence indicates that the American economy began to experience the process of modern economic growth after the War of 1812, and that by the 1840s the modern components of the economy were large enough and growing rapidly enough to have an observable impact on the rate of growth and the structure of the economy.

Gallman published the substance of this chapter as Gallman 1992; Rhode reordered and revised the text to enhance its fit and flow in this volume. Rhode also recalculated the growth rates on a continuously compounded basis, creating slight differences from the numbers appearing in Gallman (1992).

If the direct relationship between real capital and material well-being is to be examined, the capital stock series should be deflated by a consumer price index. That is, the stock should be appraised in terms of its equivalent in consumer goods. If, on the other hand, one is concerned with productive potential, proper deflation is in terms of the prices of the components of the capital stock. Both forms of deflation are employed in this chapter; the capital stock is treated as an index of both the material well-being of the society and its productive power.

The concept of capital is elastic. Some analysts have included land and investment in humans as elements of the stock. For most purposes, it is best to treat land as land and human capital as a characteristic of labor. In the present instance, the second preference makes a virtue of a necessity: there are no comprehensive estimates of human capital covering the full period of interest here. This chapter introduces a set of estimates of the land stock, but they are not treated as part of the capital stock.[1]

Although land is not included in the capital stock series of this chapter, improvements to land are. Most capital estimates include structures but omit other important improvements, such as the clearing and first breaking of land. In this chapter, a conventional series that omits the value of improvements to land is presented and is linked with estimates extending well into the twentieth century, for comparative purposes. But the series that is subjected to the most intense examination is one that includes the value of land clearing and breaking. These activities took up a substantial part of the work time of agricultural workers and made an immensely important contribution to the capital stock before 1860. They cannot properly be ignored.[2]

The United States (for convenience, the term will be applied to the colonies of 1774) began life as a debtor nation and gradually shifted to the position of a creditor nation. Ignoring recent experience, the national capital stock—which measures the net capital holdings of Americans—grew very much more rapidly over time than did the domestic capital stock, defined as capital physically located in the United States, regardless of who owned it. Most attention will be devoted to the domestic capital stock.

Section 4.2 deals briefly with the nature of the data underlying the estimates and the broad rules guiding the estimating procedure. Section 4.3 discusses estimating problems and tests of the consistency of the capital stock series before and after 1840. Section 4.4 treats the rates of growth of the real capital stock and the real capital stock per capita, with the

purpose of putting growth over shorter intervals into long-term historical perspective. Economic development involves structural shifts as well
as growth in the aggregates. Section 4.5 treats the changing composition
of the capital stock and shows its connection to the nature of American
economic development. Section 4.6 brings together estimates of all three
factor inputs and combines them into several series describing the growth
of total factor inputs. Estimates of changes in total factor productivity are
presented. Section 4.7 concludes.

## 4.2. The Estimating Procedures

In addition to capital stock figures for 1840–1900 at decade intervals, estimates were made for the years 1774, 1799, 1805, and 1815, and for various
dates in the twentieth century. The twentieth-century figures were assembled by splicing the nineteenth century estimates to Raymond Goldsmith's (1982) series, which are based on perpetual inventory procedures.
In tests conducted with data from the post–Civil War period, census-style
and perpetual inventory estimates appear to be roughly comparable.

The estimates for the years before 1840 come from a variety of sources
quite different from the censuses. This increases the risk that the capital
stock estimates based on them may not be consistent, one with the other,
and all with the figures for the years 1840 onward. (See chapter 14.) The
data that are farthest removed in type from census data are the ones underlying the capital stock figure for 1774. These data were taken chiefly from
Alice Jones's (1980) work with probate records, which value the property
of a deceased person. The figures for 1799, 1805, and 1815 rest principally
on sources that are more likely to be consistent with census records: the
direct taxes of 1799, 1813, and 1815 (Blodget 1806; Pitkin 1835; Soltow
1984). The 1805 estimate is based on the work of Samuel Blodget (1806)
and on Raymond Goldsmith's (1952) adjustments of Blodget's work. The
principal underlying source is the direct tax of 1799. Blodget apparently
carried the 1799 data forward to 1805 at a rate of growth he believed most
probable. The 1805 estimate falls out of line with those of 1799 and 1815,
and is probably too high. The history of the period leads one to expect a
higher rate of growth between 1799 and 1805 than between 1805 and 1815,
of course, but not quite so high as the Blodget data suggest. It is possible
that the 1805 figure is close to the truth and that the other two are too low;
it is also possible that the bias was introduced by the adjustment of the
Blodget data (see table 4.1). But neither seems likely.

TABLE 4.1 **Capital and wealth, estimates of Jones, Goldsmith, and Gallman, measured in current prices, 1774 and 1805, in millions of dollars**

|  | 1774 | 1774 | 1805 | 1805 |
| --- | --- | --- | --- | --- |
|  | **Jones** | **Gallman** | **Goldsmith** | **Gallman** |
| All structures |  |  | 370 | 352 |
| All land improvements |  | 180 |  | 732 |
| All privately owned real estate | 250 |  |  |  |
| Shipping |  | 8 | 40 | 80 |
| Other producers' durables | 13[a] | 15 | 32 | 65 |
| Inventories | 20 | 39 | 100 | 336 |
| Animals | 42 | 42 | 60 | 160 |
| Total domestic capital |  |  | 602 | 993 |
| International claims |  |  | −80 | −57 |
| Total national capital |  |  | 522 | 936 |
| Total domestic capital, including land clearing |  | 284 |  |  |
| Total private domestic, plus land | 327 |  |  |  |

Note: [a]Includes household equipment.
Sources: Jones 1980, 90; converted to dollars by means of the exchange rate in Jones 1980, 10; Gallman, see text; Goldsmith 1952, 315.

The 1774 through 1815 estimates depend on the sources listed above, augmented and adjusted so that the same concept of capital underlies each final aggregate figure, and so that the same estimating principles are applied in each case. The last point is an important one. While accurate estimates were sought in each instance, it seemed clear that it would be better to have a series for which the general level might be wrong, but which describes the rate of growth in a reasonably accurate way, than to have one for which the individual estimates might be closer to the truth, but which gives a more strongly biased account of the rate of growth. The choice made was always for consistency rather than for perfect accuracy.

Table 4.1 compares some of the details of the new estimates with those provided by Jones and Goldsmith. As will be evident, the adjustments made to the Jones figures were relatively unimportant, so that the new estimates tell very much the same story as do the data taken from Jones. The differences between the current estimates and Goldsmith's are greater, and are particularly pronounced with respect to inventories of all kinds. Goldsmith's estimates seem too low; for example, imports in 1805 ran around $150 million, and imports represented a relatively small part of total economic activity even in 1805. Even a very modest estimate of the fraction of imports held, on average, in inventory across the year would leave very little for inventories of domestic goods, were we to accept Goldsmith's figure for total inventories. But the question of the appropriate *level* of inventories in 1805 is perhaps not the important issue. The important point is the one made in the previous paragraph. The goals of the procedure to build the inventory estimates for all of the years, 1774–1900, have been to follow consistent methods and to pay more attention to consistency than to the specific level of any one estimate. Consistency permits appropriate comparisons to be made across time, an important desideratum. Users of capital stock series for the nineteenth century, then, would be well advised to use either Goldsmith's estimates or those presented here, but not some combination of the two.

All of the capital figures are expressed in market prices or in net reproduction costs. The two are virtually identical, where it has been possible to run a test. They are net of retirements and of capital consumption—with one exception, to be discussed below.

The cost-of-living deflator is the one assembled by Paul David and Peter Solar (1977), the only series that covers the full period. According to Claudia Goldin and Robert Margo (1989), the index rises too little or falls too much before the mid-1840s. If they are correct, the rate of growth of the capital stock deflated by this series is too high in the period before the mid-1840s, a point to which we will return. Dorothy Brady's (1966) investment goods price indexes, extended to the years before 1840 in a variety of ways, were the chief bases for the deflation of the capital stock, viewed as an input. The Brady index numbers refer to census years. They had to be adjusted modestly to make them relevant to the dates to which the capital stock estimates refer (the last day of the census year). Conceptually, these index numbers are exactly what are required. They were augmented in various ways to permit the deflation of inventories and certain types of farm improvements, for which Brady supplied no indexes.

## 4.3. Estimating Problems and Consistency Tests

This section addresses in detail the chief problems encountered during the construction of the capital stock estimates before 1840, with special attention to the difficulties of linking with the estimates from 1840 on. It also describes the tests that were run to check the estimating decisions that were made. (See also chapter 14.)

**Land Clearing and Breaking.** The largest item in the more unconventional but more meaningful concepts of capital employed in this chapter is the value imparted to land by the processes of clearing and first breaking.

The estimating procedure was simple. For each year, the following variables were established: the number of acres of improved farmland of each relevant type (land originally under forest, land originally under grass) in each state or region, the number of labor hours per acre required to improve land of each type, and the cost of farm labor in each state or region (Primack 1962; Lebergott 1964). Simple multiplication and addition produced the final figures. Constant price estimates were obtained by substituting technical coefficients and wage rates relevant to 1860 for those relevant to the current year. For the years 1840–1900, but not earlier, estimates of the value of fencing, drainage, and irrigation works were also made.

Certain characteristics of the series that may be associated with biased rates of change are immediately evident. The weight attributed to the clearing and breaking series is incorrect; it is probably too low, especially for the years before 1840. Since the clearing and breaking series exhibits relatively low rates of change over time, giving it a heavier weight would tend to reduce the rates of growth of the aggregate capital stock series, particularly before 1840. Thus the acceleration of the rate of change described previously in this chapter would be enhanced.

The weight attached to the series is too low because the estimates ignore all elements of clearing and breaking cost except labor. Labor was, no doubt, the principal cost, but it was not the only one. Second, the only improved land treated is agricultural land; no account is taken of land under houses, factories, shops, and so forth. Third, for the years before 1840, important elements of improvement—particularly fencing—had to be ignored. If it had been possible to treat all of these phenomena, the improvement series would have had a larger weight.

There are, however, certain offsets. First, the value of fencing may very well have increased faster than the value of clearing, before 1840; it is almost certainly true that the volume of land under houses and so forth increased faster than the volume of improved land in agriculture, at least after 1840. Introducing these elements into the analysis might raise the rate of change of the improvements series, though probably not by much.

Another factor may appear at first blush to be more important than any so far discussed: the estimates make allowance for land retirements (land allowed to go back to nature), but not depreciation. The reason depreciation has been ignored is that land improvements, if properly maintained, do not depreciate. Bad farming practices may erode the fertility of the land, and the opening of Western farms may reduce the value of Eastern farms, but these changes have to do mainly with the value of land, rather than with the value of improvements. Now, in a sense, this characteristic of improvements is shared with other elements of the capital stock. Properly maintained, houses and ships and even machines can last very long indeed. The difference is that most of the houses, ships, and machines that existed in eastern Pennsylvania in 1774, for example. are gone today, while much of the improved land of that period is still improved. A substantial part of it is now under houses and shopping malls and highways, rather than under maize cultivation, but it is still improved. Furthermore, in the cases of buildings, machines, and so forth, one can devise reasonable depreciation rates that properly describe the average lifetime experiences of these elements of capital, and that are roughly relevant to long reaches of history. That is not possible for land improvements.

The discussion above implicitly introduces another issue. The improvements series consists of reproduction cost estimates. Various tests have shown (see Gallman 1987) that the reproduction cost and the market value of structures and manufactured producers' durables were, on average, about the same in the nineteenth century. Is this also true of land improvements? If not, then how is the analysis affected? The few simple tests that have been run seem to suggest that they are alike. At least two efforts have been made to estimate the market value of clearing and breaking at midcentury: one by Stanley Lebergott for the Midwest, the other by Stanley Engerman and Robert Fogel for the South (Lebergott 1985; Fogel and Engerman 1977). Comparisons are not easily made, and the efforts reported here may be polluted by wishful thinking. The results suggest that estimates computed along the lines laid out above are very similar to the ones obtained by Lebergott and by Engerman and Fogel. The suggestion, then, is that the market price and the reproduction cost of land improvements were about the same, on average, at midcentury (see also chapter 7).

The same may also hold for 1774. At least it is true that when one subtracts from Alice Jones's estimate of the value of real estate, the current estimates of the value of land clearing and structures, and a rough allowance for other elements of land improvement (a relatively small part of the total), the remaining value, divided by the number of acres of land privately held (derived from Blodget 1806), yields an average price of land per acre—exclusive of improvements—that is almost identical with Blodget's estimate of the average value of unimproved land in 1774. The test is very roundabout and places much weight on a residual, but it encourages us to think that market price and reproduction cost may have been about the same, on average, at that date.

There is some evidence to the contrary, however. Specifically, Blodget's estimates of the average value of improved land per acre in 1774, 1799, and 1805 are substantially lower than the current estimates of the cost of improving land per acre. Bear in mind that Blodget's figures include the value of the land itself, while those presented here do not. The margin is so great that if Blodget's figures are truly market-price figures, and if those presented here are truly reproduction cost figures, one is left with the impression that farmers of the late eighteenth and early nineteenth centuries were behaving irrationally, improving much more land than could be justified by the market.

The estimates here are based on the assumption that all of the land improved at each of these dates had originally been forest land. That is probably not correct, and since forest land costs more to improve than grassland, this assumption probably leads to an overstatement of the value of cleared land at these dates. But the overstatement is tiny, and is surely more than offset by the fact that the cost of factors other than labor was left out of account.

It is also assumed that the labor hours per acre required for clearing were the same at these early dates as at midcentury. Primack (1962) believed that there were no important improvements in clearing techniques until after the Civil War, and while his interests were confined to the last half of the century, his remark is probably relevant to the early dates treated in this chapter as well. If this is wrong, the estimates *understate* the value of improvements at these dates, not *overstate* them.[3]

A more promising source of disparity lies in the way in which labor time was valued. It is assumed that the opportunity cost of the labor employed in clearing and first breaking could be approximated by the agricultural wage rate. In fact, however, one would suppose that clearing and first breaking would have been conducted by farmers in the off-season, when real opportunities may have been restricted to maintenance tasks around the farm, hunting, fishing, and so forth. The wage rate, then, may overstate the opportunity cost of labor. That seems not to have been the case at midcentury, when, as indicated above, reproduction cost and market value of improvements were very similar. It may be that by midcentury, clearing and breaking were more commonly hired out (e.g., to prairie sodbusters) than they had previously been, and that farmers themselves had better opportunities for off-season work. If that were the case, the estimating technique might work better for the mid-nineteenth century than for the earlier dates. But that would be a relatively unimportant matter. Our concerns are chiefly with the constant price series, which are properly a function of the techniques and wage rates of 1860. The contrast with Blodget refers exclusively to the current price estimates.

In any case, it appears that Blodget is simply wrong on the matter of the value of improved land. The check of the current estimates against Jones's estimate of the value of real estate and Blodget's estimate of the value of unimproved land seems reasonably strong. Furthermore, in comparison with Jones's estimate, Blodget's figures on the values of improved land seem very much too low. The improvements series—particularly in constant prices—arguably gives a reasonable view of what it purports to describe; it does not appear to be strongly biased in one direction or the other or as generating strongly biased rates of growth.[4]

**Structures.** The estimates for the 1850–1900 period rest chiefly on census data: for 1840 on the work of Seaman (1852), for 1815 on the direct tax of 1813–15 and the work of Pitkin (1835), for 1805 on the work of Blodget (1806) and Goldsmith (1952), for 1799 on the direct tax of 1798 and the work of Soltow (1984), and for 1774 on the work of Jones (1980). All of these data have been heavily processed, frequently with the object of extracting one element from a larger aggregate or dividing the aggregate among its components. In each case but two, however, there is a substantial component of real data that bears directly on the estimating problem. The weakest links are the ones for 1805 and 1840. There are no data expressly relevant to these dates, and the sources of evidence are Blodget and Seaman. Blodget extrapolated his estimate from an earlier date, for which real evidence is available, and Seaman both extrapolated from an earlier date and blew up partial estimates to encompass the universe. These figures have been tested, but they are less trustworthy than the rest.

We now turn to the treatment of deflation. For the years 1850–1900 there is no serious problem relating to deflation; indeed, the price index number situation is unusually good. For most of these years, Dorothy Brady's two sets of deflators—for houses and churches on the one hand, and for factories and office buildings on the other—are available. These are true price indexes, which makes them quite unusual among construction deflators. Usually it is necessary to make do with cost indexes. Brady's data need modest adjustment to make them expressly apposite to the task of deflating the capital stock, but no heroic efforts are needed to put them in proper condition for this purpose.

The serious problem appears in the years before 1850, for which Brady's indexes are not available. One possibility for this period is to follow the lead of David and Solar (1977), who linked Brady's housing price index to a construction cost index and then carried it back to the late eighteenth century. Since the relative importance of factories and office buildings before the 1840s was probably slight, and since construction techniques in this period may not have varied much between residential construction and commercial buildings (except at the cutting edge of factory design and construction), an extension of the housing price index would be an entirely adequate way to deal with the deflation problem for all kinds of structures. David and Solar, however, did not use Brady's published series; they used the unrevised figures that Brady prepared for the Income and Wealth Conference from which the 1966 volume originated. It turns out that in most instances the differences between the published and unpublished series are slight—matters of a point or two. There is one exception. In the published conference volume, Brady (1966) dropped her estimate of the price index of housing in 1839.

The Brady unpublished index falls from a level of 128 in 1839 to 94 in 1849, and then rises to 100 in 1859. Available construction cost indexes fall much more modestly and rise more sharply over these two decades, implying that, if the unpublished Brady index is correct, productivity in construction must have been rising quite dramatically. David and Solar believe that the experience reflects chiefly the diffusion of the balloon frame, which was invented in 1833. They therefore suppose that the annual rate of productivity improvement realized in the 1840s was also achieved in the period 1834–39. They construct a building cost index and employ it with the Brady price index to estimate productivity gains for the period 1839–59, and they then use it, together with their estimate of the rate of productivity improvement for the period 1839–49, to extrapolate the Brady price index number for 1839 back to 1834. They assume that there were no important productivity improvements before 1833, and extrapolate the 1834 price index number to earlier years in the century on their construction cost index. The productivity improvement for the period 1834 through 1859 implied by their calculations is a little more than 36 percent.

The procedure is ingenious, and surely adequate to the purposes of David and Solar. It is not so clear that it is adequate to the purpose of creating a deflator for the most important component of the conventional capital stock series. First there is the matter of Brady's decision to suppress her 1839 estimate. Does this mean that she had had second thoughts about the strength of that estimate? Presumably. Nonetheless, there remains evidence that Brady believed that construction prices did fall in the late 1830s and early 1840s. Her price index for factories drops very sharply between 1836 and 1844, for example. But this index refers to factories, not residences.[5]

Is it reasonable to suppose that the balloon frame led to a rise in productivity of 36 percent in the first twenty-five years of its existence? Probably not. The balloon frame saved on framing, which had accounted for about 25 percent of the cost of a building. Consequently, even if the balloon frame eliminated the expense of framing, and even if the balloon frame was adopted throughout the industry within this period, the rise in productivity could not have come close to reaching 36 percent. And neither of these conditions was actually met.[6]

The framing of a building called for many workers. Barn-raising parties were organized expressly for this purpose. The balloon frame eventually changed all that. With the new system, a man and a boy could frame a house by themselves. Thus, the innovation became immensely important to the farming community, particularly for people on the frontier, for reasons that transcended normal cost considerations. It also diffused quickly in new Western cities, places under intense demand pressure and without established artisanal power groups. (Chicago and San Francisco were both balloon-frame cities.) But it did not immediately spread to the East.

There were other innovations during this period, so that the rise in productivity that David and Solar identify need not to have been the result exclusively of the balloon frame. The principal changes that seem to have been taking place involved the transfer of some activities from the building site to mills. For example, it is said that it became more common to use manufactured nails, windows, and doors, which presumably lowered costs. But the census returns of 1810, 1850, and 1860 suggest that manufactured nails were already widely used before the 1830s. Mill-made sashes, doors, and blinds do not appear in the census returns—not separately, at least—before 1860, when their output amounted to a value of about $9.5 million in a year in which the total value of conventional construction (exclusive of railroads and canals) ran to about $345 million. Mill-made windows and so forth were therefore by no means negligible by this date, but they did not bulk large enough to suggest that their introduction led to a major improvement in productivity. Furthermore, it may well be that their contribution to productivity actually came after 1849 rather than before. At least the treatment of these lines of production by the census suggests that this was so. David and Solar find most of the productivity change (almost three-quarters of it) occurring before 1849.

The general idea behind the David and Solar treatment of construction prices is clearly reasonable, and their execution of it may have solved their problem satisfactorily. The technique is less likely to solve our problem satisfactorily, however. Unfortunately, there is no option that is clearly superior. Nonetheless, the estimation procedure uses adjusted indexes based on Brady for the years 1849 onward. It then extrapolates the adjusted 1849 (1850) index number to 1840, 1815, 1805, 1799, and 1785 on the Adams (1975) variant B (allowing for input substitutions) construction cost series. The index was extended to 1774 on a construction cost series based on the David and Solar common wage index, a Maryland farm wage rate taken from Adams (1986, 629–30), and the Bezanson-Gray-Hussey arithmetic average price index for Philadelphia (US Bureau of the Census 1975, series E-111). The last two steps need further discussion.

The Adams (1975) construction cost index was made with exceptional care from good basic data. It is an excellent construction cost index, and the version used allows for factor substitutions due to shifts in relative input prices. For present purposes, however, it has certain potential shortcomings. The ideal index is a true price index, an index that allows for changes in productivity. The Adams index does not do that, except insofar as productivity changes are associated with shifts in factor proportions. As proxy for a true price index, it will exaggerate any long-term price increases and understate any long-term price decreases, so long as productivity improvements are taking place. The capital stock series that it is used to deflate will then exhibit a rate of change that is biased in a downward direction. In the present instance, the bias would exaggerate the observed acceleration in the rate of growth of the capital stock. If the bias were serious enough, it would account fully for the acceleration. That seems highly unlikely, however. The sources of productivity improvement in construction do not appear to have been important before the mid-1830s, and even in the period between the mid-1830s and the beginning of the true price indexes in 1849, the amount of productivity improvement is unlikely to have been very great. In any case, the Adams index has other shortcomings for present purposes, and it turns out that at least one of these may introduce a compensating bias, in direction at least, and perhaps in amount as well.

The Adams index refers exclusively to Philadelphia. How successfully does it represent the United States? Two questions immediately arise.

First, housing price levels varied by region, and as time passed, the relative importance of the various regions changed. Did the shifts in regional weights affect the trend in the national average of housing prices? Probably not, and if they did, they tended to *raise* average prices a little. By ignoring the effects of the regional shift, one can perhaps compensate slightly for whatever bias is present from the use of a cost index in place of a true price index. These conclusions are based on the results of the following test.

The 1840 census requested information on the numbers of two types of houses constructed in the census year, those built of brick and stone and those built of wood, as well as the value of both types of houses taken together (US Census Office 1841, 91). Regressions using the state data generated an intercept value and coefficients for each of the two types of houses. These data were then employed to value the houses constructed in each state, and the figures thus obtained were divided through the census returns of the value of houses built to get an index number for each state (see also chapter 14). The index number compares the value of the houses constructed in the state with the value that would have obtained if prices had been at the level of the national average. Clearly, the index numbers reflect not only variations in building prices—which are required for the proposed analysis—but also differences in average size and quality of new houses, from state to state. Since cost, size, and quality were likely to have varied together—frontier areas having lower building costs, smaller houses, and houses of lower quality than the well-settled areas—the index numbers almost certainly exaggerate the regional variations in building costs, a point to be borne in mind as the analysis unfolds.

The individual state index numbers were then used to deflate the state returns of the value of real estate in 1799, according to the direct tax. The sum of the deflated returns was then divided through the aggregate current price value of real estate in 1799, according to the direct tax. The result was an index number of 0.932, which compares with the 1840 index number of 1.000. That is, according to these calculations, the shifting weights among states tended to raise, very slightly, the true price index of structures between 1799 and 1840.[7] The index numbers almost certainly overstate the true impact of the redistribution of the value of structures among states in this period, because the state index numbers probably overstate (for reasons previously given) the true variation in building costs among states. It appears unnecessary, then, to adjust the Adams cost index to take into account the effects of the shifting real-value-of-structures weights among states. This is particularly the case in view of the fact that the Adams index is a cost index and is likely, therefore, to exaggerate the extent to which the prices of buildings rose, or to understate the extent to which they fell during this period. Finally, if the bias is slight between 1799 and 1840, it is almost certainly negligible between 1774 and 1799.

There is another aspect of the regional specificity of the Adams index that must be considered. Do changes in Philadelphia costs properly represent changes in costs in other regions? The strong suggestion that one gets from looking at price and wage indexes from New England and New York (Rothenberg 1988; David and Solar 1977; Warren and Pearson 1933) is that they do not. Adams's cost index moves in step with the Bezanson-Gray-Hussey general price index for Philadelphia (US Bureau of the Census 1975, series E-97), while the Rothenberg, David-Solar, and Warren-Pearson indexes also move more or less together, but quite differently from the Philadelphia indexes. (At least these statements apply to the benchmark dates relevant here.) David and Solar report that a construction cost index they assembled from materials prices from New York (Warren and Pearson 1933) and from common wage rates from Philadelphia (Adams 1975) and the Erie Canal (Smith 1963) exhibits a less pronounced decline between 1809 and 1834 than does the Adams index. An index is constructed from Warren-Pearson materials prices and David-Solar common wages (using Adams's weights and his procedure for allowing for factor substitutions) for all the relevant dates. The Adams index shows a much more pronounced drop over time than does the index constructed from the Warren-Pearson and David-Solar series. There is the strong suggestion that, over the long run, a properly derived national construction cost index would exhibit more pronounced price increases and less pronounced price declines than would a Philadelphia index. The bias imparted to the real capital stock series from using a cost index to proxy a price index is, then, compensated for by the fact that Philadelphia prices moved differently from national average prices, at least after 1799, and probably from 1774 as well.

There is one final problem with the deflator: it represents the costs of commercial construction in a city. A substantial fraction of the stock of structures in the years 1799 through 1840 must have been built in the countryside by unprofessional labor. The matter may not be very important, however. According to Adams, Philadelphia construction and Maryland farm wage rates moved in roughly similar ways among the dates 1785, 1799, 1805, 1815, and 1840. One cannot claim great accuracy for the deflator, but on the whole it seems satisfactory.

**Animal Inventories.** There are at least two problems with the animal inventory estimates. First, they include only farm animals from 1840 onward (animals used in the mines are part of the "equipment" estimates in mining) and probably only farm animals at earlier dates as well, whereas ideally one would like to have all domestic animals throughout. The omissions are not trivial, but neither are they of overwhelming importance. In 1860, just over 12 percent of domestic animals, by value, were located off farms (US Census Office 1860, cviii, cxxvi, 192); in 1900, the fraction was just under 7 percent (US Bureau of the Census 1900, cxliv). The suggestion is that the total stock of animals increased a little more slowly than did the stock of farm animals, but correcting for this shortcoming would probably not affect very substantially the conclusions previously reached.

The second problem has to do with deflation. The constant price series was made by applying base-year prices (1860) to estimates of the numbers of animals in each year. The assumption is that a pig is a pig. In fact, pigs in 1890 were, without doubt, superior animals to pigs of 1830. The deflator, then, is biased, and deflation tends to understate the importance of the growth of the stock of animals. Furthermore, the effect is also likely to be to underplay the acceleration in the rate of growth of the per capita capital stock. The reason is that most of the gains in the quality of animals were realized after midcentury. In earlier decades there were probably periods when, on balance, the quality of animal stocks actually deteriorated. Nonetheless, numbers can reasonably proxy real values before 1840 or 1850, whereas they are less able to perform this function thereafter. There are problems with the evidence on numbers as well, but they seem less pressing and do not deserve a place in this brief treatment of the subject. On the whole, the series, despite these qualifications, is acceptable for the uses to which it has been put.

**Other Inventories.** The procedure followed is one employed by Kuznets (1946, 228). Inventories were taken as a fixed fraction of the value of imports and the value of outputs of the agricultural, manufacturing, and mining sectors. No allowance was made for changes in the efficiency with which inventories were used—a matter of limited importance, especially before the Civil War. If there were improvements in efficiency, then the estimating procedure tends to exaggerate the acceleration in the rate of change of the real per capita capital stock.

**Equipment.** The data for the years 1840 onward were derived chiefly from the census, were deflated by Dorothy Brady's true price indexes, and were tested—with considerable success—against perpetual inventory estimates (see chapter 6). For the earlier years, the chief sources were Jones (1980), Blodget (1806), Goldsmith (1952), and US Bureau of the Census (1975, for Treasury data on shipping). The series seems adequate for present purposes, but should not be trusted for much more.

In summary, it should be obvious that a substantial margin for error must be allowed for all of the estimates discussed in this book, especially those dated before 1850. On the other hand, it is not obvious that the rates of change computed from the series are subject to large biases.

## 4.3. Rates of Growth in Historical Perspective

The concern of this chapter is with American economic growth, which means that the measures of central concern to it are real measures, particularly real measures deflated by population. The current price estimates are worth a brief inspection, however. On the whole, they are less processed than the real figures, and may therefore be more reliable. Table 4.2 contains current price estimates of the capital stock, conventionally defined. Three points come through very clearly. The rates of growth are all very high; the total capital stock in 1980 was apparently about forty thousand times as large as the stock of 1774, an extraordinary figure. Although most of the rates were computed over considerable stretches of time, and therefore should not be unduly influenced by transient phenomena, they vary quite widely from one period to another. Finally, it is clear that the experience before 1860 was by no means uniform. In particular, the rates of growth are especially low from 1800 to 1840, and especially high from 1840 to 1860. The second period is short, and the rates of growth computed across it could be influenced by business cycles or long swings. But Abramovitz's (1989) chronology of long swings and protracted depressions suggests that this is probably not a problem.

The record described by table 4.2 is influenced both by real phenomena and price level changes. The price index numbers in table 4.3 allow one to judge how important the latter developments were. Between 1774 and 1900 the long-term trend of the two price indexes appears to be close to zero, but in the short-term prices were quite unstable. In the twentieth century there is additionally a pronounced upward trend. Notice, finally, that while the two indexes tend to move together, the consumer index is the more volatile. The plan to deflate by two separate price indexes, then, seems to have substantive as well as theoretical merit.

TABLE 4.2 **Indexes and average annual rates of change of the US capital stock, measured in current prices, 1774–1980**

| | Domestic capital | Domestic capital and consumer durables | National capital |
|---|---|---|---|
| **Panel A. Indexes** | | | |
| 1774 | 100 | 100 | 100 |
| 1799 | 399 | | 415 |
| 1805 | 581 | | 628 |
| 1815 | 999 | | 1,110 |
| 1840 | 1,573 | 1,503 | 1,691 |
| 1850 | 2,579 | 2,538 | 2,919 |
| 1860 | 5,298 | 5,274 | 6,000 |
| 1870 | 8,620 | 8,751 | 9,201 |
| 1880 | 11,795 | 11,761 | 12,805 |
| 1890 | 20,526 | 20,198 | 22,396 |
| 1900 | 27,386 | 26,457 | 30,886 |
| 1929 | 138,592 | 135,343 | 170,360 |
| 1953 | 444,239 | 436,493 | 541,061 |
| 1980 | 3,761,382 | 3,665,337 | 4,560,608 |
| **Panel B. Average annual rates of change (%)** | | | |
| 1774–1840 | 4.18 | 4.11 | 4.28 |
| 1774–99 | 5.54 | | 5.69 |
| 1799–1840 | 3.34 | | 3.43 |
| 1840–1900 | 4.76 | 4.78 | 4.84 |
| 1840–60 | 6.07 | 6.28 | 6.33 |
| 1860–1900 | 4.11 | 4.03 | 4.10 |
| 1900–1929 | 5.59 | 5.63 | 5.89 |
| 1929–53 | 4.85 | 4.88 | 4.82 |
| 1953–80 | 7.91 | 7.88 | 7.90 |
| 1774–1980 | 5.11 | 5.10 | 5.21 |

Sources: See text.

The deflated series appear in table 4.4. Four matters of interest strike one immediately. First, deflation does reduce the volatility of the series somewhat; part of the short-term movement observed in table 4.2 is due to price fluctuations. Second, it is clear that the real capital stock has grown more slowly in the present century than it did previously. Third, it is also clear that the rate of growth accelerated between the years before 1840 and the years thereafter. The broad pattern, then, is of an early acceleration followed by a subsequent retardation. Finally, notice that these findings emerge from all four series, the national and domestic capital stocks, deflated by the consumer price index and by the capital price index. But the detailed pattern of change differs from one series to the other. For example, compare the results obtained for the period 1929–53. The real capital stock, viewed as accumulated consuming power, grew much faster than did the real capital stock, viewed as an input to production. Between the two dates, the prices of capital goods increased faster than did consumer prices.

More interesting for present purposes is the pattern across the years 1774–1840. Notice (table 4.3) that consumer prices advanced faster than capital goods prices between 1774 and 1799, and fell faster between 1799 and 1840. Across the full span, 1774–1840, the two index numbers show roughly similar changes, so that the two capital stock series yield about the same results. But the interpretation of the subperiods before 1840 depends entirely on the system of deflation one chooses to use. And the systems of deflation view the capital stock in two quite different ways: as the value of the accumulations of the years, expressed in consumer goods, on the one hand, and as against the productive power of the capital stock, on the other hand.

No doubt the contrast is in some measure spurious, however. Items of construction compose an important part of the capital stock throughout (see table 4.8). The deflators for this component in the years before 1840 were constructed in part from data on wage rates. Wage rates tend to be less volatile than prices (see Margo 1992). The capital stock price index numbers for the period before 1840 may therefore understate the

TABLE 4.3 **Capital stock deflators, base 1860, 1774–1900**

|      | Domestic capital price index | Consumer price index |
|------|------------------------------|----------------------|
| 1774 | 81                           | 97                   |
| 1799 | 111                          | 148                  |
| 1805 | 115                          | 141                  |
| 1815 | 157                          | 185                  |
| 1840 | 91                           | 104                  |
| 1850 | 94                           | 94                   |
| 1860 | 100                          | 100                  |
| 1870 | 127                          | 157                  |
| 1880 | 112                          | 123                  |
| 1890 | 96                           | 109                  |
| 1900 | 90                           | 101                  |
| 1929 | 165                          | 205                  |
| 1953 | 357                          | 320                  |
| 1974 |                              | 589                  |
| 1980 | 1,193                        |                      |

Sources: See text.

TABLE 4.4 **Indexes and average annual rates of change of the US capital stock, measured in 1860 prices, 1774–1980**

| | Deflated by | | | |
|---|---|---|---|---|
| | capital price index | consumer price index | capital price index | consumer price index |
| **Panel A. Indexes** | | | | |
| 1774 | 100 | 100 | 100 | 100 |
| 1799 | 289 | 262 | 306 | 271 |
| 1805 | 409 | 400 | 449 | 431 |
| 1815 | 513 | 525 | 571 | 581 |
| 1840 | 1,401 | 1,472 | 1,514 | 1,571 |
| 1850 | 2,212 | 2,665 | 2,497 | 3,007 |
| 1860 | 4,292 | 5,148 | 4,849 | 5,805 |
| 1870 | 5,486 | 5,335 | 5,897 | 5,669 |
| 1880 | 8,462 | 9,318 | 9,157 | 10,071 |
| 1890 | 17,217 | 18,295 | 18,665 | 19,877 |
| 1900 | 24,552 | 26,347 | 27,632 | 29,584 |
| 1929 | 68,472 | 66,398 | 77,681 | 80,390 |
| 1953 | 102,132 | 137,182 | 114,109 | 163,571 |
| 1980 | 223,632 | | 297,638 | |
| **Panel B. Average annual rates of change (%)** | | | | |
| 1774–1840 | 4.00 | 4.07 | 4.12 | 4.17 |
| 1774–99 | 4.24 | 3.85 | 4.47 | 3.99 |
| 1799–1840 | 3.85 | 4.21 | 3.90 | 4.27 |
| 1840–1900 | 4.77 | 4.81 | 4.84 | 4.89 |
| 1840–60 | 5.60 | 6.26 | 5.82 | 6.54 |
| 1860–1900 | 4.36 | 4.08 | 4.35 | 4.07 |
| 1900–1980 | 2.76 | | 2.97 | |
| 1900–1929 | 3.54 | 3.18 | 3.56 | 3.44 |
| 1929–53 | 1.67 | 3.02 | 1.60 | 2.96 |
| 1953–80 | 2.90 | | 3.55 | |
| 1774–1980 | 3.74 | | 3.88 | |

Sources: See text.

fluctuations experienced by the prices of capital goods. It is thus possible that the measured rate of growth of the real capital stock, viewed as an input, is too high across the years 1774–99 and too low between 1799 and 1840. The matter is unlikely to be important with respect to the main point of present concern, however. It seems clear that the rate of growth of the capital stock did accelerate between the 1774–1840 period and the 1840–1900 period.

The capital stock treated so far ignores a component of investment that was important, particularly in the years before 1840: the activities of land clearing and first breaking which engaged so large a part of the working lives of American farmers (Primack 1962). Table 4.5 contains index numbers describing the change over time in the real value of the domestic capital stock, inclusive of the value of these farm-making activities. The overall rate of growth of this aggregate—3.9 percent over the 1774–1900 period—is much lower than the 4.5 percent recorded for the less comprehensive capital stock treated in table 4.4 (capital stock deflator in each case). These findings reflect the fact that farm formation was a very important part of capital, but one that increased over time much more slowly than the other components of the stock—a point to which we will return.

The acceleration shown by the data in table 4.4 reappears in table 4.5 in a more marked form. But notice that the pattern is somewhat different. The series deflated by the prices of capital now shows a higher rate of growth across the period 1799–1840 than across the period 1774–99, in contrast to the results shown in table 4.4. The explanation is that introduction of the farm-making elements of the capital stock necessarily altered the capital price index numbers. Farm making was carried out by farm

TABLE 4.5 **Indexes and average annual rates of change of the US domestic capital stock, including the value of clearing and breaking farmland, measured in 1860 prices, 1774–1900**

|  | Deflator | |
| --- | --- | --- |
|  | **Capital price index** | **Consumer price index** |
| **Panel A. Indexes** | | |
| 1774 | 100 | 100 |
| 1799 | 227 | 245 |
| 1805 | 290 | 332 |
| 1815 | 353 | 379 |
| 1840 | 913 | 1,229 |
| 1850 | 1,362 | 2,140 |
| 1860 | 2,432 | 3,980 |
| 1870 | 3,004 | 3,884 |
| 1880 | 4,520 | 6,543 |
| 1890 | 8,491 | 12,229 |
| 1900 | 11,807 | 17,253 |
| **Panel B. Average annual rates of change (%)** | | |
| 1774–1840 | 3.35 | 3.80 |
| 1774–99 | 3.28 | 3.58 |
| 1799–1840 | 3.39 | 3.93 |
| 1840–1900 | 4.27 | 4.40 |
| 1840–60 | 4.90 | 5.88 |
| 1860–1900 | 3.94 | 3.67 |

Sources: See text.

TABLE 4.6 **Indexes and average annual rates of change of the US domestic capital stock and structures, per capita, using conventional and unconventional concepts, measured in 1860 prices, 1774–1980**

| | Conventional concept | | Including land clearing | |
| --- | --- | --- | --- | --- |
| | Deflated by | | Deflated by | |
| | capital price index | consumer price index | capital price index | consumer price index |
| **Panel A. Indexes** | | | | |
| 1774 | 100 | 100 | 100 | 100 |
| 1799 | 132 | 120 | 104 | 112 |
| 1805 | 154 | 150 | 109 | 125 |
| 1815 | 143 | 147 | 99 | 106 |
| 1840 | 193 | 202 | 126 | 169 |
| 1850 | 224 | 270 | 138 | 217 |
| 1860 | 321 | 384 | 182 | 297 |
| 1870 | 323 | 315 | 177 | 229 |
| 1880 | 396 | 436 | 212 | 306 |
| 1890 | 643 | 683 | 317 | 456 |
| 1900 | 759 | 815 | 365 | 534 |
| 1929 | 1,461 | 1,461 | | |
| 1953 | 1,520 | 2,294 | | |
| 1980 | 2,735 | | | |
| **Panel B. Average annual rates of change (%)** | | | | |
| 1774–1840 | 1.00 | 1.07 | 0.35 | 0.80 |
| 1774–99 | 1.11 | 0.73 | 0.16 | 0.45 |
| 1799–1840 | 0.93 | 1.27 | 0.47 | 1.00 |
| 1840–1900 | 2.28 | 2.32 | 1.77 | 1.92 |
| 1840–60 | 2.54 | 3.21 | 1.84 | 2.82 |
| 1860–1900 | 2.15 | 1.88 | 1.74 | 1.47 |
| 1900–1929 | 1.98 | 2.01 | | |
| 1929–53 | 0.50 | 1.88 | | |
| 1953–80 | 2.18 | | | |
| 1774–1900 | 1.60 | 1.67 | | |
| 1900–1980 | 1.61 | | | |
| 1774–1980 | 1.61 | | | |

Sources: See text.

laborers, and the value of farm making is the value of the time of farm workers. Farm wage rates thus figure in the estimation of the value of land clearing and breaking, as well as in the deflation of these components of the stock. Farm wage rates rose quite pronouncedly between 1774 and 1840, and that gives the deflator an upward tilt.

All of the series discussed above refer to the aggregate capital stock. A more interesting variable, however, is the per capita capital stock. Estimates appear in table 4.6. Deflating by population produces two important results. First, the retardation of growth in the twentieth century disappears, while the acceleration between 1774–1840 and 1840–1900 becomes very much more pronounced. The acceleration appears in every variant but is particularly evident in the series describing the most comprehensive measure, deflated by capital stock prices.

The acceleration in the rate of growth of the capital stock reflects in part the increase in the investment rate and the rise in the capital-to-output ratio, which seems to have begun as early as 1800, at least in the case of the conventional measurements, but which was particularly pronounced from 1840 until 1900 (Davis and Gallman 1978; table 4.7). That does not appear to be the only source, however. The rates of growth of real national product per capita from 1840 onward were higher than the rates of growth of real capital per capita in the period before 1840, regardless of the capital concept adopted and the deflator employed (Davis and Gallman 1978; Gallman 1966). Accepting the rate of change of the capital stock series before 1840 as an upper-bound estimate of the rate of change of real national product, the evidence suggests quite clearly that the rate of growth of real national product per capita accelerated in the years before the Civil War.

These results are generally consistent with Thomas Weiss's inferences concerning income, which he derived from his labor force series (see table 4.7 and Weiss 1992). Both Weiss's figures and the capital stock data were assembled from fragmentary evidence and are subject to substantial

TABLE 4.7  **Real GDP and real domestic capital per capita, using conventional and unconventional concepts, measured in 1840 prices, 1800–1860**

|  | 1800 | 1840 | 1860 |
|---|---|---|---|
| **Real GDP per capita (in dollars)** | | | |
| Conventional, variant A | 73 | 91 | 125 |
| Conventional, variant B | 66 | 91 | 125 |
| Unconventional, variant C | 78 | 101 | 135 |
| **Real domestic capital per capita (in dollars)** | | | |
| Conventional | 104 | 157 | 262 |
| Unconventional | 175 | 219 | 316 |
| **Capital-to-output ratios** | | | |
| Conventional, variant A | 1.42 | 1.73 | 2.09 |
| Conventional, variant B | 1.57 | 1.73 | 2.09 |
| Unconventional, variant C | 2.24 | 2.16 | 2.34 |

Sources: The real GDP per capita estimates are from Weiss 1992. For the remaining estimates, see the text.

margins for error. But both series seem to tell about the same story, and that affords greater confidence that the story is a true one.[8]

## 4.5. Changing Composition of Capital Stock

Rates of change say something about the process of growth and development; data on the structure of the economy tell more. Development consists of structural change.

The conventional measure of domestic capital, in current prices, exhibits two pronounced compositional shifts: the fraction of the capital stock accounted for by animals drops very far indeed, while the share attributable to structures rises—both developments occurring chiefly after 1815 (see table 4.8). But current price data are not so useful in this context as are constant price data, which tell a very interesting story. They show that the structure of the capital stock changed very little, down to 1840. Thereafter, there were accelerating shifts. The share of animals in the total dropped precipitately and inventories dropped mildly, while the share of structures rose a little and the share of equipment rose very much. There is the strong suggestion of an economy shifting in the direction of industrial activity and modern economic growth: away from agriculture and animal power, and toward manufacturing and mechanical power. There is no question that stirrings can be identified well before 1840—Kenneth Sokoloff's (1992) work shows clearly that important industrial change can be dated to 1820 at least. But these activities could not have carried a very heavy weight in the economy much before 1840, and that is what the data in table 4.8 are showing us. Bias in the estimates may overstate the decline in the relative importance of animals after 1870, and may contribute to the finding of stability in the share of structures in the capital stock before 1840, but these matters are probably not of much importance.

The introduction of the value of farm making into the capital stock produces some expected shifts. Concentrating on the constant price data, the value of land clearing and breaking accounted for more than half of the capital stock in 1774 and something less than half in 1799. This figure dropped modestly to 1840—when it was a little less than a third—and more dramatically thereafter, reflecting the relative decline of the agricultural sector. In this variant, inventories retained roughly the same share of the capital stock after 1799, while the share of structures experienced a strong upward movement from the same date.

TABLE 4.8 Constituents of the domestic capital stock, expressed as shares in the domestic capital stock, 1774–1900

| | 1774 | 1799 | 1805 | 1815 | 1840 | 1850 | 1860 | 1870 | 1880 | 1890 | 1900 |
|---|---|---|---|---|---|---|---|---|---|---|---|
| **Panel A. Excluding the value of farmland clearing and breaking** | | | | | | | | | | | |
| **Measured in current prices** | | | | | | | | | | | |
| Structures | 0.39 | 0.33 | 0.35 | 0.41 | 0.45 | 0.47 | 0.54 | 0.54 | 0.55 | 0.61 | 0.60 |
| Equipment | 0.13 | 0.14 | 0.15 | 0.13 | 0.14 | 0.13 | 0.12 | 0.11 | 0.11 | 0.13 | 0.14 |
| Inventories[a] | 0.23 | 0.35 | 0.34 | 0.26 | 0.24 | 0.26 | 0.22 | 0.24 | 0.24 | 0.19 | 0.19 |
| Animals | 0.25 | 0.18 | 0.16 | 0.21 | 0.17 | 0.13 | 0.12 | 0.11 | 0.09 | 0.08 | 0.07 |
| **Measured in 1860 prices** | | | | | | | | | | | |
| Structures | 0.40 | 0.34 | 0.40 | 0.41 | 0.43 | 0.46 | 0.54 | 0.55 | 0.50 | 0.49 | 0.46 |
| Equipment | 0.08 | 0.09 | 0.09 | 0.07 | 0.08 | 0.09 | 0.12 | 0.13 | 0.16 | 0.25 | 0.30 |
| Inventories[a] | 0.28 | 0.35 | 0.32 | 0.29 | 0.26 | 0.27 | 0.22 | 0.22 | 0.25 | 0.21 | 0.19 |
| Animals | 0.25 | 0.23 | 0.19 | 0.22 | 0.23 | 0.17 | 0.12 | 0.10 | 0.09 | 0.06 | 0.04 |
| **Panel B. Including the value of farmland clearing and breaking** | | | | | | | | | | | |
| **Measured in current prices** | | | | | | | | | | | |
| Structures | 0.24 | 0.21 | 0.26 | 0.33 | 0.33 | 0.35 | 0.42 | 0.44 | 0.47 | 0.55 | 0.55 |
| Equipment | 0.08 | 0.09 | 0.11 | 0.10 | 0.10 | 0.10 | 0.09 | 0.09 | 0.10 | 0.11 | 0.13 |
| Inventories[a] | 0.14 | 0.23 | 0.24 | 0.21 | 0.18 | 0.20 | 0.17 | 0.20 | 0.21 | 0.17 | 0.18 |
| Animals | 0.15 | 0.11 | 0.12 | 0.17 | 0.12 | 0.10 | 0.09 | 0.09 | 0.08 | 0.07 | 0.06 |
| Land clearing | 0.40 | 0.36 | 0.28 | 0.19 | 0.28 | 0.25 | 0.22 | 0.17 | 0.14 | 0.10 | 0.08 |
| **Measured in 1860 prices** | | | | | | | | | | | |
| Structures | 0.17 | 0.19 | 0.25 | 0.27 | 0.29 | 0.33 | 0.42 | 0.44 | 0.41 | 0.44 | 0.42 |
| Equipment | 0.04 | 0.05 | 0.05 | 0.05 | 0.06 | 0.07 | 0.09 | 0.11 | 0.13 | 0.22 | 0.28 |
| Inventories[a] | 0.12 | 0.20 | 0.20 | 0.19 | 0.17 | 0.19 | 0.17 | 0.18 | 0.21 | 0.19 | 0.18 |
| Animals | 0.11 | 0.13 | 0.12 | 0.14 | 0.15 | 0.12 | 0.09 | 0.08 | 0.07 | 0.05 | 0.04 |
| Land clearing | 0.56 | 0.44 | 0.39 | 0.36 | 0.32 | 0.28 | 0.22 | 0.19 | 0.17 | 0.11 | 0.08 |

[a] Excluding animals
Sources: See text.

TABLE 4.9  **Indexes of per capita real magnitudes, measured in 1860 prices, 1774–1900**

|                  | 1774 | 1799 | 1805 | 1815 | 1840 | 1850 | 1860 | 1870 | 1880 | 1890  | 1900  |
|------------------|------|------|------|------|------|------|------|------|------|-------|-------|
| Structures       | 100  | 112  | 156  | 150  | 211  | 263  | 438  | 449  | 503  | 793   | 886   |
| Equipment        | 100  | 142  | 166  | 133  | 202  | 262  | 479  | 538  | 785  | 1,981 | 2,867 |
| Inventories[a]   | 100  | 166  | 176  | 149  | 178  | 218  | 253  | 258  | 360  | 479   | 526   |
| Animals          | 100  | 122  | 121  | 130  | 179  | 154  | 154  | 126  | 139  | 148   | 132   |
| Land clearing    | 100  | 81   | 74   | 64   | 73   | 70   | 72   | 62   | 66   | 60    | 55    |

[a]Excluding animals
Sources: See text.

Table 4.9 is another way of considering the same phenomena. It shows indexes of the per capita supply of each component of the capital stock. The growing importance of structures and, particularly, equipment comes through powerfully, while the value of the stock of land clearing and first breaking is shown to have fallen well behind the growth of population. There were two elements involved in the production of this result. First, the volume of farmland per capita declined over time, as the population became less and less rural and farm-centered. Since American agriculture was able to feed a growing population and expand its overseas sales, the decline in the value of farm improvements per capita went hand in hand with the growing productivity of agricultural land. Second, as population moved westward, out of the wooded areas, the cost of preparing land for cultivation fell. Toward the end of the nineteenth century, then, the real value of farm improvements (exclusive of structures) per acre was smaller than it had been in the eighteenth century.

On the whole, the structural evidence supports the conclusions that one might tentatively draw from the aggregate series: the American economy began to experience the process of modern economic growth in the years after the War of 1812; by the 1840s the modern components of the economy were large enough and growing rapidly enough to have an observable impact on the rate of growth and the structure of the economy.

## 4.6. The Growth of Total Factor Inputs

The measurements of the capital stock, viewed as an input to the productive process, yield information that clearly bears on the speed and nature of American economic growth. Measurements of total factor inputs would be even more useful. The assembly of the additional required inputs is not very difficult. Estimates of the volume of agricultural land (the only land input that could be taken into account) already exist. (Gallman 1972, 201–2). Weiss has generated new labor force figures for the years 1800–1900, at ten-year intervals, and they were readily extended to 1774.[9]

Table 4.10, panel A, reports the rate of growth of labor, land, and capital inputs (in total and per capita) for various periods between 1774 and

TABLE 4.10  **Rates of growth of factor supplies, factor supplies per capita, and total factor productivity, 1774–1900**

|  | 1774–1800 | 1800–40 | 1840–1900 | 1840–60 |
|---|---|---|---|---|
| **Panel A** | | | | |
| Labor force (LF) | 3.09 | 3.09 | 2.72 | 3.41 |
| LF/population | –0.08 | 0.11 | 0.20 | 0.31 |
| Land | 2.26 | 2.80 | 2.17 | 2.87 |
| Land/population | –0.91 | –0.18 | –0.35 | –0.23 |
| Capital (K) | 3.39 | 3.45 | 4.40 | 5.17 |
| K/population | 0.22 | 0.48 | 1.88 | 2.07 |
| **Panel B** | | | | |
| Total factor inputs, LF | 3.10 | 3.18 | 3.20 | 3.91 |
| Total factor inputs/ population, LF | –0.07 | 0.20 | 0.68 | 0.81 |
| Total factors, inputs, LFQV | 3.21 | 3.44 | 3.75 | 4.78 |
| Total factor inputs/ population, LFQV | 0.04 | 0.46 | 1.23 | 1.69 |
| Total factor inputs, LFQF | 3.25 | 3.47 | 3.57 | 4.41 |
| Total factor inputs/ population, LFQF | 0.08 | 0.49 | 1.05 | 1.31 |
| **Panel C** | | | | |
| Total factor productivity | | | | |
| GDP, LF | | 0.46 | | 0.82 |
| GNP, LF | | | 0.80 | 0.70 |
| GDP, LFQV | | | 0.25 | –0.17 |
| GDP, LFQF | | | 0.43 | 0.20 |

Sources: The real GDP estimates underlying the first set of total factor productivity estimates (panel C) are from Weiss 1992 (broad concept, variant C). They are expressed in 1840 prices, as are the capital stock estimates (domestic capital) used with them to estimate total factor productivity.

The real GNP estimates (panel C) were derived from those underlying Gallman 1966. They are expressed in 1860 prices and include the value of all land improvements made in the given year and the value of home manufactures. The capital stock estimates used in the analysis involving the GNP refer to the national capital stock. The labor input series is based on Weiss's labor force figures. LF refers to this series in unadjusted form. LFQV means that the labor force has been adjusted to take into account differences in work time and labor quality, both among sectors and over time (1840 onward); that is, the sectoral "weights" are variable. LFQF means that the labor force figures have been adjusted to take into account differences in time and quality among sectors, but not across time; that is, the sectoral "weights" are fixed. (In fact, the weights employed are those of 1880; only two sectors are distinguished in the fixed weight variant: "agriculture" and "all other.") See text.

The rates of growth of the capital stock, 1840–1900, were computed from the series that incorporates the value of fencing.

The weights assigned to the rates of growth of the individual factors of production are labor, 0.68; land, 0.03; and capital, 0.29. These weights are intended to reflect income shares. Land improvements are treated as capital.

1900. Notice that the labor force grew slightly more slowly than population between 1774 and 1800 and a little faster between 1800 and 1840. Thereafter, with the expansion of immigration and its effect on the structure of population, the labor force participation rate rose faster than before. On the whole, the patterns of change of the other inputs are similar. The volume of agricultural land per capita actually declined throughout, but the rate of decline was less after 1800 than before, while the quantity of capital increased faster than population, the rate rising persistently over time. The strong suggestion of these data is that the per capita supply of all inputs, taken together, must have grown very slowly, if at all, down to 1800, when it began to increase, the increase becoming more marked as time passed.

This, in fact, is what is shown by table 4.10, panel B, which sets out the rates of change of all three factors combined. The rates of growth of total inputs and inputs per capita accelerated over time, the change in the per capita rates being particularly striking.

There are three series describing rates of change of aggregate inputs. In the first, the underlying labor input is measured by the numbers of workers, without regard to the length of the work year or the differential quality of the workers. In the second (LFQV) and third (LFQF), very crude efforts have been made to adjust the labor supply for quality change. (The techniques employed to make the LFQV and LFQF estimates are described in the next subsection.) The adjustments are almost certainly too large. That is, the rates of change represented by LFQV—and possibly by LFQF as well—are probably too large. The three sets of figures, however, may very well establish boundaries within which the rates of change of a properly adjusted labor input series would lie.

### 4.6.1. Labor Quality Adjustments

This subsection describes the time-quality adjustments that were made to the labor force estimates to create LFQV and LFQF. These adjust, in admittedly crude ways, the labor supply for sectoral differences in the work year, trends over time in the work year, and differences among sectors in the "quality" of workers. In series LFQV, the weights by which the rates of change of the three input series are combined (estimated factor income shares) vary from one year to the next; in series LFQF, the weights are fixed at the 1880 levels. Thus, the Q stands for varying weights, and F for fixed weights.

The adjustments were made in two steps. First, the farm labor force figures were adjusted to take into account changes in the farm work year.[10] Then quality-time weights were devised for the two remaining sectors that could be readily distinguished: mining, manufacturing, and hand trades, and all others. The weights consisted of the ratio of labor income per worker in the relevant sector to labor income per worker in agriculture. Since two of the important factors accounting for sectoral differences in labor income per worker are the relative duration of the labor year in each sector and the relative quality of workers in each sector, one is perhaps justified in referring to these ratios as time-quality weights. Unfortunately, however, other factors irrelevant to the time-quality adjustment also affect intersectoral differences in labor income per worker. Sectoral labor income deviations arose out of shortterm disequilibria in labor markets, as well as from enduring quality differences among workers. Furthermore, some part of the variations in labor income surely reflected regional and urban/rural price differences, rather than real income disparities. It is likely that both of these factors typically operated to widen the gaps between labor incomes in agriculture and the other two identified sectors, each of which enjoyed higher labor incomes per worker than did the agricultural sector. Since the labor forces attached to these two sectors were growing faster than the agricultural labor force, the excessive time-quality weights given these sectors mean that the rates of change of the time-quality adjusted labor series are biased upward. The present status of regional and urban/rural price series does not permit an appropriate deflating of the labor income series, and there is no way of knowing how serious the bias arising out of disequilibria in labor markets is.

There are other difficulties with these measurements.

1. It would be helpful to have detailed breakdowns of the labor force and labor earnings so that a more fully articulated weighting scheme might be developed, but adequate data simply are not available.
2. Sectoral labor income estimates were developed from value-added data. Value-added estimates involve some double-counting. If the extent of double-counting varied from one sector to another, the labor income estimates would not be good indexes of the true relative sectoral labor incomes. It is quite unlikely that this problem is serious.
3. The labor income estimates were taken as residuals, the difference between total sectoral income and sectoral property income. Property income was estimated as the product of the value of capital and land and estimated rates of

TABLE 4.11  **Average sectoral rates of return, percentages per annum**

|                          | 1840 | 1860 | 1880 | 1900 |
|--------------------------|------|------|------|------|
| Agriculture              | 11.6 | 11.0 | 9.4  | 7.6  |
| Manufacturing and Mining | 13.0 | 12.6 | 10.9 | 9.4  |
| All other                | 13.2 | 12.5 | 10.7 | 8.9  |

Source: See text.

return. Since the estimates of inventories could not be distributed among sectors, property income was computed against the value of land and fixed capital only. If the relative importance of inventories varied by sector, the sectoral property estimates are biased. Unfortunately, there is no way to be sure that this was not the case, although it is unlikely that it is a major source of bias.

4. More important, the system of estimating property incomes involved the assumption that the rate of return on property *of a given type* was the same in all sectors. In fact, this is unlikely to have been the case. Bateman and Weiss (1981, 107–8, 114) show that the returns to property in the antebellum South were much higher in manufacturing than in agriculture. The rates of return do vary from one sector to another, as the structure of the capital stock varies; only the rates for individual types of property are constant. But the differences in the average rates that have emerged are small, compared with those observed by Bateman and Weiss. Table 4.11 displays the average rates of return by sector. Bateman and Weiss (1981, 116) report rates of return for large manufacturing firms of 17 percent in 1850, and 21 percent in 1860. Unfortunately, there is no good basis for producing different sectoral rates of return for all types of property for all sectors in all years. We can be quite sure, however, that the procedure followed to produce labor income estimates has led to an exaggeration of the relative levels of labor income in the "mining, manufacturing, and hand trades" sector, and probably in the "all other" sector as well. This in turn means that the time-quality weights attached to the nonfarm sector labor forces are too high and that, therefore, the rates of change of the adjusted labor series are biased upward.

The sectoral value-added series (current prices) were taken from Gallman (1960, 47, 54, 56, 63) and from Gallman and Weiss (1969, 305), and were adjusted in the following ways. The estimates of farmland improvements were dropped from farm value-added, and new estimates derived from data in Brady (1966) were substituted for them.[11] Value added by the "all other" sector was estimated from the value added by construction from Gallman (1960, variant A) plus the total value added by services from Gallman and Weiss (1969), minus the value of shelter and value added by the hand trades. The value of shelter was dropped because the production of shelter involves the use of practically no labor, and therefore the value of shelter should not figure in the estimation of sectoral labor quality weights. Value added by the hand trades was added to value added by manufacturing and mining, taken from Gallman (1960).

The gross rate of return for each type of property is composed of the net rate plus depreciation, if any. The following depreciation rates were assumed: Land, 0; animals, 0; buildings, fences, irrigation, and drainage works, 2 percent; land clearing and breaking, 0; tools and equipment, 6.67 percent. The net rate of return was taken to be 10 percent in 1860, and was adjusted in the other years on the basis of an index number of the rate of return on New England municipal bonds (Homer 1963, 287–88, linked at 1857–59 to Boston City 5s, 305).

The labor force data were drawn from Weiss (1992). The division of the nonfarm labor force between the two nonfarm sectors was based on Lebergott (1964).

The adjustment for changes in agricultural work hours was based on data in Gallman (1975, 73), and the David, Lebergott, and Weiss series. From Gallman (1975, 73, inclusive of improvements, variant B) and the David and Lebergott farm labor force series, it was possible to compute an index of the hours worked by farm laborers in 1800, 1850, and 1900. With this index and the Weiss farm labor force in each of these three years, an index of the number of hours worked per worker was computed. Index numbers for the missing intermediate years were interpolated on a straight line. The index for 1774 was assumed to be the same as the index for 1800. The aggregate quality-adjusted labor force series were then adjusted for changes in the number of hours worked by multiplying them by the index of hours worked per worker.

### 4.6.2. Output Elasticities

The section takes up the estimation of the elasticities of output with respect to factor inputs. The procedure adopted to make estimates of the elasticities of output was similar to the one by which labor and property incomes were computed for the three sectors. The only difference was that the calculations were made at the national and not the sectoral level, and that components of capital left out of the sectoral calculations—inventories, the international sector—were here added back in.

These elasticities are necessary to weight the factors of production to make estimates of the combined inputs and total factor productivity changes. The weights assigned to the rates of growth of the individual factors of production are as follows: labor, 0.68; land 0.03; and capital, 0.29. Land improvements are treated as capital. These weights are intended to reflect income shares and the elasticities of output with respect to factor inputs.

### 4.6.3. Growth Accounting

In any case, the rates of change of the combined input series do describe the same general pattern: an acceleration in the supply of inputs and especially inputs per capita. For the period following 1800, these findings once again parallel Weiss (table 4.7). Furthermore, there was an acceleration not only in the rate of change of aggregate inputs, but also in total factor productivity: the long-term rate of gain was substantially higher after 1840 than before (table 4.10, panel C).

These results are surely not surprising. The period from 1774 through 1815 encompassed years in which the young country engaged twice in major wars. When peace was achieved, American products were frequently prevented from entering their natural markets under reasonably free conditions. There was one period of booming trade, when the Napoleonic Wars created great opportunities for American merchants—opportunities ended by the Embargo of 1807 and then the War of 1812. With the return of peace, the factory system began to spread in earnest, and by 1840 the production of textiles had been virtually completely transferred out of the home and the shop and into the factory. The variety of American manufacturing activities increased markedly in the 1840s and 1850s, and machine building began to assume the central position it was to occupy in American industrialization for the rest of the century. The aggregate statistics are simply the embodiment of these well-known developments. The degree to which the benefits of economic growth were offset by costs unrecorded here, and the extent to which the benefits were shared among Americans, are matters of considerable importance.

## 4.7. Conclusions

The conclusions of this chapter are readily summarized. The capital stock series suggest that the pace of American economic growth accelerated in the decades before the Civil War. The evidence for this statement is to be found in the real per capita capital stock figures, the various estimates of aggregate real inputs per capita, and the changing structure of the capital stock. The components that make up the series have their weaknesses, but the review conducted above turned up no compelling reasons to believe that the computed rates of growth and structural changes are biased in important ways.

The acceleration of the rate of growth should not be allowed to obscure the progress made before 1840. The series assembled in this chapter support the view that per capita GDP increased in the decades between 1800 and 1840. Furthermore, the per capita supply of capital seems to have been increasing since 1774, and the combined supply of all factors of production seems to have increased at least as fast as population between the beginning of the American Revolution and 1800. There were bad times as well as good ones, and the standard of life surely sometimes declined, perhaps for extended periods. But if these series are to be believed, the trend was mildly favorable between 1774 and 1799/1800, more clearly favorable from 1799/1800 until 1840, and even more pronouncedly favorable thereafter.

Combining the results of this chapter with those in chapter 3, we observed that expansion of the real capital stock in the United States was more rapid in the 1840–1900 period than in the 1744–1840 period or in the post-1900 period. The next two chapters examine capital formation from a different perspective; namely, from Gallman's series on annual product flows.

# Gallman's Annual Product Series, 1834–1909

## 5.1. Introduction

Gallman's annual series on the US gross national product over the 1834–1909 period represent one of the underground classics of American economic history. Building on over a decade of labor, he assembled his national product estimates in the mid-1960s to provide a clearer picture of long-run performance of the US economy. They offer a valuable additional perspective on the rate of capital formation, and how it changed over the nineteenth century. The data were originally published as overlapping decade averages in Gallman (1966), and the data became known as his volume 30 annual series. Over the next three decades, Gallman continued to refine and elaborate his value added and final flow estimates.

Gallman never published his annual data, in part because he worried that they would be used to analyze business cycle fluctuations and compare their changes over time. These were purposes for which the series were not designed. He always emphasized that (1) the series contained major derived components that did not move at business cycle frequencies, and (2) the methods of data construction before and after the Civil War differed in fundamental ways. A large part of the apparent differences in annual income dynamics between the antebellum and postbellum periods reflected differences in the estimation techniques, most particularly with respect to the residential service flows. Gallman's volume 30 annual series simply were not suitable for business cycle analysis, as tempting as

Rhode wrote this chapter.

that was. In the best scholarly tradition, Gallman did make his numbers available through the avenue of personal correspondence, with the appropriate caveats, to other economists and economic historians "for testing purposes."

This chapter presents his two major annual series for US GNP calculated on the final flow (i.e., spending) side for the long nineteenth century: (1) US national product (excluding inventory changes) and the main subcomponents in 1860 prices over the 1834–59 and 1869–1909 periods, and (2) national product in current prices over the 1869–1909 period.[1] It goes beyond the spreadsheets that have circulated since the mid-1960s by incorporating Gallman's work on inventory changes and discussing whether their inclusion is justified.

Gallman's numbers are about the best we have for the nineteenth century, and they provide important material for any attempt to create better national product estimates. In his modest way, Gallman gave a sense of their value in his 1996–97 "Notes for the File on National Accounts":

> The annual series underlying Volume 30 have several virtues . . . It has been extended into the ante-bellum years—on an annual basis, to 1834, and on an intermittent basis, to 1800—and it links with twentieth century series, rendering a quantitative account of virtually the entire national history of the United States; in most of the period with which we are principally concerned, it is available in considerable detail, distinguishing the various forms of consumption and of capital formation; [and] it lies within a consistent scheme of national accounting, which includes both the sectoral values added series . . . and the capital stock estimates. . . .[2]

Indeed, the volume 30 annual series were the product decades of painstaking labor and careful judgment by one of the best economic historians. One way to prevent the abuse of these series is greater openness, publicizing their limitations as indicators of the business cycle while highlighting their value for other scholarly endeavors.

In this chapter, the section 5.2 introduces Gallman's annual series and documents why these figures, among those in Gallman's files, are his most "finished" product. It also uncovers and corrects a small number of errors appearing in the circulated spreadsheets. Sections 5.3 and 5.4 discuss Gallman's efforts to construct and further develop the volume 30 annual series. Section 5.5 lays out the limitations on their usefulness for business-cycle analysis. Section 5.6 compares the volume 30 annual series to other available pre-1909 series for GNP and the implicit price deflator. Major findings from the series and the components are explored in section 5.7. Section 5.8 discusses Gallman's extensions and section 5.9 concludes

## 5.2. The Volume 30 Annual Series

Tables 5.1 and 5.2 show Gallman's annual series in constant 1860 prices for national product and its major spending subcomponents over the 1834–59 and 1869–1909 periods, respectively. The 1834–59 series are for census years—that is, 1839 refers to 1 June 1839 to 31 May 1840—and those for 1869–1909 are for calendar years.[3] Table 5.2 also includes Gallman's newer (1990s) estimates of annual changes in inventories for the 1870–1909 period, and reports on various corrections to the postbellum real income series. Table 5.3 displays Gallman's series on annual national product and its major spending subcomponents over the 1869–1909 period in current prices. Gallman did not develop annual current-value national product series for the antebellum period in volume 30 because the relevant price deflators were available only intermittently.[4] Because Gallman made a number of revisions over time, the series reported in this chapter differ somewhat from those underlying the published decadal averages. Gallman's practice remained to refer to these numbers as the "volume 30 series."

The data in table 5.1 are, with Gallman's minor revisions, fundamentally the same as those underlying the overlapping decennial series published in Gallman (1966). The differences resulted from (1) small discrepancies in rounding and (2) small revisions to the estimates for manufactured producers' durables in the postbellum period, especially for the 1884–1903 period.[5]

Apart from the inventory investment estimates, the figures using the 1860 prices are from a typeset mimeograph found in Gallman's files dated June 1965, with "Master-Final Version" penciled in his hand.[6] We have several solid pieces of evidence that Gallman considered these series his most "finished." First, he was using these spreadsheets as the basis for his work on national product and capital formation in the 1980s and 1990s. One copy has a pencil note: "Checked—May 24, 1993." Second, he apparently sent the 1860-price national product series for 1834–59 from the June 1965 sheets to Robert Margo as late as 7 February 1996.[7] Third, Gallman sent the 1834–1909 national product series to Benjamin Friedman as late as 15 August 1995.[8]

There seems little doubt that Gallman intended to revise the annual series underlying volume 30 to include the newer inventory investment estimates. In the document "Notes for the File on National Accounts," he states, "The annual series underlying Volume 30 . . . has an important, but easily eliminated, shortcoming: it does not include changes in the value of inventories. New estimates have now been made, however, removing this shortcoming."[9] Indeed, Gallman (2000, 6–8) incorporated the inventory changes. Moreover, he included his later estimates of annual inventory changes in the series sent to Friedman.

The current price series for the 1869–1909 period are from hand-written spreadsheets dated June 1967, found in Gallman's files.[10] Again, there is evidence that he used these sheets as the basis for his subsequent work.

Gallman at various times reported statistics based on net national product (NNP) over decade-long periods. Recall that NNP equals GNP minus capital consumption. Gallman does not appear to have estimated NNP annually for his constant price series.[11] Instead, he appears to have generated capital consumption estimates from the capital stock estimates available every ten years. Gallman (2000, 25) describes estimating capital consumption from the variant B capital stock figures using straight-line depreciation techniques, assuming that the lifespan of structures is fifty years and of equipment is fifteen years, and that the average age of structures is ten years and of equipment is five years. He refers to the results as approximate. Gallman (1992, 100) asserted that the investments in land improvement do not depreciate.

Gallman's efforts to construct and improve his national product estimates spanned more than five decades. The paper trail he left, while not complete, is amazingly thick. There are feet upon feet of files, containing drafts of articles and huge paper accounting spreadsheets filled with hand-written entries, calculations, and source notes. Many of the exercises are repeated ad infinitum, with numbers transferred by hand from one sheet to the next. Gallman and his research assistants were usually very thorough in outlining the steps used to produce a given number on a given sheet, but less helpful in bridging between the sheets or dating the calculations. And because the numbers created or used in one branch of his work built on and required modifications to numbers created or used in other branches, the records are not always in chronological order. There are several instances where gaps appear in the paper trail.[12] Research leaves, changes in research assistants, and movements between offices no doubt

TABLE 5.1 **Gallman's annual national product series, measured in 1860 prices, 1834–59, in millions of dollars**

| | Value of goods flowing to consumers | | | | | |
|---|---|---|---|---|---|---|
| Census year | Perishable goods | Semidurble goods | Durable goods | Total goods | Services | Total consumption |
| 1834 | 753.6 | 124.8 | 25.5 | 903.9 | 419 | 1,322.9 |
| 1835 | 703.3 | 148.5 | 30.7 | 882.5 | 426 | 1,308.5 |
| 1836 | 688.7 | 113.9 | 28.8 | 831.4 | 432 | 1,263.4 |
| 1837 | 754.6 | 99.9 | 34.4 | 888.9 | 440 | 1,328.9 |
| 1838 | 718.5 | 150.9 | 36.7 | 906.1 | 449 | 1,355.1 |
| 1839 | 826.3 | 107.8 | 31.1 | 965.2 | 457 | 1,422.2 |
| 1840 | 832.7 | 125.3 | 29.0 | 987.0 | 465 | 1,452 |
| 1841 | 859.5 | 140.6 | 36.2 | 1,036.3 | 474 | 1,510.3 |
| 1842 | 894.1 | 89.0 | 40.0 | 1,023.1 | 484 | 1,507.1 |
| 1843 | 1,044.6 | 146.7 | 41.8 | 1,233.1 | 493 | 1,726.1 |
| 1844 | 1,008.7 | 217.4 | 51.9 | 1,278.0 | 502 | 1,780.0 |
| 1845 | 1,057.7 | 209.4 | 60.2 | 1,327.3 | 514 | 1,841.3 |
| 1846 | 1,022.1 | 218.8 | 68.4 | 1,309.3 | 531 | 1,840.3 |
| 1847 | 1,133.2 | 302.6 | 82.9 | 1,518.7 | 550 | 2,068.7 |
| 1848 | 1,144.7 | 298.2 | 90.3 | 1,533.2 | 570 | 2,103.2 |
| 1849 | 1,145.4 | 334.9 | 96.6 | 1,576.9 | 594 | 2,170.9 |
| 1850 | 1,178.0 | 402.1 | 108.5 | 1,688.6 | 616 | 2,304.6 |
| 1851 | 1,270.5 | 401.4 | 127.8 | 1,799.7 | 647 | 2,446.7 |
| 1852 | 1,409.2 | 498.1 | 156.6 | 2,063.9 | 682 | 2,745.9 |
| 1853 | 1,513.1 | 598.6 | 162 | 2,273.7 | 721 | 2,994.7 |
| 1854 | 1,457.0 | 445.9 | 162.3 | 2,065.2 | 758 | 2,823.2 |
| 1855 | 1,551.7 | 555.2 | 177 | 2,283.9 | 790 | 3,073.9 |
| 1856 | 1,496.1 | 565.5 | 187 | 2,248.6 | 828 | 3,076.6 |
| 1857 | 1,617.1 | 433.3 | 184.2 | 2,234.6 | 863 | 3,097.6 |
| 1858 | 1,824.5 | 567.4 | 197.5 | 2,589.4 | 892 | 3,481.4 |
| 1859 | 1,825.9 | 622.5 | 200.4 | 2,648.8 | 919 | 3,567.8 |

N.B. When citing these series, include the following statement: "These series were not constructed for analysis as annual series."
Sources: Gallman Papers

explain some of these gaps. Though one cannot exactly replicate the series from the background material available, one can usually come close, and the published documentation of the sources and procedures employed is remarkably good.

As noted above, there are a handful of errors in Gallman's original data underlying tables 5.2 and 5.3. The most notable errors occur in the data on gross investment in new railroad construction in 1860 prices for the 1875–77 period. The supporting documents suggest that the problem

| Capital formation, less change in inventories | | | | | | | Correction | | |
| --- | --- | --- | --- | --- | --- | --- | --- | --- | --- |
| Manuf. producers' durables | Gross new construction | | | | Changes in claims against | Total capital formation | (excluding inventory changes) | For Pennsylvania mainline | |
| | Railroad | Canal | Other | Total | foreigners | | | Canal | GNP |
| 32.0 | 9.3 | 5.5 | 66.7 | 81.5 | −33.5 | 80.0 | 1,402.9 | 3.9 | 1,401 |
| 33.7 | 11.2 | 5.1 | 80.9 | 97.2 | −61.7 | 69.2 | 1,377.7 | 4.7 | 1,377 |
| 31.7 | 13.9 | 7.5 | 75.1 | 96.5 | −20.9 | 107.3 | 1,370.7 | 7.4 | 1,370 |
| 33.3 | 16.1 | 12.3 | 101.4 | 129.8 | −5.0 | 158.1 | 1,487 | 11.9 | 1,487 |
| 33.9 | 16.9 | 15.6 | 118.2 | 150.7 | −46.9 | 137.7 | 1,492.8 | 15.1 | 1,492 |
| 27.1 | 15.1 | 16.9 | 108.1 | 140.1 | 33.2 | 200.4 | 1,622.6 | 16.6 | 1,622 |
| 25.5 | 12.6 | 16.3 | 111.0 | 139.9 | −8.3 | 157.1 | 1,609.1 | 16.1 | 1,609 |
| 31.2 | 10.0 | 9.5 | 111.0 | 130.5 | 7.0 | 168.7 | 1,679.0 | 9.5 | 1,679 |
| 32.4 | 6.5 | 2.7 | 104.3 | 113.5 | 26.8 | 172.7 | 1,679.8 | 2.7 | 1,680 |
| 34.2 | 5.8 | 1.3 | 107.1 | 114.2 | 5.7 | 154.1 | 1,880.2 | 1.2 | 1,880 |
| 44.4 | 7.2 | 1.9 | 136.4 | 145.5 | 4.2 | 194.1 | 1,974.1 | 1.8 | 1,974 |
| 51.0 | 10.1 | 2.4 | 164.0 | 176.5 | 0.9 | 228.4 | 2,069.7 | 2.4 | 2,069 |
| 59.9 | 16.9 | 4.2 | 187.4 | 208.5 | 27.0 | 295.4 | 2,135.7 | | |
| 75.5 | 27.2 | 5.8 | 184.5 | 217.5 | 5.8 | 298.8 | 2,367.5 | | |
| 68.6 | 33.4 | 4.8 | 177.1 | 215.3 | 8.8 | 292.7 | 2,395.9 | | |
| 66.5 | 35.1 | 5.0 | 177.3 | 217.4 | −25.7 | 258.2 | 2,429.1 | | |
| 75.7 | 41.9 | 5.7 | 211.7 | 259.3 | −4.4 | 330.6 | 2,635.2 | | |
| 86.9 | 55.3 | 4.7 | 252 | 312 | −14.1 | 384.8 | 2,831.5 | | |
| 102.6 | 72.3 | 4.1 | 292.2 | 368.6 | −57.9 | 413.3 | 3,159.2 | | |
| 112.3 | 86.8 | 4.7 | 326.4 | 417.9 | −34.2 | 496 | 3,490.7 | | |
| 124.1 | 78.1 | 5.5 | 346.9 | 430.5 | −12.2 | 542.4 | 3,365.6 | | |
| 143.1 | 61.4 | 5.1 | 375.4 | 441.9 | −10.0 | 575.0 | 3,648.9 | | |
| 154.7 | 62.3 | 4.1 | 414 | 480.4 | −14.8 | 620.3 | 3,696.9 | | |
| 138.3 | 62.7 | 3.4 | 394.5 | 460.6 | 21.5 | 620.4 | 3,718.0 | | |
| 124.1 | 54.4 | 2.5 | 346.1 | 403 | −25.7 | 501.4 | 3,982.8 | | |
| 133.1 | 44.3 | 1.6 | 345.9 | 391.8 | 7.2 | 532.1 | 4,099.9 | | |

arose because a research assistant misplaced the decimal point when deflating the current dollar investment series by the construction cost index.[13] There were several typos and inconsistencies in Gallman's inventory investment series.[14] Given that the original data are used in much of Gallman's later work, it seems desirable to present them without revision and to include my suggested corrections separately (in the bottom rows and far right columns of the tables). The corrections, while important for the component series, have a negligible effect on the estimated total income; the differences in the resulting GNP estimates are always less that

TABLE 5.2  **Gallman's annual national product series, measured in 1860 prices, 1869–1909, in millions of dollars**

| Value of goods flowing to consumers | | | | | Total consumption | Capital formation, less changes in inventories | |
| --- | --- | --- | --- | --- | --- | --- | --- |
| | | | | | | Manufactured producers' durables | Gross new construction |
| Perishable goods | Semidurables | Durable goods | Total goods | Services | | | Railroad |
| 2,166 | 669 | 349 | 3,184 | 1,009 | 4,193 | 360 | 158 |
| 2,103 | 734 | 330 | 3,167 | 958 | 4,125 | 375 | 233 |
| 2,095 | 831 | 325 | 3,251 | 975 | 4,226 | 375 | 196 |
| 2,449 | 876 | 425 | 3,750 | 1,059 | 4,809 | 537 | 189 |
| 2,577 | 810 | 442 | 3,829 | 1,112 | 4,941 | 564 | 125 |
| 2,697 | 806 | 389 | 3,892 | 1,195 | 5,087 | 431 | 47 |
| 2,595 | 894 | 450 | 3,939 | 1,254 | 5,193 | 384 | <u>282</u> |
| 2,772 | 921 | 447 | 4,140 | 1,373 | 5,513 | 427 | <u>292</u> |
| 2,991 | 1,020 | 486 | 4,497 | 1,449 | 5,946 | 441 | <u>338</u> |
| 3,187 | 1,023 | 474 | 4,684 | 1,481 | 6,165 | 517 | 75 |
| 3,456 | 1,170 | 550 | 5,176 | 1,638 | 6,814 | 583 | 69 |
| 3,958 | 1,385 | 595 | 5,938 | 1,791 | 7,729 | 869 | 149 |
| 3,891 | 1,304 | 673 | 5,868 | 1,741 | 7,609 | 1,052 | 230 |
| 4,204 | 1,429 | 737 | 6,370 | 1,846 | 8,216 | 1,166 | 184 |
| 4,240 | 1,420 | 752 | 6,412 | 1,832 | 8,244 | 1,108 | 117 |
| 4,497 | 1,368 | 758 | 6,623 | 1,851 | 8,474 | 889 | 97 |
| 4,470 | 1,524 | 867 | 6,861 | 1,866 | 8,727 | 845 | 75 |
| 4,421 | 1,575 | 998 | 6,994 | 1,857 | 8,851 | 1,254 | 92 |
| 4,505 | 1,567 | 1,077 | 7,149 | 1,854 | 9,003 | 1,555 | 119 |
| 4,494 | 1,597 | 1,092 | 7,183 | 1,836 | 9,019 | 1,448 | 103 |
| 4,686 | 1,665 | 1,088 | 7,439 | 1,837 | 9,276 | 1,571 | 96 |
| 4,492 | 1,763 | 1,162 | 7,417 | 1,820 | 9,237 | 1,643 | 102 |
| 4,921 | 1,800 | 1,183 | 7,904 | 1,918 | 9,822 | 1,813 | 118 |
| 4,904 | 1,886 | 1,253 | 8,043 | 1,979 | 10,022 | 1,928 | 255 |
| 5,381 | 1,723 | 1,114 | 8,218 | 1,978 | 10,196 | 1,895 | 267 |
| 5,248 | 1,671 | 988 | 7,907 | 1,925 | 9,832 | 1,474 | 106 |
| 5,626 | 1,973 | 1,206 | 8,805 | 2,145 | 10,950 | 1,844 | 11 |
| 5,608 | 1,913 | 1,187 | 8,708 | 2,154 | 10,862 | 2,162 | 0 |
| 5,998 | 2,058 | 1,270 | 9,326 | 2,306 | 11,632 | 1,758 | 0 |
| 6,137 | 2,044 | 1,230 | 9,411 | 2,348 | 11,759 | 1,832 | 0 |
| 6,727 | 2,290 | 1,403 | 10,420 | 2,602 | 13,022 | 2,297 | 41 |
| 6,762 | 2,301 | 1,335 | 10,398 | 2,682 | 13,080 | 2,696 | 48 |
| 7,586 | 2,549 | 1,429 | 11,564 | 3,008 | 14,572 | 2,793 | 38 |
| 7,337 | 2,643 | 1,523 | 11,503 | 3,087 | 14,590 | 3,190 | 26 |
| 7,783 | 2,774 | 1,546 | 12,103 | 3,296 | 15,399 | 3,626 | 13 |
| 7,791 | 2,801 | 1,521 | 12,113 | 3,394 | 15,507 | 3,083 | 54 |
| 8,013 | 2,941 | 1,734 | 12,688 | 3,625 | 16,313 | 3,637 | 66 |
| 8,910 | 3,172 | 1,968 | 14,050 | 4,016 | 18,066 | 4,559 | 93 |
| 9,155 | 3,128 | 1,886 | 14,169 | 4,165 | 18,334 | 4,810 | 112 |
| 8,265 | 3,137 | 1,633 | 13,035 | 4,057 | 17,092 | 3,328 | 225 |
| 9,046 | 3,427 | 2,043 | 14,516 | 4,429 | 18,945 | 3,778 | 248 |
| As corrected | | | | | | | |
| | | | | | | | 28 |
| | | | | | | | 29 |
| | | | | | | | 34 |

N.B. When citing these series, include the following statement: "These series were not constructed for analysis as annual series."
Notes: Examination of the underlying spreadsheets converting current-value railroad investment estimates into constant-value estimates reveals that a decimal-place error occurs in the original calculations for 1875–77. The affected series are indicated by underlining. The corrected series adjusted railroad construction, total construction, total capital formation, and GNP.
The Gallman revised railroad construction estimates can be used to replace this original series. The revised inventory series differs by rounding and errors in the underlying data.
Sources: Gallman papers

| Other | Total | Changes in foreign claims | Total capital formation | GNP (excluding inventory changes) | Inventory changes Original | GNP Revised | Railroad construction Revised |
|---|---|---|---|---|---|---|---|
| 772.0 | 930.0 | −136 | 1,154.0 | 5,347.0 | | | |
| 734.0 | 967.0 | −112 | 1,230.0 | 5,355.0 | | | 202 |
| 663.3 | 859.3 | −143 | 1,091.3 | 5,317.3 | 113 | 112 | 232 |
| 957.1 | 1146.1 | −194 | 1,489.1 | 6,298.1 | 392 | 392 | 208 |
| 915.1 | 1040.1 | −84 | 1,520.1 | 6,461.1 | 169 | 168 | 128 |
| 838.3 | 885.3 | −84 | 1,232.3 | 6,319.3 | −20 | −19 | 69 |
| 855.2 | 1,137.2 | −88 | 1,433.2 | 6,626.2 | 71 | 71 | 69 |
| 809.0 | 1,101.0 | 17 | 1,545.0 | 7,058.0 | 132 | 133 | 80 |
| 783.1 | 1,121.1 | 3 | 1,565.1 | 7,511.1 | 304 | 305 | 77 |
| 765.0 | 840.0 | 123 | 1,480.0 | 7,645.0 | 250 | 249 | 122 |
| 785.1 | 854.1 | 85 | 1,522.1 | 8,336.1 | 349 | 349 | 197 |
| 807.9 | 956.9 | 39 | 1,864.9 | 9,593.9 | 631 | 631 | 315 |
| 1,054.6 | 1,284.6 | 21 | 2,357.6 | 9,966.6 | 38 | 37 | 407 |
| 1,050.8 | 1,234.8 | −82 | 2,318.8 | 10,534.8 | 653 | 653 | 384 |
| 1,130.1 | 1,247.1 | −25 | 2,330.1 | 10,574.1 | 172 | 171 | 203 |
| 1,289.0 | 1,386.0 | −19 | 2,256 | 10,730.0 | 308 | 309 | 131 |
| 1,250.5 | 1,325.5 | −43 | 2,127.5 | 10,854.5 | 404 | 289 | 209 |
| 1,494.7 | 1,586.7 | −90 | 2,750.7 | 11,601.7 | 634 | 584 | 397 |
| 1,602.8 | 1,721.8 | −127 | 3,149.8 | 12,152.8 | 374 | 409 | 376 |
| 1,559.5 | 1,662.5 | −155 | 2,955.5 | 11,974.5 | 102 | 234 | 229 |
| 1,573.1 | 1,669.1 | −90 | 3,150.1 | 12,426.1 | 633 | 631 | 201 |
| 2,278.5 | 2,380.5 | −116 | 3,907.5 | 13,144.5 | 235 | 235 | 197 |
| 2,086.2 | 2,204.2 | −27 | 3,990.2 | 13,812.2 | 611 | 612 | 168 |
| 2,700.3 | 2,955.3 | −56 | 4,827.3 | 14,849.3 | 50 | 51 | 159 |
| 2,175.2 | 2,442.2 | −42 | 4,295.2 | 14,491.2 | −235 | −238 | 119 |
| 2,141.2 | 2,247.2 | 2 | 3,723.2 | 13,555.2 | 1,729 | −297 | 79 |
| 2,242.0 | 2,253.0 | −142 | 3,955.0 | 14,905.0 | −1,291 | 736 | 77 |
| 1,883.4 | 1,883.4 | 100 | 4,145.4 | 15,007.4 | 136 | 136 | 94 |
| 2,162.0 | 2,162.0 | 156 | 4,076.0 | 15,708.0 | 438 | 438 | 133 |
| 1,997.0 | 1,997.0 | 443 | 4,272.0 | 16,031.0 | 242 | 242 | 194 |
| 1,887.2 | 1,928.2 | 280 | 4,505.2 | 17,527.2 | 779 | 778 | 235 |
| 2,135.8 | 2,183.8 | 412 | 5,291.8 | 18,371.8 | 164 | 164 | 268 |
| 2,372.8 | 2,410.8 | 337 | 5,540.8 | 20,112.8 | 806 | 807 | 298 |
| 2,621.2 | 2,647.2 | 150 | 5,987.2 | 20,577.2 | 314 | 315 | 305 |
| 2,471.1 | 2,484.1 | 221 | 6,331.1 | 21,730.1 | 635 | 634 | 248 |
| 2,443.3 | 2,497.3 | 148 | 5,728.3 | 21,235.3 | −135 | −136 | 215 |
| 2,543.3 | 2,609.3 | 153 | 6,399.3 | 22,712.3 | 746 | 747 | 262 |
| 2,750.5 | 2,843.5 | 137 | 7,539.5 | 25,605.5 | 1,477 | 1,478 | 283 |
| 2,876.7 | 2,988.7 | 104 | 7,902.7 | 26,236.7 | 5 | 5 | 220 |
| 2,650.6 | 2,875.6 | 201 | 6,404.6 | 23,496.6 | −1,459 | −1,459 | 182 |
| 2,963.4 | 3,211.4 | −134 | 6,855.4 | 25,800.4 | 960 | 1,199 | 206 |
| | 883.2 | | 1,179.2 | 6,372.2 | | | |
| | 838 | | 1,282 | 6,795 | | | |
| | 817.1 | | 1,261.1 | 7,207.1 | | | |

TABLE 5.3. **Gallman's annual national product series, measured in current prices, 1869–1909, in millions of dollars**

### Value of goods flowing to consumers

| Calendar year | Perishable goods | Semidurables | Durable goods | Total goods | Services | Total consumption |
|---|---|---|---|---|---|---|
| 1869 | 3,319 | 940 | 401 | 4,660 | 1,499 | 6,159 |
| 1870 | 3,036 | 992 | 398 | 4,426 | 1,427 | 5,853 |
| 1871 | 3,029 | 1,090 | 417 | 4,536 | 1,466 | 6,002 |
| 1872 | 3,111 | 1,251 | 537 | 4,899 | 1,587 | 6,486 |
| 1873 | 3,321 | 1,126 | 506 | 4,953 | 1,608 | 6,561 |
| 1874 | 3,570 | 1,063 | 459 | 5,092 | 1,656 | 6,748 |
| 1875 | 3,430 | 1,124 | 471 | 5,025 | 1,686 | 6,711 |
| 1876 | 3,495 | 1,053 | 440 | 4,988 | 1,753 | 6,741 |
| 1877 | 3,634 | 1,123 | 444 | 5,201 | 1,845 | 7,046 |
| 1878 | 3,486 | 1,047 | 418 | 4,951 | 1,884 | 6,835 |
| 1879 | 3,571 | 1,188 | 460 | 5,219 | 2,046 | 7,265 |
| 1880 | 4,543 | 1,623 | 606 | 6,772 | 2,310 | 9,082 |
| 1881 | 4,519 | 1,472 | 611 | 6,602 | 2,280 | 8,882 |
| 1882 | 5,112 | 1,604 | 661 | 7,377 | 2,425 | 9,802 |
| 1883 | 5,079 | 1,543 | 656 | 7,278 | 2,422 | 9,700 |
| 1884 | 4,956 | 1,403 | 638 | 6,997 | 2,456 | 9,453 |
| 1885 | 4,352 | 1,504 | 659 | 6,515 | 2,484 | 8,999 |
| 1886 | 4,171 | 1,569 | 726 | 6,466 | 2,495 | 8,961 |
| 1887 | 4,406 | 1,567 | 745 | 6,718 | 2,531 | 9,249 |
| 1888 | 4,501 | 1,606 | 747 | 6,854 | 2,541 | 9,395 |
| 1889 | 4,737 | 1,666 | 765 | 7,168 | 2,598 | 9,766 |
| 1890 | 4,450 | 1,764 | 827 | 7,041 | 2,576 | 9,617 |
| 1891 | 4,854 | 1,771 | 855 | 7,480 | 2,710 | 10,190 |
| 1892 | 4,594 | 1,864 | 890 | 7,348 | 2,717 | 10,065 |
| 1893 | 5,404 | 1,674 | 763 | 7,841 | 2,795 | 10,636 |
| 1894 | 4,792 | 1,451 | 661 | 6,904 | 2,718 | 9,622 |
| 1895 | 5,068 | 1,671 | 767 | 7,506 | 3,003 | 10,509 |
| 1896 | 4,819 | 1,601 | 733 | 7,153 | 3,031 | 10,184 |
| 1897 | 5,255 | 1,741 | 782 | 7,778 | 3,264 | 11,042 |
| 1898 | 5,607 | 1,779 | 817 | 8,203 | 3,357 | 11,560 |
| 1899 | 6,247 | 2,086 | 981 | 9,314 | 3,780 | 13,094 |
| 1900 | 6,696 | 2,232 | 1,019 | 9,947 | 3,992 | 13,939 |
| 1901 | 7,491 | 2,333 | 1,111 | 10,935 | 4,533 | 15,468 |
| 1902 | 7,711 | 2,471 | 1,214 | 11,396 | 4,742 | 16,138 |
| 1903 | 8,089 | 2,664 | 1,275 | 12,028 | 5,154 | 17,182 |
| 1904 | 8,299 | 2,689 | 1,277 | 12,265 | 5,379 | 17,644 |
| 1905 | 8,657 | 2,974 | 1,474 | 13,105 | 5,819 | 18,924 |
| 1906 | 9,447 | 3,476 | 1,743 | 14,666 | 6,519 | 21,185 |
| 1907 | 10,262 | 3,588 | 1,817 | 15,667 | 6,875 | 22,542 |
| 1908 | 9,528 | 3,357 | 1,559 | 14,444 | 6,796 | 21,240 |
| 1909 | 10,927 | 3,823 | 1,370 | 16,120 | 7,540 | 23,660 |

N.B. When citing these series, include the following statement: "These series were not constructed for analysis as annual series."

Notes: Revised inventory series corrects for typos and adjusts the livestock values over the 1869–79 period. The original series used *Historical Statistics* livestock prices, which are in gold dollars. The revised series uses prices in greenback dollars to maintain consistency.

Sources: Gallman papers, and annual reports of the US commissioner of agriculture, 1869–78.

| Capital formation, less change in inventories | | | | | Inventory changes | |
| Manufactured producers' durables | Gross new construction | Changes in foreign claims | Total capital formation | GNP (excl. inventory changes) | Original | Revised |
|---|---|---|---|---|---|---|
| 359 | 1,064 | −187 | 1,236 | 7,395 | | |
| 334 | 1,103 | −149 | 1,288 | 7,141 | 232 | −45 |
| 322 | 1,003 | −192 | 1,133 | 7,135 | 186 | −150 |
| 520 | 1,409 | −252 | 1,677 | 8,163 | 269 | 432 |
| 566 | 1,314 | −108 | 1,772 | 8,333 | 52 | 39 |
| 404 | 1,028 | −107 | 1,325 | 8,073 | −180 | −147 |
| 354 | 1,004 | −105 | 1,253 | 7,964 | −117 | −33 |
| 359 | 946 | 19 | 1,324 | 8,065 | −164 | −289 |
| 334 | 896 | 3 | 1,233 | 8,279 | 202 | 180 |
| 356 | 920 | 133 | 1,409 | 8,244 | −150 | −450 |
| 395 | 953 | 88 | 1,436 | 8,701 | 304 | 665 |
| 652 | 1,184 | 44 | 1,880 | 10,962 | 1,047 | 1067 |
| 699 | 1,603 | 24 | 2,326 | 11,208 | 285 | 109 |
| 758 | 1,584 | −94 | 2,248 | 12,050 | 855 | 855 |
| 660 | 1,552 | −28 | 2,184 | 11,884 | 219 | 218 |
| 457 | 1,658 | −21 | 2,094 | 11,547 | 36 | 36 |
| 401 | 1,526 | −43 | 1,884 | 10,883 | 197 | −197 |
| 567 | 1,818 | −88 | 2,297 | 11,258 | 129 | 129 |
| 682 | 1,932 | −124 | 2,490 | 11,739 | 459 | 458 |
| 633 | 1,867 | −155 | 2,345 | 11,740 | 333 | 335 |
| 657 | 1,830 | −90 | 2,397 | 12,163 | 309 | 308 |
| 678 | 2,598 | −115 | 3,161 | 12,778 | 191 | 191 |
| 682 | 2,314 | −26 | 2,970 | 13,160 | 536 | 536 |
| 705 | 3,001 | −53 | 3,653 | 13,718 | −383 | −383 |
| 677 | 2,490 | −41 | 3,126 | 13,762 | 84 | 85 |
| 520 | 2,160 | 2 | 2,682 | 12,304 | −1179 | −1,179 |
| 590 | 2,091 | −126 | 2,555 | 13,064 | 108 | 108 |
| 617 | 1,769 | 86 | 2,472 | 12,656 | −86 | −85 |
| 585 | 1,938 | 139 | 2,662 | 13,704 | 700 | 698 |
| 674 | 1,887 | 408 | 2,969 | 14,529 | 534 | 535 |
| 892 | 2,090 | 266 | 3,248 | 16,342 | 1,109 | 1,108 |
| 1,054 | 2,536 | 412 | 4,002 | 17,941 | 1,324 | 1,326 |
| 1,074 | 2,682 | 334 | 4,090 | 19,558 | 722 | 723 |
| 1,247 | 3,023 | 153 | 4,423 | 20,561 | 647 | 646 |
| 1,324 | 2,909 | 225 | 4,458 | 21,640 | 774 | 774 |
| 1,166 | 2,879 | 152 | 4,197 | 21,841 | 246 | 248 |
| 1,373 | 3,271 | 165 | 4,809 | 23,733 | 735 | 734 |
| 1,729 | 3,990 | 149 | 5,868 | 27,053 | 1,684 | 1,684 |
| 1,871 | 4,428 | 119 | 6,418 | 28,960 | 1,340 | 1,341 |
| 1,253 | 4,062 | 235 | 5,550 | 26,790 | −1,114 | −1,116 |
| 1,498 | 4,467 | −161 | 5,804 | 29,464 | 1,744 | 1,743 |

TABLE 5.4 **Shares of consumption, measured in 1860 prices**

| Percent | Perishable goods | Semidurables | Durable goods | Total goods | Services | Total consumption |
|---|---|---|---|---|---|---|
| 1869–78 | 51.1 | 17.2 | 8.2 | 76.4 | 23.6 | 100 |
| 1874–83 | 51.1 | 17.0 | 8.3 | 76.4 | 23.6 | 100 |
| 1879–88 | 51.0 | 17.3 | 9.7 | 78.0 | 22.0 | 100 |
| 1884–93 | 50.5 | 17.8 | 11.4 | 79.7 | 20.3 | 100 |
| 1889–98 | 51.1 | 17.9 | 11.3 | 80.3 | 19.7 | 100 |
| 1894–1903 | 51.6 | 17.6 | 10.5 | 79.8 | 20.2 | 100 |
| 1899–1908 | 50.3 | 17.8 | 10.2 | 78.4 | 21.6 | 100 |

Source: See text.

3.5 percent. All of the subsequent discussion in this chapter will be based on Gallman's original annual series.

The estimates for consumption did not change. Table 5.4 uses the data from table 5.2 to calculate, at a three-digit level, the shares of key components—perishables, semiperishables, durables, and services—of consumption for overlapping decadal periods from 1869 to 1908. The shares are based on the constant (1860) price series. The numbers, adjusted for precision, exactly match those published in Gallman (2000).

## 5.3. Construction of the Volume 30 Annual Series

Gallman produced his estimates for the 1834–59 and 1869–1909 periods using the same basic methodological framework, but those for the antebellum period required substantially more original work. Construction of the series generally involved establishing solid benchmarks every five or ten years and then using a less comprehensive set of annual time series to interpolate values for the intervening years.

For the postbellum period, Gallman largely adjusted estimates made by Simon Kuznets (1946), who in turn had built up his estimates from the work of William H. Shaw (1947).[15] Gallman made the following adjustments to the Kuznets series: (1) substituting new estimates for firewood, animal products, and federal excise taxes for Shaw's series (thereby substantially raising estimated income in 1869 and lowering growth rates over the 1870s and 1880s relative to Kuznets series); (2) incorporating new estimates of distribution costs based on Harold Barger (1955); (3) splitting off railroad construction from other building activity and creating a more appropriate markup series; and (4) deflating the current-value GNP series by final price indexes (using an 1860 base) from Dorothy Brady (1966).[16]

Gallman constructed his antebellum national product series by (1) taking his benchmark figures for commodity (agriculture, mining, and manufacturing) production for the years 1834, 1836, 1839, 1844, 1849, 1854, and 1859; (2) adding estimates for the value of services based largely on capital stock series;[17] and (3) interpolating the series in the intervening years using scattered annual data on numerous economic activities. The appendix of volume 30 extensively documents the procedures employed. The "major" benchmarks (1839, 1849, and 1859) were primarily based on materials from the US Census, whereas the "minor" benchmarks (1834, 1836, 1844, and 1854) used several state censuses. The benchmarks for commodity production relied primarily on the sectoral value-added data described in Gallman (1960). There were only small adjustments and shifts of commodity production between categories.

Two points deserve our attention here. The first is that these series incorporated the most up-to-date data available in the early 1960s. Gallman (1966) thanked Albert Fishlow, who generously provided his unpublished statistics on the annual production of locomotives and estimates of investments in railroad construction; Paul David, for his unpublished series on agricultural implement production; Robert Fogel, for his iron output series; Maurice Gottlieb, for figures on residential construction; and Dorothy Brady, for her final price series. These are not the final word. Gallman would have heartily applauded serious research to collect and analyze real data, such as Davis 2004, for the nineteenth-century US economy.

Second, the annual national product series between the benchmark years are interpolated or extrapolated using a less comprehensive set of products. The main issue is not the number of series used—for his antebellum estimates, Gallman (1966, 65–70) employed data on more than thirty commodities drawn from an amazing array of primary and secondary sources—but how representative their movements are. Regarding his use of interpolators and extrapolators, Gallman (1966, 64–71) noted that the statistics on net imports "receive relatively too much weight," that industrial equipment is "inadequately represented," that many of the major groups rely on one or a few underlying series, and that the flow of materials into production (e.g., wheat, corn, raw cotton and wool, and lumber) tended to dominate the series. He adds that lest these warnings "raise too many doubts, [one should] bear in mind that the interpolations and extrapolations generally carry over only four years, and frequently fewer years than this. The estimates produced are only used in decade averages . . . to reduce our dependence on benchmark year estimates to establish prewar levels of performance."

The main point is that these interpolation and extrapolation procedures are useful for determining long-run trends but, as Gallman noted, problematic for analyzing business-cycle fluctuations.[18] This is especially true for investigations of the changing volatility of the macro-economy, or for comparison of one specific cycle with another. This message carries double weight for analyses contrasting the behavior of the antebellum and postbellum series, which at the detailed level are constructed in fundamentally different ways. One key difference is in how noncommodity production is estimated. As Gallman was keenly aware, the results of business-cycle analysis on the annual volume 30 data would depend more on artifact than on fact.[19]

## 5.4. Gallman's Subsequent Work Related to the Volume 30 Annual Series

From the mid-1960s on, Gallman produced a long stream of articles—often in collaboration with Lance Davis, Edward Howle, or Thomas Weiss—that further developed and analyzed the volume 30 national product estimates (see table 1.1). Gallman (1965) added estimates of annual changes in inventories (based on decadal averages of differences in the capital stocks as estimated in his work with Howle). He generally judged data on inventory investments to be "relatively weak," even "hazardous" (Davis and Gallman 1974, 439–40, 455). Gallman and Howle (1971) explored the sectoral distribution of income in greater detail.

Davis and Gallman (1973) reported new estimates of capital consumption and net investment flows, although this development seems overshadowed by the article's other important contributions.[20] Calculating these figures involved depreciating the annual investment flows of equipment and structures estimated in the volume 30 series. Gallman (1972) took the next logical step by generating estimates of net national product for every decade from 1840 on. Davis and Gallman (1978) used the net investment and net national product statistics to provide evidence on the timing and extent of the rise of capital formation. In each case, the article fundamentally was a work of economic analysis and interpretation, but there was usually some "value added" to the income or investment concept under examination.

Davis and Gallman (1973) also began to incorporate the research of Gallman and Weiss (1969) on the service sector. In his summary appraisal of the volume 30 antebellum series, Gallman (1966, 62) had observed:

> Of all the estimates, the poorest are those of the value of services flowing to consumers. We do not know what margin for error to assign to these figures. If they are in error, the chances are that they are too high. Services account for roughly one-quarter of GNP in the prewar years. Consequently, an error as large as 20 per cent in the service component would throw GNP off by only 5 per cent.

Around 1966, Gallman started to work with Thomas Weiss to create new estimates of noncommodity production. These efforts led to the decadal estimates of the value added of the service sector from 1839 to 1899 reported in Gallman and Weiss (1969), a chapter in volume 34 of the *Studies in Income and Wealth*. Given that the new series used data from a far more comprehensive collection of service activities, they regarded these estimates as "stronger" that those derived from the volume 30 statistics (Gallman and Weiss 1969, 290).

The volume 30 series for services was reported in volume 34 as variant 1. It was calculated as a residual of national product minus net income originating from agriculture (including firewood production), manufacturing, mining, and construction. In addition to services, it included fishing and forestry exclusive of firewood production. The new series built up from data on components of the service sector was labeled variant 2. Table 5.5 compares the two variants.

As Gallman had anticipated, the volume 30 current-price series for the service sector was 5 to 18 percent higher than the new series over the 1839–79 period, and about 10 percent lower over the 1889–99 period. Consequently, the growth rate of service output as revealed by the new series was faster than that shown in the old, especially over the late nineteenth century. The difference was meaningful, but modest in the big picture. The average rate of growth over the 1839–99 period was 4.13 percent per annum for old variant 1 series, and 4.36 percent per annum for new variant 2 series. Subsequent articles used the volume 34 service sector series to make adjustments to decade averages (as an example, Davis and Gallman 1974). But Gallman did not systematically incorporate the

TABLE 5.5. **Revised estimates of the service sector: Comparison of two estimates of output, measured in current prices**

| | Variant 1, vol. 30, in billions of dollars | Variant 2, vol. 34, in billions of dollars | Ratio of variant 1 to variant 2 | Share of variant 2 in GNP percentage |
|---|---|---|---|---|
| 1839 | 0.68 | 0.65 | 1.05 | 39 |
| 1849 | 1.11 | 0.94 | 1.18 | 38 |
| 1859 | 2.01 | 1.75 | 1.15 | 41 |
| 1869 | 3.32 | 2.93 | 1.13 | 37 |
| 1879 | 4.34 | 3.87 | 1.12 | 42 |
| 1889 | 5.80 | 6.50 | 0.89 | 46 |
| 1899 | 8.14 | 8.91 | 0.91 | 47 |

Source: Gallman and Weiss 1969, 288–89, 291.

volume 34 revisions in his underlying annual estimates. The volume 30 series continue to form the core of our best estimates of US GNP, NNP, and capital formation in the nineteenth century.

## 5.5. Limitations on the Uses of the Estimates

During his long career, Gallman circulated his unpublished volume 30 annual series to other scholars, but he almost always included a warning. As a 1963 mimeographed document put it: "NOTE: These figures should not be regarded as reliable, annual estimates. They were derived for the purpose of computing decade averages and are supplied to interested technicians for testing, not for analysis as annual series."[21] While this warning was not included in the June 1965 mimeo that is the source for the data presented here, there is little doubt that his feelings had not changed substantially. Gallman's background materials underlying chapter 3 ("Appendix US Estimates of National Product") in Davis and Gallman (2001) reiterated these concerns. These drafts noted that neither Simon Kuznets nor John Kendrick published their annual GNP series: "Kuznets thought the series would be useful in the study of trends and long swings, but he had doubts with respect to their ability to properly describe business cycles. For this reason, he never published annual series for the years before 1889. These annual series were available in mimeographed form, however, and have been used by other scholars in their work on national product." Gallman further wrote that the explanation for publishing the volume 30 series "only in the form of decade average . . . was the same as Kuznets had used earlier."[22]

Because the research community abhors a vacuum as much as nature does, analyses of the annual volume 30 series did appear in print. Gallman did allow Milton Friedman and Anna Schwartz to publish a "somewhat revised" version of his series over the 1869–1909 period. Essentially, Friedman and Schwartz (1982, 99–101, 122–26) created a net product series from Gallman's volume 30 annual series by adding inventory changes back in, estimating and deducting depreciation, and shifting the price base to 1929. Gallman's 1834–59 national product series were never published in annual form.

Gallman's objective in creating his annual series was exactly the opposite of business-cycle analysis. He wanted to control for short-run fluctuations so that they would not cloud our assessment of longer-run economic performance. Simple comparisons of the benchmark estimates, available only on a five- or ten-year basis, risked comparing peaks with troughs. Table 5.6 provides a better sense of differences resulting from using the benchmark estimates and the decadal averages. As it shows, especially in the antebellum period, the growth rates calculated over the decadal averages are less volatile than those based on comparisons of the single-year benchmarks.[23]

TABLE 5.6 **Comparison of benchmark and decade average growth rates in Gallman's 1860-price GNP series**

| | Value, measured in millions of 1860 dollars | | | Growth rates per annum over decade | |
|---|---|---|---|---|---|
| | Single year | Decade average | Ratio | Single years | Decade averages |
| 1834 | 1,403 | — | — | — | — |
| 1839 | 1,623 | 1,560 | 1.04 | 2.91% | — |
| 1844 | 1,974 | 1,941 | 1.02 | 3.92% | 4.37% |
| 1849 | 2,429 | 2,549 | 0.95 | 4.14% | 5.45% |
| 1854 | 3,366 | 3,296 | 1.02 | 6.52% | 5.15% |
| 1859 | 4,100 | — | — | 3.94% | — |
| 1869 | 5,347 | — | — | — | — |
| 1879 | 8,336 | 8,417 | 0.99 | 4.44% | — |
| 1889 | 12,426 | 12,604 | 0.99 | 3.99% | 4.04% |
| 1899 | 17,527 | 17,353 | 1.01 | 3.44% | 3.20% |
| 1909 | 25,800 | — | — | 3.87% | — |

Notes: Decade averages are centered ten-year moving averages. That is, 1839 is the average from 1834 to 1843. Sources: Tables 5.1 and 5.2.

## 5.6. Comparisons with Other Estimates

To assess the volume 30 annual series more fully, it is useful to compare them with the other available annual series. One obvious set of comparisons for the antebellum period is Thomas Berry (1978, 1988). Berry constructed income estimates for the 1789–1889 period using regression analysis and back-projection. Berry found several long time-series of economic variables that were available during the period when reliable national product estimate existed, and which extend back into the earlier "statistical dark age." Berry empirically estimated the relationship between these variables and the national product series during the period of overlap, and then used these coefficients to backcast the product series for the earlier period. This procedure is problematic if these relationships shift over time—that is, if, as almost every observer attests, the US economy experienced significant structural change over this period. Given that Gallman's income estimates over the 1834–59 period are based on a firmer empirical foundation than Berry's numbers, this comparison is best viewed as a test of Berry.

Figure 5.1 and 5.2 compares the annual constant-dollar product 1978 and 1988 estimates of Thomas Berry with those of Robert Gallman over the 1889–34 and 1834–59 periods respectively. For the early period, figure 5.1 includes income estimates from Gallman (2000, table 3) for 1793, 1800, 1807, 1810, 1820, and 1830 (which added estimates for inventory changes). For the later period, figure 5.2 compares the Gallman and Berry series directly.[24] For the 1834–59 period, Gallman's series starts lower than either of the Berry's series; it displays considerably more variability than the Berry 1978 series, but less than the Berry 1988 series. Also note that for the earlier 1789–1834 period, Berry's figures are initially lower than Gallman's, implying higher rates of growth.

Making comparisons for the postbellum period is more difficult because there are now numerous alternative series. Among the series predating the volume 30 series are those of Kuznets and Kendrick. Kendrick's main contribution was to adjust the concepts underlying Kuznets's series to make the national product estimates more comparable to the official Department of Commerce series. Specifically, Kendrick treated the government sector differently. This adjustment resulted in unimportant changes over the late nineteenth century, because government spending was small. Figure 5.3 compares the real Kuznets variant I annual GNP

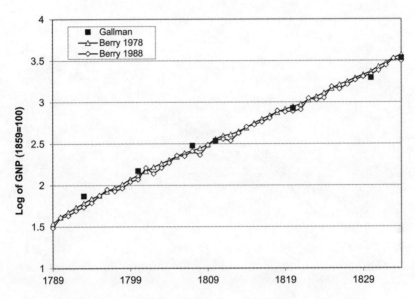

FIGURE 5.1 Comparison of antebellum GNP series, 1789–1834. Sources: See text.

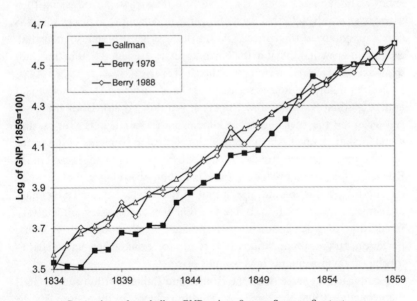

FIGURE 5.2 Comparison of antebellum GNP series, 1834–59. Sources: See text.

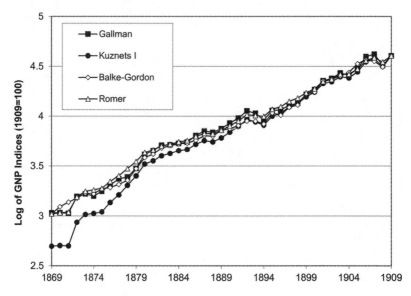

FIGURE 5.3 Comparison of postbellum GNP series, 1869–1909. Sources: See text.

series with Gallman's counterpart over the 1869–1909 period, using 1909 as the base date. (Note that Kuznets aggregated using 1929 prices whereas Gallman employed 1860 prices.) As the discussion in volume 30 indicated, the rate of growth implicit in the Kuznets series exceeded that in the Gallman series during the period after the Civil War.

Postdating the volume 30 series are those of Christina D. Romer (1989) and of Nathan S. Balke and Robert J. Gordon (1989). Both these series accepted the revisions that Gallman made to Kuznets's series, and made further changes which affected the cyclical movements of the series rather than its general trend. Romer used regression analysis to replace Kuznets's less formal procedure for establishing the relationship between commodity production and the output of the service sector. To estimate noncommodity production, Balke-Gordon also used regression analysis. In addition, they developed new interpolators for the construction, transportation, and communications sectors and constructed new annual deflators based on movements in consumer prices.

Comparing his series with the Romer and Balke-Gordon series, Gallman concluded that the three series "differ chiefly in the methods used to estimate noncommodity production, and the differences in methods chiefly affect undulations in the series, not trends." Figure 5.3 also includes the Romer and Balke-Gordon constant-value GNP series. As Gallman observed, there were important differences in the annual movements of the series around 1894 and again in 1903/04, but over the long run the series tell roughly similar stories. He further argued that because only the volume 30 style series offered details regarding the composition of GNP, it retained substantial value.[25] Elsewhere, Gallman concluded that the three series exhibited "quite similar" decennial rates of change. The most visible discrepancies occurred in the 1870s, when the Balke-Gordon series displays a markedly different pattern from the Romer, Gallman, or Kuznets series. However, correcting the typos in Gallman's railroad construction series in the 1875–77 period creates a series closer to that of Balke-Gordon during the second half of the 1870s.

Another important point of comparison between the various national product estimates for the nineteenth century is their implicit price deflators relating current-dollar to constant-dollar income. Figure 5.4 graphs the deflators (set at 100 in 1909) implicit in the Gallman, Kuznets variant I, Balke-Gordon, and Romer product estimates for the postbellum period.[26] The Gallman and Romer series follow roughly similar patterns. As Balke and Gordon (1898, 71–75) note, their deflator, which is based primarily on the consumer price indexes of Hoover and Rees, displays

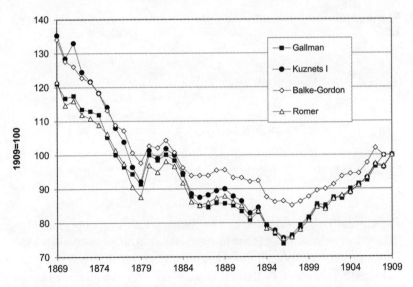

FIGURE 5.4 Implicit price deflators for postbellum income estimates. Source: See text.

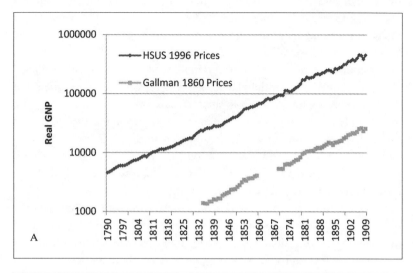

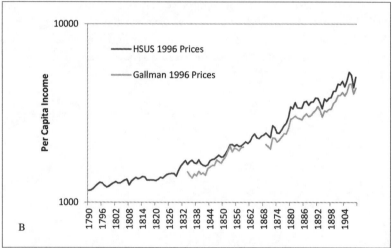

FIGURE 5.5 Comparison of Gallman and HSUS real GNP series: (a) total income; (b) per capita income in 1996 prices (1996 = 100, 1860 = 6.54). Sources: See text.

a consistently different picture. The Kuznets series initially tracks the Balke-Gordon series, but shifts to the Gallman-Romer pattern from the 1880s on. The year-to-year movements of all four series largely coincide.

Figure 5.5 compares Gallman's constant-price series with the series appearing in Carter et al. (2006), series Ca9 (hereafter, HSUS). To facilitate the examination of the two series for total income, the Gallman series is left in 1860 prices, whereas the HSUS series is left in 1996 prices. For the two series on per capita income, the Gallman series is converted to 1996 = 100 prices (on the assumption that 1860 = 6.54). In making the comparisons, one must note that the construction of the HSUS series likely depends in part on the Gallman series. The two estimates are not independent.

## 5.7 Major Findings

Gallman's annual product series yields new insights about the changing importance of capital goods in US output flows over the nineteenth century. Figure 5.6 graphs the share of annual product by major categories: services, consumer perishables and semidurables, consumer durables, producer durables, railroad and canal construction, and other construction. Commodity production (everything except services) was generally on the rise, especially over the antebellum period. The commodity share rose from about two-thirds of output in 1834 to about four-fifths in the late 1880s, then plateaued and declined gradually. Production of capital goods generally rose from 1834 on. Internal improvements such as investments

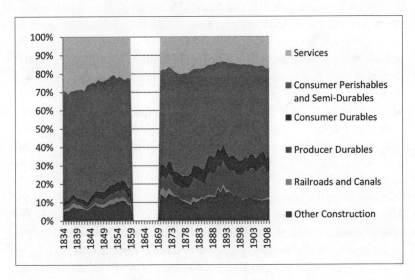

FIGURE 5.6 Composition of output, constant price series, 1834–1909. Source: See text.

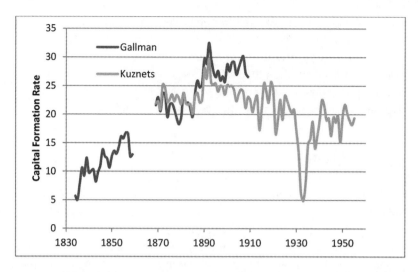

FIGURE 5.7 US capital formation rate, 1834–1955. Sources: constant price series from Gallman 1966 and text, and Kuznets 1961a and underlying T-tables.

in railroad and canals do not appear to drive this increase, except in the immediate post–Civil War period.

Figure 5.7 places Gallman's series on US capital formation rate for the 1834–1909 period into a longer context. The figure relates Gallman's series with those from 1869 to 1955 of Simon Kuznets, Gallman's mentor. In the capstone volume of his ambitious *Capital in the American Economy* project, Kuznets (1961a, 8–11) concluded that the share of gross capital formation in US gross national product measured in current prices was very stable—at about 20 percent—between the 1870s and the 1950s. This finding served as one of the foundations for Nicholas Kaldor's (1961) stylized macroeconomic constants. But Kuznets's fixed-price series (plotted in figure 5.7) revealed a different pattern: an uneven rise from 1869 to early 1890s and then a gradually declining trend. This trend was interrupted by fluctuations, such as the investment collapse in the Great Contraction, when the rate of capital formation fell to about 5 percent in 1933. The stability that Kuznets noted was predicated on the rebound of the rate to about 20 percent in the early post–World War II period.

Gallman (1966) numbers, which pushed the series back to 1834, completely undermined any picture of a constant rate of capital formation. According to Gallman's main series (displayed in figure 5.7), the share of real gross capital formation in GNP rose from "roughly one-tenth in the late 1830s and early 1840s to about one-quarter" in the 1886–1900 period (Davis and Gallman 1973, 437). The capital formation rate grew by a factor of two or three. The largest change occurred during the 1860s, the Civil War decade.[27] Numerous scholars (Abramovitz and David 1973a, 1973b; Davis and Gallman 1973, 1978, 1994; Williamson 1974) have sought to explain these patterns.

## 5.8. Extensions

Gallman considered the annual estimates of nineteenth-century US national product that he made in the 1960s to be "incomplete." He worked over the subsequent decades to make improvements. A memo from 20 May 1985 highlighted the following limitations with the volume 30 income series:

(a) They are missing one element of investment—changes in inventories.
(b) There is a gap in the series from 1859 to 1869.
(c) The current price components of the series are intermittent before the Civil War.
(d) The series do not extend back of 1834.
(e) There are no net national product estimates.
(f) Also, it would be helpful to complete estimates expressed in, say, 1929 prices to facilitate long-term analysis.[28]

Gallman and his research assistants engaged in a project in the summer of 1985 to address several of these issues, specifically a, b, and c. With the exception of the estimation of inventory changes, these initiatives apparently did not reach such a finished stage as to merit incorporation in the annual series that Gallman sent to scholars in the 1990s.

Most of this work in the mid-1980s focused on adjustments relevant to Gallman's capital stock project. For example, to create estimates comparable to those of Raymond Goldsmith and to check his own census-based capital stock estimates, Gallman (1987) pursued the perpetual inventory approach of accumulating and depreciating annual investment flows. As part of this research, he produced and published a variety of new annual series on investment in manufactured producers' durables and construction. This endeavor required filling the gap in his annual product series during the Civil War decade and projecting the series back from 1834 to 1790 (addressing points b and d above). For this purpose, Gallman relied on Berry's 1978 national product series, which explains in part his thoroughgoing analysis of this work. Gallman (1987, 217) concluded that the Berry series suffered from two weaknesses: (1) investment was derived as residual of product minus consumption, and (2) "the empirical bases for the Berry estimates become ever more fragile as the series extends into the early nineteenth century and the late eighteenth." This project produced several new investment series, but there is little or no evidence that Gallman believed that these should replace the figures in his volume 30 series. Indeed, regarding the perpetual inventory estimates, Gallman (1987, 254) wrote: "I publish the annual data with some misgiving—in view of the weaknesses of the evidence on which they are based—and refuse to warrant them for any particular purpose. Future users are on their own and are asked not to blame me if the series do not perform up to expectations. On the other hand, I am willing to accept the credit if they do."

Gallman also actively but intermittently worked to revise his transportation investment series. The original volume 30 estimates of the value of railroad construction relied on the work of Melville Ulmer (1960), which never truly satisfied Gallman. Gallman (1966, 37–38) reported using Ulmer's cost index with "some hesitancy." In the mid-1980s he set his research assistants on the task of recalculating antebellum canal and railroad investment. Part of the goal was to incorporate Fishlow's superior construction cost estimates. Another part was to correct problems in Cranmer's canal investment series, which, as Segal noted, included some of the Pennsylvania Mainline System's early investments in railroads. More generally, Gallman wanted to derive series on railroad construction consistent with his decadal railroad capital stock estimates. A notebook from the mid-1980s entitled "Measurement of U.S. Nineteenth Century National Product" concluded that these adjustments were "not of great quantitative significance."[29]

Spurred on by communications with Richard Sutch in 1993 and 1994, Gallman revisited his attempts to revise capital formation estimates in American railroads over the late nineteenth century.[30] The nature of the problem in the volume 30 annual series is apparent in the constant-value railroad construction series appearing in table 5.2. In the process of disaggregating postbellum construction into railroad and nonrailroad components, Gallman used Ulmer's estimates of gross capital expenditures

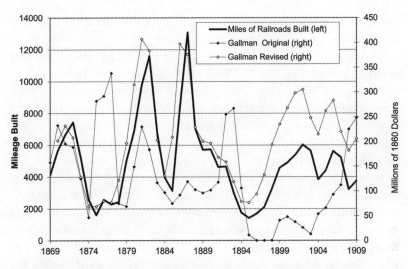

FIGURE 5.8  Railroad mileage and construction estimates. Source: See text.

(excluding land) by steam railroads, and then subtracted estimates of equipment spending based on Shaw's output data to derive his series of annual gross investment for railroad construction (Gallman 1966, 37, note 45; Ulmer 1960, 256, 274). This procedure apparently yielded negative residuals in the 1896–98 period, leading Gallman to replace these estimates with the zeros shown in the table. (As noted above, the original series also contain errors resulting from misplacing the decimal point during the 1875–77 period.) As figure 5.8 illustrates, the timing of the original residual-based series is poorly correlated with numbers of mileage constructed available from *Railway Age*.[31] Over the 1869–1909 period, the correlation coefficient was only 0.07.

Based on better data on the cost of construction from Albert Fishlow and information on the number of miles of railroads built, Gallman produced in 1994 through 1996 a revised series on railroad construction investment over the 1870–1909 period.[32] Although Gallman did create some GNP series using the revised figures, it is questionable whether these data should be considered a "finished product." Gallman believed that reestimating railroad investment was a fruitful subject for research. For the convenience of those who would prefer to use the revised series and avoid the obvious problems inherent in the original railroad series, table 5.2

includes Gallman's 1994–96 revisions for railroad construction. Again, the effects on the annual GNP estimates are small.

Throughout his work, Gallman relied on what he considered the best available price series, chiefly Dorothy Brady's numbers. But he clearly noted that the "prices count a lot," and that having "more reliable" price series would improve our ability to form better estimates of both constant and current GNP.[33] The differences between the movements of the implicit price deflators displayed in figure 5.4 highlight the importance of treating prices with care.

Another area that seems ripe for reconsideration is the estimation of the product of the service sector, especially for the antebellum period. As noted above, the estimation of noncommodity production and its impact on measured volatility figure prominently in the debates between Romer, Balke-Gordon, and others. Moreover, Gallman considered the service sector estimates for the antebellum sector the weakest in the series, and he worked with Thomas Weiss to improve the benchmark estimates in their volume 34 paper (Gallman and Weiss 1969). The volume 34 decadal estimates, which include data on distribution, transportation, public utilities, banking, insurance, professional and personal services, education, government, and housing, could usefully serve as benchmarks for more comprehensive interpolations and extrapolations than those conducted to estimate the service flows in volume 30.[34]

Another area that warrants further examination is the estimation of inventory changes over the 1870–1909 period. During the 1990s, Gallman endeavored to supplement his decadal inventory estimates with annual figures (see below). By differencing the inventory stocks, Gallman formed estimates of annual inventory investment, which he added to his volume 30 annual series to create a GNP series closer to the conventional definition. The work to estimate inventory levels was conducted, principally by his research assistants, in the mid-1990s and has not been subject to the same scrutiny as the volume 30 annual series.

An additional concern centers on how the inventory stocks were estimated. The stocks of animals (cattle, swine, sheep, horses, and mules) were estimated separately from those of other goods (imported goods, crops, mined and manufactured goods). Gallman (1992, 109) notes that the procedure for estimating inventories of other goods followed "one employed by Kuznets (*National Product since 1869*, 1946, 228) [in which] inventories were taken as a fixed fraction of the value of imports and the value of outputs of the agricultural, manufacturing, and mining sectors."

Note that this procedure, while reasonable over long periods, builds properties into the high-frequency time series that may be misleading. Specifically, it assumes that the relationship between production and inventory accumulation does not vary over the business cycle.

Also note that if the ratios translating output into inventories fail to capture the effects of improvements in transportation and communications or organizational changes (such as the rise of modern business enterprise), these inventory figures may paint a misleading picture of secular growth. Gallman (1966, 39) observed that

> Kuznets' estimates of changes in inventories are, in considerable measure, extrapolations on rates of change of output. Since we have altered these rates of change, the inventory figures should be adjusted. But Kuznets himself has limited confidence in the procedures he used. Application of these procedures to pre–Civil War data would appear to be even more dubious, but no other method is presently available. Consequently, we decided to leave this component out of both the pre– and post–Civil War series.

He cited Kuznets (1961a, 159–60), who expressed concern that using the inventory-output ratios from the 1920s "may have introduced a false stability" into key economic relationships. Others may judge whether to include or exclude the series on annual inventory changes. This discussion serves to highlight that assembling and analyzing data on the evolution of inventory-output relationships over the nineteenth century is potentially a high-value area for future research.

Finally, Gallman made a number of estimates of the value of nonconventional output, including the value of improvements to farmland and of home production activities. To evaluate economic performance over the nineteenth century requires paying full attention to these important activities, and to the shifts between market and nonmarket production.

Table 5.7 displays data on the composition of gross investment flows from Gallman (2000), the last time that he reported statistics derived from the volume 30 series. These conventional measures incorporate changes in the value of inventories ($\Delta INV$) to the investment series, and may be compared to the GNP series that also includes changes in the value of inventories.[35] Column 2 of the table also displays the rise in the share in gross investment of manufactured durables, such as machinery, when measured in constant prices. The flow data are consistent with the stock data reported in figure 1.1.[36]

TABLE 5.7 **Percentage shares of gross investment flow series, measured in current and 1860 prices**

| | (1) | (2) | (3) | (4) | (5) | (6) | (7) | (8) | (9) |
|---|---|---|---|---|---|---|---|---|---|
| | Conventional manufactured durables | | Construction | | Change in inventories | | Change in claims on foreigners | | Unconventional land clearing |
| | Current prices | 1860 prices | Current prices | 1860 prices | Current prices | 1860 prices | Current prices | 1860 prices | 1860 prices |
| 1834–43 | | 17 | | 63 | | 26 | | –5 | 41 |
| 1839–48 | 19 | 16 | 57 | 58 | 23 | 23 | 1 | 4 | 22 |
| 1844–53 | 20 | 18 | 60 | 62 | 23 | 22 | –3 | –2 | 15 |
| 1849–58 | 20 | 20 | 59 | 66 | 23 | 17 | –2 | –3 | 17 |
| 1869–78 | 26 | 28 | 71 | 62 | 9 | 15 | –6 | –4 | 8 |
| 1874–83 | 26 | 33 | 63 | 52 | 11 | 15 | 0 | 0 | 6 |
| 1879–88 | 25 | 39 | 66 | 48 | 11 | 14 | –2 | –2 | 4 |
| 1884–93 | 21 | 42 | 73 | 55 | 8 | 6 | –3 | –2 | 3 |
| 1889–98 | 20 | 42 | 71 | 52 | 8 | 6 | 1 | 1 | 2 |
| 1894–1903 | 25 | 46 | 66 | 45 | 4 | 5 | 5 | 4 | 2 |
| 1899–1908 | 27 | 54 | 65 | 41 | 4 | 2 | 5 | 3 | 1 |

Note: Columns 1–8 relate to conventional forms of investment. Ignoring discrepancies due to rounding, (1) + (3) + (5) + (7) =100, and (2) + (4) + (6) + (8) =100. Column 9 is land improvements (variant I) divided by the sum of constant-price manufacturing durables, construction, change in inventories, change in claims on foreigners, and land improvements (variant I). The numbers in Gallman 2000, 39, are derived from Gallman 1966, 34–35.

Source: Gallman 2000, 39, table 1.12.

## 5.9. Conclusion

The volume 30 annual series form a key part of our best estimates of nineteenth-century US GNP, NNP, and capital formation, and thus underlie much of what we know about America's economic growth. In his modest, scholarly way, Gallman wanted to make his volume 30 estimates better before releasing them to the world. Even without all the improvements he hoped to make, they remain among the best numbers we have for this period. But it is important to recall Gallman's own caveat: "These data were not constructed for analysis as annual series."

## CHAPTER SIX

# Investment Flows and Capital Stocks

## 6.1. Introduction

There are two ways to estimate the value of the capital stock: by cumulating investment flows, following the perpetual inventory procedures developed by Raymond Goldsmith (1955); or by taking a census of the existing stock, enumerating each element, and placing a value on it (as in the preceding chapters). With identical concepts in each case and perfectly accurate measurements, the two sets of results ought to be the same. In practice, measurements are never perfectly accurate, and historically the concepts embedded in perpetual inventory and census-style estimates have often differed, so that one or the other had to be adjusted to permit close comparisons. Given these incongruities, the degree of consistency observed between US capital stock estimates of the two types is encouraging. Census-style and perpetual inventory series have exhibited similar levels and trends, so that for many analytical purposes it matters little which type is used. Quite the contrary obtains, however, when the focus is on short periods; in such cases the two series often trace discrepant courses (Kendrick 1964, 24–25; Kuznets 1946, 1961a; Davis and Gallman 1973). In the study of business cycles or Kuznets cycles, it matters a great deal which form of evidence is adopted.

The two types of estimates differ in other respects. Censuses of wealth have been taken only intermittently, so that capital series assembled from them are discontinuous, whereas perpetual inventory series can be continuous, a great advantage for many purposes. Economists have worked

Gallman published the substance of this chapter as Gallman 1987. Rhode has revised it modestly for clarity and consistency with the rest of this volume.

out several useful concepts of value and systems of measuring capital consumption. Perpetual inventory procedures can be readily adapted to generate, from a given set of flow data and prices, a variety of capital stock estimates reflecting different systems of valuation, average service lives, distributions of service lives, and systems of capital consumption. It is much more difficult—virtually impossible in some cases—to manipulate census-style capital data to achieve similar ends.

Census-style estimates, however, are likely to be the more comprehensive than perpetual inventory estimates. Perpetual inventory estimates depend upon measurements of investment flows. Such measurements are almost bound to be more complete with respect to repetitive, market-bound events than with respect to their opposite. Should a farmer build a log cabin or a split-rail fence, his activity would probably not be captured in any official record of investment on which perpetual inventory estimates are based. But his log cabin and his fence would almost certainly turn up in a census of wealth, should one be taken. In modern economies, homemade cabins and fences are so few as to be negligible sources of discrepancy between aggregate stock and flow capital series. That would not have been the case in earlier days, when agriculture accounted for a larger fraction of activity, when the raw materials of construction lay within the reach of many farmers, when mechanization had not yet smoothed out the seasonal demand for farm labor, and when markets were so incompletely articulated that off-season work away from the farm was not widely available. In those days, farmers built many a fence and cabin in the off-season from the materials drawn from farm woodlots.

There is ample reason, then, to attempt to build two sets of capital stock estimates: one based on perpetual inventory and the other on census-style procedures. We can check one against the other and lay the basis for sensitivity testing with respect to analyses involving investment and the capital stock (e.g., analyses of the share of investment in income, the rate of growth of the capital stock, the sources of economic growth, or the structure of the capital stock). Furthermore, in view of the existing range of analytical requirements—for gross and net series, for acquisition-cost, reproduction-cost, and market-value series—and the degree of uncertainty as to appropriate capital service lives and the pattern by which capital loses value as it ages, there is reason to produce a wide array of perpetual inventory series, resting on a variety of assumptions with respect to these matters. Such considerations motivated the work of this chapter.

Chapter 3 detailed the estimates of capital stock figures at decade intervals from 1840 through 1900. But many of the details depend upon
census-style evidence—evidence that leaves something to be desired, in
part because the capital concepts involved are not always perfectly clear.
A central part of this chapter is devoted to tests comparing the census-
style estimates and perpetual inventory estimates assembled specifically
for that purpose, and to a consideration of the implications of the results
for the history of the US capital stock. The perpetual inventory series are
also used to explore the effects of choices with respect to average service
life, retirement schedule, and depreciation technique on the level and rate
of change of the measured capital stock.

The perpetual inventory series encompass two elements: manufactured producers' durables (i.e., tools, equipment, machines) and "other
construction" (i.e., construction other than railroads, canals, farmland
clearing, and construction carried out with farm materials). They are important elements, accounting for 80 to 90 percent of the conventionally
defined nineteenth-century US domestic capital stock (exclusive of inventories), and 50 to 70 percent of the same stock, including the value of
farmland clearing and first ground breaking. Unfortunately, the ultimate
source for these series is production data, which do not provide the sectoral evidence available in the census-style series.

The perpetual inventory series are imperfect in other respects, as well.
The basic annual investment series from which they were derived were
initially assembled chiefly to establish secular levels of investment. As
noted in the previous chapter, their authors were doubtful that they could
be depended upon to pick out year-to-year movements accurately (Gallman 1966, 39–41, 64–71).[1] For present purposes, however, that is not so
serious a problem. Perpetual inventory capital stock series, after all, are
cumulations of investment over several years. They are not likely to be
unduly sensitive to spurious annual perturbations in the investment series, so long as errors more or less offset each other, and so long as the
series are reliable indicators of, for instance, quinquennial or decennial
levels. The basic annual investment series probably pass that test satisfactorily; at least their authors believed this to be so, because they published
quinquennial and decennial averages.

A more serious problem is that the basic series cover only the years
1834 through 1859 and 1869 through 1909. To fill the gap of the Sixties,
and to extend the evidence backward to the late eighteenth century
(necessarily if estimates of the stock of "other construction" were to be

produced for the mid-nineteenth century), the basic series (hereafter, the Gallman series) had to be pieced out with evidence from Berry's (1978) monograph. Because Berry's work consisted of carrying Kuznets's series backward from the late nineteenth century to 1790, and because the Gallman series are also linked to Kuznets's work (at 1909), this procedure seems reasonable enough. But the nature of the Berry series poses some problems. It was derived as the difference between national product and consumption (including government), and therefore has all the weaknesses of a series composed of residuals. Furthermore, components of investment are not distinguished, which means that the bases for carrying the two elements of the Gallman series, individually, across the 1860s and into the years before 1834 are by no means so strong as one could wish. Finally, the empirical bases for the Berry estimates become ever more frail as the series extends into the early nineteenth century and the late eighteenth.

These matters are important, but perhaps not quite so important as they seem at first. Presumably, the most doubtful elements of the pieced-together Berry-Gallman series are those that relate to the earliest period. But given the rapid rate at which the US economy was growing, these elements bear only very modest weights in the determination of the capital stock estimates discussed in this chapter—estimates beginning in 1840. So long as the remote Berry-Gallman figures pick up the trend level of investment at least roughly, there is no serious problem. Although it is true that one should cast a more distrustful eye on the perpetual inventory estimates for 1840 than on the rest. The rest also deserve their share of suspicion. None of the investment flow evidence underlying the perpetual inventory estimates—whether of Berry, Gallman, or Kuznets—can be regarded as being of exceptionally high quality.

The tests to be described here are thus tests of consistency between two series, both of which must be regarded with some suspicion. They are intended as checks on both series, rather than on just one. The required consistency tests are not easily made. As noted earlier, there are certain types of investment that appear in only one of the two series—either census-style or perpetual inventory. Thus, adjustments are called for before proper comparisons can be drawn. Furthermore, the conceptual content of the census-style estimates is not perfectly clear, and that must also be clarified before proper comparisons can be made.

The chapter proceeds by first considering the conceptual problem, in section 6.2. Section 6.3 then takes up the questions of the appropriate service life of capital, the retirement schedule, and the depreciation procedure. Section 6.4 considers elements of the capital stock omitted from the two series, proposes appropriate adjustments, and exhibits the final comparisons. The final section pulls things together.

## 6.2. The Conceptual Problem

Capital stocks can be valued at acquisition cost, reproduction cost, or market value. Each measure has its own special analytical uses. Acquisition cost is backward-looking. A capital stock estimate so valued might be used to study savings behavior, since in this view the stock can be regarded as accumulated savings. Reproduction cost concerns the present. It conceives of the capital stock as the value of inputs required to reproduce it, given current factor prices and production techniques.[2] Such measures are useful in the study of production relationships. Market value is forward-looking. It is the discounted stream of anticipated returns to capital, and it would serve well, for example, in the analysis of aggregate consumption. It would be good to have all three types of measure, but commonly it is necessary to make do with one or two.

Market value is a net concept, since it takes into account only the remaining earning life of existing capital. Acquisition cost and reproduction cost can be measured as both gross and net. The questions about whether net measures should be produced—and, if so, how—are vexing; neither would be appropriately addressed here. The subsequent sections rest on the assumption that both gross and net measures are legitimate, as are conventional methods of obtaining net measures.

If the economy were perpetually in equilibrium, if prices and productivity never changed, and if depreciation allowances accurately described the decline in the earning power of capital as time passed, then net acquisition cost would always equal net reproduction cost, which in turn would always equal market value. In fact, these conditions do not obtain, and therefore the three measures are not equal.

These matters would be of no present importance were it certain that the perpetual inventory and census-style estimates embraced the same valuation scheme. But that is not the case. The perpetual inventory series, which are expressed in constant (1860) prices, closely approximate reproduction cost, deviating from that standard only to the extent that the markets for new capital goods were out of equilibrium in 1860. The meaning of the census-style figures is less clear, and may in fact differ from one figure or one year to the next.

The principal but not exclusive source of these data is the federal census, which collected wealth data from individuals, business firms (including farms), and tax officials. From the latter, the census requested statements of "true value," a concept that is itself ambiguous. While it is often understood by outsiders to refer to market value, tax officials seem to have something else in mind: perhaps what market value would be, were it not subject to temporary fluctuations proceeding from transitory interest rate shifts or from cyclical booms and busts.

Businessmen might be thought to have provided the census takers with acquisition-cost values: book values, either gross or net. But one must remember that capital accounting was a new phenomenon in the nineteenth century. Most businessmen charged off capital as a current expense. For these people, tax records would have constituted the only "books" from which the answers to the census taker's questions could be drawn. The census instructions are not a great help in guiding one as to the meaning of value, and different modern analysts have interpreted them in different ways. There is strong support for the notion that the census was seeking acquisition cost—probably gross—when it approached businesses. However, the evidence indicates that net reproduction cost or market value was most often meant, at least in the latter part of the century. Consider the following definition of value, drawn from the 1890 manufacturing census questionnaire: value "should be estimated at what the works would cost in 1890, if then erected, with such an allowance for depreciation as may be suitable in the individual case (US Census Office 1892, 10)."[3]

But however the matter is judged, it must be regarded as being still in doubt. Thus, if consistency tests are to be run between the two sets of capital estimates, and if the conceptual content of one set is uncertain, it behooves the analyst to consider first—before comparisons are drawn—the forces at work during the century driving acquisition, reproduction, and market values apart, and the strength of these forces. Only with this information in hand can the comparison of the two series be properly interpreted.

The acquisition cost and reproduction cost of a capital stock will differ if capital goods prices have changed over time, and if the changes have not offset each other. For example, if capital goods prices persistently rise, a capital stock will be smaller if measured in acquisition costs than if measured in reproduction costs. If capital goods prices persistently fall, the reverse will be true.

What happened to capital goods prices across the nineteenth century? Interestingly enough, the prices of construction goods apparently rose and fell periodically, but exhibited no clear long-term trend (see table 6.1, columns 1 and 2). Thus one would suppose that acquisition costs and reproduction costs would differ little at the census dates, and that any differences that emerged would place acquisition costs sometimes above and sometimes below reproduction costs.

Experiments show that this is precisely what happened. In the experiments, the constant-price annual flow series was cumulated to produce constant-price reproduction-cost estimates of the "other construction" capital stock, at decade intervals, from 1839 through 1899. The series was then inflated using construction price index numbers relevant to the benchmark years 1839, 1849, and so on. To form acquisition-cost estimates of the same capital stock for the same years, the annual flow series was first inflated and then cumulated. The resulting ratios of the current-price acquisition-cost estimates to the current-price reproduction-cost estimates are given in column 3 of table 6.1.[4] It will be observed that the ratios are all close to a value of one. In every case but one, acquisition cost is within 6 percent of reproduction cost. That must be regarded as very close, particularly given the fairly wide margins for error that must be allowed for all capital stock estimates in the nineteenth century. In view of these considerations, it is a matter of small importance whether the census measured "other construction" capital projects at acquisition costs or at reproduction costs.

The situation with respect to manufactured producers' durables was very different, however. The prices were more variable, and they dropped throughout the century, but particularly sharply in the 1880s (see table 6.2). Consequently, in 1890, acquisition cost (gross and net) was well above reproduction cost—a quarter to a third higher in the net variants, and two-fifths to almost three-fifths in the gross variants. But by 1900 the two measures produced roughly the same values. No doubt acquisition cost was also slightly higher in 1850 and 1880 (but not in 1860), and perhaps more pronouncedly so in 1870, but not to the degree exhibited in 1890. It does matter, then, whether the census returns of the stock of manufactured producers' durables were measured in acquisition cost or reproduction cost. To interpret the census wealth estimates for 1890, one must know the concept that guided the collection of the evidence in that year. It is less important, but useful, to have this information for other years as well.

TABLE 6.1 **Construction price indexes, 1789–98 through 1889–98 (base: 1860), and estimates of the ratio of acquisition cost to reproduction cost for "other construction" capital stock, 1839–99**

| | (1) | (2) | (3) |
|---|---|---|---|
| Dates | Index of residential bldg. costs in Philapdelphia | Index of total US construction costs | Ratio of acquisition cost to reproduction cost (gross) |
| 1789–98 | 96 | | |
| 1794–03 | 110 | | |
| 1799–08 | 110 | | |
| 1804–13 | 118 | | |
| 1809–18 | 121 | | |
| 1814–23 | 126 | | |
| 1819–28 | 108 | | |
| 1824–33 | 102 | | |
| 1829–38 | 101 | | |
| 1834–43 | 97 | | 1.06 (1839) |
| 1839–48 | | 95 | |
| 1844–53 | | 95 | 1.05 (1949) |
| 1849–58 | | 97 | |
| 1854–63 | | 110 | 1.00 (1859) |
| 1859–68 | | 117 | |
| 1864–73 | | 125 | 0.93 (1869) |
| 1869–78 | | 107 | |
| 1874–83 | | 109 | 0.96 (1879) |
| 1879–88 | | 118 | |
| 1884–93 | | 109 | 1.00 (1889) |
| 1889–98 | | 100 | |
| 1894–03 | | 104 | 1.05 (1899) |

Sources:
Column 1: Adams 1975. 813. Variant B, linked to Brady-Gallman index (implicit index of "new construction," able A-3 in Gallman 1966, 34) at census year 1839. The link was established in the following way. The Adams (calendar year) index numbers for 1839 and 1840 were averaged (1839, weight of 7; 1840, weight of 5) to approximate an index number for census year 1839 (86.3). This number was divided through the Brady-Gallman index number for census year 1839 (97.9), resulting in the ratio 1.134. The Adams index numbers. 1789–1839 (decade averages, unweighted), were multiplied by 1.134 and then rounded, to produce the values in column 1, which refer to calendar years. The Adams variant B series was accepted in preference to variant A, because the weighting scheme adopted by Adams in variant B is similar to the one underlying the Brady-Gallman series.

Column 2: Figures for 1839–48 through 1849–58 and 1869–78 through 1894–1903 are derived from Gallman 1966 (see notes to column 1) and refer to all new construction. Figures for 1839–48 through 1854–63 are three-item averages, referring to 1839, 1844, 1849 (1839–48), 1844, 1849, 1854 (1844–53), etc. The years are census years, except 1863, which is a calendar year. Figures for 1869–78 through 1894–1903 are weighted decade averages and refer to calendar years. Figures for 1859–68 (calendar years) are based on interpolations of the Brady-Gallman estimates of 1860 and 1869, carried out on a construction-cost series derived for the purpose. The construction-cost series was computed from the David-Solar (1977) index of the common wage and the Warren and Pearson price index of building materials. The weights used were the same as Adams's variant B weights.

Column 3: See text. The service life adopted was fifty years, except for 1839, in which case I used forty years. The price index numbers used to inflate the constant-price flow series are the index numbers contained in columns L and 2. (These inflators were required only for the years prior to 1869, since the Gallman flow series are available in both current and constant prices, 1869–1909.) Flows across each decade were inflated by decade average index numbers. The index numbers used to inflate the reproduction-cost stock series—1869, 1879, 1889, and 1899—refer expressly to "other construction" and were derived from data underlying the data in column 2. The figures for 1879, 1889, and 1899 are weighted averages of prices for calendar years 1878 and 1879, etc., to approximate the census year. Such an adjustment was impossible for 1869, which refers to the calendar year. The index numbers used to inflate the reproduction-cost series—1839, 1849, and 1859—are the appropriate figures underlying column 2.

TABLE 6.2 **Manufactured producers' durables price indexes, 1839–48 through 1899–1908 (base 1860), and estimates of the ratio of acquisition cost to reproduction cost, 1890, 1900, and 1908**

| | (1) | (2) | (3) | (4) | (5) |
|---|---|---|---|---|---|
| | | Ratios of acquisition cost to reproduction cost | | | |
| | | Net valuation | | Gross valuation | |
| **Dates** | **Price index** | 13 years[a] | 18 years[a] | 13 years[a] | 18 years[a] |
| 1839–48 | 114 | | | | |
| 1844–53 | 109 | | | | |
| 1849–58 | 108 | | | | |
| 1869–78 | 88 | | | | |
| 1874–83 | 72 | | | | |
| 1879–88 | 55 | | | | |
| 1884–93 | 42 | 1.24 (1890) | 1.31 (1890) | 1.42 (1890) | 1.56 (1890) |
| 1889–98 | 35 | | | | |
| 1894–1903 | 37 | 0.92 (1900) | 0.96 (1900) | 1.03 (1900) | 1.09 (1900) |
| 1899–1908 | 38 | 0.99 (1908) | 0.99 (1908) | 1.02 (1908) | 1.02 (1908) |

[a] Service lives.
Sources:
Column 1: See the source notes for column 2 of table 6.1.
Column 2: See the source notes for column 3 of table 6.1. The net valuations depend upon straight-line depreciation.

Market price might deviate from net reproduction cost for any cause or development that (1) could throw the new capital goods markets out of equilibrium, (2) alter the distribution of expected earnings among capital goods of differing age, or (3) alter the appraisal of a given income stream. The first type of development is not of great interest here, since the measures of net reproduction cost used here are probably affected by disequilibrium in new capital goods markets, and are thus a kind of mixture of reproduction cost and market value. The other two types of developments could be allowed for in forming net reproduction-cost estimates, with service lives and depreciation systems being adjusted to reflect the changing market reality. But insofar as these decisions were left unchanged over extended periods, market value and net reproduction cost could and would diverge.

The distribution of earnings among capital goods of differing vintage might presumably change in response to technical changes, but no account can be offered about precisely how earnings streams were altered and, thus, how the pattern of market capital values was affected in the nineteenth century. It is possible, however, to say something about the third and probably most powerful development listed above: changes in the appraisal of the income streams flowing from capital.

The market value of the capital stock represents the discounted anticipated income flowing from capital. A rise in the discount rate—the rate of interest—will tend to reduce the market value of capital, ceteris paribus, while a decline will tend to increase it. To judge the effect of changes in interest rates on the value of capital, one needs to know which interest rates are relevant, the extent to which they changed, and the age distribution of the capital stock beforehand. With this information and an annuity table, one can readily compute the change in the market value of capital.

The focus here is on the capital stock values derived from census wealth data. The question is this: If the census had appraised capital at market value, how far would the interest rate changes across the nineteenth century have altered census capital stock values, relative to what they would have been had capital been appraised at net reproduction cost with fixed estimating parameters from one census to the next? For example, assume that in 1840 the market value of the stock of manufactured producers' durables had been equal to the net reproduction cost of this capital, the latter computed on the assumption of a thirteen-year average service life and straight-line depreciation. How far would this equality have been disturbed by the observed interest rate changes of the nineteenth century?

To answer this question, one must imagine how census appraisers (officials or respondents) went about their task. It may be safely assumed that if they attempted to place market values on capital, they were well aware of the influence of interest rates on capital values and therefore took interest rates into account. Whether they would have looked to nominal or real interest rates is by no means certain, but both possibilities were considered. Surely they would have been concerned not with the interest rate on the morning of the day on which their appraisals were made, but rather with the general level of the interest rate in the census year, and perhaps even the year or two preceding it. That is, it may be assumed that they would have left out of account what they regarded as temporary, short-run movements.

With these considerations in mind, one can examine interest rate changes from one census year to the next, coming to the following conclusions concerning patterns of change summarized in table 6.3.[5] The table suggests that the period from 1870 onward is worthy of examination. From 1870 to 1880, the nominal rate fell pronouncedly, from roughly 7 percent to 5 percent. From 1880 to 1890, the real rate fell pronouncedly, from

TABLE 6.3 **Interest rate movements**

| Intercensal periods | Real | Nominal |
|---|---|---|
| 1840–50 | Fell | No change |
| 1850–60 | Rose | Fell modestly |
| 1860–70 | Rose modestly | Fell modestly |
| 1870–80 | Fell | Fell pronouncedly |
| 1880–90 | Fell pronouncedly | Fell |
| 1890–1900 | Fell very pronouncedly | Fell |

Sources: See text.

7 percent to 5 percent; and from 1890 to 1900, the real rate fell very pronouncedly, from 5 percent to 1 percent. In each episode the market price
of the capital stock must have gone up. Assuming that the market price
had been equal to net reproduction cost before each rise, how far would
the former have increased above the latter as a result of the interest rate
change? Answers to this question were worked out with an annuity table
and the perpetual inventory estimates, using a service life of thirteen years
(manufactured producers' durables) and straight-line depreciation. The
ratio of market value to net reproduction cost emerging from a change
from 7 percent to 5 percent is 1.10. The ratio for a change from 5 percent
to 1 percent is 1.24.

One's first impression is that these differences are small. This is particularly the case if one is concerned chiefly with the probable differences
between the perpetual inventory series and the measures taken from the
wealth census. Some part of the effect of falling interest rates on the value
of capital—the part that has to do with the pricing of new capital—is
reflected in the perpetual inventory series. Thus, if the census wealth and
perpetual inventory series were in all ways consistent, except in mode
of valuation, and if the census-of-wealth data were expressed in market
value and the perpetual inventory series in net reproduction cost of the
form previously attributed to it, then the ratios in the tabulation would
actually overstate the quantitative differences between the two series.

Second thoughts suggest the following qualifications. The service life
selected above, thirteen years, may not be unrepresentative of manufactured producers' durables, but it is short for improvements. Changes in
interest rates have greater effects on long-lived capital. Thus, for improvements (construction), computed changes in value would surely be greater
than those recorded above. Furthermore, since the interest rate seems to

have been falling from at least 1870 to 1900, it is possible that the deviation between reproduction cost and market value would continue to grow from one census date to the next, in which case the two might diverge in 1900 by as much as 50 percent ($1.10 \times 1.10 \times 1.24 = 1.50$). (This assumes that the experiences of the decades 1870–80 and 1880–90 were similar, and it ignores the qualification advanced in the previous paragraph.) Such a conclusion surely goes too far, however, since it rests on the implicit assumption that reproduction cost would remain unchanged. In fact, with the interest rate falling and investment being encouraged, one would expect some tendency for reproduction cost to rise (relative to market price) toward a new equilibrium. This would be a factor counteracting the widening of the gap between market price and reproduction cost. Furthermore, the calculations carried out above rest on the implicit assumption that the income-earning capacity of capital remained unchanged. But, ceteris paribus, one would expect that a flood of new investment would tend to lower income, and thus reduce the market value of capital.

Clearly, the calculations are less than conclusive, especially since they take into account only one element affecting market value. Nonetheless, the modest change in market value occasioned by a fall from a rate of 7 percent to one of 5 percent remains impressive and, despite all qualifications, even the effects of a change from 5 percent to 1 percent appear rather modest. In terms of the practical problems to be discussed in the next section, it seems possible to conclude that at the decennial census dates 1840–90, reproduction cost and the market price of capital were unlikely to have been very far apart—though at the last of these dates, and perhaps the one before as well, market price probably exceeded reproduction cost. This was also almost certainly true in 1900, and the margin between these two measures was the greater at that date.

In summary, the constant-price perpetual inventory series approximate the reproduction-cost series, while the series derived from the census wealth data may be valued at reproduction cost, at market value, or at acquisition cost. The possible conceptual differences are apparently empirically unimportant for the antebellum period. The question of whether construction is measured at acquisition cost or at reproduction costs is also unimportant for most of the postbellum period. Where conceptual differences *are* important, reproduction cost is a smaller value than acquisition cost (for example, for manufactured producers' durables in 1890) and market value (for example, for all capital in 1900). With this background, the relevant comparisons can be examined.

## 6.3. The Service Life of Capital

To compute perpetual inventory estimates, one must establish service
lives for the relevant types of capital, the pace at which each type of capital lost value as time passed (the depreciation schedule), and the pattern
in which capital retirements took place. Since the perpetual inventory estimates under discussion were assembled to test the census wealth data, it
was necessary to make allowance for casualty losses and to keep in mind,
while choosing among depreciation schedules, the manner in which the
census wealth data were assembled. That is, census wealth data are net of
casualty losses. Comparable perpetual inventory estimates must therefore
also be net of casualty losses. Census wealth data represent appraisals by
owners or officials. Thus, comparable perpetual inventory estimates must
capture the mental processes of nineteenth-century appraisers.

The service lives have not been computed from nineteenth-century
evidence, although there are surely data among census and business records by which such computations could be made. For example, the Tenth
Census (1880) contains data from which the service lives of railroad rails
and ties of various specifications have been computed (Fogel 1964, 172).
Davis, Hutchins, and Gallman (1987) assembled a set of data concerning
the New Bedford whaling fleet, from which service lives and the incidence
of casualty losses have been calculated. There must be much more evidence of this type, particularly in business records. But I have not been
able to assemble a full set of such data, and have therefore accepted guid-
ance from the work of Simon Kuznets and Raymond Goldsmith—both
of whom, however, have been concerned chiefly with twentieth-century
experience, not nineteenth-century experience.

In his research on the late nineteenth century, Kuznets adopted a service life of thirteen years for manufactured producers' durables, and fifty
years for improvements—figures that include an allowance for losses by
fire, but not for other types of casualty losses.[6] Furthermore, the improvements include railways and waterways, unusually long-lived capital that
is excluded from the perpetual inventory series discussed in this chapter. Thus, fifty years may be an excessive service life for this exercise. As
a check, Goldsmith's service life data, drawn from IRS bulletin F, were
weighted up, by sector and type of capital, with data from the census-
style capital stock series (Goldsmith 1951, 14–17, 20–24).[7] These calculations yielded values of seventeen years for durables and fifty-two years for

improvements (exclusive of railroads and canals); neither figure includes an allowance for casualty losses.

Perpetual inventory producers' durables series based on both thirteen- and seventeen-year service lives were computed, but while the latter presumably consists of upper-limit estimates in each year, the former may not constitute lower limits, in view of Kuznets's evidence. With respect to improvements, series using forty- and fifty-year service lives were computed. It is possible that these two values do describe limits within which the appropriate service life lies, although one can be more sure with respect to the upper bound than with respect to the lower.

It is possible that average service lives changed across the nineteenth century. Experiments with weighting up the bulletin F evidence revealed no shifts in average lives occasioned by changes in weights (i.e., changes in the structure of the stock of durables and improvements). But the information used for this purpose is not detailed as to types of capital. In any case, there may have been shifts in durability or in the rate of obsolescence which influenced average service life by type of capital. That must be borne in mind when the two sets of capital stock estimates are compared.

Estimates were made based on three systems of capital consumption: straight-line, declining-balances, and BLS concave. The first system would presumably come closest to replicating census values, if census enumerators or their respondents in fact estimated the cost of reconstructing each piece of capital, chose a service life, and then computed the depreciation to be deducted from the value of that piece of capital. But it is possible that estimators did not go through all of these steps, at least not consciously. It is also possible that they used rules of thumb that in fact reflected a different depreciation scheme. Certainly, it would not be surprising if they believed that capital lost value with particular rapidity—or, for that matter, with particular slowness—in the first years of life, thus adopting in this way attitudes that are embodied in declining-balances and BLS concave procedures. Therefore, while it was expected that the best results would come from the first technique, computations were carried out for all of them.

Two separate retirement schedules were made. The first rests on the assumption that all pieces of capital of a given type were retired at the same age. For example, in the case of the lower-bound durables estimates, it was assumed that all durables lasted exactly thirteen years. The second set of estimates makes provision for both early and late retirements.[8] While it is based on twentieth-century rather than nineteenth-century experience, it is more realistic than the assumption of a uniform retirement age. But it poses a problem: it is a formidable consumer of data. Thus, producing estimates of the value of improvements for years before 1889, on the basis of a fifty-year service life, requires data running deep into the eighteenth century—data that do not appear to exist. Estimates can be produced, of course, if zeroes are entered for missing values, and such computations were made. Given the rapid pace at which investment grew in the nineteenth century, and given the nature of the retirement distribution, these estimates are unlikely to deviate very far from true values in the years with which this chapter is concerned. But they are biased downward, and the bias is more serious the earlier the date to which the estimate refers. For this reason, one set of estimates was computed resting upon these procedures, and another was computed depending upon the assumption of a common retirement age. The two *sets* of estimates, in fact, differ little with respect to level, and even less with respect to trend. Consequently, it matters little, for present purposes, which set of estimates is employed.

Table 6.4 contains the results of a first effort to compare the perpetual inventory and census-style capital stock estimates. Each entry expresses one of the former estimates as a ratio of one of the latter. Both gross and net perpetual inventory estimates were prepared; the gross figures represent each of the four average service lives deemed relevant: forty years and fifty years, in the case of improvements; thirteen years and seventeen years, in the case of producers' durables (machinery and equipment). Only the net calculations that produced the closest fits to the census-style estimates figure in the ratios computed for the table. At least one estimate for each service life is included. A common age of retirement was assumed in the case of improvements, to avoid the computational problem discussed above. In the cases of the producers' durables, that assumption was unnecessary.

Even a casual study of the table reveals several important points. All of the ratios in the columns headed "gross" are greater than one—several substantially so—while this is not true of the ratios in the columns headed "net." *Gross* and *net* refer to the perpetual inventory estimates. Since the net values correspond more closely to the values derived from census data, the results are consistent with the notion that the census returns are expressed in net values. This does not preclude the idea that the census data are gross, and that they or the perpetual inventory data are subject to serious measurement errors leading either the former to be understated

TABLE 6.4 **Ratios of gross and net perpetual inventory capital stock estimates to census-style capital stock estimates, 1840–1900**

**Panel A. Gross estimates**

| | Improvements service life | | Producers' durables service life | |
|---|---|---|---|---|
| | 40 yrs. | 50 yrs. | 13 yrs. | 17 yrs. |
| 1840 | 1.19 | 1.21 | 1.21 | 1.35 |
| 1850 | 1.45 | 1.48 | 1.31 | 1.54 |
| 1860 | 1.40 | 1.43 | 1.26 | 1.43 |
| 1870 | 1.67 | 1.73 | 1.89 | 2.17 |
| 1880 | 2.20 | 2.31 | 2.10 | 2.42 |
| 1890 | 1.89 | 1.99 | 1.51 | 1.73 |
| 1900 | 2.15 | 2.31 | 1.47 | 1.76 |
| Mean | 1.71 | 1.78 | 1.54 | 1.77 |

**Panel B. Net estimates**

| | Improvements | | | Producers' durables, straight-line depreciation service life |
|---|---|---|---|---|
| | Straight-line depreciation service life | | Declining balance service life | |
| | 40 yrs. | 50 yrs. | 50 yrs. | 13 yrs. |
| 1840 | 0.90 | 0.96 | 1.79 | 0.77 |
| 1850 | 1.05 | 1.14 | 0.92 | 0.83 |
| 1860 | 1.02 | 1.1 | 0.89 | 0.77 |
| 1870 | 1.12 | 1.24 | 0.97 | 1.31 |
| 1880 | 1.49 | 1.65 | 1.29 | 1.22 |
| 1890 | 1.28 | 1.42 | 1.12 | 0.95 |
| 1900 | 1.46 | 1.61 | 1.25 | 0.86 |
| Mean | 1.19 | 1.3 | 1.03 | 0.96 |

Sources: See text.

or the latter overstated. These possibilities cannot be excluded, but they seem less probable. It is likely that the census data are truly net.

Assuming that this judgment is correct, what do the net ratios reveal about the degree of consistency between the two sets of series? Since the two sets of series do not contain precisely the same components (see above), the data underlying table 6.4 need to be adjusted before a final answer to this question can be given. A preliminary answer can be offered, however, if an appropriate standard of consistency can be established.

Suppose that the margin for measurement error in each series were as low as 10 percent—it may very well be higher—and that none of the series were biased, so that in any given year a positive error were as likely as a negative error. The maximum relative deviation between the two series in two successive years would then appear if a set of errors were as follows:

|                     | Year 1 | Year 2 |
|---------------------|--------|--------|
| Perpetual inventory | −10%   | +10%   |
| Census style        | +10%   | −10%   |

Now supposing that the two series were perfectly consistent, except for these random errors, the ratios for the two years—corresponding to those in table 6.4—would be 0.82 in the first year and 1.22 in the second. That is, 0.82 and 1.22 are values that can occur even if the two types of estimates are fundamentally consistent, but subject to independent measurement errors of as much as ±10 percent.

Now notice that of the thirty-five "net" ratios in table 6.4, twenty fall within this range and another five are within five percentage points of the limits of this range. Is that good or bad? It seems moderately good—that is, it suggests consistency—though the test is not very demanding.

There are also some details in table 6.4 that are worth noticing. Of the five ratios for 1900 that lie in the net columns, four exceed the value of 1, three exceed the values recorded for 1890, and the other two fall only moderately short of the 1890 values. Abstracting from the possible errors discussed in the preceding paragraph, the ratios for 1900 would have been lower than those for 1890, and it might also have been expected that they would fall well below a value of 1 *if census returns had been expressed in market values* (see section 6.2, above). One of the two producers' durables ratios for 1890 also exceeds a value of 1, while the other is very close to 1. Had the census valued capital at acquisition cost, both of these ratios would have been well below a value of 1. The ratios for 1890 and 1900, thus, are inconsistent with the idea that the census valued capital at acquisition cost or market value, and they are consistent with the idea that capital was valued at net reproduction cost. That suggests that no differences in valuation criteria stand in the way of the comparison of the perpetual inventory and census-style capital stock estimates. It also indicates that the census-style estimates can be treated, for analytical purposes, as net reproduction-cost estimates, though one should bear in mind that for the antebellum years, and in some measure for the postbellum years as well (see section 6.2), the three different systems of valuation are likely to have yielded very similar values.

Introducing the possibility of measurement error, of course, blurs the clear outlines of these conclusions. But the outlines are probably not completely erased. The results of the consistency tests square with what informed students might have supposed before the fact. It is therefore reasonable to accept the view that the census-style figures are truly net and are truly valued at reproduction cost (at those few dates where the valuation concept matters); at least these conclusions can be accepted in the preliminary way in which even the strongest research results should be accepted.

## 6.4. Omitted Components

The census-style data include all capital in each sector covered, regardless of where it was produced and regardless of the materials used. The perpetual inventory series are more narrowly conceived. They include, under the heading "producers' durables," only the products of census establishments, adjusted for foreign trade in durables. They exclude durables made by very small firms and implements produced at home or on the farm. These omissions are unimportant throughout, but they were more important at the beginning of the period under consideration than at the end. Thus, the perpetual inventory series should increase faster than the census-style series, as they do (see table 6.4). The upward bias imparted to the rate of change of the perpetual inventory improvements series is probably more serious. The estimates include all improvements, except railroads and canals, carried out with construction materials produced by census firms—again, adjusted for foreign trade flows. The census-style capital stock estimates, however, also include residences, sheds, barns, and the like produced from farm materials. For example, log cabins and barns are included in the census-style estimates, but not in the perpetual inventory estimates.[9] Since these types of capital were more important earlier in the period than later, one would expect the perpetual inventory series to exhibit higher rates of growth than the census-style series—as, in fact, they do (see table 6.4).

While the census-style data are comprehensive with respect to the industrial sectors covered, they do not cover all sectors. The principal omission consists of highways and highway bridges. Insofar as these projects were constructed from materials returned by the census, the value of such capital is included in the perpetual inventory improvements series. It seems likely that highways and bridges, so constructed, increased in relative importance over time, which is yet another reason why the perpetual inventory improvements series could be expected to exhibit higher rates of growth than the census-style series.

In summary, were it possible to remove these elements of incomparability lying between the perpetual inventory and census-style series, the ratios contained in the "net" columns of table 6.4 would probably be closer to values of 1, although they would certainly not all achieve a value of 1.

Finally, the two sets of series from which the ratios of table 6.4 were computed treat the losses of capital during the Civil War differently: the census-style estimates are net of such losses, while the perpetual inventory estimates are not. Removal of this inconsistency might further diminish the differences between the two sets of series.

The best estimate of Civil War destruction of capital is one prepared by Goldin and Lewis (1975, 308).[10] It covers only Southern losses—the implication is that Northern losses were negligible—and its authors regard it as an upper-bound estimate. However, if Northern losses were in fact more than negligible, the figure may not constitute an excessive appraisal of the losses of North and South combined. The North was not the theater of much of the war, although Southern raiders did do some damage. Greater losses were suffered at sea. Southern cruisers appear to have injured the US whaling fleet seriously, and to have induced the transfer of part of the merchant marine to foreign ownership, a transfer that was not immediately reversed with the end of the war. The real value of US shipping was only slightly greater in 1870 than in 1860. Presumably, the transfer of ownership of vessels simply changed the form in which US capital was held, thus diminishing the value of shipping and producing a compensatory change in net claims on foreigners. But because the latter claims are unrepresented in the series underlying table 6.4, and because the former value is reflected only in the postwar census-style estimates, the transfer is a source of difference between the two sets of estimates forming the numerators and denominators of the ratios. It does not stretch the meaning of words too far to attribute this element of the difference to northern wartime "losses" of capital.

If the Goldin and Lewis estimate exaggerates Southern losses—as they believe it does—it probably does not exaggerate Southern and Northern

losses taken together, especially if the element of "loss" discussed immediately above is included. Indeed, it may even understate the true total.
For present purposes, that is a matter of small importance, since this bias
is offset by the fact that the Goldin and Lewis figure includes the value
of certain types of destroyed capital (railroads, animal inventories) that
have no bearing whatsoever on the ratios displayed in table 6.4. Whether
the biases precisely offset each other cannot be established, but in what
follows it is assumed that they do.

Table 6.5 contains ratios from table 6.4, recomputed to bring the numerators and denominators into closer conceptual conformity. Specifically,
estimated Civil War losses, appropriately depreciated, were deducted from
the numerators. To make the computations, it was assumed that total losses
came to $1.5 billion (Goldin and Lewis's estimate of $1.487 billion, rounded
up), and that four-fifths of the capital destroyed ($1.2 billion) consisted of
improvements while one-fifth ($0.3 billion) consisted of manufactured pro-
ducers' durables.

It was also assumed that the improvements destroyed were distributed
among vintages in the same proportions as were improvements in general, that the average service life of all improvements was forty years, and
that destruction was centered on the year 1864. In the case of producers'
durables, it was assumed that while the average service life of the stock
as a whole was thirteen years, the lost property—since it must have consisted disproportionately of shipping, farm vehicles, and other long-lived
equipment—had an expected average service life of twenty years, perhaps an upper bound. It was assumed that the losses centered on the year
1863, a date lying between the time of the principal transfer of shipping
to foreign ownership and the period of greatest military destruction in the
South.[11]

The adjustments improve the results of table 6.4 by reducing the ratios
for 1870 and 1880 and bringing the mean ratios closer to values of 1. That
two of the ratios for improvements fall below 1 in 1870—well below, in
one case—is a little bit troubling. The 1870 census is widely believed to
have been short, particularly in the South (Ransom and Sutch 1975, 10).
One would therefore expect to find the 1870 ratio to be larger than 1, even
after adjustment of the perpetual inventory series for Civil War losses.

Nonetheless, given the nature of the data—and particularly given that
the 1870 and 1840 perpetual inventory estimates are heavily dependent on
disparate series patched together—the degree of consistency attained by the
two sets of series is moderately reassuring. Notice that the declining-balances

TABLE 6.5 **Ratios of net perpetual inventory capital stock estimates (adjusted for Civil War losses) to census-style capital stock estimates, 1840–1900**

**Panel A. Improvements**

| | Straight-line depreciation | | Declining balance | Means of columns 1 and 2 |
|---|---|---|---|---|
| | Service life | | | |
| | 40 yrs. | 50 yrs. | 50 yrs. | |
| 1840 | 0.90 | 0.96 | 0.79 | 0.93 |
| 1850 | 1.06 | 1.14 | 0.92 | 1.10 |
| 1860 | 1.02 | 1.10 | 0.89 | 1.06 |
| 1870 | 0.95 | 1.07 | 0.79 | 1.01 |
| 1880 | 1.42 | 1.57 | 1.22 | 1.50 |
| 1890 | 1.27 | 1.41 | 1.11 | 1.34 |
| 1900 | 1.46 | 1.61 | 1.25 | 1.54 |
| Mean | 1.15 | 1.27 | 1.00 | 1.21 |

**Panel B. Producers' durables**

| | Straight-line depreciation | | Means of columns 1 and 2 |
|---|---|---|---|
| | Service life | | |
| | 13 yrs. | 17 yrs. | |
| 1840 | 0.77 | 0.89 | 0.83 |
| 1850 | 0.83 | 0.98 | 0.91 |
| 1860 | 0.77 | 0.91 | 0.84 |
| 1870 | 1.22 | 1.40 | 1.31 |
| 1880 | 1.22 | 1.48 | 1.35 |
| 1890 | 0.95 | 1.11 | 1.03 |
| 1900 | 0.86 | 1.05 | 0.96 |
| Mean | 0.95 | 1.12 | 1.00 |

**Panel C. Improvements and producers' durables**

| | Weighted means of | |
|---|---|---|
| | panel A, column 4 and panel B, column 3 | panel A, column 3 and panel B, column 3 |
| 1840 | 0.90 | 0.79 |
| 1850 | 1.05 | 0.92 |
| 1860 | 1.02 | 0.88 |
| 1870 | 1.08 | 0.91 |
| 1880 | 1.46 | 1.25 |
| 1890 | 1.23 | 1.08 |
| 1900 | 1.29 | 1.13 |
| Mean | 1.15 | 0.99 |

Sources: See text.

improvements series (panel A, column 3) and the mean of the two producers' durables series track the two census-style series reasonably well, particularly when one allows for the incompleteness of each set of series.

Happily, the degree of consistency improves when the level of aggregation is increased. That is as it should be, in view of the fact that several
of the census-style estimates were made by distributing a total between
its improvements and producers' durables components. Errors made at
that level wash out with aggregation. Panel C of table 6.5 shows that the
weighted average ratios are better than the component ratios from which
they were assembled, and that the combination of the declining-balances
improvements estimates and the straight-line producers' durables estimates yields a fairly plausible set of ratios; the one large outlier appears in
1880. Even that value lies only barely outside the boundaries established
by assuming that each series is subject to errors as large as 10 percent, and
that the errors are distributed among years randomly (see above).

The position of 1880 as outlier calls for a little further consideration.
Are there peculiarities surrounding the evidence for that year that account
for the differences between the two sets of series? So far as the producers'
durables series are concerned, we know nothing. It is true that the prices
of producers' durables fell very dramatically in the postwar years. If the
weighting schemes underlying the deflation for the two series differed,
that might produce contrasting results of the sort we observe. Given the
nature of the series, this is a difficult possibility to check. Nonetheless, the
patterns of change described by the implicit deflators of the census-style
stock estimates and the flow data underlying the perpetual inventory series
move nicely in parallel, picking out precisely the same periods of rapid and
slow decline. The 1880 problem does not appear to be rooted in deflation.

The annual construction-flow data for the years 1869 to 1909 that underlie the perpetual inventory improvements estimates are based on a
series prepared by Simon Kuznets for *Capital in the American Economy*.
To calculate the estimates here, this series was reworked, distinguishing
its components and altering the total construction flows, particularly for
the earlier years (Gallman 1966, 37–39). Were these adjustments well advised? Did they influence importantly the "other" construction component relevant to the present discussion? There are two ways to approach
these questions: by recomputing the perpetual inventory estimates on the
basis of the Kuznets series, to see whether a better fit with the census-style
estimates can be obtained; and by considering the rationale for the original adjustments to the Kuznets series.

In computing the census-style estimates, I have departed from the practice of Raymond Goldsmith. In his own work with the nineteenth-century capital stock, Goldsmith has assumed that nonfarm residences typically accounted for three-quarters of the value of nonfarm residential real estate. It has been assumed here that the figure was probably closer to 64 percent. Clearly, had Goldsmith's example been followed, the census-style capital stock estimate for 1880 would have been higher, and the ratios in columns 1 and 3 of table 6.5 for 1880 would have been lower. But presumably the ratios for all the other years would also be lower, which would not be an altogether desirable result.

Table 6.6 was assembled to test the proposition that shifting to the original Kuznets flow data and adjusting the census-style estimates to reflect Goldsmith's judgment as to the relative importance of structures in nonfarm residential real estate would markedly improve the quantitative fit of the perpetual inventory and census-style estimates. Panel A, which incorporates only the adjustment of the census-style estimates to bring them into closer conformity with Goldsmith's views, shows that the adjustment does not altogether solve the 1880 "problem." As to the ratios for the other years, some are improvements on those appearing in table 6.5, but others are not. The test does not provide a secure basis for choosing between the Goldsmith and Gallman judgments on this point. The differences between the Gallman estimates and the set that would be substituted for them in the event that we accepted Goldsmith's view are not very large, after all, and the test is by no means a refined one.

The ratios in panel B are only rough approximations of the ratios that would have emerged had the perpetual inventory estimates been reworked using Kuznets's data. To recompute the perpetual inventory series, it would be necessary to distribute the Kuznets flow estimates between the two components, "railroad construction" and "other construction," since Kuznets did not himself distinguish these components. For purposes of the computations underlying panel B, it was assumed that the ratio of this total construction-flow estimate to Kuznets's would be an appropriate basis for adjusting the "other construction" flow data to a basis consistent with the Kuznets's series (Gallman 1966, table A-6). That assumption almost certainly resulted in too large an adjustment (for reasons to be discussed below), so that the contrasts between the relevant table 6.5 and table 6.6 ratios are, in fact, too great.

With that qualification in mind, it can be said that the "Kuznets adjustment" does improve the fit between the perpetual inventory and census-

TABLE 6.6 **Ratios of net perpetual inventory capital stock estimates (adjusted for Civil War losses) to census-style capital stock estimates, 1840–1900**

| | Straight-line depreciation | | Declining balance | Mean of columns 1 and 2 |
|---|---|---|---|---|
| | 40 yrs. | 50 yrs. | 50 yrs. | |
| **Panel A. Goldsmith adjustment to census-style estimates** | | | | |
| 1840 | 0.85 | 0.91 | 0.75 | 0.88 |
| 1850 | 0.99 | 1.05 | 0.86 | 1.02 |
| 1860 | 0.95 | 1.02 | 0.82 | 0.99 |
| 1870 | 0.89 | 1.00 | 0.74 | 0.95 |
| 1880 | 1.32 | 1.46 | 1.13 | 1.39 |
| 1890 | 1.18 | 1.31 | 1.02 | 1.25 |
| 1900 | 1.37 | 1.5 | 1.16 | 1.44 |
| Mean | 1.08 | 1.18 | 0.93 | 1.13 |
| **Panel B. Kuznets adjustment to perpetual inventory series** | | | | |
| 1840 | 0.90 | 0.96 | 0.79 | 0.93 |
| 1850 | 1.06 | 1.14 | 0.92 | 1.10 |
| 1860 | 1.02 | 1.10 | 0.89 | 1.07 |
| 1870 | 0.88 | 1.00 | 0.72 | 0.95 |
| 1880 | 1.18 | 1.33 | 0.98 | 1.26 |
| 1890 | 1.11 | 1.22 | 0.94 | 1.17 |
| 1900 | 1.37 | 1.49 | 1.08 | 1.44 |
| Mean | 1.07 | 1.18 | 0.90 | 1.13 |
| **Panel C. Goldsmith and Kuznets adjustments** | | | | |
| 1840 | 0.85 | 0.91 | 0.75 | 0.88 |
| 1850 | 0.99 | 1.05 | 0.86 | 1.02 |
| 1860 | 0.95 | 1.02 | 0.82 | 0.99 |
| 1870 | 0.82 | 0.93 | 0.68 | 0.88 |
| 1880 | 1.10 | 1.23 | 0.91 | 1.17 |
| 1890 | 1.02 | 1.13 | 1.15 | 1.08 |
| 1900 | 1.28 | 1.39 | 1.08 | 1.34 |
| Mean | 1.00 | 1.09 | 0.89 | 1.05 |

Sources: See text.

style series in the 1880–1900 period, but in two of the variants it produces a much poorer fit in 1870.

Despite the seeming overall improvement occasioned by the adjustments underlying panel B, there are good reasons why they should be rejected. There are three differences between the annual construction-flow estimates of Kuznets and Gallman. In each of these cases, Gallman benefited from the work done by other scholars after the publication of the Kuznets estimates. Harold Barger worked out margin estimates for wholesale and retail trade, Dorothy Brady assembled final price index estimates, and Melville Ulmer and Albert Fishlow estimated railroad construction series. Kuznets had generated his nineteenth-century construction-flow series by extrapolating his twentieth-century series backward to 1869 on constant-price materials flows and then inflating the series. There is the implicit assumption here that trade margins and value added by construction constituted a constant fraction of final product, at least in constant prices.

The assumption was clearly the best one available when the estimates were made, particularly in view of the deflators available to Kuznets. But given the data of Barger (1955), Brady (1966), Fishlow (1966c), and Ulmer (1960)—and particularly Brady's true price indexes—this assumption no longer has to be made. Following the work of Barger, the materials flows for trade margins were marked up. Distinctions were made between flows into railroad construction and all others, because value added by construction is much more important in heavy construction—for example, in railroads—than elsewhere in the sector. The materials for construction were marked up using census current-price ratios and the Fishlow work on railroads, and they were deflated using the final price indexes developed by Brady and Ulmer. The series thus rests on improved evidence and procedures. It does yield much larger estimates of construction flows, especially in the 1870s. But the main explanation for this is not that my "other" construction series deviated far from what Kuznets's procedures would have yielded, but that the estimates distinguish railroad construction, where the ratio between final product flows and materials inputs is very large. The great margin of my total construction series in the 1870s over Kuznets's reflects, chiefly, the fact that railroad construction was very important in that decade.

The conclusions are that the data underlying table 6.5 are the best series feasible given currently available evidence, and that they are reasonably consistent. But clearly, the two sets of series are far from identical. How far would the historical narrative of US economic growth in the nineteenth century be affected by the choice, on the part of the narrator, of one of these sets of series over the other? The question is a large one, and a detailed answer is best left to another occasion. However, table 6.7 gathers together a few data that bear on the question. The estimates from which they were drawn refer to the national capital stock-land improvements and producers' durables of all kinds, as well as inventories and net claims on

TABLE 6.7 **Rates of growth, structure of the capital stock, and capital-to-output ratios: Two versions measured in 1860 prices, 1840–1900**

**Panel A. Rates of growth**

|  | Census-style | Perpetual inventory |
|---|---|---|
| 1840–50 | 4.2 | 4.6 |
| 1850–60 | 5.8 | 5.5 |
| 1860–70 | 1.6 | 1.8 |
| 1870–80 | 4.2 | 6.0 |
| 1880–90 | 6.3 | 5.5 |
| 1890–1900 | 3.8 | 4.2 |
| 1840–60 | 5.0 | 5.1 |
| 1860–80 | 4.0 | 3.9 |
| 1880–1900 | 4.8 | 4.8 |
| 1840–1900 | 4.3 | 4.6 |

**Panel B. Shares of "other" improvements and producers' durables**

|  | Improvements | | Durables | | Improvements and durables | |
|---|---|---|---|---|---|---|
|  | Census-style | Perpetual inventory | Census-style | Perpetual inventory | Census-style | Perpetual inventory |
| 1840 | 0.24 | 0.21 | 0.05 | 0.05 | 0.29 | 0.26 |
| 1850 | 0.27 | 0.25 | 0.06 | 0.06 | 0.33 | 0.31 |
| 1860 | 0.34 | 0.32 | 0.09 | 0.08 | 0.43 | 0.40 |
| 1870 | 0.37 | 0.31 | 0.11 | 0.15 | 0.49 | 0.46 |
| 1880 | 0.34 | 0.37 | 0.13 | 0.15 | 0.47 | 0.52 |
| 1890 | 0.37 | 0.40 | 0.22 | 0.22 | 0.60 | 0.62 |
| 1900 | 0.37 | 0.43 | 0.27 | 0.24 | 0.64 | 0.66 |

**Panel C. Capital-to-output ratios**

|  | Census-style | Perpetual inventory |
|---|---|---|
| 1840 | 2.8 | 2.6 |
| 1850 | 2.7 | 2.7 |
| 1860 | 2.9 | 2.8 |
| 1870 | 2.8 | 2.9 |
| 1880 | 2.6 | 2.9 |
| 1890 | 3.2 | 3.3 |
| 1900 | 3.4 | 3.7 |

Sources: See text. For methods by which panel C was computed, see Gallman 1987.

foreigners. One set of estimates is based chiefly on census-style data. In the other set, the perpetual inventory data underlying table 6.5, panel A, column 3, and panel B, column 3 have been substituted for the census-style "other" improvements and producers' durables. Remember, both sets of total capital stock estimates include all the conventional components of the capital stock, as well as the value of land clearing, breaking, and fencing.

The two sets of estimates tell essentially the same story of the long-term growth of the capital stock, of shifts in its structure, and of the level and direction of change of the capital-to-output ratio. The capital stock grew rapidly—except over the decade of the 1860s—and the pace was particularly pronounced in the 1850s, 1870s, and 1880s. According to the census-style series, the rate of growth was higher in the 1880s than in the 1870s, while according to the other series the reverse was true. The differences are not great, but they are great enough to affect the analysis of the business cycle and the Kuznets cycle over this period.

The structural findings drawn from the two series (panel B) are also similar. The shares in total capital of "other" improvements and durables increase in both series, the change being particularly pronounced in the case of durables. Once again, the timing of the changes in shares is a little different from one series to the next—particularly with respect to improvements across the 1860s—but not much different.

The same kinds of results emerge from panel C. The levels of the capital-to-output ratios and their broad trends are similar in the two cases, the two being distinguished only by very modest differences in the timing of the changes—this time across the 1870s.

Clearly, much more needs to be done along these lines. But the data in table 6.7 suggest that the most consistent sets of census-style and perpetual inventory estimates—estimates plausible on other grounds (e.g., average service life, system of depreciation) as well—do tell roughly the same story about the nineteenth-century capital stock.

What happens, however, when less consistent perpetual inventory estimates are selected? Table 6.8 was put together as a first step toward answering this question. Panels A and C compare levels of gross and net estimates computed following a variety of plausible procedures, while panels B and D compare rates of growth. (None of these series, incidentally, has been corrected for Civil War losses, since the adjustment is not required for present purposes.)

The table shows that while the levels of the series differ from one case to the next—declining-balances series are always very much lower than

TABLE 6.8 **Levels and decennial rates of change of stocks of "other" improvements and producers' durables, measured in 1860 prices, perpetual inventory estimates, various versions, 1840–1900**

**Panel A. Producers' durables estimates expressed as ratios of net estimates, seventeen-year service life, straight-line depreciation**

|      | 17-year service life | | | 13-year life |
|------|---------------------|------------------------------|-------|--------------|
|      | Declining-balance | Bureau of Labor Statstics | Gross | Straight-line |
| 1840 | 0.74 | 1.15 | 1.51 | 0.86 |
| 1850 | 0.75 | 1.16 | 1.57 | 0.85 |
| 1860 | 0.73 | 1.16 | 1.57 | 0.85 |
| 1870 | 0.78 | 1.13 | 1.46 | 0.88 |
| 1880 | 0.73 | 1.18 | 1.64 | 0.83 |
| 1890 | 0.75 | 1.16 | 1.55 | 0.85 |
| 1900 | 0.73 | 1.18 | 1.69 | 0.82 |

**Panel B. Producers' durables, decennial rates of growth (%)**

|           | 17-year service life | | | | 13-year life |
|-----------|---------------|-------------------|------------------------------|-------|--------------|
|           | Straight-line | Declining-balance | Bureau of Labor Statstics | Gross | Straight-line |
| 1840–50   | 96% | 99% | 96% | 103% | 93% |
| 1850–60   | 130 | 124 | 132 | 129 | 129 |
| 1860–70   | 132 | 147 | 124 | 116 | 141 |
| 1870–80   | 83  | 71  | 91  | 105 | 72 |
| 1880–90   | 138 | 143 | 134 | 126 | 145 |
| 1890–1900 | 64  | 59  | 68  | 78  | 58 |

**Panel C. Other improvements estimates expressed as ratios of net estimates, fifty-year service life, straight-line depreciation**

|      | Declining-balance | Bureau of Labor Statistics | Gross |
|------|-------------------|----------------------------|-------|
| 1840 | 0.82 | 1.16 | 1.27 |
| 1850 | 0.81 | 1.18 | 1.30 |
| 1860 | 0.81 | 1.18 | 1.30 |
| 1870 | 0.78 | 1.23 | 1.40 |
| 1880 | 0.79 | 1.23 | 1.40 |
| 1890 | 0.79 | 1.22 | 1.40 |
| 1900 | 0.78 | 1.24 | 1.43 |

*continues*

TABLE 6.8 (*continued*)

**Panel D. "Other" improvements, decennial rates of growth (%)**

|           | Straight-line | Declining-balance | Bureau of Labor Statstics | Gross |
|-----------|---------------|-------------------|---------------------------|-------|
| 1840–50   | 101%          | 97%               | 104%                      | 106%  |
| 1850–60   | 116           | 116               | 116                       | 116   |
| 1860–70   | 45            | 40                | 51                        | 55    |
| 1870–80   | 83            | 84                | 82                        | 83    |
| 1880–90   | 74            | 76                | 74                        | 74    |
| 1890–1900 | 64            | 60                | 65                        | 67    |

Sources: See text.

BLS concave series, for example—the various durables series move in parallel, as do the various improvements series. There are differences, of course, and they emerge where one would expect to find them. Thus, the durables declining-balances series shows an unusually large increase across the 1860s, as compared with the other series, because the postwar investment boom receives a much larger weight in the 1870 value in this series than in the others. Similarly, the gross series and the BLS concave series exhibit especially small rates of growth across the same decade, because the poor wartime investment experience figures importantly in the 1870 value in these series.

These expected contrasts aside, the ratios in panels A and C are quite stable, and the rates of change in panels B and D—particularly D, which has to do with longer-lived property—are quite similar. These are fortunate findings, since they suggest that analytical results depending upon rates of change of the capital stock are unlikely to be very sensitive to the choice of service life and depreciation scheme, the exceptions to the rule being quite obvious.

## 6.5. Conclusion

What has been learned from all of these data and calculations? The statistical tests suggest that nineteenth-century census-style capital stock estimates reflect net values—a useful result in view of the previous disagreements in the literature about this matter.

In most of the census years, net acquisition cost, net reproduction cost, and market value are unlikely to have differed much; in those few years in which they did, the statistical tests show that the census-style data are probably expressed in reproduction cost. The statistical finding, in this case, has support in literary evidence. Once again, this result bears on a subject on which scholars have previously disagreed. The results of the consistency tests could reflect no more than compensatory errors. Nonetheless, the evidence suggests that the tests do have merit, that both sets of estimates are in fact net, and that where the valuation scheme matters, both are valued in reproduction costs.

When plausible assumptions are made with respect to service lives and depreciation schedules, and when appropriate allowances are made for differences in coverage, the levels of the perpetual inventory series and census-style series appear roughly similar. There are some suspicious results: the ratios of perpetual inventory to census-style estimates seem always rather low in 1840 and high in 1880, the latter being the more important deviation. The ratio for durables also seems high in 1870, and the ratio for improvements seems high in 1890 and especially 1900. The 1840 results should not be surprising, since both sets of estimates are relatively weak at that date, while the deviations in 1870, 1890, and 1900 disappear when durables and improvements are aggregated, leaving 1880 as the one remaining major puzzle.

Combined with other elements of the capital stock, the census-style and perpetual inventory series imply essentially the same pattern of long-term evolution of the US capital stock, although moderate differences as to timing and short-period developments also emerge. The student of economic fluctuations who plans to introduce capital into his or her analysis would be well advised to examine both the perpetual inventory and the census-style series.

Finally, experiments with the perpetual inventory series show that decisions concerning whether capital should be measured gross or net, as well as decisions regarding the appropriate service life and system of capital consumption, affect the level of the measured capital stock much more than they do the rates of change. This is particularly true with long-lived capital, but it also holds, to a lesser degree, with respect to the relatively short-lived manufactured producers' durables. The greatest deviations occur across periods in which the flow of investment varied very widely—such as the decade of the 1860s, during the beginning of which capital formation was unusually low, and at the end of which it was unusually high. Under these circumstances, the differences in the weighting schemes between a declining-balance series and a BLS concave series will give rise to fairly marked differences in computed rates of change between the two series. But, such unusual circumstances aside, the rates of change traced by the various types of series are remarkably similar—a fortunate result, since it means that more conclusive findings with respect to the evolution of the capital stock can be obtained than would otherwise be possible.

# Appendix to Chapter Six

The Gallman annual estimates of the flows of producers' durables and "other construction" into the US economy (1834–59, 1869–1909), in constant prices, were interpolated and extrapolated to the missing years 1860–68 and 1791–1833 on Berry's annual estimates of gross private domestic investment, also in constant prices. All calendar-year estimates (Berry, throughout; Gallman, 1869–1909) were first converted to an approximation of census-year values by computing two-year moving averages. Each series was then decomposed into a time trend and a cyclical component. Through least-squares analysis, the Gallman trends and cyclical movements were associated with the like characteristics of the Berry series. The predicted values of the cyclical part of the Gallman series were then combined with the predicted values of the trend relationship to produce estimates for the years missing in the original Gallman series. All these calculations were carried out in logarithms. The last step consisted of taking the antilogarithms.

The new series were then used to generate perpetual inventory capital stock estimates in the manner described in the text. The panels of table 6.app I that follow exhibit the various annual cumulations produced. The net series are intended to be net of capital consumption, including all casualty losses, *except for war losses.* The only important losses of this type during the period considered were Civil War losses. Capital was also destroyed during the war by neglect and lack of maintenance, especially in the South. This type of loss was also left out of account in the assembly of the tables.

Thus, all the values in the tables are gross of important elements of capital consumption that took place during the Civil War. The values computed on the assumption that average service lives of seventeen years

TABLE 6.APP1 **Annual perpetual inventory cumulations, at midyear points of years indicated, in millions of 1860 dollars**

**Panel A. Manufactured producers' durables, service life of 13 years, retirement age of 13**

|  | Gross | Net straight-line | Net BLS concave | Net declining balance |
|------|-------|-------------------|-----------------|----------------------|
| 1840 | 305.8 | 193.3 | 225.8 | 138.2 |
| 1841 | 319.5 | 195.3 | 230.9 | 136.4 |
| 1842 | 338.2 | 201.9 | 240.2 | 140.5 |
| 1843 | 357.6 | 208.3 | 249.1 | 145.1 |
| 1844 | 376.6 | 215.0 | 257.8 | 150.4 |
| 1845 | 403.1 | 230.4 | 274.8 | 164.7 |
| 1846 | 433.4 | 250.4 | 296.2 | 182.7 |
| 1847 | 470.3 | 277.0 | 324.4 | 206.0 |
| 1848 | 513.8 | 316.3 | 365.6 | 239.8 |
| 1849 | 548.7 | 345.4 | 398.0 | 260.1 |
| 1850 | 583.5 | 369.7 | 426.7 | 274.6 |
| 1851 | 625.9 | 400.5 | 462.7 | 295.3 |
| 1852 | 678.9 | 439.2 | 507.8 | 323.3 |
| 1853 | 754.4 | 489.6 | 565.7 | 361.9 |
| 1854 | 841.2 | 543.9 | 628.5 | 403.0 |
| 1855 | 934.1 | 603.3 | 697.2 | 447.5 |
| 1856 | 1,044.8 | 674.5 | 778.7 | 502.4 |
| 1857 | 1,165.3 | 748.8 | 864.4 | 558.2 |
| 1858 | 1,259.2 | 797.5 | 925.0 | 586.2 |
| 1859 | 1,332.3 | 824.7 | 964.3 | 594.3 |
| 1860 | 1,405.5 | 855.4 | 1,006.1 | 609.2 |
| 1861 | 1,462.0 | 879.2 | 1,040.5 | 619.2 |
| 1862 | 1,447.6 | 821.0 | 992.9 | 549.9 |
| 1863 | 1,408.1 | 736.7 | 915.2 | 466.9 |
| 1864 | 1,379.4 | 675.4 | 854.7 | 419.2 |
| 1865 | 1,421.2 | 697.9 | 873.4 | 461.8 |
| 1866 | 1,687.7 | 957.7 | 1,127.7 | 735.5 |
| 1867 | 2,075.4 | 1,327.9 | 1,500.6 | 1,087.0 |
| 1868 | 2,438.4 | 1,655.3 | 1,843.0 | 1,357.0 |
| 1869 | 2,703.7 | 1,876.2 | 2,090.3 | 1,495.1 |
| 1870 | 2,916.5 | 2,035.7 | 2,285.0 | 1,565.0 |
| 1871 | 3,153.2 | 2,186.4 | 2,478.0 | 1,630.0 |
| 1872 | 3,485.1 | 2,399.8 | 2,739.3 | 1,764.6 |
| 1873 | 3,902.5 | 2,682.2 | 3,075.8 | 1,967.3 |
| 1874 | 4,268.1 | 2,879.5 | 3,335.5 | 2,077.7 |
| 1875 | 4,621.3 | 2,958.7 | 3,481.3 | 2,081.5 |
| 1876 | 4,999.8 | 3,008.7 | 3,589.3 | 2,084.2 |
| 1877 | 5,386.8 | 3,058.1 | 3,680.8 | 2,113.6 |
| 1878 | 5,737.1 | 3,122.7 | 3,767.6 | 2,177.6 |
| 1879 | 5,918.1 | 3,231.4 | 3,880.1 | 2,285.4 |
| 1880 | 6,144.0 | 3,502.2 | 4,153.1 | 2,540.3 |
| 1881 | 6,617.5 | 3,990.1 | 4,657.3 | 2,981.2 |
| 1882 | 7,318.0 | 4,590.0 | 5,295.8 | 3,490.7 |
| 1883 | 8,087.5 | 5,164.1 | 5,928.2 | 3,932.5 |
| 1884 | 8,711.0 | 5,540.5 | 6,377.2 | 4,150.3 |
| 1885 | 9,122.0 | 5,737.4 | 6,651.8 | 4,189.7 |
| 1886 | 9,621.0 | 6,085.2 | 7,079.6 | 4,398.2 |
| 1887 | 10,528.0 | 6,749.7 | 7,838.0 | 4,925.0 |

TABLE 6.APP1 (*continued*)

**Panel A. Manufactured producers' durables, service life of 13 years, retirement age of 13**

|      | Gross | Net straight-line | Net BLS concave | Net declining balance |
|------|-------|-------------------|-----------------|-----------------------|
| 1888 | 11,622.0 | 7,441.3 | 8,643.9 | 5,452.9 |
| 1889 | 12,726.0 | 8,056.8 | 9,384.9 | 5,887.0 |
| 1890 | 13,899.0 | 8,684.9 | 10,141.5 | 6,332.9 |
| 1891 | 15,148.0 | 9,343.7 | 10,927.9 | 6,811.1 |
| 1892 | 16,468.5 | 10,049.0 | 11,756.7 | 7,335.5 |
| 1893 | 17,654.0 | 10,693.7 | 12,519.3 | 7,789.4 |
| 1894 | 18,378.0 | 11,020.2 | 12,961.2 | 7,914.2 |
| 1895 | 18,928.0 | 11,265.5 | 13,319.9 | 7,980.1 |
| 1896 | 19,794.0 | 11,812.5 | 13,983.8 | 8,375.6 |
| 1897 | 20,755.5 | 12,249.9 | 14,551.7 | 8,660.4 |
| 1898 | 21,683.5 | 12,448.3 | 14,874.7 | 8,733.5 |
| 1899 | 22,698.5 | 12,844.8 | 15,362.9 | 9,050.7 |
| 1900 | 23,790.5 | 13,595.3 | 16,182.7 | 9,716.6 |
| 1901 | 25,033.5 | 14,509.8 | 17,176.8 | 10,496.4 |
| 1902 | 26,515.5 | 15,575.6 | 18,341.6 | 11,372.8 |
| 1903 | 28,316.5 | 16,944.0 | 19,829.2 | 12,490.6 |
| 1904 | 29,943.0 | 18,120.3 | 21,158.2 | 13,332.0 |
| 1905 | 31,432.5 | 19,177.0 | 22,398.7 | 14,008.5 |
| 1906 | 33,619.0 | 20,857.1 | 24,296.1 | 15,289.9 |
| 1907 | 36,619.0 | 22,955.5 | 26,668.1 | 16,925.2 |
| 1908 | 39,029.0 | 24,207.7 | 28,241.5 | 17,631.9 |
| 1909 | 40,579.0 | 24,758.4 | 29,116.5 | 17,664.8 |

**Panel B. Manufactured producers' durables, average service life of 13 years, diverse retirement ages (Winfrey distribution)**

|      | Gross | Net straight-line | Net BLS concave | Net declining balance |
|------|-------|-------------------|-----------------|-----------------------|
| 1840 | 300.2 | 190.2 | 222.0 | 136.2 |
| 1841 | 313.5 | 191.9 | 226.6 | 134.5 |
| 1842 | 330.9 | 198.2 | 235.3 | 138.7 |
| 1843 | 347.6 | 204.5 | 243.6 | 143.3 |
| 1844 | 364.2 | 211.3 | 252.2 | 148.7 |
| 1845 | 388.8 | 227.2 | 269.5 | 163.1 |
| 1846 | 417.8 | 247.8 | 291.8 | 181.1 |
| 1847 | 453.6 | 275.0 | 321.1 | 204.3 |
| 1848 | 503.3 | 315.1 | 363.9 | 238.3 |
| 1849 | 544.2 | 344.2 | 397.1 | 258.4 |
| 1850 | 581.9 | 368.0 | 425.7 | 272.5 |
| 1851 | 627.6 | 397.9 | 461.0 | 293.1 |
| 1852 | 683.6 | 435.4 | 504.3 | 320.8 |
| 1853 | 753.9 | 483.9 | 559.4 | 358.6 |
| 1854 | 832.2 | 536.5 | 619.6 | 398.6 |
| 1855 | 919.8 | 594.6 | 686.2 | 442.3 |
| 1856 | 1,023.6 | 664.8 | 765.8 | 496.3 |
| 1857 | 1,135.4 | 738.3 | 850.2 | 551.0 |
| 1858 | 1,226.2 | 786.5 | 910.2 | 578.3 |

*continues*

TABLE 6.APPI (*continued*)

**Panel B. Manufactured producers' durables, average service life of 13 years, diverse retirement ages (Winfrey distribution)**

|      | Gross | Net straight-line | Net BLS concave | Net declining balance |
|------|-------|-------------------|-----------------|-----------------------|
| 1859 | 1,297.9 | 813.4 | 949.7 | 586.1 |
| 1860 | 1,372.7 | 843.7 | 991.5 | 601.5 |
| 1861 | 1,440.5 | 867.3 | 1,025.6 | 612.6 |
| 1862 | 1,423.6 | 807.9 | 975.6 | 543.7 |
| 1863 | 1,372.2 | 723.3 | 895.8 | 461.6 |
| 1864 | 1,332.7 | 663.5 | 835.4 | 415.9 |
| 1865 | 1,367.0 | 689.3 | 856.6 | 460.6 |
| 1866 | 1,634.0 | 953.1 | 1,115.9 | 735.7 |
| 1867 | 2,024.1 | 1,326.7 | 1,494.4 | 1,084.5 |
| 1868 | 2,395.2 | 1,655.6 | 1,842.6 | 1,349.0 |
| 1869 | 2,684.7 | 1,875.6 | 2,094.9 | 1,482.1 |
| 1870 | 2,933.5 | 2,030.9 | 2,290.4 | 1,548.9 |
| 1871 | 3,189.9 | 2,172.9 | 2,476.7 | 1,611.4 |
| 1872 | 3,528.4 | 2,374.5 | 2,724.4 | 1,743.9 |
| 1873 | 3,955.0 | 2,642.6 | 3,040.4 | 1,944.9 |
| 1874 | 4,319.0 | 2,823.0 | 3,271.7 | 2,052.7 |
| 1875 | 4,577.7 | 2,884.6 | 3,382.8 | 2,049.6 |
| 1876 | 4,811.8 | 2,925.0 | 3,465.4 | 2,045.9 |
| 1877 | 5,146.2 | 2,977.3 | 3,551.5 | 2,071.2 |
| 1878 | 5,288.0 | 3,058.0 | 3,658.6 | 2,135.3 |
| 1879 | 5,562.5 | 3,192.9 | 3,814.2 | 2,255.8 |
| 1880 | 5,969.3 | 3,484.1 | 4,123.9 | 2,525.8 |
| 1881 | 6,577.0 | 3,978.8 | 4,643.1 | 2,973.7 |
| 1882 | 7,303.1 | 4,574.3 | 5,277.6 | 3,477.7 |
| 1883 | 8,034.8 | 5,139.7 | 5,900.8 | 3,907.2 |
| 1884 | 8,609.4 | 5,507.4 | 6,344.0 | 4,112.2 |
| 1885 | 9,039.0 | 5,696.9 | 6,617.4 | 4,146.7 |
| 1886 | 9,637.8 | 6,034.1 | 7,037.7 | 4,359.6 |
| 1887 | 10,575.3 | 6,677.6 | 7,766.6 | 4,885.6 |
| 1888 | 11,585.6 | 7,342.3 | 8,527.9 | 5,402.4 |
| 1889 | 12,569.7 | 7,934.3 | 9,226.3 | 5,822.6 |
| 1890 | 13,606.3 | 8,546.4 | 9,950.6 | 6,256.5 |
| 1891 | 14,711.7 | 9,198.6 | 10,720.4 | 6,724.3 |
| 1892 | 15,899.0 | 9,907.0 | 11,552.5 | 7,240.1 |
| 1893 | 17,056.3 | 10,564.0 | 12,339.3 | 7,692.1 |
| 1894 | 17,908.9 | 10,903.9 | 12,812.6 | 7,825.4 |
| 1895 | 18,658.2 | 11,153.2 | 13,186.8 | 7,907.1 |
| 1896 | 19,675.1 | 11,690.5 | 13,836 | 8,316.2 |
| 1897 | 20,568.0 | 12,106.8 | 14,361.2 | 8,597.2 |
| 1898 | 21,215.1 | 12,290.2 | 14,646.3 | 8,655.1 |
| 1899 | 22,043.9 | 12,696.3 | 15,138.1 | 8,969.6 |
| 1900 | 23,219.1 | 13,473.0 | 15,995.2 | 9,649.5 |
| 1901 | 24,557.9 | 14,406.7 | 17,021.0 | 10,436 |
| 1902 | 26,064.0 | 15,483.1 | 18,207.8 | 11,307.6 |
| 1903 | 27,903.6 | 16,858.4 | 19,716.6 | 12,417.7 |
| 1904 | 29,621.6 | 18,033.6 | 21,062.6 | 13,249.0 |
| 1905 | 31,286.7 | 19,076.3 | 22,304.3 | 13,920.3 |
| 1906 | 33,626.6 | 20,724.0 | 24,168 | 15,197.2 |
| 1907 | 36,489.3 | 22,769.4 | 26,466.4 | 16,803.5 |

TABLE 6.APP1 *(continued)*

**Panel B. Manufactured producers' durables, average service life of 13 years, diverse retirement ages (Winfrey distribution)**

|  | Gross | Net straight-line | Net BLS concave | Net declining balance |
|---|---|---|---|---|
| 1908 | 38,665.7 | 23,967.4 | 27,964.6 | 17,471.2 |
| 1909 | 40,243.9 | 24,475.9 | 28,780.2 | 17,495.0 |

**Panel C. Manufactured producers' durables, service life of 17 years, retirement age of 17**

|  | Gross | Net straight-line | Net BLS concave | Net declining balance |
|---|---|---|---|---|
| 1840 | 341.6 | 225.3 | 259.9 | 166.7 |
| 1841 | 359.4 | 230.7 | 268.9 | 167.2 |
| 1842 | 382.3 | 240.8 | 282.3 | 173.2 |
| 1843 | 405.4 | 250.7 | 295.4 | 179.5 |
| 1844 | 429.1 | 261.1 | 308.9 | 186.6 |
| 1845 | 461.7 | 280.2 | 331.1 | 202.8 |
| 1846 | 500.2 | 304.1 | 358.0 | 223.1 |
| 1847 | 547.1 | 334.5 | 391.7 | 249.3 |
| 1848 | 607.4 | 377.8 | 438.6 | 287.1 |
| 1849 | 658.1 | 410.7 | 475.6 | 312.3 |
| 1850 | 703.9 | 438.5 | 507.8 | 331.5 |
| 1851 | 756.6 | 472.8 | 546.7 | 356.9 |
| 1852 | 811.5 | 515.2 | 594.2 | 389.1 |
| 1853 | 880.4 | 570.1 | 655.2 | 432.2 |
| 1854 | 961.0 | 630.6 | 723.2 | 478.8 |
| 1855 | 1,051.8 | 698.1 | 799.8 | 530.3 |
| 1856 | 1,161.0 | 779.4 | 891.6 | 593.1 |
| 1857 | 1,288.6 | 865.8 | 990.6 | 658.7 |
| 1858 | 1,401.4 | 928.3 | 1,067.1 | 698.4 |
| 1859 | 1,494.3 | 969.9 | 1,123.2 | 717.7 |
| 1860 | 1,595.0 | 1,015.1 | 1,182.7 | 743.1 |
| 1861 | 1,692.8 | 1,053.3 | 1,234.7 | 763.4 |
| 1862 | 1,702.6 | 1,007.9 | 1,202.4 | 702.4 |
| 1863 | 1,678.6 | 934.8 | 1,139.2 | 622.7 |
| 1864 | 1,665.7 | 883.1 | 1,093.4 | 574.1 |
| 1865 | 1,718.9 | 913.8 | 1,127.0 | 613.3 |
| 1866 | 2,019.4 | 1,181.7 | 1,397.6 | 887.5 |
| 1867 | 2,452.9 | 1,563.0 | 1,787.5 | 1,252.6 |
| 1868 | 2,864.3 | 1,905.7 | 2,147.8 | 1,550.3 |
| 1869 | 3,185.8 | 2,145.7 | 2,412.9 | 1,724.9 |
| 1870 | 3,450.7 | 2,325.8 | 2,623.0 | 1,831.8 |
| 1871 | 3,713.4 | 2,497.8 | 2,828.5 | 1,929.8 |
| 1872 | 4,045.3 | 2,735.4 | 3,102.9 | 2,093.6 |
| 1873 | 4,452.7 | 3,047.9 | 3,457.4 | 2,326.6 |
| 1874 | 4,795.5 | 3,283.5 | 3,743.2 | 2,471.5 |
| 1875 | 5,064.7 | 3,408.9 | 3,925.3 | 2,506.2 |
| 1876 | 5,346.1 | 3,516.5 | 4,091.5 | 2,534.7 |
| 1877 | 5,647.0 | 3,636.0 | 4,269.5 | 2,586.9 |
| 1878 | 5,994.1 | 3,782.8 | 4,474.8 | 2,676.5 |
| 1879 | 6,489.8 | 3,980.2 | 4,730.0 | 2,829.2 |

*continues*

TABLE 6.APP1 *(continued)*

**Panel C. Manufactured producers' durables, service life of 17 years, retirement age of 17**

| | Gross | Net straight-line | Net BLS concave | Net declining balance |
|---|---|---|---|---|
| 1880 | 7,188.8 | 4,324.5 | 5,126.3 | 3,137.2 |
| 1881 | 8,102.3 | 4,862.1 | 5,710.2 | 3,633.1 |
| 1882 | 9,082.6 | 5,494.5 | 6,386.3 | 4,199.0 |
| 1883 | 9,850.6 | 6,097.2 | 7,034.0 | 4,693.7 |
| 1884 | 1,0349.0 | 6,516.3 | 7,510.4 | 4,968.3 |
| 1885 | 10,729.0 | 6,774.5 | 7,840.3 | 5,071.8 |
| 1886 | 11,370.0 | 7,192.9 | 8,339.1 | 5,347.9 |
| 1887 | 12,407.0 | 7,928.6 | 9,163.1 | 5,941.1 |
| 1888 | 13,533.5 | 8,700.3 | 10,036.3 | 6,543.6 |
| 1889 | 14,587.0 | 9,413.7 | 10,863.8 | 7,060.0 |
| 1890 | 15,643.5 | 10,162.6 | 11,740.2 | 7,591.6 |
| 1891 | 16,874.0 | 10,970.4 | 12,694.2 | 8,169.6 |
| 1892 | 18,337.0 | 11,848.3 | 13,734.2 | 8,811.0 |
| 1893 | 19,843.0 | 12,681.2 | 14,738.2 | 9,399.3 |
| 1894 | 21,093.5 | 13,198.4 | 15,430.0 | 9,672.1 |
| 1895 | 22,273.5 | 13,616.6 | 16,013.7 | 9,876.2 |
| 1896 | 23,726.5 | 14,309.4 | 16,856.7 | 10,389.6 |
| 1897 | 24,960.5 | 14,873.8 | 17,562.0 | 10,772.7 |
| 1898 | 25,795.0 | 15,200.5 | 18,022.0 | 10,918.7 |
| 1899 | 26,750.5 | 15,747.6 | 18,696.6 | 11,302.9 |
| 1900 | 28,110.0 | 16,670.6 | 19,753.3 | 12,060.6 |
| 1901 | 29,856.0 | 17,761.6 | 20,995.1 | 12,964.2 |
| 1902 | 31,980.5 | 18,996.8 | 22,390.9 | 13,990.7 |
| 1903 | 34,339.0 | 20,523.6 | 24,077.4 | 15,270.4 |
| 1904 | 36,289.0 | 21,858.2 | 25,582.7 | 16,284.6 |
| 1905 | 38,147.5 | 23,083.5 | 27,000.1 | 17,148.7 |
| 1906 | 40,736.0 | 24,937.6 | 29,065.1 | 18,623.1 |
| 1907 | 43,813.5 | 27,225.8 | 31,597.3 | 20,460.5 |
| 1908 | 46,154.5 | 28,717.6 | 33,379.7 | 21,404.2 |
| 1909 | 47,837.0 | 29,555.6 | 34,534.2 | 21,683.4 |

**Panel D. Manufactured producers' durables, average service life of 17 years, diverse retirement ages (Winfrey distribution)**

| | Gross | Net straight-line | Net BLS concave | Net declining balance |
|---|---|---|---|---|
| 1840 | 335.7 | 221.6 | 255.4 | 163.9 |
| 1841 | 352.6 | 226.6 | 263.7 | 164.2 |
| 1842 | 374.3 | 236.2 | 276.5 | 170.2 |
| 1843 | 396.1 | 245.8 | 289.0 | 176.5 |
| 1844 | 418.6 | 255.9 | 301.9 | 183.6 |
| 1845 | 450.0 | 274.8 | 323.5 | 199.8 |
| 1846 | 486.4 | 298.5 | 350.0 | 220.0 |
| 1847 | 530.0 | 329.0 | 383.4 | 245.9 |
| 1848 | 587.6 | 372.4 | 430.3 | 283.3 |
| 1849 | 636.2 | 405.5 | 467.7 | 307.9 |
| 1850 | 680.9 | 433.5 | 500.6 | 326.7 |
| 1851 | 733.2 | 468.0 | 540.4 | 351.7 |

TABLE 6.APPI  (*continued*)

**Panel D. Manufactured producers' durables, average service life of 17 years, diverse retirement ages (Winfrey distribution)**

|  | Gross | Net straight-line | Net BLS concave | Net declining balance |
|---|---|---|---|---|
| 1852 | 795.0 | 510.6 | 588.8 | 384.1 |
| 1853 | 870.7 | 565.0 | 649.8 | 427.2 |
| 1854 | 955.0 | 624.5 | 716.9 | 473.3 |
| 1855 | 1,049.1 | 690.6 | 791.8 | 524.0 |
| 1856 | 1,160.0 | 769.8 | 880.9 | 586.0 |
| 1857 | 1,281.0 | 853.9 | 976.4 | 650.1 |
| 1858 | 1,383.6 | 914.0 | 1,049.4 | 688.0 |
| 1859 | 1,469.0 | 953.7 | 1,102.6 | 706.0 |
| 1860 | 1,560.6 | 997.2 | 1,159.4 | 730.5 |
| 1861 | 1,647.1 | 1,034.1 | 1,209.3 | 750.2 |
| 1862 | 1,650.7 | 988.2 | 1,175.8 | 688.9 |
| 1863 | 1,623.1 | 915.1 | 1,112.1 | 610.3 |
| 1864 | 1,610.5 | 864.2 | 1,066.5 | 563.8 |
| 1865 | 1,672.9 | 896.3 | 1,100.5 | 605.8 |
| 1866 | 1,969.2 | 1,165.3 | 1,370.7 | 881.0 |
| 1867 | 2,389.4 | 1,547.1 | 1,760.5 | 1,243.4 |
| 1868 | 2,788.9 | 1,890.0 | 2,121.7 | 1,535.6 |
| 1869 | 3,103.5 | 2,129.6 | 2,389.1 | 1,704.3 |
| 1870 | 3,371.9 | 2,309 | 2,602.2 | 1,806.5 |
| 1871 | 3,642.6 | 2,479.3 | 2,810.0 | 1,901.2 |
| 1872 | 3,991.2 | 2,713.8 | 3,084.9 | 2,063.0 |
| 1873 | 4,430.6 | 3,020.9 | 3,436.7 | 2,294.8 |
| 1874 | 4,808.4 | 3,247.4 | 3,713.6 | 2,438.1 |
| 1875 | 5,088.8 | 3,360.3 | 3,879.5 | 2,469.8 |
| 1876 | 5,362.3 | 3,454.0 | 4,025.1 | 2,495.8 |
| 1877 | 5,658.5 | 3,560.0 | 4,179.4 | 2,547.3 |
| 1878 | 5,990.4 | 3,693.5 | 4,357.2 | 2,636.7 |
| 1879 | 6,375.2 | 3,878.5 | 4,582.9 | 2,783.0 |
| 1880 | 6,901.2 | 4,216.8 | 4,959.4 | 3,080.9 |
| 1881 | 7,629.0 | 4,758.3 | 5,542.2 | 3,565.6 |
| 1882 | 8,485.6 | 5,404.6 | 6,239.9 | 4,124.2 |
| 1883 | 9,351.8 | 6,027.5 | 6,927.1 | 4,623.2 |
| 1884 | 10,055.4 | 6,460.0 | 7,435.6 | 4,905.6 |
| 1885 | 10,597.0 | 6,718.9 | 7,776.1 | 5,012.3 |
| 1886 | 11,277.7 | 7,127.7 | 8,266.6 | 5,282.1 |
| 1887 | 12,278.3 | 7,850.0 | 9,075.0 | 5,866.0 |
| 1888 | 13,359.5 | 8,607.4 | 9,932.3 | 6,458.7 |
| 1889 | 14,435.6 | 9,306.1 | 10,744.5 | 6,969.8 |
| 1890 | 15,586.4 | 10,036.4 | 11,598.4 | 7,499.9 |
| 1891 | 16,828.6 | 10,817.3 | 12,512.2 | 8,069.2 |
| 1892 | 18,177.3 | 11,665.0 | 13,502.0 | 8,692.3 |
| 1893 | 19,529.6 | 12,471.5 | 14,460.2 | 9,260.2 |
| 1894 | 20,612.4 | 12,968.8 | 15,116.0 | 9,516.3 |
| 1895 | 21,614.0 | 13,376.0 | 15,677.5 | 9,709.2 |
| 1896 | 22,897.9 | 14,068.2 | 16,516.9 | 10,215.4 |
| 1897 | 24,078.2 | 14,641.4 | 17,237.8 | 10,598.9 |
| 1898 | 25,037.0 | 14,980.6 | 17,721.0 | 10,757.5 |
| 1899 | 26,204.8 | 15,534.7 | 18,407.5 | 11,160.6 |

*continues*

TABLE 6.APPI  (*continued*)

**Panel D. Manufactured producers' durables, average service life of 17 years, diverse retirement ages (Winfrey distribution)**

|      | Gross | Net straight-line | Net BLS concave | Net declining balance |
|------|-------|-------------------|-----------------|-----------------------|
| 1900 | 27,716.2 | 16,452.8 | 19,451.9 | 11,928.5 |
| 1901 | 29,370.8 | 17,529.4 | 20,660.2 | 12,819.2 |
| 1902 | 31,191.5 | 18,754.4 | 22,030.1 | 13,817.0 |
| 1903 | 33,359.4 | 20,287.0 | 23,725.2 | 15,076.7 |
| 1904 | 35,401.8 | 21,635.4 | 25,261.7 | 16,089.0 |
| 1905 | 37,380.4 | 22,866.7 | 26,701.2 | 16,950.8 |
| 1906 | 40,010.2 | 24,716.6 | 28,776.0 | 18,412.5 |
| 1907 | 43,132.7 | 26,992.4 | 31,309.4 | 20,229.0 |
| 1908 | 45,580.9 | 28,460.6 | 33,079.7 | 21,153.0 |
| 1909 | 47,450.9 | 29,263.1 | 34,202.1 | 21,424.0 |

**Panel E. Improvements (other than canals, railroads, farmland clearing, and improvements constructed with farm materials), service life of 50 years, retirement age of 50**

|      | Gross | Net straight-line | Net BLS concave | Net declining balance |
|------|-------|-------------------|-----------------|-----------------------|
| 1840 | 1,354.8[*] | 1,070.3[*] | 1,246.0[*] | 878.71[*] |
| 1841 | 1,465.8[*] | 1,154.2[*] | 1,345.6[*] | 945.75[*] |
| 1842 | 1,576.8 | 1,235.9 | 1,444.2 | 1,009.46 |
| 1843 | 1,679.4 | 1,308.7 | 1,534.9 | 1,063.16 |
| 1844 | 1,784.8 | 1,382.2 | 1,627.3 | 1,116.95 |
| 1845 | 1,919.3 | 1,482.9 | 1,747.9 | 1,197.3 |
| 1846 | 2,081.3 | 1,608.5 | 1,894.9 | 1,301.3 |
| 1847 | 2,265.9 | 1,754.3 | 2,063.7 | 1,423.4 |
| 1848 | 2,447.2 | 1,893.5 | 2,228.1 | 1,536.5 |
| 1849 | 2,621.1 | 2,021.6 | 2,383.3 | 1,636.5 |
| 1850 | 2,794.9 | 2,146.5 | 2,537.1 | 1,731.7 |
| 1851 | 3,002.9 | 2,302.3 | 2,723.5 | 1,856.5 |
| 1852 | 3,250.9 | 2,494.3 | 2,948.2 | 2,015.3 |
| 1853 | 3,538.6 | 2,721.4 | 3,210.7 | 2,206.4 |
| 1854 | 3,860.1 | 2,977.1 | 3,504.9 | 2,422.0 |
| 1855 | 4,201.2 | 3,246.8 | 3,816.8 | 2,647.3 |
| 1856 | 4,569.7 | 3,538.1 | 4,154.1 | 2,889.8 |
| 1857 | 4,975.6 | 3,860.7 | 4,526.7 | 3,158.7 |
| 1858 | 5,361.0 | 4,155.7 | 4,876.3 | 3,394.5 |
| 1859 | 5,698.1 | 4,394.6 | 5,174.1 | 3,570.2 |
| 1860 | 6,035.0 | 4,626.6 | 5,468.3 | 3,736.8 |
| 1861 | 6,360.5 | 4,840.2 | 5,747.3 | 3,883.6 |
| 1862 | 6,579.5 | 4,941.7 | 5,916.9 | 3,917.3 |
| 1863 | 6,722.7 | 4,963.5 | 6,007.9 | 3,874.0 |
| 1864 | 6,847.6 | 4,965.4 | 6,078.7 | 3,815.7 |
| 1865 | 6,977.5 | 4,972.1 | 6,153.6 | 3,767.4 |
| 1866 | 7,203.6 | 5,075.0 | 6,324.2 | 3,820.2 |
| 1867 | 7,550.9 | 5,298.1 | 6,615.6 | 3,994.7 |
| 1868 | 8,036.4 | 5,654.9 | 7,043.5 | 4,301.1 |

TABLE 6.APPI *(continued)*

**Panel E. Improvements (other than canals, railroads, farmland clearing, and improvements constructed with farm materials), service life of 50 years, retirement age of 50**

|      | Gross | Net straight-line | Net BLS concave | Net declining balance |
|------|-------|-------------------|-----------------|-----------------------|
| 1869 | 8,636.1 | 6,117.7 | 7,581.9 | 4,707.6 |
| 1870 | 9,365.6 | 6,698.0 | 8,243.9 | 5,223.4 |
| 1871 | 10,040.8 | 7,209.3 | 8,844.8 | 5,659.1 |
| 1872 | 10,826.4 | 7,818.7 | 9,550.4 | 6,184.4 |
| 1873 | 11,736.7 | 8,538.2 | 10,374.1 | 6,809.2 |
| 1874 | 12,586.1 | 9,180.2 | 11,129.7 | 7,343.3 |
| 1875 | 13,402.9 | 9,775.2 | 11,846.6 | 7,820.4 |
| 1876 | 14,202.9 | 10,339.3 | 12,540.0 | 8,258.8 |
| 1877 | 14,964.3 | 10,851.3 | 13,188.3 | 8,639.2 |
| 1878 | 15,699.6 | 11,326.0 | 13,805.2 | 8,978.3 |
| 1879 | 16,433.0 | 11,787.1 | 14,413.7 | 9,301.1 |
| 1880 | 17,185.2 | 12,254.9 | 15,034.0 | 9,629.1 |
| 1881 | 18,066.2 | 12,842.5 | 15,778.7 | 10,074.9 |
| 1882 | 19,064.6 | 13,533.8 | 16,633.9 | 10,619.6 |
| 1883 | 20,093.2 | 14,243.0 | 17,514.7 | 11,174.4 |
| 1884 | 21,232.1 | 15,050.7 | 18,502.2 | 11,819.7 |
| 1885 | 22,435.1 | 15,895.8 | 19,536.9 | 12,493.1 |
| 1886 | 23,726.8 | 16,819.7 | 20,660.0 | 13,234.8 |
| 1887 | 25,200.5 | 17,893.9 | 21,944.5 | 14,115.8 |
| 1888 | 26,680.2 | 18,971.1 | 23,244.5 | 14,983.1 |
| 1889 | 28,128.3 | 20,003.7 | 24,513.8 | 15,790.8 |
| 1890 | 29,946.0 | 21,367.0 | 26,127.1 | 16,918.4 |
| 1891 | 32,017.4 | 22,950.4 | 27,978.1 | 18,246.1 |
| 1892 | 34,299.6 | 24,703.3 | 30,018.9 | 19,718.3 |
| 1893 | 36,633.1 | 26,455.1 | 32,081.0 | 21,161.4 |
| 1894 | 38,684.2 | 27,880.6 | 33,838.1 | 22,253.1 |
| 1895 | 40,739.4 | 29,298.5 | 35,603.2 | 23,321.4 |
| 1896 | 42,638.1 | 30,546.4 | 37,214.8 | 24,205.4 |
| 1897 | 44,473.4 | 31,716.4 | 38,763.1 | 25,003.3 |
| 1898 | 46,368.4 | 32,906.4 | 40,345.5 | 25,818.0 |
| 1899 | 48,133.4 | 33,921.1 | 41,766.1 | 26,455.0 |
| 1900 | 49,967.6 | 34,970.0 | 43,230.0 | 27,129.7 |
| 1901 | 52,010.2 | 36,224.9 | 44,908.6 | 28,011.1 |
| 1902 | 54,255.2 | 37,681.7 | 46,801.4 | 29,088.0 |
| 1903 | 56,509.1 | 39,142.8 | 48,715.0 | 30,156.8 |
| 1904 | 58,639.9 | 40,469.8 | 50,512.7 | 31,080.6 |
| 1905 | 60,786.3 | 41,790.3 | 52,321.2 | 31,992.7 |
| 1906 | 63,057.8 | 43,221.5 | 54,258.5 | 33,010.9 |
| 1907 | 65,457.4 | 44,773.9 | 56,337.7 | 34,141.7 |
| 1908 | 67,826.6 | 46,228.4 | 58,343.5 | 35,167.3 |
| 1909 | 70,287.5 | 47,678.9 | 60,367.0 | 36,188.9 |

*continues*

TABLE 6.APP1  *(continued)*

**Panel F. Improvements (other than canals, railroads, farmland clearing, and improvements constructed with farm materials), average service life of 50 years, diverse retirement ages (Winfrey distribution)**

|      | Gross | Net straight-line | Net BLS concave | Net declining balance |
|------|-------|-------------------|-----------------|-----------------------|
| 1890 | 29,219.0 | 20,943.9 | 25,534.1 | 16,614.7 |
| 1891 | 31,248.0 | 22,505.0 | 27,356.0 | 17,923.8 |
| 1892 | 33,480.4 | 24,233.6 | 29,366.4 | 19,374.0 |
| 1893 | 35,750.0 | 25,958.8 | 31,396.8 | 20,791.4 |
| 1894 | 37,729.1 | 27,355.4 | 33,122.7 | 21,855.1 |
| 1895 | 39,730.4 | 28,743.4 | 34,857.2 | 22,897.5 |
| 1896 | 41,589.0 | 29,960.1 | 36,437.1 | 23,757.2 |
| 1897 | 43,398.2 | 31,097.8 | 37,952.3 | 24,533.6 |
| 1888 | 45,254.1 | 32,254.9 | 39,499.3 | 25,327.8 |
| 1889 | 46,960.2 | 33,235.8 | 40,882.3 | 25,944.3 |
| 1900 | 48,720.2 | 34,251.0 | 42,307.7 | 26,599.5 |
| 1901 | 50,707.0 | 35,473.3 | 43,948.5 | 27,464.3 |
| 1902 | 52,925.1 | 36,896.6 | 45,802.6 | 28,526.9 |
| 1903 | 55,177.5 | 38,322.8 | 47,674.2 | 29,582.6 |
| 1904 | 57,327.8 | 39,612.8 | 49,424.2 | 30,494.6 |
| 1905 | 59,493.1 | 40,893.7 | 51,177.0 | 31,395.2 |
| 1906 | 61,792.1 | 42,283.7 | 53,049.4 | 32,402.6 |
| 1907 | 64,243.2 | 43,792.2 | 55,054.6 | 33,524.6 |
| 1908 | 66,623.7 | 45,199.8 | 56,971.4 | 34,538.0 |
| 1909 | 69,033.5 | 46,601.3 | 58,893.8 | 35,542.8 |

[*]Assuming no investment in the years 1791 (1 July 1790–30 June 1791) and 1792 (1 July 1791–30 June 1792)—years for which data are not available.
Sources: See text.

and fifty years respectively characterized producers' durables and improvements are also almost certainly too large (see the text). The other estimates, associated with average service lives of thirteen and forty years, may or may not be too low. Only the thirteen-, seventeen-, and fifty-year estimates are shown here.

## CHAPTER SEVEN

# Agriculture

## 7.1. Introduction

This chapter focuses on agriculture, detailing the estimation of the current-price and constant-price (1860) values of the capital stock on a decadal basis from 1840 to 1900. It includes buildings, equipment, animal inventories, and land improvements.

## 7.2. Buildings

### 7.2.1. Coverage

Barns, sheds, residences, and all other farm structures are included in the estimates of the capital stock. Capital formed by other types of improvements to the land—initial clearing and breaking, draining, irrigating, and fencing—is discussed in the section below headed "Other Improvements to Farmland."

### 7.2.2. Sources of Evidence

From 1850 through 1900, census enumerators were to ask farmers to estimate the value of the farms they worked. In 1850 and 1860 the "cash value" of the farm was to be returned; in 1870 the "present cash value"; in 1880 and 1890 the value ("fair market value," according to the 1890 instructions to enumerators) "including land, fences, and buildings"; and

---

Gallman wrote this chapter. "We" and "our" refers to Gallman and Howle. Rhode made minor revisions and contributed the epilogue.

in 1900 the "value . . . of the entire farm (including all owned or leased land contained therein, together with the value of buildings and other permanent improvements)." While the wording of the questions and the instructions to enumerators changed somewhat, it appears that the under-lying concept—market value of farmland and permanent improvements thereto—did not change over the years (Wright 1900, 235–38, 278, 293; US Bureau of the Census 1902, 758–59; Kuznets 1946, 213). Furthermore, the question was asked of the person most likely to know the answer, and the concept of value selected made the answer easier to come by, in most cases, than alternative concepts would have made it. We believe that these are among the more reliable of the census wealth returns.

In 1900, for the first time, the census asked for a separate statement of the value of farm buildings. Our main problem of estimation was there-fore to devise a way to extract the value of buildings from the larger aggre-gate, "the value of farms," for 1850 through 1890. We faced a similar—but somewhat less severe—problem with respect to 1840. The 1840 census did not return the value of farms. However, a reliable, well-informed con-temporary student of that census, Ezra Seaman, prepared a plausible esti-mate of the value of farm and nonfarm residences and outbuildings (pre-sumably including barns). We used his estimate, but again had to extract the value of farm buildings from a larger aggregate (Seaman 1852, 282).

### 7.2.3. Estimating Procedures

Three scholars have previously attempted estimates of the value of farm buildings in the nineteenth century. Simon Kuznets (1946, 202) extrapo-lated the ratio of the value of farm buildings to the value of farm real estate from the twentieth century back to 1880, and then used the extrapolated ratio to estimate the value of farm buildings in 1880 and 1900. Martin Pri-mack (1962) followed a similar procedure, but improved it by employing nineteenth-century data (from a number of states) on the ratio of farm building value to farm real estate value. Alvin Tostlebe (1957, 54–57, 66–69) estimated the values of farm buildings (1870 onward) based on the assump-tion that the real value of buildings per farm remained constant prior to 1900.[1] The Kuznets and Primack estimates are very close. The Primack and Tostlebe figures, though at different levels, describe similar trends. This consistency is reassuring. We chose to use Primack's figures because they cover the full period, 1850–1900, and because they rely much more on nineteenth-century evidence than do the Kuznets and Tostlebe estimates.

The procedure we adopted to separate farm from nonfarm buildings in 1840 is described in chapter 9 (especially table 9.9).

### 7.2.4. Deflation

The best available deflator is Dorothy Brady's (1966, 110–11) index of the prices of houses, churches, and schools, which is a true price index, a rarity among construction indexes. It presents several problems, however.

First, it is an index of the prices of new structures, whereas the stock of farm buildings, the value of which we wished to deflate, consisted of both new and old structures. Of course, one would expect the prices of new and old structures to move roughly together, but not precisely so. In particular, changes in the rate of interest lead to changes in the age structure of the prices of capital goods. But we know of no index of prices of old and new structures, let alone one properly weighted for our present purposes, and we were therefore obliged to make do with an index of the prices of new structures.

Second, Brady's index numbers before 1860 refer to census years, which run from 1 June in a year ending in nine to 31 May in a year ending in zero; after 1860, they refer to the calendar years ending in nine. Census capital valuations, however, refer to 1 June in years ending in zero. Thus, the Brady index numbers are centered on dates either six months or eleven months prior to the census valuation dates. We dealt with this problem by building up, at each relevant calendar and census year, a construction cost index number (1860 = 100) based on input prices, and by adjusting Brady's price index on the basis of this series. For example, according to this series, construction prices were 0.9 percent higher in calendar year 1850 than in census year 1849. We therefore raised Brady's census year 1849 price index number by 0.9 percent, to convert it to a price index for calendar year 1850, and we accepted the calendar indexes as adequate proxies for the required 1 June indexes. All of the required adjustments are modest.[2]

A third problem is that Brady's index numbers refer to a group of structures ("houses, churches, and schools") that differs from the group of structures ("farm houses, barns, and sheds") whose value is to be deflated. Presumably "farm houses, barns, and sheds"—particularly in the early years of the period—would often have been built by farm labor, unlike the nonfarm houses, churches, and schools represented in the price

TABLE 7.1  **Building price and cost indexes, measured in 1860 prices, 1840–1900**

|  |  | Calendar year | | | | | | |
|---|---|---|---|---|---|---|---|---|
|  |  | 1840 | 1850 | 1860 | 1870 | 1880 | 1890 | 1900 |
| 1 | Adjusted Brady price index |  | 96 | 100 | 128 | 130 | 135 |  |
| **Building costs indexes** | | | | | | | | |
| 2 | Artisan labor | 81 | 89 | 100 | 172 | 135 | 152 | 162 |
| 3 | Farm wage | 81 | 85 | 100 | 133 | 98 | 111 | 112* |
| 4 | Weighted average | 81 | 86 | 100 | 146 | 117 | 132 | 137 |

Note: *1899
Sources: Lines 1, 2, and 4, see text. Line 3, the Warren-Pearson building materials index (see text) and the
Lebergott (1964, 539) farm wage index were used; the weighting scheme is described in the text for the "artisan
labor" index. Lebergott has no farm wage rate for 1840. We estimated an 1840 value by averaging the 1830 and
1850 figures.

index. In order to test the proposition that this would be important if true, we assembled two construction cost indexes: one depending on artisan labor, the other on farm labor. The two tell somewhat different stories of the evolution of construction costs (table 7.1). However, the adjusted Brady index does not track the "artisan labor" index much better than it does the "farm labor" index; in two of the four nonbase years, the adjusted Brady index lies between the "artisan labor" and "farm labor" indexes. We experimented and found that weights shifting from 3 to 1 in 1850 ("farm labor" to "artisan labor"), to 2 to 1 in 1860 and 1870, and to 1 to 1 in 1880 through 1900 produced a set of averages that parallel the Brady index numbers better than does either cost index by itself. The direction in which these weights shift—away from "farm labor" and toward "artisan labor"—is certainly appropriate, given the history of farm construction. The test, therefore, although not powerful, does tend to support our using the Brady index as a deflator for the farm building series.

The final problem posed by the Brady series is that it contains no index numbers for the years 1840 and 1900. We chose to estimate these values by extrapolation on the weighted average construction cost index discussed in table 7.1. We used the following regression:

$Y = 40.8 + 0.663X$

where the Y's are the Brady index numbers and the X's are from the weighted index in table 7.1. The results are plausible: The index numbers for 1880, 1890, and 1900 are very close, a result also obtained by Kuznets

(1946, 216); the deflated value for 1840 implies a ratio of the real value of structures to the volume of improved farm land only modestly below the 1850 figure.

## 7.3. Agricultural Equipment

### 7.3.1. Coverage

This category includes all machinery, tools, and other equipment used in agriculture. See table 7.2.

### 7.3.2. Derivation of Estimates

**1850–1900.** The current value estimates were taken directly from the censuses of agriculture. We believe that they represent market value, and therefore we have deducted no depreciation.

**1840.** The constant price estimate for 1840 was obtained by extrapolation, and then inflated to yield a current price estimate. The value of agricultural buildings (1860 prices) increased 104.6 percent from 1850 to 1860, while our constant value equipment estimate rose by 115.8 percent. Assuming the same relationship between the two rates of change between 1840 and 1850, our building rate of increase of 42.8 percent for that period indicates an equipment rate of increase of 47.4 percent. These data and

TABLE 7.2  **Value of agricultural buildings and equipment, measured in current and 1860 prices, 1840–1900, in millions of dollars**

|   |   | 1840 | 1850 | 1860 | 1870 | 1880 | 1890 | 1900 |
|---|---|------|------|------|------|------|------|------|
| **Agricultural buildings** | | | | | | | | |
| 1 | Value, at current prices | 415 | 599 | 1,277 | 1,949 | 2,115 | 2,760 | 3,560 |
| 2 | Price index (1860 = 100) | 95 | 96 | 100 | 128 | 130 | 135 | 132 |
| 3 | Value, at 1860 prices | 437 | 624 | 1,277 | 1,523 | 1,627 | 2,044 | 2,697 |
| **Agricultural equipment** | | | | | | | | |
| 4 | Value, at current prices | 119 | 152 | 246 | 337 | 407 | 494 | 750 |
| 5 | Price index (1860 = 100) | 152 | 132 | 100 | 117 | 84 | 64 | 55 |
| 6 | Value, at 1860 prices | 78 | 115 | 246 | 288 | 485 | 772 | 1,364 |

Sources: Lines 1–4, see text. Line 5, see text; the Brady index numbers were adjusted on the basis of data in US Senate 1893, 21112 (hereafter the *Aldrich Report*) (scythes, shovels) and US Bureau of the Census 1949, series L-9 and L-10. The adjustments were made multiplying the Brady price index numbers by the following ratios: 1839, 0.97; 1849, 1.00; 1869, 0.90; 1879, 1.10; 1889, 1.00; and 1899, 1.00. Line 6: 1840, see text. 1850–1900: 100 × line 4 ÷ line 5.

the 1850 equipment estimate of \$115 million imply an equipment valuation of \$78 million in 1840, expressed in 1860 dollars.

### 7.3.3. Deflation

The estimates were deflated (1840 inflated) by averages of Brady's (1966, 110–11) price indexes of "agricultural machines" and "agricultural implements" (equal weights). Since Brady has no "implements" index number for either 1839 or 1849, we interpolated between 1834 and 1844 and between 1844 and 1854 on the "machines" index to obtain the combined "implements" and "machines" index number for these dates. As indicated in section 7.2.4 above, the dates of the Brady index numbers are not entirely apposite for our purposes. We adjusted them according to a method described in the notes to table 7.2.

## 7.4. Animal Inventories

### 7.4.1. Coverage

This category includes all cattle, horses, mules, sheep, and swine on farms and ranges. See table 7.3.

### 7.4.2. Estimating Procedures

**1870–1900.** For the period 1870 through 1900, the most consistent and satisfactory source of evidence is the US Department of Agriculture, which provides information on the number of animals of each type in stock and the average value per head.[3] We preferred these figures to those provided by the census, which are less consistent from one decade to the next. Unfortunately, the USDA data refer to 1 January, whereas we require 1 June data. With respect to cattle and swine, there is a satisfactory method for translating 1 January numbers into 1 June numbers, and we have made use of it (US Department of Agriculture 1925, 838, 899).[4] However, there is no adequate way to convert the average value data or the numbers of horses, mules, and sheep into 1 June equivalents. Consequently, we left them unadjusted. Thus, our post–Civil War animal inventory estimates are not entirely consistent with either our estimates of other components of the capital stock or our figures on pre–Civil War animal inventories. These inconsistencies are not important, however. Sheep accounted for

TABLE 7.3  **Value of animal inventories, measured in current and 1860 prices, 1840–1900**

| | | 1840 | 1850 | 1860 | 1870 | 1880 | 1890 | 1900 |
|---|---|---|---|---|---|---|---|---|
| **Cattle[a]** | | | | | | | | |
| 1 | Number, in millions[c] | 20.0 | 24.5 | 34.1 | 32.8 | 45.7 | 63.4 | 63.3 |
| 2 | Price, in dollars per head | 8.03 | 10.00 | 13.78 | 22.84 | 17.80 | 16.95 | 26.5 |
| 3 | Value at current prices, in millions of dollars | 160.6 | 245 | 469.9 | 749.2 | 813.5 | 1,074.6 | 1,669.5 |
| 4 | Value at 1860 prices, in millions of dollars | 275.6 | 337.6 | 469.9 | 452.0 | 629.7 | 873.6 | 868.1 |
| **Swine[b]** | | | | | | | | |
| 5 | Number, in millions[c] | 26.3 | 30.4 | 33.5 | 40.1 | 52.5 | 57.0 | 60.6 |
| 6 | Price in dollars per head | 1.49 | 1.29 | 2.92 | 5.64 | 4.40 | 4.80 | 5.36 |
| 7 | Value at current prices, in millions of dollars | 39.2 | 39.2 | 97.8 | 226.2 | 231.0 | 273.6 | 324.8 |
| 8 | Value at 1860 prices, in millions of dollars | 76.8 | 88.8 | 97.8 | 117.1 | 153.3 | 166.4 | 177.0 |
| **Sheep** | | | | | | | | |
| 9 | Number, in millions[c] | 32.0 | 36.0 | 36.0 | 36.4 | 44.9 | 42.7 | 45.1 |
| 10 | Price in dollars per head | 1.40 | 1.55 | 2.70 | 1.87 | 2.18 | 2.29 | 2.97 |
| 11 | Value at current prices, in millions of dollars | 44.8 | 55.8 | 97.2 | 68.1 | 97.9 | 97.8 | 133.9 |
| 12 | Value at 1860 prices, in millions of dollars | 86.4 | 97.2 | 97.2 | 98.3 | 121.2 | 115.3 | 121.8 |
| **Horses** | | | | | | | | |
| 13 | Number, in millions[c] | 4.24 | 4.77 | 6.87 | 7.63 | 10.90 | 15.73 | 17.86 |
| 14 | Price in dollars per head | 40.62 | 44.37 | 48.12 | 66.99 | 53.74 | 69.27 | 43.56 |

*continues*

TABLE 7.3 *(continued)*

|    |                                                              | 1840  | 1850  | 1860    | 1870    | 1880    | 1890    | 1900    |
|----|--------------------------------------------------------------|-------|-------|---------|---------|---------|---------|---------|
| **Horses** | | | | | | | | |
| 15 | Value at current prices, in millions of dollars             | 172.2 | 211.6 | 330.6   | 511.3   | 585.8   | 1089.6  | 778.0   |
| 16 | Value at 1860 prices, in millions of dollars                | 204   | 229.5 | 330.6   | 367.2   | 524.5   | 756.9   | 859.4   |
| **Mules** | | | | | | | | |
| 17 | Number in millions[c]                                        | 0.539 | 0.615 | 1.266   | 1.245   | 1.878   | 2.322   | 3.139   |
| 18 | Price in dollars per head                                    | 52.07 | 56.87 | 61.68   | 89.71   | 61.74   | 77.61   | 51.46   |
| 19 | Value at current prices, in millions of dollars             | 28.1  | 35.0  | 78.1    | 111.7   | 115.9   | 180.2   | 161.4   |
| 20 | Value at 1860 prices, in millions of dollars                | 33.2  | 37.9  | 78.1    | 76.8    | 115.8   | 143.2   | 193.6   |
| **Total** | | | | | | | | |
| 21 | Value in millions of current dollars                        | 444.9 | 586.6 | 1,073.6 | 1,666.3 | 1,844.1 | 2,715.8 | 3,067.7 |
| 22 | Value, in millions of 1860 dollars                          | 676   | 791   | 1,073.6 | 1,111.4 | 1,544.5 | 2,055.4 | 2,219.9 |
| 23 | Implicit price index                                        | 65.8  | 74.2  | 100     | 149.9   | 119.4   | 132.1   | 138.2   |

Notes: Estimated from January 1 numbers, 31.1 million, 43.3 million, 60.0 million, and 59.7 million respectively. See text. Ratio of June 1 to January 1 values = 1.056. [b]Estimated from January 1 numbers, 33.8 million, 44.3 million, 48.1 million, and 51.1 million respectively. See text. Ratio of June 1 to January 1 values = 1.186. [c]As of June 1, except number of sheep, horses and mules, 1870–1900; prices, 1870–1900.
Sources: See text.

only a small part of the value of animal inventories, and the 1 June and 1 January values for horses and mules are unlikely to have differed by much.

**1840–60.** The census data on the numbers of each type of animal on farms and ranges in 1840, 1850, and 1860 have been tested by Gallman (1956), who concluded that the numbers of swine returned approximated 1 June inventories, while the numbers of cattle, horses, and mules returned were less than 1 June inventories by about 25 percent, 10 percent, and 10 percent respectively. We accepted the judgments of Gallman (1956, 114–15, 130–31); adjusted the cattle, sheep, horse, and mule inventories accordingly; and used his prices for each type of animal.

### 7.4.3. Constant Price Series

The constant price series were constructed by multiplying the number of each type of animal in each year by the 1860 average value of that type of animal. No allowance was made for changes in the quality of animals from one census date to the next. It is probable that the average quality of animals improved over time, except perhaps between 1860 and 1870. Thus, the constant price series probably understates the true long-term increase in the animal stock, but may overstate the increase between 1860 and 1870.

## 7.5. Other Improvements to Farmland

### 7.5.1. Coverage

Farmers improved land for agricultural purposes by clearing trees; breaking virgin land with the plow; and fencing, draining, irrigating, and constructing farm buildings. Buildings have been treated in section 7.2 above. The other elements of improvements are taken up in this section. The irrigation of rice land and other types of land are distinguished, since they called for quite different types of works in the nineteenth century.

### 7.5.2. Sources of Evidence and General Procedures

The censuses of 1850 through 1900 contain estimates of the value of farms, made by those who farmed them. We extracted the value of farm buildings from these figures, following a procedure developed by Primack (see section 7.2). Although in principle we might have estimated the value of other improvements in the same way, we chose instead to work out detailed estimates of the cost of these improvements, based on the value of physical inputs (current year and base year techniques).

Again we made use of methods devised by Primack, modified in two respects (Gallman 1956, ch. 2 and 4–6, appendix, 152–61, 196–98, 202–8, 214–18, 224–28, 231–32). Primack was concerned with investment flows, rather than with stocks. However, he provided enough evidence so that stock estimates could be worked out, and we did so. Also, Primack concerned himself exclusively with labor inputs to land improvement. Labor contributed the lion's share to the value of land clearing and breaking, draining, irrigating, and even fencing with farm materials, and in each of these instances we followed Primack and ignored nonlabor inputs.[5] Our estimates should therefore be slightly too low. In the case of fences made with nonfarm materials (e.g., boards, wire), ignoring nonlabor inputs would have produced important errors. We therefore estimated the volume and value of the principal materials used in these fences.

The procedures described above give reproduction cost estimates. That is, the current price figures show the cost of reproducing the existing stock of capital, given current-year techniques of production and input prices; the constant price figures show the cost of reproducing the existing stock, given 1860 techniques of production and prices. Thus, these estimates differ conceptually from all our other estimates of the value of agricultural capital and land, which are market-value estimates. In order to diminish the degree of conceptual heterogeneity, it was necessary for us to translate our gross reproduction cost estimates into net reproduction cost estimates; i.e., it was necessary for us to consider the matter of depreciation.

The improvements composed of land clearing and breaking do not physically deteriorate, so long as the land is properly maintained. The fertility of the soil may be depleted; but, strictly speaking, this process affects the land itself, not the improvements to it. Changes in markets may drive some land out of production so that, e.g., trees once again grow up on it. But this does not necessarily happen to any given piece of land, and most of the improved land in production today was probably first improved more than a century ago. One cannot, then, work out reasonable depreciation schedules for these improvements, and we therefore left them undepreciated. Our estimating procedure removed retirements (land allowed to go back to nature) from the stock, however.

With perhaps less warrant, we also left stone fences, hedges, and draining and irrigation works undepreciated. In each case it seemed reasonable to suppose that proper maintenance and repair would make good all physical deterioration of nineteenth-century improvements of these types. Obsolescence is unlikely to have affected them in a sufficiently systematic way to warrant applying a depreciation schedule. Retirements were excluded from the stock by our procedures.

Worm, post and rail, board, and wire fences were all subject to depreciation. We assumed a twenty-year service life (see below).

### 7.5.3. Detailed Estimating Procedures: Clearing and Breaking

(a) Introduction. The inputs required to clear and break land depend on its vegetation and on the techniques used to clear and break it. Primack points out that different types of forests posed different kinds of problems, that prairies and plains were unequally receptive to the plow, and that techniques varied across regions. But the data are inadequate to permit all of these distinctions to be made in an empirically meaningful way. Thus, Primack distinguished only among three types of improved land: land formerly forested, land formerly grassland or desert, and land cleared a second time from abandoned land grown up in forest (Gallman 1956, ch. 2). He measured the effect of changes in techniques of clearing and breaking, but did not deal with geographic variation in technique at a given moment. We generally followed Primack, but did not distinguish between land cleared of original forest, and land abandoned to forest and then subsequently cleared again—a distinction relevant if one is interested in investment flows (as Primack was), but not if one is interested in capital stock.

(b) Acres of forested and nonforested land cleared, 1850–1900. Primack established the number of improved farm acres at each census date, 1850–1900, from the reports of the Census of Agriculture. We also adopted these totals, except for the year 1880, at which census some meadowland (improved) was double-counted in the Middle Atlantic states (Gallman 1972a, 201).[6] We removed the duplication. We accepted Seaman's estimate of improved land for 1840 (Gallman 1972a, 201–2).[7]

Primack used a map in the *Atlas of American Agriculture*, together with census county data, to establish the original ground cover of land cleared in the period 1850–1900 (US Department of Agriculture 1924, 4–5). We used the same sources, but chose to work at regional and state levels rather than at the county level.

Some states were originally covered entirely in forest or grass, or at least virtually so. In these instances, assigning improved land to one of our two categories of original ground cover posed no problem. It was more often the case, however, that a state was originally covered partly in forest and partly in grass. Where a state first entered the census records after 1850, we distributed improved land between land originally forested and land originally in grass along lines established by Primack. Primack shows gross increments of each type of improved land between each pair of census years, and net increments of the two types of land taken together. We estimated the net acres of grassland improved during each decade using Primack's gross grassland increment, and his ratio of net to gross increment of forest and grassland together, the ratio being assumed to hold for each type of land as well as for the two taken together. We then cumulated the net figures for improved grassland, and derived net improved forest land figures as residuals.[8] In several of the Southern states, the volume of improved land fell between 1860 and 1870. We assumed that former grasslands and former forests were retired in equal proportions.

Where a state was already in the census records by 1850, it was necessary to distribute the 1850 total of improved land between land originally forested and land originally in grass. We did this in the following way.

First, we established the entire land area of the state, in acres. Then, with a ruler and the *Atlas* map (US Department of Agriculture 1924), we established the fraction of the state originally covered in grass. Multiplying this fraction by the entire land area produced an estimate of the number of acres originally under grass. Finally, we cumulated Primack's decadal increments to improved grassland, 1850–1910, and subtracted this figure from our estimate of the total grassland in the state. This gave us a rough estimate of the amount of grassland improved before 1850. These estimates are subject to error because the procedure ignores the possibility that some grassland was never broken or was first broken after 1910 (an unimportant source of error), and because it ignores "retirements" of grassland. But it is the best procedure available and is probably adequate. Its underlying assumption is that, ceteris paribus, grassland would be selected for clearing and breaking ahead of forest, because the investment involved would be smaller.

In the case of Mississippi, which had some prairie but also much rich, forested river bottom, one might expect the latter to be cleared and broken before the former, because it would be better cotton land. We checked our procedure to make sure that it did not produce results inconsistent with this view of things, and it did not. Our estimate of grassland cleared before 1850 in Mississippi is only a small fraction of the forest (presumably chiefly river bottom) cleared by that date.

In Missouri, by contrast, this procedure did not produce sensible results. We assumed that improved land in 1850 in that state was divided between land originally forested and land originally under grass in the same proportion as was the land cleared in the 1850s (according to Primack).

A number of ad hoc decisions were made.

Primack shows no prairie cleared in Arkansas after 1850, and it is doubtful that any was cleared before that date. Yet Arkansas does contain small amounts of prairie. We chose to ignore this land, which means, ceteris paribus, that our estimates of the value of land improvements in Arkansas are slightly too high. (Improvements to forest land cost more per acre than did improvements to prairie.)

Only five thousand acres were clear in Minnesota in 1850. We assumed that it had all been prairie. We also assumed that all California land improved as of 1850 had formerly been under grass, and all Texas and Oregon land improved as of that date had been under forest.

Primack's data on Oklahoma are inconsistent. We assumed that the total on Primack's page 153 was correct, and divided it between forest and grassland in the proportions shown on Primack's pages 157 and 159.

There are a number of small inconsistencies in Primack's work: tables that do not sum to the totals given, and so on. To correct them all would have required redoing much work, with little substantive gain. Instead, we chose between inconsistent results on the best bases we could find for judgment. We do not believe that these shortcuts substantially reduced the accuracy of our final estimates.

(c) Acres of forested and nonforested land cleared, 1840. We accepted Seaman's estimate of the number of improved acres in 1840 and made a rough division of it among New England, the Middle Atlantic States, the South Atlantic, the East and West North Central, and the East and West South Central, on the assumptions that the totals increased only slightly in the first three regions between 1840 and 1850, more pronouncedly in the fourth and fifth, and quite dramatically in the last two. We assumed that all the improved land in the first three regions in 1840 had formerly been forested land. We distributed the totals between the two types of land in the last four regions in the proportions in which they were distributed in 1850. The estimates are very rough, much more so than is true of the other years.

Table 7.4 contains our estimates of improved land, 1840–1900, by region and by type of original ground cover. The regional definitions follow those of US Bureau of the Census (1960), series A-123 to A-180, rather than those of Primack, for reasons that will become apparent.

(d) Physical inputs into clearing and breaking land. It is probable that most of the cost of clearing and breaking was labor cost. We took into account only the labor requirements, ignoring costs of capital such as oxen, horses, and various tools.

According to Primack (1962, 28), it took about 32 man-days to clear an acre of forest land in 1860 (and earlier); this figure gradually dropped to 26 man-days by 1900 as techniques improved. Grassland was much

TABLE 7.4 **Improved land in farms, by region and by type of original ground cover, 1840–1900, in millions of acres**

|                     | 1840 | 1850   | 1860   | 1870   | 1880   | 1890   | 1900   |
|---------------------|------|--------|--------|--------|--------|--------|--------|
| **Forest cover**    |      |        |        |        |        |        |        |
| New England         | 10.0 | 11.15  | 12.22  | 12.00  | 13.15  | 10.74  | 8.13   |
| Middle Atlantic     | 19.5 | 22.80  | 26.77  | 29.12  | 30.74  | 31.60  | 29.79  |
| East North Central  | 11.2 | 17.17  | 29.47  | 38.30  | 53.66  | 57.57  | 63.85  |
| West North Central  | 0.8  | 1.20   | 2.12   | 4.30   | 8.06   | 10.25  | 13.02  |
| South Atlantic      | 28.5 | 30.01  | 34.90  | 30.20  | 36.16  | 41.67  | 46.10  |
| East South Central  | 8.8  | 17.25  | 24.02  | 22.71  | 29.04  | 33.77  | 38.09  |
| West South Central  | 1.5  | 3.02   | 6.94   | 6.48   | 14.02  | 21.89  | 26.18  |
| Mountain            | —    | 0      | 0      | 0      | 0      | 0      | 0      |
| Pacific             | —    | 0.13   | 1.91   | 2.97   | 5.5    | 6.43   | 6.85   |
| Totals              | 80.3 | 102.73 | 138.35 | 146.08 | 190.33 | 213.92 | 232.01 |
| **Grass cover**     |      |        |        |        |        |        |        |
| East North Central  | 2.8  | 5.74   | 11.72  | 16.60  | 21.93  | 21.20  | 22.82  |
| West North Central  | 1.2  | 2.57   | 9.00   | 19.20  | 53.20  | 95.27  | 122.63 |
| South Atlantic      | 0    | 0      | 0      | 0.01   | 0.01   | 0.01   | 0.02   |
| East South Central  | 1.0  | 1.77   | 1.87   | 1.51   | 1.78   | 1.96   | 2.15   |
| West South Central  | 0    | 0      | 0.40   | 0.39   | 4.96   | 8.66   | 13.59  |
| Mountain            | —    | 0.18   | 0.24   | 0.58   | 2.21   | 5.46   | 8.40   |
| Pacific             | —    | 0.03   | 1.54   | 4.56   | 7.85   | 11.13  | 12.91  |
| Totals              | 5.0  | 10.29  | 24.77  | 42.85  | 91.94  | 143.69 | 182.52 |
| **Grand total**     | 85.3 | 113.02 | 163.12 | 188.93 | 282.27 | 357.61 | 414.53 |

Sources: See text. Primack's data do not square exactly with census data. We adjusted them to cope with this problem. We also adjusted the census data of 1880 to eliminate double counting by the census (see Gallman 1972).

easier to improve, taking about 1.5 man-days per acre in 1860 and earlier, and only 0.5 man-days by 1900. We converted these coefficients to man-months (26 days per month) per acre—which, when applied to the data in table 7.4, yield estimates of the total man-months required to clear, remove tree trunks, and break the improved land reported at each census year, given the techniques of that year. A second set of calculations was made showing the total man-months required to carry out the same procedures, given the techniques of 1860.

These estimates (not shown) clearly overstate the true reproduction cost of land improvements, since they rest on the assumption that all improved land reported at each census had been cleared of trees and stumps and been broken. In fact, however, stumps were typically left in the ground to rot for five to twenty-five years before they were removed (see chapter 4). Thus, a substantial part of the improved land reported in any given census year probably contained stumps. Furthermore, Primack's antebellum estimate of stump-clearing requirements depends on slender evidence and seems somewhat high, while his more abundant postbellum evidence can be given a more optimistic reading than he gave it.

For these reasons we decided that, for our purpose, Primack's stump-clearing estimates should be reduced. How far they should be reduced is by no means clear. We marked them down to one-third of their original value. The adjusted estimates appear in table 7.5.

(e) Valuation. We used Lebergott's (1964, 141, 262, 539) rates of monthly wages paid to farm laborers, adjusted upward by one-half to include the value of board. The Lebergott series have the great virtue of being available at the regional level, and we made use of these regional averages. Lebergott does not have data for 1840 or 1900. For 1840 we used the means of the 1830 and 1850 wage rates; for 1900 we used 1899 wage rates. There is no average for the Mountain region for 1870; we used the Pacific average to fill the gap. The Mountain wage rates for 1850 and 1860

TABLE 7.5  **Labor embodied in the clearing and breaking of improved land, using current techniques and techniques of 1860, 1840–1900, in millions of man-months**

|                       | 1840     | 1850   | 1860   | 1870   | 1880   | 1890   | 1900   |
|-----------------------|----------|--------|--------|--------|--------|--------|--------|
| **A. Current techniques** |      |        |        |        |        |        |        |
| New England           | 9.23     | 10.29  | 11.28  | 10.92  | 11.80  | 9.36   | 6.88   |
| Middle Atlantic       | 18.00    | 21.05  | 24.71  | 26.51  | 27.58  | 27.55  | 25.21  |
| East North Central    | 10.50    | 16.18  | 27.88  | 35.51  | 48.78  | 50.81  | 54.47  |
| West North Central    | 0.81     | 1.26   | 2.48   | 4.65   | 8.77   | 11.69  | 13.38  |
| South Atlantic        | 26.31    | 27.07  | 32.22  | 27.49  | 32.45  | 36.33  | 39.01  |
| East South Central    | 8.18     | 16.03  | 22.28  | 20.73  | 26.11  | 29.50  | 32.27  |
| West South Central    | 1.38     | 2.79   | 6.43   | 5.91   | 12.72  | 19.34  | 22.41  |
| Mountain              |          | 0.01   | 0.01   | 0.02   | 0.06   | 0.16   | 0.16   |
| Pacific               |          | 0.12   | 1.85   | 2.88   | 5.16   | 5.93   | 6.04   |
| Totals                | 74.41    | 95.43  | 129.14 | 134.62 | 173.43 | 190.67 | 199.83 |
| **B. Techniques of 1860** |      |        |        |        |        |        |        |
| New England           | 9.23     | 10.29  | 11.28  | 11.08  | 12.14  | 9.91   | 7.50   |
| Middle Atlantic       | 18.00    | 21.05  | 24.71  | 26.88  | 28.38  | 29.17  | 27.50  |
| East North Central    | 10.50    | 16.18  | 27.88  | 36.31  | 50.80  | 54.36  | 60.26  |
| West North Central    | 0.81     | 1.26   | 2.48   | 5.08   | 10.51  | 14.96  | 19.09  |
| South Atlantic        | 26.31    | 27.70  | 32.22  | 27.88  | 33.38  | 38.47  | 42.56  |
| East South Central    | 8.18     | 16.03  | 22.28  | 21.05  | 26.91  | 31.29  | 35.28  |
| West South Central    | 1.38     | 2.79   | 6.43   | 6.00   | 13.23  | 20.71  | 24.95  |
| Mountain              |          | 0.01   | 0.01   | 0.03   | 0.13   | 0.32   | 0.48   |
| Pacific               | no data  |        |        |        |        |        |        |
| Totals                | 74.41    | 95.43  | 129.14 | 137.31 | 181.01 | 205.77 | 224.69 |

Sources: See text.

TABLE 7.6 **Monthly farm wage rates, including the value for board, 1840–1900, in dollars**

|  | 1840 | 1850 | 1860 | 1870 | 1880 | 1890 | 1900 |
|---|---|---|---|---|---|---|---|
| New England | 18.44 | 19.47 | 22.10 | 29.76 | 20.91 | 26.67 | 27.30 |
| Middle Atlantic | 14.77 | 16.76 | 19.13 | 26.84 | 20.57 | 23.64 | 23.97 |
| East North Central | 15.13 | 17.16 | 20.69 | 25.41 | 23.22 | 23.88 | 25.35 |
| West North Central | 16.61 | 18.00 | 20.64 | 25.65 | 22.32 | 23.76 | 27.06 |
| South Atlantic | 11.52 | 12.30 | 16.62 | 14.93 | 13.22 | 14.19 | 13.98 |
| East South Central | 14.23 | 14.40 | 21.09 | 19.17 | 15.24 | 15.87 | 16.08 |
| West South Central |  | 16.92 | 23.30 | 21.08 | 19.35 | 19.26 | 17.79 |
| Mountain |  | 11.18 | 26.20 | 43.79* | 37.11 | 32.51 | 39.50 |
| Pacific |  | 102.00 | 51.24 | 43.79 | 37.16 | 33.96 | 37.65 |

Note: *Mountain 1870 based on Pacific 1870.
Sources: See text.

are weighted averages of the wage rates for New Mexico and Utah, the weights being drawn from the relative amounts of improved land in the two states.

The wage data are displayed in table 7.6. Table 7.7 contains our estimates of the value of farm land improvements (clearing and breaking), in current and constant prices, derived from tables 7.5 and 7.6. Both input prices and techniques were held constant in producing the estimates expressed in 1860 values.

### 7.5.4 Detailed Estimating Procedures: Fences

(a) Introduction. We began by establishing the rods of fencing of each type (worm, post and rail, stone, hedge, board, wire) in existence at each census date; the labor required to replace this fencing, given current and 1860 techniques of construction; the materials needed to carry out the replacements; the cost of the required labor and materials, expressed in current and constant (1860) prices; and the depreciation that the fencing had experienced. With this information, we were able to work our gross and net reproduction cost estimates for farm fences. Because tests suggested that these estimates were too low, we derived an adjustment to improve them.

(b) Rods of fencing. We used Primack's estimates of rods of fencing of each type (1962, 206–7) for the census years 1850 through 1880. For 1890 and 1900, Primack (1962, 207) provides the necessary information for every region except New England and the Middle Atlantic, for which Primack (1962, 197) shows only the total rods of fencing of all types.

We extended his 1880 proportions among types in these two regions to 1890 and 1900, modifying them slightly according to the pattern of prior change and Primack's (1962, 208) notes to his table.[9] We estimated the number of improved acres by region (Primack's definitions) in 1840, along lines described in Section 7.5.3.c, and assumed that the rods of fencing per improved acre were the same in each region in 1840 as in 1850. We then distributed fencing (by region) among types of fencing as we had done for 1890 and 1900.

Since plain and barbed wire fences used different amounts and qualities of material per rod, we were obliged to divide wire fencing between

TABLE 7.7 **Value of agricultural land improvements (clearing and breaking), measured in current and 1860 prices, 1840–1900, in millions of dollars**

|  | 1840 | 1850 | 1860 | 1870 | 1880 | 1890 | 1900 |
|---|---|---|---|---|---|---|---|
| **Value, at current prices** | | | | | | | |
| New England | 170.2 | 200.3 | 249.3 | 325.0 | 246.7 | 249.6 | 187.8 |
| Middle Atlantic | 265.9 | 352.8 | 472.7 | 711.5 | 567.3 | 651.3 | 604.3 |
| East North Central | 158.9 | 277.6 | 576.8 | 902.3 | 1,132.7 | 1,213.3 | 1,380.8 |
| West North Central | 13.5 | 22.7 | 51.2 | 119.3 | 195.7 | 277.8 | 362.1 |
| South Atlantic | 303.1 | 340.7 | 535.5 | 410.4 | 429.0 | 515.5 | 545.4 |
| East South Central | 116.4 | 230.8 | 469.9 | 397.4 | 397.9 | 468.2 | 518.9 |
| West South Central | 19.6* | 47.2 | 149.8 | 124.6 | 246.1 | 372.5 | 398.7 |
| Mountain | 0 | 0.1 | 0.3 | 0.9 | 2.2 | 5.2 | 6.3 |
| Pacific | 0 | 12.2 | 94.8 | 126.1 | 191.7 | 201.4 | 227.4 |
| Totals | 1,047.6 | 1,484.4 | 2,600.3 | 3,117.5 | 3,409.3 | 3,954.8 | 4,231.7 |
| **Value, at 1860 prices** | | | | | | | |
| New England | 204.0 | 227.4 | 249.3 | 244.9 | 268.3 | 219.0 | 165.8 |
| Middle Atlantic | 344.3 | 402.7 | 472.7 | 514.2 | 542.9 | 558.0 | 526.1 |
| East North Central | 217.2 | 334.8 | 576.8 | 751.3 | 1,051.1 | 1,124.7 | 1,246.8 |
| West North Central | 16.7 | 26.0 | 51.2 | 104.9 | 216.9 | 308.8 | 394.0 |
| South Atlantic | 437.3 | 460.4 | 535.5 | 463.4 | 554.8 | 639.4 | 707.3 |
| East South Central | 172.5 | 338.1 | 469.9 | 443.9 | 567.5 | 659.9 | 744.1 |
| West South Central | 32.2 | 65.0 | 149.8 | 139.8 | 308.3 | 482.5 | 581.3 |
| Mountain | 0 | 0.3 | 0.3 | 0.8 | 3.4 | 8.4 | 12.6 |
| Pacific | 0 | 6.1 | 94.8 | 153.7 | 283.4 | 337.2 | 362.3 |
| Totals | 1,424.2 | 1,860.8 | 2,600.3 | 2,816.9 | 3,796.6 | 4,337.9 | 4,740.3 |

*Valued using the average wage for the East South Central region.
Sources: Derived from tables 7.5 and 7.6. See text.

these two types.[10] We did this by cumulating the production of barbed wire, assuming that it all went into agriculture and that no barbed wire fence was retired before 1900. The tendency of the procedure to lead to an overestimate of barbed wire fencing in place is at least partly offset by our inability to establish production before 1880 (production began in 1874 or 1876). For present purposes the estimates, while rough, are certainly adequate.[11]

Table 7.8, panel A, contains our estimates of rods of fencing, 1840–1900, by type.

TABLE 7.8 **Derivation of estimates of the value of fencing, measured in current and 1860 prices, 1840–1900**

| | | 1840 | 1850 | 1860 | 1870 | 1880 | 1890 | 1900 |
|---|---|---|---|---|---|---|---|---|
| **A. Rods of fencing, in millions** | | | | | | | | |
| 1 | Worm | 634.40 | 861.75 | 1,019.5 | 1,031.80 | 1,232.90 | 1,177.3 | 1,147.30 |
| 2 | Post and Rail | 63.60 | 98.91 | 1,22.09 | 150.07 | 173.83 | 133.92 | 92.58 |
| 3 | Hedge | | | 23.14 | 54.08 | 76.52 | 38.48 | 57.61 |
| 4 | Stone | 56.40 | 74.41 | 85.43 | 89.00 | 91.92 | 57.04 | 54.51 |
| 5 | Board | 26.44 | 53.37 | 107.2 | 186.71 | 369.67 | 625.81 | 758.57 |
| 6 | Wire | | | | | | | |
| a | Plain | | | 46.64 | 108.58 | 177.79 | 285.74 | 863.55 |
| b | Barbed | | | | | | 519.17 | 1,229.30 |
| **B. Labor requirements, in thousands of man-months, using current techniques** | | | | | | | | |
| 1 | Worm | 9,760 | 13,258 | 15,684 | 15,873 | 18,967 | 18,112 | 17,651 |
| 2 | Post and Rail | 832 | 1,293 | 1,597 | 1,962 | 2,273 | 1,751 | 1,211 |
| 3 | Hedge | | | 329 | 770 | 1,089 | 548 | 820 |
| 4 | Stone | 4,338 | 5,724 | 6,572 | 6,846 | 7,071 | 4,388 | 4,193 |
| 5 | Board | 203 | 411 | 825 | 1,436 | 2,844 | 4,814 | 5,835 |
| 6 | Wire | | | 161 | 376 | 547 | 2,477 | 4,829 |
| 7 | Total | 15,133 | 20,686 | 25,168 | 27,263 | 32,791 | 32,090 | 34,539 |
| **C. Labor requirements, in thousands of man-months, using 1860 techniques** | | | | | | | | |
| 1 | Wire | 0 | 0 | 161 | 376 | 615 | 2786 | 7244 |
| 2 | Total, B(1) (5) + C(1) | 15,133 | 20,686 | 25,168 | 27,263 | 32,859 | 32,399 | 36,954 |
| **D. Average monthly wage** | | 15.09 | 17.26 | 20.42 | 23.72 | 19.25 | 20.94 | 21.52 |
| **E. Labor cost of fences, value at current prices, in millions of current dollars (line B7 × line D)** | | 228.36 | 357.04 | 513.93 | 646.68 | 631.23 | 671.96 | 743.30 |
| **F. Labor cost of fences, value at 1860 prices, in millions of 1860 dollars (line C2 × Line D for 1860)** | | | 309.02 | 422.41 | 513.93 | 556.71 | 670.98 | 661.59 | 754.60 |

TABLE 7.8 (*continued*)

| | 1840 | 1850 | 1860 | 1870 | 1880 | 1890 | 1900 |
|---|---|---|---|---|---|---|---|
| G. Rods of board (in millions) in board and wire fences (line A5 × 4.5 + line A6 × 3) | | | | | | | |
| | 118.98 | 240.17 | 622.32 | 1,165.90 | 2,196.90 | 5,230.90 | 9,692.10 |
| H. Rods of plain wire (mil) in plain wire fences (line A6a × 7) | | | | | | | |
| | 0 | 0 | 326.48 | 760.06 | 1,244.50 | 2,000.20 | 6,044.80 |
| I. Rods of barbed wire (mil) in barbed-wire fences (line A6b × 4) | | | | | | | |
| | 0 | 0 | 0 | 0 | 0 | 2,076.70 | 4,917.20 |
| Price per rod of | | | | | | | |
| J. board | 0.189 | 0.1706 | 0.1786 | 0.2851 | 0.2181 | 0.231 | 0.2296 |
| K. plain wire | | | 0.0578 | 0.0733 | 0.055 | 0.0367 | 0.0326 |
| L. barbed wire | | | | | 0.1094 | 0.406 | 0.0364 |
| M. Value of board in fences, at current prices, in millions of dollars, panel G × panel J | | | | | | | |
| | 22.49 | 40.97 | 111.15 | 332.41 | 479.14 | 1,208.30 | 2,225.30 |
| N. Same, at 1860 prices | 21.25 | 42.89 | 111.15 | 208.24 | 392.36 | 934.24 | 1,731.00 |
| O. Value of plain wire in fences, at current prices, in millions of dollars, panel H × panel K | | | | | | | |
| | 0 | 0 | 18.87 | 55.71 | 68.45 | 73.41 | 197.06 |
| P. Same, at 1860 prices | 0 | 0 | 18.87 | 43.93 | 71.93 | 115.61 | 349.39 |
| Q. Value of barbed wire in fences, at current prices, in millions of dollars, panel I × panel L | | | | | | | |
| | 0 | 0 | 0 | 0 | 0 | 84.31 | 177.51 |
| R. Same, at 1860 prices | 0 | 0 | 0 | 0 | 0 | 120.03 | 284.21 |
| S. Total value of fences, gross reproduction cost, at current prices, in millions of dollars, panels E + M + O + Q | | | | | | | |
| | 250.85 | 398.01 | 643.95 | 1,034.8 | 1,178.8 | 2,038.0 | 3,343.2 |
| T. Same, at 1860 prices, panels F + N + P + R | | | | | | | |
| | 330.27 | 465.3 | 643.95 | 808.88 | 1,135.3 | 1,831.5 | 3,119.2 |
| U. Adjusted value of fences gross reproduction cost, at current prices, in millions of dollars | | | | | | | |
| | 502.2 | 769.93 | 1,205.0 | 1,747.6 | 1,876.5 | 2,792.0 | 4,163.9 |
| V. Same, at 1860 prices | | | | | | | |
| | 669.86 | 936.82 | 1,205.0 | 1,415.3 | 1,866.8 | 2,555.1 | 3,894.0 |
| W. Adjusted net value of fences reproduction cost, at current prices, in millions of dollars | | | | | | | |
| | 318.06 | 432.44 | 718.86 | 956.78 | 1,149.1 | 1,596.4 | 2,588.5 |
| X. Same, at 1860 prices | | | | | | | |
| | 424.24 | 526.17 | 718.86 | 774.88 | 1,143.2 | 1,461.0 | 2,420.8 |

Sources: See text.

(c) Labor requirements. Primack (1962, 82) gives estimates of man-days required to build a rod of fencing, by type of fence, at each census date. The estimates include the labor time required to prepare farm materials, when appropriate: felling trees, splitting rails, removing stones from fields, and so on. For these types of fences (worm, post and rail, hedge, stone), there was no need to develop materials cost estimates. For plain, barbed, and woven wire fences, table 7.9 provides the estimated required man-days per rod in each period. We converted Primack's coefficients to man-months by dividing through by twenty-six. We then multiplied the results by the number of rods of each type of fence in place at each census date, to produce estimates of the man-months of labor required to reproduce farm fencing.[12] Since labor requirements for wire fence declined over time with improved techniques, we made two sets of estimates, one given current techniques, the other given techniques of 1860. The results are contained in table 7.8, panels B and C.

(d) Labor costs. Once again we used Lebergott's wage data as described in section 7.5.3.e, weighted by regional labor requirements. We computed weights for 1850 and 1880 from regional data on labor requirements for fencing, and interpolated and extrapolated these weights to the other years. The Lebergott (wage data) and Primack (weights) regional definitions are virtually identical for the New England, Middle Atlantic, South Atlantic (Southeast), and Pacific regions, and for all practical purposes they are very close for the Mountain and East South Central (South Central) regions. We matched Lebergott's East North Central to Primack's North Central, Lebergott's West North Central to Primack's Prairie and Lake, and Lebergott's West South Central to Primack's Southwest. This array comes close to achieving a weighting scheme precisely appropriate for the problem at hand. The regional weights are summarized in table 7.10. The weighted average wage rates (adding one-half to take account of the value of board) are contained in table 7.8, panel D. Panels E and F

TABLE 7.9  **Estimated required man-days per rod of fencing, 1850–1900**

|        | 1850 | 1860 | 1870 | 1880 | 1890 | 1900 | 1910 |
|--------|------|------|------|------|------|------|------|
| Plain  | 0.09 | 0.09 | 0.09 | 0.08 | 0.08 | 0.06 | 0.04 |
| Barbed |      |      |      | 0.08 | 0.08 | 0.06 | 0.04 |
| Woven  |      |      |      |      | 0.09 | 0.06 | 0.04 |

Source: Primack 1962, 82.

TABLE 7.10 **Regional weights, 1840–1900**

|  | 1840 | 1850 | 1860 | 1870 | 1880 | 1890 | 1900 |
|---|---|---|---|---|---|---|---|
| New England | 0.24 | 0.22 | 0.19 | 0.16 | 0.14 | 0.12 | 0.10 |
| Middle Atlantic | 0.27 | 0.25 | 0.23 | 0.21 | 0.19 | 0.17 | 0.15 |
| East North Central | 0.18 | 0.17 | 0.17 | 0.17 | 0.17 | 0.17 | 0.17 |
| West North Central | 0 | 0.02 | 0.05 | 0.08 | 0 | 0.12 | 0.14 |
| South Atlantic | 0.17 | 0.16 | 0.16 | 0.16 | 0.16 | 0.16 | 0.16 |
| East South Central | 0.14 | 0.14 | 0.15 | 0.16 | 0.17 | 0.18 | 0.19 |
| West South Central | 0 | 0.03 | 0.04 | 0.05 | 0.06 | 0.07 | 0.08 |
| Mountain | 0 | 0 | 0 | 0 | 0 | 0.005 | 0.005 |
| Pacific | 0 | 0.01 | 0.01 | 0.01 | 0.01 | 0.005 | 0.005 |

Sources: See text.

contain the labor component of the reproduction cost of farm fencing, 1840 through 1900, expressed in current (panel E) and constant (panel F) values.

(e) Materials requirements. The values in panels E and F of table 7.8 contain allowances for the labor costs of preparing farm materials for use in fencing, but not for materials acquired outside the farm sector, which we were obliged to estimate. We took account only of boards, posts and wire.

According to the data gathered by the commissioner of agriculture, board fences called for four or five rods of material per rod of fence; we assumed 4.5.[13] Posts and boards were normally made of different types of lumber (black locust was preferred for posts), but we were unable to assemble the price information necessary to make use of this fact. Some fence posts were made of steel or cement; many were made from farm materials, even when board for the fence was purchased. We had no way of introducing these variations into our estimating procedure in an effective way. We doubt that the errors due to neglecting these matters are at all large.

According to Danhof (1944), plain wire fencing (normally number 9, 10, or 11) was usually built with four to eight strands. For swine, eight strands were required; for other animals, "six would be sufficient and even less." We used an average of seven. For posts, supports, and gates, we assumed that an average of three rods of lumber per rod of fence was required.

Hayter mentions barbed wire fences of three and four strands (Hayter 1925, 194–95). Barbed wire was also sometimes used to top off a board, or plain wire or woven wire fence. We assumed that allowing four rods of barbed wire per rod of barbed wire fence would be adequate. We also allowed three rods of lumber per rod of barbed wire fence.

The materials required to build the existing board and wire fences, 1840–1900, are given in panels G, H, and I of table 7.8.

(f) Prices of board and wire. We took wire prices for the period 1860 through 1890 from the *Aldrich Report*, selecting 1 July prices as the closest of those available to the census date to which the capital stock figures apply (US Senate 1893, 183, 190). We extrapolated to 1900 on prices of nails in US Bureau of the Census 1960, series E-109.

We computed an average lumber price for 1871 (weighted by regional requirements) from evidence in a farmers' survey compiled in the *Report of the Commissioner of Agriculture*, and assumed that it held for 1870 (US Bureau of the Census 1960, 508). We then extrapolated this average to 1840, 1850, 1860, and 1890 on a weighted average of July prices of one-inch spruce and pine boards (US Senate 1893, 230, 238).[14] Since spruce was favored in New England and the Middle Atlantic, and pine in the North Central, Lake, and Southeast, we derived weights for spruce and pine prices from the total lumber requirements of these regions. We extrapolated these prices to 1900 on a building materials price index in US Bureau of the Census 1960, series E-21. Prices were then converted to per-rod figures, which are recorded in panels J, K, and L of table 7.8.

(g) Gross value of fences. We estimated the value of materials in fences (current and constant prices) by multiplying the volume of materials of each type by the relevant price. The results are displayed in table 7.8, panels M, N, O, P, Q, and R. The total value of fences (labor plus materials), derived in the ways described, is contained in panel S (current prices) and panel T (constant prices) of table 7.8.

(h) A test of the estimates. The 1871 *Report of the Commissioner of Agriculture* contains an estimate of the value of fences in the US of $1,748 million, substantially higher than our figure for 1870 (table 7.8, panel S) (US Bureau of the Census 1960, 510). Unfortunately, the commissioner does not explain the concept of value he has in mind, but the context suggests that it is gross reproduction cost, the same concept we used. The commissioner had access to considerable evidence, and his work seems careful. We therefore decided to investigate the difference between his figure and ours.

The commissioner worked with the returns of a survey of farmers in all parts of the country, a survey that returned the cost per rod for each type of fencing in each state (US Bureau of the Census 1960, 509). With these materials and Primack's data on the regional distribution of fences in 1870, we produced a weighted national average cost per rod for worm ($0.79), post and rail ($1.14), board ($1.37), and stone ($2.02) fencing.[15] These may be compared with the Gallman-Howle-Primack estimates for worm ($0.36), post and rail ($0.31), board ($1.47), and stone ($1.82) fencing.

In each case in which the fence materials came from the farm, our Gallman-Howle-Primack estimate is much below that drawn from the survey of the commissioner of agriculture. In the one case in which materials (board fence) were purchased, the two estimates are very close. We also found that the difference between our estimate of the gross reproduction cost of all fences in 1870 and that of the commissioner can be fully accounted for by differences between our estimates and his of the average cost per rod of worm, post and rail, and stone fences alone. We take these results to mean that our aggregate estimate is too low, chiefly because we have underestimated the cost per rod of the three types of fences that use farm-produced materials. We do not think it is the commissioner who is mistaken, because in the one case in which we were obliged to estimate the cost of materials directly, our estimate and the commissioner's are very close. Furthermore, while the data are not conceptually unambiguous, it is clear that the commissioner had more primary evidence from his survey than we were able to draw from Primack.

We chose, then, to accept the commissioner's estimate, and to date it to 1870. We then multiplied our estimates of the cost of worm, post and rail, and stone fences in each year (in current and constant prices) by the ratio of the survey average cost per rod to ours. These adjusted figures were combined with our estimates of the cost of hedge, board, and wire fence, and the aggregate series was used as an extrapolator. (Specifically, the commissioner's 1870 figure was extrapolated to all other years on the current price extrapolating series. The 1860 figure thus obtained was then extrapolated to all other years on the constant price extrapolating series [table 7.8, panels U and V].) Thus, Primack's very useful evidence on trends in labor expended per rod of fence affects the movement of the series over time, while the level of the series is adjusted to the evidence from the commissioner's survey.

(i) Net value of fences. We assumed that properly maintained hedge and stone fences do not depreciate. According to Danhof (1944, 173), nineteenth-century wooden fences had a service life of twenty to twenty-five years; just before World War I, Humphrey (1916, 32) placed the service life of wire fence at twenty-two years.

TABLE 7.11 **Derivation of estimates of the value of work directed toward drainage, irrigation, and irrigation for rice, measured in current and 1860 prices, 1840–1900**

| | 1840 | 1850 | 1860 | 1870 | 1880 | 1890 | 1900 |
|---|---|---|---|---|---|---|---|
| **A. Drainage works** | | | | | | | |
| 1 Acres drained, in thousands | 0 | 153 | 386 | 1,253 | 3,526 | 11,011 | 17,955 |
| 2 Man-months of labor | 0 | 17.7 | 44.5 | 144.6 | 406.8 | 1,270.5 | 2,071.7 |
| 3 Average wage rate | 0 | 16.95 | 19.62 | 25.98 | 22.72 | 23.85 | 25.38 |
| 4 Value, at current prices, in millions of dollars: (A2 × A3 ÷ 1000) | 0 | 0.300 | 0.873 | 3.757 | 9.241 | 30.301 | 52.579 |
| 5 Value at 1860 prices, in millions of dollars: (A2 × A3 for 1860 ÷ 1000) | 0 | 0.347 | 0.873 | 2.837 | 7.981 | 24.927 | 40.647 |
| **B. Irrigation works** | | | | | | | |
| 1 Acres irrigated (000) | 0 | 63 | 96 | 349 | 1,600 | 3,631 | 7,537 |
| 2 Man-months of labor | 0 | 14.5 | 22.2 | 80.5 | 369.2 | 837.9 | 1,739.3 |
| 3 Average wage rate | 0 | 11.47 | 27.62 | 43.79 | 37.12 | 33.2 | 38.98 |
| 4 Value, at current prices, in millions of dollars: (B2 × B3 ÷ 1000) | 0 | 0.166 | 0.614 | 3.525 | 13.705 | 27.667 | 67.801 |
| 5 Value at 1860 prices, in millions of dollars: (B2 × B3 for 1860 ÷ 1000) | 0 | 0.400 | 0.614 | 1.982 | 10.197 | 23.143 | 48.039 |
| **C. Irrigation for rice** | | | | | | | |
| 1 Acres irrigated (000) | 218 | 358 | 291 | 140 | 174 | 161 | 338 |
| 2 Man-months of labor | 419.2 | 688.5 | 559.6 | 269.2 | 334.6 | 309.6 | 650 |
| 3 Average wage rate | 11.79 | 12.72 | 17.02 | 16.58 | 13.77 | 15.11 | 15.32 |
| 4 Value, at current prices, in millions of dollars: (C2 × C3 ÷ 1000) | 4.942 | 8.758 | 9.524 | 4.463 | 4.607 | 4.678 | 9.956 |
| 5 Value at 1860 prices, in millions of dollars: (C2 × C3 for 1860) | 7.135 | 11.718 | 9.524 | 4.582 | 5.695 | 5.269 | 11.063 |

Sources: Lines A1, B1, C1, 1850 1900, Primack 1962, 214–18, 226, 228; 1840, extrapolated from 1850 on output of rice, Gallman 1960, 47. Line A2: line A1 × 15 to convert to rods (Primack 1962, 222) × 0.2 man-days per rod (p. 224) ÷ 26 (days per month). Line B2: line B1 × 6 (man-days per acre; Primack 1962, 231) ÷ 26 (days per month). C2: Line C1 × 50 (man-days per acre; Primack 1962, 232) ÷ 26 (days per month). A3, B3, C3, see text. A4 and A5, B4 and B5, C4 and C5, see body of table.

We adopted a service life of twenty years for all fences, and computed depreciation in the following ways, beginning with values expressed in 1860 prices. We assumed that two-thirds of the fence in place in 1840 had been built in the 1830s, the other third in the 1820s. We assumed that fence built in the 1830s was an average of four years old in 1840, while fence built in the 1820s was fourteen years old. Thus, fence built in the 1830s had a depreciated value of 0.8 times, and fence built in the 1820s a depreciated value of 0.3 times, its 1840 reproduction cost. Fence built in the 1830s was assumed still to be in the stock in 1850, but then to be fourteen years old on average, with a depreciated value 0.3 times its 1850 reproduction cost. The difference between the gross reproduction cost of all fence in 1850 and that of fence built in the 1830s was taken to be the gross reproduction cost of fence built in the 1840s. Fence built in the 1830s was taken to have a depreciated value of 0.3 times its gross reproduction cost, fence built in the 1840s a value of 0.8 times its gross reproduction cost, and so on. In this manner, we estimated the depreciated value of fence (expressed in prices of 1860) for each census date.

The proportion of depreciated to undepreciated value was computed at each date, and applied to the current price values to derive the depreciated value expressed in current prices (table 7.8, panel W).

### 7.5.5 Detailed Estimating Procedures: Drainage, Irrigation, Irrigation for Rice

Once again we used data from Primack, to estimate labor requirements, and from Lebergott, to estimate labor costs. The Lebergott regional wage rates (augmented by one-half to allow for board) were weighted up by man-months of labor to produce appropriately weighted average wage rates. Only labor costs were counted. No depreciation was allowed, on the grounds that properly maintained work of this type did not depreciate. Details are contained in Table 7.11.

## 7.6. Land

The value of farmland was computed by subtracting from the value of farms the value of buildings, clearing and breaking land, fences (depreciated), drainage, irrigation, and irrigation of rice lands.[16] The figures appear in table 7.12, which presents estimates from 1850 to 1900. Since

TABLE 7.12  **Value of farmland at current prices, 1850–1900**

|                                          | 1850 | 1860  | 1870  | 1880  | 1890  | 1900  |
|------------------------------------------|------|-------|-------|-------|-------|-------|
| Total value, in millions of dollars      | 748  | 2,039 | 3,226 | 3,496 | 4,905 | 6,104 |
| Dollars per acre                         |      |       |       |       |       |       |
|   Farmland                     | 2.55 | 5.01  | 7.91  | 6.55  | 7.87  | 7.26  |
|   Improved land                | 6.62 | 12.50 | 17.08 | 12.39 | 13.72 | 14.73 |

Sources: See text.

farms were valued at market values while many of the improvements were valued at reproduction cost, the residual—the value of farm land—is conceptually ambiguous and clearly subject to error. In all likelihood, the estimates are too low.

The value of farmland per acre of land in farms and per acre of improved land in farms implied by these data also appears in table 7.12. The increases between 1850 and 1860 seem rather rapid, but in other respects the average values behave plausibly. Between 1860 and 1870, events in the South tended to depress land values while general inflation tended to raise them; apparently, inflation was the more powerful force. Thereafter, prices in general declined until the mid-1890s, but the stock of land in the United States did not increase and the economy was experiencing rapid growth—factors that might be expected to raise farmland prices. This may be why our average values fall to 1880 and rise modestly thereafter.

On the whole, then, while the land value data might be expected to be relatively weak, they at least are not inconsistent with the data on the quantity of land, or with reasonable expectations concerning the development of land prices.

There is no good basis for estimating the value of land in 1840.

## 7.7. Tests of the Estimates of Land Improvements

The census returned the cash value of farms and the number of acres of improved and unimproved land, the two types of land being distinguished. With this information, the total value of improvements per improved acre can be derived by regression analysis. Several estimates of this type have been made, and they can be used to check our figures of the value of improvements. The two sets of estimates, however, are conceptually somewhat different and subject to somewhat different measurement problems. These matters must be considered before the tests are discussed.

The census returns of farm value probably refer to market value. Thus, the value of improvements obtained by regression analysis describes market value. Three of the four elements of our estimates, however, are expressed in reproduction cost. Market value may equal, exceed, or fall short of reproduction cost, depending upon the state of the market. But market value is always net, whereas two elements of our estimates are gross. Thus, a consideration of conceptual differences alone leads one to suppose that our figures of the aggregate value of land improvements might usually exceed estimates derived by regression analysis.

A second reason for believing that this might be the case springs from the nature of several of our series. Most farmland was probably cleared, broken, fenced, drained, or irrigated with resident labor—either family workers or slaves. The value we placed on the work of improvement accomplished by this labor reflects our perception of opportunity costs, based on wage rates, and the value of room and board established in markets. But land clearing and breaking was probably mainly an off-season activity, pursued when local labor markets were slack. It is possible, then, that our estimates of opportunity cost are too high. Certainly, they are more likely to be too high than too low.

There is also some reason to believe that the value of improvements obtained by regression is also too high (Anderson and Gallman 1977). The underlying assumption of the regression analysis is that the improved land and unimproved land on a farm are of equal quality, so far as location and adaptability to agriculture are concerned. But that is unlikely to have been the case. The best land is likely to have been improved first, so that the regression coefficient intended to measure the value of improvements probably also picks up other qualitative differences between the two types of land. The bias is unlikely to be large, however.

For these reasons, the test of our estimates against the regression estimates cannot be expected to be very conclusive. But it is the best overall test available, and well worth considering.

Stanley Lebergott (1985, 188–89) reported regression coefficients for six Midwestern states for 1850, based on census county data, while Robert Fogel and Stanley Engerman (1977, 284) worked out figures for cotton county farms in 1860, computed from the Parker-Gallman sample of farms and plantations. Neither of these two sets of estimates is in the ideal form for comparison with our work, but Lebergott's is close to being so.

Four of his states are from the East North Central region, the one missing state being Ohio. For purposes of comparison with his figures, we assembled an estimate of the total value of improvements per acre, based in part (land clearing and breaking) on our figure for the East North Central region, and in part (buildings and fences) on evidence relating expressly to Lebergott's four states.[17] For Lebergott's four states, the weighted average is $21 per acre for all farmland. The Gallman-Howle-Primack average is $24 per acre. The check is reasonably close, particularly when one recalls that the clearing and breaking experience of Ohio affects our estimate but not Lebergott's. Ohio was originally relatively heavily forested, a factor that probably raised the per acre cost of clearing and breaking above the level of the average cost for the region.

Our estimate checks even more closely with a second set prepared by Lebergott. Lebergott assumed a fixed price for unimproved land in his four states, based on federal land sales records. He then was able to compute the unimproved value of all land in each state and subtract this value from the total value of farms, to obtain the value of land improvements ($23 per acre for improved land).

The check against our figure ($24 per acre) could hardly be closer, especially when one allows for the presence of Ohio data in our estimate. The suggestion is that the market price and reproduction cost of farm improvements were very similar in the East North Central region in 1850, that net and gross values for clearing and breaking were also similar, and that the bias from our calculation of opportunity cost is not serious—all of which is gratifying.

The results obtained by Fogel and Engerman ($18.01 per acre) are more difficult to compare with ours, since they refer to the cotton counties of the South, a geographic entity that we are unable to extract from our data. We are obliged to draw comparisons with our estimates for three large census regions which do not closely approximate the cotton counties of the South. The contrast here (see column 1 in table 7.13) is much greater than in the case of the comparisons with the Lebergott figures.

A possible explanation is that the regions covered by the two sets of estimates are quite different, as previously mentioned. One way to work around this problem is to attempt to apply Lebergott's second method directly to census data for the South. According to Fogel and Engerman, the average value of unimproved land in the cotton South was $4.288 per acre, but this figure is an average, struck from a very high value ($12.613) for farms with more than fifty slaves, and more moderate values for the

TABLE 7.13  **Consistency check for Southern states**

|  | Gallman-Howle-Primack | Value of improved land per acre, given the following prices of unimproved land | | |
|---|---|---|---|---|
|  |  | 2.5 | 2.9 | 4.288 |
| South Atlantic | 22.99 | 21.20 | 19.88 | 15.74 |
| East South Central | 27.52 | 28.68 | 27.52 | 23.51 |
| West South Central | 32.79 | 37.33 | 34.92 | 26.56 |
| Weighted average | 27.10 |  |  |  |

Sources: The methods by which the Gallman-Howle-Primack estimates were computed were similar to those described in the text. But the weights (number of farms) for the weighted average were drawn from "Efficiency and Farm Interdependence in an Agricultural Export Region: Size and Scope of the Matched Sample" (Gallman and Swan 1966). They reflect the regional weights of the Parker-Gallman sample.

more numerous farms with fewer than fifty-one slaves: $2.572, $2.533, and $2.931 for farms with no slaves, one to fifteen slaves, and sixteen to fifty slaves respectively. In columns 2 through 4 in table 7.13, we have applied Lebergott's second procedure, based on three separate assumptions about the average value of unimproved land in the South.

On the whole, these results are much better. The progression of the estimates from one region to the next follows a similar pattern in each column. And the column based on the assumption that unimproved land was worth $2.90 an acre—not an unreasonable assumption—is almost identical with the column exhibiting our estimates. Clearly, these tests leave much to be desired. Nonetheless, they provide modest support for the levels of the estimates described in this section.

## Epilogue

Gallman's procedures for making the 1840 estimates are more opaque than in other years. This is understandable because the census did not enumerate the number, acreage, or value of farms until 1850. In his earlier work on agricultural productivity, Gallman made estimates of the 1840 farmland stock. As noted in the text, Gallman (1972a, 201–2) accepted Seaman's assertion that there were five acres of improved farmland per inhabitant in the United States. This generated the estimate of 85.3 million acres of improved land in 1840 that is reported in table 7.4. Gallman

(1972a, 202) added: "The ratio of unimproved to improved land was about 1:6, in 1850, and 1:5, in 1860. I assumed that the ratio was 1:7 in 1840 and therefore was able to estimate the number of acres of unimproved land at that date." As written, this statement is in error. It would be correct if the colon were replaced by a decimal point. In 1850 the acreage of unimproved land was 1.6 times that of improved land; in 1860 it was 1.5 times. Correcting the typo yields an assumed ratio of 1.7 in 1840 and an estimate of 145.0 million acres of unimproved farmland (1.7 × 85.3 million) and 230.3 million acres of total farm land (2.7 × 85.3 million).

In a 1981–82 grant proposal, Gallman included figures implying that the value of farm real estate in 1840 was $2,222 million (Gallman papers). The estimation method was not reported, and the subcomponent for buildings differ slightly (by 2 percent) from those reported in this chapter. His numbers for 1850 and 1860 match the aggregates reported here. If one accepts that the current value of farm real estate in 1840 was $2,222, and then subtracts the value of structures and land improvements reported in this chapter, the residual value of raw land was $436 million in 1840. The implied value was $1.89 per acre. Gallman obviously did not consider this estimate satisfactory. He writes above: "There is no good basis for estimating the value of land in 1840." Having an 1840 "raw land" price to use in combination with Gallman's conjectured farm acreage would be of great value.

## CHAPTER EIGHT

# Mining and Manufacturing

## 8.1. Introduction

This chapter focuses on mining and manufacturing, detailing the estimation of the current-price and constant-price (1860) values of the capital stock on a decadal basis from 1840 to 1900.

## 8.2. Mining

### 8.2.1. Introduction

The estimates are based on modified US census data. They distinguish improvements, equipment, and land. "Improvements" are buildings and other immovables; "equipment" is tools, machinery, livestock, and other moveable durable assets. The concept of "value" adopted by the census is discussed below, in section 8.2.4.

### 8.2.2. Value of Capital and Land

**1870–1890.** We based our estimates on the work of Creamer, Dobrovolsky, and Borenstein (1960, 304–14), who used census data but modified it by excluding the value of leased land. Since we wished to include the value of leased land, we used the Creamer-Dobrovolsky-Borenstein series as an extrapolator, to which we applied estimating ratios designed both

---

The substance of this chapter was written by Gallman. "We" and "our" refers to Gallman and Howle.

to distinguish the values of improvements, equipment, and land, and to introduce the value of leased land into the final estimates.

**1900.** There are no census capital figures for 1900. We obtained estimates for that year by interpolating between 1890 and 1909 on output. Since mining industries operated at less than full capacity in some years, we computed each capital-to-output ratio from the output figure in the relevant year, or from the highest previous output where that was higher (see table 8.1).

**1850–60.** Mining and manufacturing industries were reported in the same tables in the censuses of 1850 and 1860. Most of the important mining industries could be distinguished, but industries accounting for roughly 5 percent of total mining capital (7 percent in 1870, 3.1 percent in 1840) could not. We increased our final estimates to account for this factor.

Mining statistics prior to 1880 are of poor quality (see section 8.2.3 below). In several instances we adjusted the 1850 and 1860 figures upward. For details, see the notes to table 8.3.

**1840.** The 1840 census combined some mining and manufacturing operations. For example, the smelting, casting, and forging of metals were apparently all included in the returns of the mining industries. In these instances, we used data from later censuses to distribute capital between mining and manufacturing (see table 8.2).


*8.2.3. Estimates of Improvements, Equipment, and Land*

The only year for which separate valuations of improvements, equipment, and land are available is 1890, a year in which land was the most important of the three assets (US Census Office 1892a). Creamer, Dobrovolsky, and Borenstein (1960, 285) cite evidence to indicate that the "ratio of land value (excluding leased land) to capital fell from 57.4 percent in 1890 to 48 percent in 1922." However, they show that this overall decline can be explained by the relatively faster growth of those mining industries (e.g., petroleum) in which land value was less important. Had land value ratios for individual industries remained unchanged, shifts in the relative importance of mining industries would have produced a decline in the land-to-capital ratio from 57.4 percent in 1890 to 41.7 percent in 1922, a sharper drop than the true ratios show (Creamer, Dobrovolsky, and Borenstein 1960, 285–86). Relying on this evidence, we assumed that the ratios of the individual components of capital within industries did not change

TABLE 8.1  **Capital to-output ratios and the value of capital in mining, 1890, 1900, and 1909**

| | 1890 | 1900 | 1909 |
|---|---|---|---|
| **A. Capital-to-output ratios** | | | |
| Anthracite coal | $\frac{105}{46.6}$ | $\frac{150}{60.4}$ | $\frac{247}{85.6}$ |
| Bituminous coal | $\frac{146}{111}$ | $\frac{363}{212}$ | $\frac{961}{395}$ |
| Iron mining | $\frac{74.6}{160}$ | $\frac{137}{273}$ | $\frac{301}{517}$ |
| Copper mining | $\frac{60.7}{130}$ | $\frac{150}{303}$ | $\frac{302}{563}$ |
| Stone quarrying | $\frac{75}{50}$ | $\frac{79}{52}$ | $\frac{133}{77}$ |
| Petroleum wells | $\frac{82.4}{45.8}$ | $\frac{118}{63.6}$ | $\frac{408}{183}$ |
| Natural gas wells | $\frac{16.3}{-}$ | $\frac{61}{128}$ | $\frac{275}{481}$ |
| **B. Value of capital (in millions of dollars)** | | | |
| Gold and silver | 447 | 474 | 501 |
| Industries listed in lines 1–7 | 560 | 1,058 | 2,627 |
| Line 8 plus line 9 | 1,007 | 1,532 | 3,128 |
| Value of total mining capital | 1,035 | 1,589 | 3,280 |
| Ratio of line 10 to line 11 | 0.973 | 0.964 | 0.954 |

Note: These figures are used as the basis for final capital estimates; see table 8.3. Top value is capital; bottom value is output.

Sources: Lines 1–8: Value of capital 1890 and 1909, Creamer, Dobrovolsky, and Borenstein 1960, 304–8), in millions of dollars. Creamer et al. give only the total capital in gas and petroleum. We divided it in proportion to the capital figures in US Bureau of the Census 1913, 265. The 1890 Creamer, Dobrovolsky, and Borenstein estimate for natural gas wells includes independently owned pipelines. We deducted \$31.6 million to remove this element (see chapter 10.7, below). The 1909 figure excludes independently owned pipelines; see US Bureau of the Census 1913, 264.

Lines 1–8, output: US Bureau of the Census 1960, 351–68). The output of stone quarries is expressed in dollar value (millions of dollars); all other outputs are in physical units, which vary from case to case. Each figure represents the output of the year indicated, or the highest previous annual output, where that is larger. Lines 1–6, value of capital, 1900: The ratios of 1890 and 1909 were interpolated on output to 1900 and multiplied by the output figures to produce estimates of the value of capital. (That is, the change in the capital-to-output ratio, 1890–1900, was taken to be the same proportion of the change, 1890–1909, as the change in output, 1890–1900, was of the change in output, 1890–1909.)

Line 7, Value of capital, 1900: Extrapolated from 1909 and subsequent years on output. Line 8, 1900: Straight-line interpolation. Line 9, 1890, 1900, 1909: Sum of capital values in lines 1–7. Line 10, 1890, 1900, 1909: line 8 + line 9. Line 11, 1890, 1909: Creamer, Dobrovolsky, and Borenstein 1960, 304–8.

Line 11, 1900: line 10 ÷ line 12. Line 12, 1890, 1909: Line 10 ÷ line 11. Line 12, 1900: Straight-line interpolation.

TABLE 8.2  **Value of mining capital, measured in current prices, 1840, in millions of dollars**

| 1 | Iron | 1.43 |
|---|------|------|
| 2 | Gold | 0.23 |
| 3 | Anthracite coal | 3.20 |
| 4 | Bituminous coal | 1.87 |
| 5 | Stone | 2.54 |
| 6 | Lead | 1.05 |
| 7 | Other metals | 0.18 |
| 8 | Total | 9.60 |

Note: These figures are used as the basis for final estimates; see table 8.3.

Sources: The data on the value of capital were taken from US Department of State 1841, 354, 355, 361; and Schaefer 1967, 69. In several cases it was necessary to estimate the division of the value of capital between mining and manufacturing. We based these estimates on data drawn from the census figures from 1850 through 1870. The estimating ratios are as follows: line 1, 0.07; line 2, 0.994 (the 1870 census data used refer to gold and silver); line 6, 0.113 (the 1870 census data used refer to lead mining plus the manufacture of lead bar, pig, pipe, and shot); line 7, 0.75 (predominantly copper and silver). Salt mining is included with manufacturing.

from 1840 to 1900. We adjusted for shifts among industries by applying the 1890 ratios of land, improvements, and equipment for each significant mining industry to the corresponding capital figures for each census year. Improvements, equipment, and land values were then totaled for each year, and the totals increased to account for minor industries for which we did not develop separate ratios. (The total valuation of the significant industries was divided by the ratio of their capital to the total capital of all mining industries.) In every year the capital of industries for which we did develop ratios accounted for at least 93 percent of the total mining capital.

The derivation of the mining estimates is shown in table 8.3. The final series was increased by 10 percent for the 1840 to 1870 period to compensate for the likely exclusion of borrowed capital from the total capital estimates of that period. (See the remarks in 8.3.2 below.)

## 8.2.4. Deflation

The capital estimates to which we applied our ratios do not represent precisely the same thing in all years. Prior to 1880, census marshals were instructed to determine the amount of capital used in the business, a

TABLE 8.3 **Value of mining capital by asset type and industry, measured in current prices, 1840–1900, in millions of dollars**

| | | 1840 | 1850 | 1860 | 1870 | 1880 | 1890 | 1900 |
|---|---|---|---|---|---|---|---|---|
| 1 | "Capital" in anthracite coal mining | 3.2 | 5.1 | 13.9 | 50.9 | 100.4 | 105 | 150 |
| 2 | (1) × 0.350 = Improvements | 1.12 | 1.79 | 4.87 | 17.8 | 35.1 | 36.8 | 52.5 |
| 3 | (1) × 0.135 = equipment | 0.43 | 0.69 | 1.88 | 6.9 | 13.6 | 14.2 | 20.3 |
| 4 | (1) × 0.995 = land | 3.18 | 5.07 | 13.83 | 50.7 | 100 | 104.6 | 149.4 |
| 5 | "Capital" in bituminous coal mining | 1.87 | 3.2 | 15.5 | 59.1 | 78.6 | 145.9 | 363 |
| 6 | (5) × 0.187 = Improvements | 0.35 | 0.6 | 2.9 | 11.1 | 14.7 | 27.3 | 67.9 |
| 7 | (5) × 0.144 = equipment | 0.27 | 0.46 | 2.23 | 8.5 | 11.3 | 21 | 52.3 |
| 8 | (5) × 0.837 = land | 1.57 | 2.68 | 12.97 | 49.5 | 65.8 | 122.1 | 303.8 |
| 9 | "Capital" in iron Mining | 1.43 | 3.3 | 7.4 | 17.8 | 45.9 | 74.6 | 137 |
| 10 | (9) × 0.103 = Improvements | 0.15 | 0.34 | 0.76 | 1.8 | 4.7 | 7.7 | 14.1 |
| 11 | (9) × 0.108 = equipment | 0.15 | 0.36 | 0.8 | 1.9 | 5 | 8.1 | 14.8 |
| 12 | (9) × 1.05 = land | 1.5 | 3.47 | 7.77 | 18.7 | 48.2 | 78.3 | 143.9 |
| 13 | "Capital" in gold and silver mining | 0.23 | 1.8 | 12 | 50 | 225.8 | 447 | 474 |
| 14 | (13) × 0.235 = Improvements | 0.05 | 0.42 | 2.82 | 11.8 | 53.1 | 105 | 111.4 |
| 15 | (13) × 0.020 = alternative Improvements | 0 | 0.04 | 0.24 | 1 | 4.5 | 8.9 | 9.5 |
| 16 | (13) × 0.034 = equipment | 0.01 | 0.06 | 0.41 | 1.7 | 7.7 | 15.2 | 16.1 |
| 17 | (13) × 0.249 = alternative equipment | 0.06 | 0.46 | 2.99 | 12.5 | 56.2 | 111.3 | 118 |
| 18 | (13) × 0.756 = land | 0.17 | 1.36 | 9.07 | 37.8 | 170.7 | 337.9 | 358.3 |
| 19 | "Capital" in copper mining | | 2.8 | 8.5 | 7.8 | 30.9 | 60.7 | 150 |
| 20 | (19) × 0.096 = Improvements | | 0.27 | 0.82 | 0.7 | 3 | 5.8 | 14.4 |
| 21 | (19) × 0.056 = equipment | | 0.16 | 0.48 | 0.4 | 1.7 | 3.4 | 8.4 |
| 22 | (19) × 0.825 = land | | 2.31 | 7.01 | 6.4 | 25.5 | 50.1 | 123.8 |
| 23 | "Capital" in petroleum and natural gas | | | | | 43.1 | 98.7 | 179 |
| 24 | (23) × 0.65 = improvements | | | | | 28 | 64.2 | 116.4 |
| 25 | (23) × 0.077 = equipment | | | | | 3.3 | 7.6 | 13.8 |
| 26 | (23) × 0.50 = land | | | | | 21.6 | 49.4 | 89.5 |
| 27 | "Capital" in stone quarrying | 2.54 | 4 | 9.2 | 11.2 | 20.7 | 74.6 | 79 |
| 28 | (27) × 0.145 = improvements | 0.37 | 0.59 | 1.33 | 1.6 | 3 | 10.8 | 11.5 |
| 29 | (27) × 0.195 = equipment | 0.5 | 0.8 | 1.79 | 2.2 | 4 | 14.5 | 15.4 |
| 30 | (27) × 0.721 = land | 1.83 | 2.96 | 6.63 | 8.1 | 14.9 | 53.8 | 57 |
| 32 | Total capital above | 9.27 | 20.22 | 66.5 | 196.8 | 545 | 1,007 | 1,532 |
| 32 | Total capital, all mining | 9.6 | 21.15 | 70.51 | 211.7 | 558 | 1,035 | 1,589 |
| 33 | Ratio line 31 to line 32 | 0.966 | 0.956 | 0.943 | 0.93 | 0.977 | 0.973 | 0.964 |
| 34 | Improvements, above | 2.04 | 4.01 | 13.5 | 44.8 | 141.6 | 257.6 | 388.2 |
| 35 | Alternative improvements, above | 1.99 | 3.63 | 10.92 | 34 | 93 | 161.5 | 286.9 |
| 36 | Total improvements | 2.11 | 4.19 | 14.32 | 48.2 | 144.9 | 264.7 | 402.7 |
| 37 | Alternative total improvements | 2.06 | 3.8 | 11.58 | 36.6 | 95.2 | 166 | 297.6 |
| 38 | Equipment, above | 1.36 | 2.53 | 7.59 | 21.6 | 46.6 | 84 | 141.1 |
| 39 | Alternative equipment, above | 1.41 | 2.92 | 10.17 | 32.4 | 95.1 | 181.1 | 243 |
| 40 | Total equipment | 1.41 | 2.65 | 8.05 | 23.2 | 47.7 | 86.3 | 146.4 |
| 41 | Alternative total Equipment | 1.46 | 3.05 | 10.79 | 34.8 | 97.3 | 186.1 | 252.1 |

*continues*

TABLE 8.3 (*continued*)

| | 1840 | 1850 | 1860 | 1870 | 1880 | 1890 | 1900 |
|---|---|---|---|---|---|---|---|
| 42 Land above (owned and leased) | 8.25 | 17.85 | 7.28 | 171.2 | 446.7 | 796.2 | 1225.7 |
| 43 Total land (owned and leased) | 8.54 | 18.67 | 60.74 | 184.1 | 457.2 | 818.3 | 1271.4 |
| 44 Total improvements, adjusted for borrowed Capital | 2.32 | 4.61 | 15.75 | 53 | 144.9 | 264.7 | 402.7 |
| 45 Total equipment, adjusted for borrowed capital | 1.55 | 2.92 | 8.86 | 25.5 | 47.7 | 86.3 | 146.4 |
| 46 Total land, adjusted for borrowed capital | 9.39 | 20.54 | 66.83 | 202.5 | 457.2 | 818.3 | 1271.4 |

Sources:

Lines 1, 5, 9, 13, 19, 23 and 27: N.B. These series are extrapolators, not final estimates of capital.

1840, table 8.2, above.

1850–60: All except the iron figure (line 9) are from US Census Office 1872, 399, 408, which summarizes the 1850 and 1860 data. The introduction to the 1860 census points out that the census figures for iron mining include only independent mines. A product estimate for the other mines is given, and we have assumed the same capital/ton ratio as for the mines included in the census. We also assumed that the same ratio of reported to unreported iron mines applied to 1850. Thus we increased both the 1850 and 1860 census estimates to include "captive" mines. The anthracite estimate is from "A Quantitative Description and Analysis of the Growth of the Pennsylvania Anthracite Coal Industry, 1820 to 1865" (Schaefer 1967, 69), "owned land plus equipment and improvements."

1870–90, Creamer, Dobrovolsky, and Borenstein 1960, 304–14 (except petroleum and natural gas, which is from table 8.1, above). Capital in stone quarrying in 1870 consists of Creamer's "total stone," plus "total misc.," less "asphalt" and "other," an aggregate roughly comparable to Creamer's "total stone" in 1880 and 1890.

1900, table 8.1 above.

Lines 2, 3, 4, 6, 7, 8, 10, 11, 12, 14, 15, 16, 17, 18, 20, 21, 22, 28, 29, and 30: These ratios were derived from the valuation of assets in the 1890 Census of Mineral Industries and the total capital estimates from the same source, that have been adjusted by Creamer, Dobrovolsky, and Borenstein (1960, 304–14) to exclude leased land. Improvements include buildings and fixtures, while equipment includes tools, machinery, and livestock. For gold and silver mining, a separate category for "underground improvements" was listed. Kuznets's estimates (1946, 202, 213) apparently include this category under equipment. We included it under improvements, but derived alternative estimates (lines 15, 17, 35, 37, 39, and 41), which treat gold and silver underground improvements as Kuznets does.

Lines 24, 25, 26: The 1890 census provides inadequate data to make these divisions. We therefore based them on data in the census of 1880 (US Census Office 1884b, 143–47, data for Bradford and Lowes Counties, Pennsylvania). We treated rigs, drive pipe, casing, tubing, and the cost of drilling as elements in the value of improvements; engines and boilers, as equipment. The distribution of the value of capital and land that we thereby obtained was: land, 38.1 percent; improvements, 55.4 percent; and equipment, 5.7 percent. We used these proportions to distribute the total census value of capital and land in 1890 among asset types. (We included in this total the value of oil and gas land, and the value of oil and gas rigs, etc.) We then computed the ratio of the value of each asset type in 1890 to the value contained in line 23, and rounded. The ratio relating to the value of improvements was also adjusted downward, and the ratio relating to the value of equipment was adjusted upward, to take into account the fact that the 1880 census data (which refer to current investment rather than to the stock of capital) almost certainly overstate the value of improvements and understate the value of equipment.

Lines 31, 34, 35, 38, 39, and 42: These lines are totals of the corresponding categories in the listed mining industries, above.

Line 32: 1840, table 8.2, above. 1850–1860, These estimates were obtained by dividing line 31 by line 33. See notes to line 33, 1850–60.

1870–90: Creamer, Dobrovolsky, and Borenstein 1960, 304. This total also excludes leased land. Note that they lowered the 1870 census total by $10 million, to account for an error in the quicksilver returns. In 1890, 31.6 million is subtracted for gas pipelines.

1900, table 8.1.

Line 33: 1840, line 31 ÷ line 32.

1850–60, interpolated between 1840 and 1870. The omission of copper mining from the separately listed categories in 1840 evidently does not appreciably affect the interpolation.

1870–90, line 31 ÷ line 32.

1900, table 8.1, above.

Lines 36, 37, 40, 41, and 43: Lines 34, 35, 38, 39 and 42, respectively, were divided by line 33.

Lines 44, 45, and 46: For 1840–70, lines 36, 40, and 43 were adjusted upward by 10 percent to account for borrowed capital. For 1880–1900, these lines are identical to lines 36, 40, and 43.

question that—in the absence of further instructions—might have elic-
ited answers about equity in the business; the market or par value of
outstanding stocks and bonds; or the reproduction cost, market value, or
book value of the firm's property:

> If the question is simply, How much capital is employed in your business? it
> may be considered an inquiry into a strictly private matter; the answer may
> refer to what would remain after the debts were paid; or some such unsubstan-
> tial thing such as "the goodwill of the business" may be included. In case the
> producer is an incorporated company, the answer will be the amount of share
> capital at par (US Census Office 1886, xxvi–xxvii).

An effort was made at standardization in 1880. According to the introduction to the 1880 census, the following questions were asked:

> What is the value of the mineral real estate attached to the mine? What is the
> value of the plant? and how much is usually employed as working capital (US
> Census Office 1886, xxvi–xxvii)?

Apparently, market values were being sought. Thus "plant" was defined
as follows:

> The "plant" means all machinery, improvements, personal property (not sup-
> plies), animals, fixtures, etc. An estimate of this should be based on actual val-
> ues, not cost, and should exclude all antiquated and idle machinery (US Census
> Office 1886, 801).

The 1890 census is of particular interest, as the source of the asset ratios we used to distribute property among types in all other years. In-
quiry forms specified that values should represent what the property was
presently worth or what it would cost in 1890. The form used for gold
and silver asked, among other things, for the present actual cash value
of buildings. It thus appears that the census collected estimates of either
market value or reproduction cost—depending in each case on whether
the enumerator and the person being interviewed were more struck by
the question that emphasized the former or by the question that emphasized the latter. Since Kuznets (1946, 192–93) and Creamer, Dobrovolsky,
and Borenstein (1960, 204) tell us that the census figures contain little
undeducted depreciation, we may assume that net reproduction cost was

TABLE 8.4 **Underground improvements deflators, 1840–1900**

| | 1840 | 1850 | 1860 | 1870 | 1880 | 1890 | 1900 |
|---|---|---|---|---|---|---|---|
| **1 Coal** | | | | | | | |
| a Daily wage rate | | | 1.00 | 1.66 | 1.66 | 1.87 | 1.93* |
| b Value of improvements (in millions of dollars) | — | — | 7.77 | 28.90 | 49.80 | 64.10 | 120.40 |
| c Ratio (1b ÷ 1a) | | | 7.77 | 17.40 | 30.00 | 34.30 | 62.40 |
| **2 Iron** | | | | | | | |
| a Daily wage rate | | | 1.00 | 1.90 | 1.90 | 1.91 | 2.00* |
| b Value of improvements (in millions of dollars) | — | — | 0.76 | 1.80 | 4.70 | 7.70 | 14.10 |
| c Ratio (2b ÷ 2a) | | | 0.76 | 0.90 | 2.50 | 4.00 | 7.10 |
| **3 Gold** | | | | | | | |
| a Daily wage rate | | | 3.10 | 3.00 | 2.70 | 3.00 | 3.10* |
| b Value of improvements (in millions of dollars) | — | — | 2.82 | 11.80 | 53.10 | 105.00 | 111.40 |
| c Ratio (3b ÷ 3a) | | | 0.91 | 3.90 | 19.70 | 35.00 | 35.90 |
| 4 Sum of 1b + 2b + 3b | | | 11.35 | 42.50 | 107.60 | 176.80 | 254.90 |
| 5 Sum of 1c + 2c + 3c | | | 9.44 | 22.20 | 52.20 | 73.30 | 105.40 |
| 6 Weighted average wage rate Ratio of line 4 to line 5 | | | 1.2 | 1.91 | 2.06 | 2.41 | 2.42 |
| 7 Underground improvement deflator (base = 1860) | 85 | 120 | 100 | 159 | 172 | 201 | 202 |

Note: *1902

Sources: Line 1a: The daily wage rate of Pennsylvania coal miners (Lebergott 1964, 529) was reduced to the US level according to the ratio for 1860 (Lebergott 1964, 318). Line 1b: Sum of lines 2 and 6, table 8.3. Lines 1c, 2c, 3c: These divisions convert the improvements estimates into their equivalents in labor time. Thus, the average wage rate (line 6) is a weighted average, in which the labor time equivalents of the underground improvements serve as weights. Line 2a: Lebergott 1964, pp. 319 (1860) and 529 (1880–1902). Information for 1870 was extrapolated from 1880 on line 1a. Line 2b: Line 10, table 8.3. Line 3a: The value for 1890 is the weighted average daily wage rate of below-ground miners, laborers, and boys in deep precious-metals mines (US Census Office 1892a, 34; $3.04, rounded to $3.00). This value was extrapolated to 1902 on the wage rates of coal and iron miners, lines 1a and 2a ($3.12 rounded to $3.10) and to 1880 on the average wage of all deep-mine precious metals workers (US Census Office 1892a, 34. $2.97) and the 1880 census (US Census Office 1885, 157, $2.67). The 1880 value, in turn, was extrapolated to 1870 on the average annual income of all deep-mine precious metals workers (US Census Office 1885, 157, $766) and the 1870 census (US Census Office 1872, 760, $838, "gold quartz" and "silver quartz"). The 1870 value was extrapolated to 1860 on the average annual income of all gold and silver mine workers (US Census Office 1872, 401, 404, 760, gold quartz, silver quartz, placer, hydraulic). Line 3b: Line 14, table 8.3. Line 7: 1840, 1850, 1860, Lebergott (1964, 317–18), converted to a set of index numbers on the base 1860. 1860, 1900: Line 6, converted to a set of index numbers on the base 1860.

reported more often than gross reproduction cost. Market and net reproduction cost figures—especially in an industry that is growing very rapidly, as mining was—are likely to be similar. The price deflators we used are reasonably apposite for both (Gallman 1987).

The estimates for the years before 1880 are a different matter. We have applied our 1890 ratios to capital figures that must have been at least partly expressed in book values. There is no sure way to cope with this problem, though it is probably not serious in any case. This was a period of dynamic expansion of mining investment. In *each* ten-year period from 1840 to 1880, mining capital investment more than doubled (see table 8.3). Thus, even if book values made up a large portion of our conglomerated total capital estimates, the quantity of older capital was small enough to exert only a minor influence on the valuation of the total. To make a long story short, we deflated our 1840–70 estimates as though they were market (or net reproduction cost) values, not book values. This seems appropriate for 1880–1900. For the earlier period it may or may not be appropriate, but the quantitative significance of the matter is surely slight.

TABLE 8.5  **Value of reproducible durable mining capital and land, current and 1860 prices, 1840–1900, in millions of dollars**

|   |   | 1840 | 1850 | 1860 | 1870 | 1880 | 1890 | 1900 |
|---|---|---|---|---|---|---|---|---|
| 1 | Improvements (excl. pet. and gas), at current prices | 2.82 | 4.61 | 15.75 | 53 | 116.9 | 200.5 | 286.3 |
| 2 | Price index | 95 | 113 | 100 | 127 | 143 | 146 | 146 |
| 3 | Improvements (excluding. petroleum and gas), at 1860 prices | 2.44 | 4.08 | 15.75 | 41.7 | 81.7 | 137.3 | 196.1 |
| 4 | Petroleum and gas improvements (e.g., wells), at current prices |  |  |  |  | 28 | 64.2 | 116.4 |
| 5 | Price index |  |  |  |  | 83 | 75 | 54 |
| 6 | Petroleum and gas improvements, at 1860 prices |  |  |  |  | 33.7 | 85.6 | 215.6 |
| 7 | Total improvement, at current prices | 2.82 | 4.61 | 15.75 | 53 | 144.9 | 264.7 | 402.7 |
| 8 | Total improvements, at 1860 prices | 2.44 | 4.08 | 15.75 | 41.7 | 115.4 | 222.9 | 411.7 |
| 9 | Equipment, at current prices | 1.55 | 2.92 | 8.86 | 25.5 | 47.7 | 86.3 | 146.4 |
| 10 | Price index | 103 | 105 | 100 | 102 | 83 | 75 | 54 |
| 11 | Equipment, at 1860 prices | 1.5 | 2.78 | 8.86 | 25 | 57.5 | 115.1 | 271.1 |
| 12 | Total reproducible durable capital, at 1860 prices | 3.94 | 6.86 | 24.61 | 66.7 | 172.9 | 338 | 682.8 |
| 13 | Land, at current prices | 9.39 | 20.54 | 66.83 | 202.5 | 457.2 | 818.3 | 1,271.4 |

Sources: Line 1: line 44 – line 24, table 8.3. Line 2: The adjusted Brady index for factories and stores (see notes to table 8.9) and the underground improvement deflator (table 8.4) receive equal weights. Line 3: 100 × line 1 ÷ line 2. Line 4: line 24, table 8.3. Line 5: The adjusted price index of machine shop products (table 8.9), the railroad equipment price index (table 10.9), and the price index of horses (derived from table 7.3, above), equally weighted. Line 6: 100 × line 4 ÷ line 5, multiplied by 100. Line 7: line 1 + line 4. Line 8: line 3 + line 6. Line 9: line 45, table 8.3. Line 10: See Line 5. Line 11: 100 × line 8 ÷ line 9. Line 12: line 7 + line 10. Line 13: line 46, table 8.3.

Table 8.5 shows the deflation of our estimates (accompanying notes give details). We made use of the Brady factory price index, but also developed a price index of underground improvements based on the cost of mining labor, their chief input (see table 8.4). The two indexes were combined to form a deflator for mining improvements. Petroleum and gas were exceptions; we decided that the improvements in these sectors were more appropriately deflated by an equipment index (see table 8.5).

### 8.2.5. Evaluation of Mining Estimates

Those who have worked with the censuses before 1880 agree that the mining data probably understate the true value of mining capital. Thereafter, census data are doubtless better, but a substantial margin for error must still be allowed. Creamer, Dobrovolsky, and Borenstein (1960) present an excellent critique of the census capital data in the years after 1860. Rather than repeat their remarks, we refer readers to them.

## 8.3. Manufacturing

### 8.3.1. Introduction

Our estimating procedure for manufacturing was simpler than that for mining. By modifying census data, we first obtained an estimate of total capital in all manufacturing. For 1890 and 1900 the land, buildings, and equipment breakdowns are from the censuses, with appropriate adjustments to include rented property. For earlier years, we extrapolated the ratio of each of these assets to total capital from later census figures. Applying the ratios to the total capital estimates gives the asset estimates for 1840 through 1880.

### 8.3.2. Total Capital in Manufacturing

For all years we used adjusted census data to obtain a capital estimate that includes borrowed capital but excludes rented property. (Rented property was added back in at a later stage in the estimating procedure.) Two initial adjustments of the census data were necessary:

(1) The 1840–60 censuses recorded mining and manufacturing together. Since we had already estimated mining capital, we simply deducted it from the total to obtain manufacturing capital.

TABLE 8.6  **Value of manufacturing capital, measured in current prices, 1840–1900, in millions of dollars**

|   |   | 1840 | 1850 | 1860 | 1870 | 1880 | 1890 | 1900 |
|---|---|------|------|------|------|------|------|------|
| 1 | Manufacturing and mining | 305.7 | 533.2 | 1,009.9 | | | | |
| 2 | Less mining | 9.6 | 21.2 | 70.5 | | | | |
| 3 | Manufacturing | 296.1 | 512 | 939.4 | 2,118.2 | 2,790.3 | | |
| 4 | Borrowed capital | 29.6 | 51.2 | 93.9 | 211.8 | 279.0 | | |
| 5 | Total manufacturing capital, census definition | 325.7 | 563.2 | 1,033.3 | 2,330 | 3,069.3 | 6,525.2 | 9,817.4 |

Sources: Line 1: 1840, US Department of State 1841, 354–55, 361. 1850 and 1860, US Census Office 1872, 392–93. Line 2: Table 8.3, line 32, above. Line 3: For 1840–60, line 3 = line 1 - line 2; for 1870–80, the line 3 figures are from the respective censuses of manufacturing. Line 4: Ten percent of line 3; see text. Line 5: For 1840–80, line 5 = line 3 + line 4. The 1890 and 1900 estimates are taken directly from the census.

TABLE 8.7  **Indexes (1890 = 100) of capital-to-output ratios in mining and manufacturing, 1870–90**

|   |   | 1870 | 1880 | 1890 |
|---|---|------|------|------|
| 1 | Manufacturing: capital unadjusted | (74) | (81) | 100 |
| 2 | Mining: capital unadjusted | (54) | 92 | 100 |
| 3 | Manufacturing: adjusted for borrowed capital | 81 | 89 | 100 |
| 4 | Mining: adjusted for borrowed capital | 66 | 92 | 100 |

Sources: Capital estimates are from table 8.3 (lines 31, 44, 45, and 46) and table 8.6, above. The mining output figures are taken from Creamer, Dobrovolsky, and Borenstein 1960, 304 (all mining value of output). The manufacturing output estimates are from Gallman's value added series (1960, 56).

(2) Before 1890, census officials asked for "total capital invested" by the firm. In 1890 and 1900, the censuses asked detailed questions regarding the value of each kind of asset. For the first time, the 1890 census specifically stated that borrowed capital should be included. It appears that, when the owner of an establishment was asked merely for "capital invested," he usually excluded borrowed capital.[1] Since borrowed capital amounted to about 12.6 percent of owned capital in 1890, we increased the estimates for earlier years by 10 percent to compensate for the tendency on the part of the census to exclude this item (US Census Office 1892b). The capital figures resulting from these adjustments are shown in table 8.6.

We are now able to compare manufacturing and mining capital-to-output ratios (table 8.7). The comparison supports our adjustment of the earlier estimates to compensate for the exclusion of borrowed capital. The detailed questions concerning capital were first adopted by the mining census in 1880, and by the manufacturing census in 1890. The ratios corresponding to the old form of questioning are enclosed in parentheses. To make a comparison of manufacturing and mining easier, the ratios have been put into index form, with 1890 = 100. There is a considerable jump in the unadjusted series when the method of questioning was changed (i.e., between 1880 and 1890 for manufacturing, and between 1870 and 1880 for mining), which confirms the notion that, prior to this, borrowed capital had been omitted, at least in part.

### 8.3.3. Buildings, Equipment, and Land

The censuses of 1890 and later reported the values of buildings, equipment, and land separately. Rented real estate was excluded. The value of the omitted real estate was estimated in the introduction to the Census of Manufactures in 1890 and again in 1900 (US Census Office 1892a, xcix, c). We divided rented real estate between land and improvements (see notes to table 8.8) and added the resulting estimates to the owned land and improvements figures. The ratios of buildings, land, and equipment to total capital were extrapolated to the period prior to 1890 and applied to our adjusted capital estimates. See table 8.8.

### 8.3.4. Deflation

Are our estimates expressed in book or current values? There is no simple answer, because the questions asked by census agents varied from time to time. Thus, in no year (except perhaps 1890) can the returns be considered precisely as either market, reproduction cost, or book values. The year 1890 is of particular interest; we use evidence from this year to extrapolate the asset ratios. The wording of the 1890 census questionnaire is quite clear. Enumerators were directed to collect net reproduction cost data:

> The value should be estimated at what the works would cost in 1890, if then to be erected, with such an allowance for depreciation as may be suitable in the individual case (US Census Office 1892b, 10).

As to the years 1840 to 1880, the comments in section 8.2.4 on deflation with respect to mining capital apply as well to manufacturing. It is probable that the census figures reflect in part book values (most often for incorporated businesses) and in part estimated market values (for small

TABLE 8.8  **Value of capital in manufacturing, current prices, 1840–1900, in millions of dollars**

|   |                    | 1840  | 1850  | 1860  | 1870  | 1880  | 1890  | 1900  |
|---|--------------------|-------|-------|-------|-------|-------|-------|-------|
| 1 | Census definition  | 325.6 | 563.2 | 1,033 | 2,330 | 3,069 | 6,525 | 9,817 |
| 2 | Buildings          | 74.9  | 129.5 | 238   | 536   | 706   | 1,493 | 2,150 |
| 3 | Equipment          | 70.0  | 123.9 | 232   | 536   | 737   | 1,584 | 2,543 |
| 4 | Land               | 86.1  | 142.5 | 250   | 536   | 671   | 1,318 | 1,522 |

Sources: Line 1: table 8.6, line 5, above. Line 2: 1890–1900: The 1890 and 1900 censuses reported separate
valuations of owned buildings and land (US Bureau of the Census 1902, xcvii). In addition, they estimated the
value of rented real property (buildings and land together; US Bureau of the Census 1902, c). We divided the
rented property between buildings and land by applying the owned property ratio of these two assets. 1840–80:
The ratio of buildings (owned and rented) to total capital (excluding rented property) was taken from 1890
and 1900 and applied to the earlier years. The 1890 ratio was 0.224; in 1900 it was 0.235. We used 0.23 for the
earlier periods. The small change in the ratio between 1890 and 1900 was not considered an adequate basis for
an extrapolated trend. Information on total rented real estate was lacking in the 1909 and 1919 censuses. Line 3:
1890–1900: The equipment estimates were taken directly from the census. 1840–1880: Paul Douglas (1934, 116)
developed ratios of equipment to total capital for the period 1879–1919, based on census asset data for 1890 and
later (i.e., the asset data we used for 1890 and 1900, and data from the censuses of 1909 and 1919). We extrapolated
the ratio of machinery and equipment to total capital to 1840:

| Douglas estimates |      |       |       |       | | Extrapolation |      |       |       |
|-------------------|------|-------|-------|-------|-|---------------|------|-------|-------|
| 1919 | 1909 | 1900 | 1890 | 1880 | | 1870 | 1860 | 1850 | 1840 |
| 0.295 | 0.281 | 0.259 | 0.243 | 0.240 | | 0.230 | 0.225 | 0.220 | 0.215 |

These ratios were applied to our total capital estimates (1840–80) to estimate machinery and equipment.
Line 4: 1890–1900: See notes to line 2. 1840–80: The value of land is a rough estimate based on the extrapolation of
the land to buildings ratio from 1890 and 1900.

| Census data |      | | Extrapolation |      |      |      |      |
|-------------|------|-|---------------|------|------|------|------|
| 1900 | 1890 | | 1880 | 1870 | 1860 | 1850 | 1840 |
| 70.8 | 88.3 | | 95 | 100 | 105 | 110 | 115 |

See notes to line 2 for details of the 1890 and 1900 asset figures.

firms with poor bookkeeping). Businesses were probably often forced to
rely on tax appraisal data, which are closer to the market value concept
than to the book value concept.

What the figures in the 1900 census represent is not clear. The asset
ratios and the ratio of fixed to short-term assets do not change much from
1890 to 1900, which suggests that the census value concept may have been
the same in these two years. The 1900 census says:

The value of capital represented by buildings and machinery (supposed to
be returned as the valuation of the property upon the inventories of the census year) is too variable to permit statistical accuracy. The return is, strictly
speaking, a return of estimated market value, rather than capital invested. The
amount of the latter is affected by many causes—by depreciation requiring
additional investment, by throwing out old machinery and substituting new,
by business failures, and by other causes. So that in the case of most of the old
and successful manufacturing concerns in the country the total investment in
the plant has been much greater than the present market value, as estimated by
assessors (US Census Office 1902, xcix).

Unfortunately, the case is not as clear-cut as the above quotations indicate. Creamer, Dobrovolsky, and Borenstein (1960, 12) conclude that the census figures in both 1890 and 1900 are book values, quoting from the 1900 census to support this conclusion:

> Capital invested: The answer must show the total amount of capital both owned and borrowed. All the items of fixed and live capital may be taken at the amounts carried on the books. If land or buildings are rented, that fact should be stated and no value given . . . The value of all items of live capital, cash on hand, bills receivable, unsettled ledger accounts, value of raw materials on hand, materials in process of manufacture, and finished products on hand, etc., should be given as of the last day of the business year reported. (US Census Office 1902, xcvii).

The statistics of capital invested at the two censuses (1890 and 1900) show totals which are perfectly comparable (US Census Office 1902, xcviii). Creamer, Dobrovolsky, and Borenstein (1960, 13) then write, quoting the italicized part from the census, that for 1890, "the respondents were instructed to make '*such allowance for depreciation as may be suitable in the individual case. . . .*'"

From these statements, Creamer and coauthors conclude that the returns in both 1890 and 1900 were of book values and that, at least in part, they referred to depreciated values. Yet their last quotation, placed in italics, is only the last part of the sentence appearing in this census. The first part of the sentence, which has already been quoted above, reads: "The value should be estimated at what the works would cost in 1890, if then to be erected" (US Census Office 1892b, 10). Creamer, Dobrovolsky, and Borenstein are clearly incorrect regarding the 1890 census, which expressly sought net reproduction cost, not net book value.

The quotations for the 1900 census are conflicting. The case of Creamer, Dobrovolsky, and Borenstein for 1900 stands chiefly on the statement in the questionnaire that the items of fixed and live capital may be taken at the amounts carried on the books. This statement is subject to a new interpretation, however, when our earlier quotation is taken into account: "The value of capital represented by buildings and machinery (supposed to be returned as the valuation of the property upon the inventories of the census year) is too variable to permit statistical accuracy" (US Census Office 1902, xcix). "Books" may refer to tax appraisal books.

Our asset ratios were extrapolated from 1890, when the valuations were clearly current values (depreciated replacement cost). The total cap-

TABLE 8.9  **Value of manufacturing equipment, buildings, and land, measured in current and 1860 prices, 1840–1900, in millions of dollars**

|  |  | 1840 | 1850 | 1860 | 1870 | 1880 | 1890 | 1900 |
|---|---|---|---|---|---|---|---|---|
| **Equipment** | | | | | | | | |
| 1 | Value, at current prices | 70 | 123.9 | 232 | 536 | 737 | 1,584 | 2,543 |
| 2 | Price index | 145 | 138 | 100 | 105 | 76 | 32 | 28 |
| 3 | Value, at 1860 prices | 48.3 | 89.8 | 232 | 510 | 970 | 4,950 | 9,082 |
| **Buildings** | | | | | | | | |
| 4 | Value, at current prices | 74.9 | 129.5 | 238 | 536 | 706 | 1,493 | 2,150 |
| 5 | Price index | 107 | 108 | 100 | 90 | 114 | 91 | 89 |
| 6 | Value, at 1860 prices | 70 | 119.9 | 238 | 596 | 619 | 1,641 | 2,416 |
| **Land** | | | | | | | | |
| 7 | Value, at current prices | 86.1 | 142.5 | 250 | 536 | 671 | 1,318 | 1,522 |

Sources: Line 1: table 8.8, line 3, above. Line 2: Dorothy Brady's price index numbers of machine shop products, adjusted to bring them into line with the correct calendar year (see section 8.2.4 above). The adjustments were based on data in US Senate, *Aldrich Report* (1893), 181–82, 184, 187–89, 195, 197, 209, 211–13, 217, for prices of anvils, augers, axes, chisels, files, hammers, meat cutters, planes, circular saws, six-foot crosscut saws, scythes, shovels, vises (unweighted means of percentage changes); and US Bureau of the Census 1949, series L-9 and L-10 (1839, 1840, 1899, 1900). The adjustments were made by multiplying the Brady index numbers by the following ratios: 1839 = 0.97; 1849 = 1.00; 1869 = 0.93; 1879 = 1.07; 1889 = 1.00; 1899 = 1.00. Line 3: 100 × line 1 ÷ line 2. Line 4: table 8.8, line 2, above. Line 5: Brady's price index of new factory and store construction, 1850–1890, adjusted in the manner (and for the reasons) described in chapter 8.2.4 above (Brady 1966, 110–11). The 1840 and 1900 figures were obtained by extrapolation on the series in table 7.2. Line 6: 100 × line 4 ÷ line 5. Line 7: table 8.8, line 4.

ital estimates for earlier years are at best a conglomeration. Either the 1900 data are net reproduction costs, or net reproduction costs and book values were virtually the same in that year, because of the similarity of the 1890 and 1900 asset ratios.

We treated all the capital estimates as though they were net reproduction costs—an assumption as nearly correct as any other, and one that considerably simplified the computation of our constant value series. In any case, the question is not as important as it may appear. As long as our asset ratios are for net reproduction cost, it makes surprisingly little difference whether total capital is in book or current terms. Several factors contribute to this result.

(1) Almost half of total capital is short-term capital. This is always in current values.

(2) The remaining half would have to be deflated by three price indexes: indexes for land, for equipment, and for buildings. Both the buildings and equipment price indexes generally declined over time (see table 8.9). No land index has been developed, but the value of land in the vicinity of a mill would generally rise as a result of the very fact that the mill has been constructed, and the current value for the land would generally be above the book or cost valuation. Thus there is probably a tendency for

these diverse influences to bring book values and current values of total capital closer together.

(3) The rapid rate of growth of manufacturing capital in the 1800s (often more than doubling in ten years) diminishes the influence of old assets in the total valuation.

If the census valuations are really net reproduction cost valuations, then Brady's price indexes are appropriate means for deflating our manufacturing capital stock estimates, and we therefore made use of them. Details are contained in table 8.9.

### 8.3.5. Evaluations

The census capital figures for manufacturing appear to be only slightly better than the mining data. It is quite possible that they are low, particularly prior to 1880. The reader is invited to read the discussion of the quality of the census data in Creamer, Dobrovolsky, and Borenstein (1960, 195–221). In general, we may say that our 1890 and 1900 estimates are reasonably accurate, the 1880 estimate is only slightly less so, but the 1840–1870 estimates are of considerably poorer quality, and are more likely to understate valuations than to overstate them.

## 8.4. Conclusion

This chapter discusses the estimates of the capital stock in mining and manufacturing. It addresses important debates over valuation.

## CHAPTER NINE

# Nonfarm Real Estate and Trade[*]

## 9.1. Introduction

This chapter details the estimation of the current-price and constant-price (1860) capital stock on a decadal basis from 1840 to 1900 for nonfarm residential and trade real estate and equipment. It also provides estimates for churches and schools, and government buildings.

The "residential" category is self-explanatory. The "trade" category is a residual made up primarily of the property of commercial and financial establishments and vacant lots. (Kuznets [1946, 206] refers to it as "other industrial.") Only in 1900 does the census report residential and trade real estate separately. For other years we were forced to make the division on the basis of the proportional distribution observed in 1900. Since the residential category makes up about 75 percent of the total, an error in the estimated residential/trade ratio would affect the accuracy of the residential category much less than it would the trade estimate. If, for example, we were to use a ratio of 75 percent, and the true ratio were 70 percent, the error in our residential estimate would be only about 6 percent, while the error in our trade estimate would be 20 percent. The method thus leaves open the possibility of considerable error in our earlier (prior to 1880) trade estimates. We have therefore attempted to use 1840 census data on capital in trade to test the relevance of the 1900 ratio for the earlier period.

At the time Kuznets and Goldsmith developed their wealth estimates, one of the major unresolved problems they faced was the accurate

---

[*] The substance of this chapter was written by Gallman. "We" and "our" refers to Gallman and Howle.

estimation of nonfarm land values in the nineteenth century. Since the census figures include both land and improvements, it was necessary to deduct the value of land in order to estimate improvements. Their divergence of opinion was great: Kuznets (1946, 206) assumed that land values made up about 50 percent of the total, Goldsmith, 25 percent (Goldsmith 1952, 259).

We have limited information, extending back as far as 1850, on the land-to-improvements ratio in nonagricultural real estate. Since this ratio is crucial to our estimates, it is appropriate that we first look into this problem.

## 9.2. Deduction of Land Values

In developing his 1900 land-to-improvements ratio for trade and residential real estate, Kuznets (1946, 206) first obtained a ratio for all taxable nonutility real estate, as follows:

> The ratio of the value of land to the total value of real estate is extrapolated from 1922—by the comparable ratio for five sample states. The data for the latter ratio in 1922 are the percentages for California, Colorado, Indiana, Minnesota, and West Virginia (National Wealth and Income), weighted by the value of taxable property reported for those states (Estimated National Wealth); the data for the 1900 ratio are from Wealth Debt and Taxation (Special Report of the Census Office, Washington, 1907, table 2).

In this way he was able to estimate the value of all nonutilities improvements. Then, by deducting the value of improvements in agriculture, mining, and manufacturing, he obtained the value of trade (his "other industrial") and residential improvements. Land values were computed similarly.

There is considerable evidence, however, that the 1922 Federal Trade Commission ratios are too high. (e.g. see Keller 1939). Kuznets's 1900 ratio would not be affected by this if the 1922 ratios for his five sample states were overstated to the same extent. If the 1900 ratios for the sample are accurate, Kuznets's extrapolation would compensate for any uniform overstatement of the 1922 ratios.

The 1900 ratios were computed by the census from tax appraisal data together with ratios for manufacturing for the same five states (US Bureau of the Census 1907, table 2). The census compares the manufacturing ratios with those obtained from the Census of Manufactures:

If the five states are taken as a whole the value of land as shown by the census of manufactures constitutes 47.8 percent of the total (of land and improvements), while the assessed valuation gives to that land a percentage of 56.6. Considered in this way the figures seem to indicate that in these states the land connected with manufacturing establishments is assessed at a higher proportion of its true value than are the buildings and other improvements (US Bureau of the Census 1907, table 2).

It is possible that this was true of the residential property in these states as well. In fact, in view of the doubt as to the level of the 1922 ratios (also based on tax data), one may well conclude that tax assessments generally allot to land a disproportionately large share of total valuation.

Winnick (1953) used an alternative approach to establish the proportion of land in nonagricultural residential real estate. He estimated this ratio on the basis of Federal Housing Administration data for the years 1936 to 1949, and data for a limited number of cities before 1936. He used no source material prior to 1907, but extrapolated the ratio from 1907 to 1890. Winnick shows the share of land in total residential real estate declining from 40 percent in 1890 and 36.3 percent in 1900 to 18 percent in 1950.

Winnick also points out that the aggregate nonfarm ratio (i.e., residential and nonresidential) in fifteen cities in 1936 ran about 40 percent above the residential ratio. This could not be true for the earlier period. Between 1840 and 1900, residential real estate made up roughly three-quarters of all residential and trade real estate. If the ratio of land to land-and-improvements were 40 percent higher for all real estate than for residential real estate alone, the nonresidential ratio would be impossibly high: 94 percent.

We accepted Winnick's residential ratio of 36.3 percent for 1900, but we could not accept an aggregate ratio 40 percent above it (50.8 percent). Instead we set the trade ratio at 65 percent, which is as high as seems reasonable for this period. Since residential real estate made up about three-fourths of residential and trade real estate, the 36.3 percent ratio for residential and the 65 percent ratio for trade yield an aggregate ratio of 43.5 percent for residential and trade real estate together—a value a little lower than the one adopted by Kuznets, but higher than the one preferred by Goldsmith. This seems to be the largest land value ratio that the data on residential real estate will allow for 1900.

We next extrapolated the 1900 ratios to 1840. We had tax appraisal ratios for a few states, from which we computed a series intended to describe the trend in the national ratio. The variation in this series from year to year is small. No clear trend is indicated. We therefore used our 1900 ratios (0.363 for residential and 0.650 for other commercial) for all previous years.

## 9.3. Ratio of Residential to Residential and Trade Real Estate

E. A. Keller (1939, 116–18) estimated the value of nonfarm residential real estate—both owned and rented—for 1922. The owned property estimate was based on the number of owner-occupied houses and their median value, the rented estimate on the capitalization of rentals (at 8.5 percent). A comparison of residential with other commercial and non-farm real property indicates that residences alone made up 0.793 of the total. This seems high, and it may be that the capitalization rate was inappropriate for this period.

A corresponding ratio for 1900 was estimated by the census to be 0.75: "The values arbitrarily assigned to 'general residence property' and 'other business property' are respectively three-fourths and one-fourth of the difference obtained by subtracting from the total value of 'all taxed real property and improvements' the sum of the value of taxed farm realty, the value of land and buildings in factories, and the arbitrary and of course imperfect estimate of the value of mining realty" (US Bureau of the Census 1907, 18).

Grebler, Blank, and Winnick (1956, 365) estimate that nonfarm residential real estate was worth $14,974 million in 1890, a figure close to Kuznets's $14,423 million, although derived in a very different way. (They base their figure on estimates of the number and average value of dwellings.) It is roughly 76.3 percent of our estimate of trade and residential real estate, which suggests that the 1900 ratio of 0.75, established by the census, was a good guess. We used 0.75 for all years, since we believe the available information inadequate to extrapolate a trend.

## 9.4. Improvements and Land

**1880–1900.** The censuses of this period contain aggregate estimates of all taxable nonutility real estate, as well as estimates of some of their components. The aggregates appear to be expressed in market values. In order to obtain estimates of trade and nonagricultural residential real estate,

TABLE 9.1 **Value of trade and nonagricultural residential real estate, measured in current prices, 1880–1900, in millions of dollars**

|   |   | 1880 | 1890 | 1900 |
|---|---|------|------|------|
| 1 | Taxable nonutility real estate | $9,811[a] | $35,711.20[b] | $46,324.80 |
| 2 | Agricultural real estate | [a] | 13,279.30 | 16,440.40 |
| 3 | Mining real estate | [a] | [b] | 1,674.10 |
| 4 | Manufacturing real estate | 1,377 | 2,811.00 | 3,670.80 |
| 5 | Trade and nonagricultural residential real estate | 8,504 | 19,620.90 | 24,541.50 |

Notes: [a]1880 total excludes agriculture and mining. [b]1890 total excludes mining.
Sources: 1880, line 1: US Census Office 1884a, 11. Lines 2 and 3: excluded in total. Line 4: line 2 + line 4, table 8.8. Line 5: line 1 – line 4. [Rhode: The 1880 census places the value of "residential and business real estate, including water-power" at $9,881m.] 1890, line 1: US Census Office 1895c, 5, 13. Line 2: US Bureau of the Census 1949, series E-3. Line 3: US Census Office 1895c, 7, makes clear that the mining real estate is omitted. Line 4: line 2 + line 4, table 8.8. Line 5: line 1 – line 2 – line 4. 1900, line 1: US Bureau of the Census 1907, 16. Line 2: US Bureau of the Census 1907, 16. This is the same sum used in chapter 7, less $174.3 million for tax-exempt agricultural real estate not included in line 1. Line 3: line 44 + line 46, column 7, table 8.3. Line 4: table 8.8 above, less a deduction for tax-exempt property. Line 5: line 1 – line 2 – line 3 – line 4. [Rhode: There is a small discrepancy here.]

we had only to subtract our estimates of the other categories of real estate included in the aggregates. In each case, it is fairly clear from the census context which categories were included.[1] The derivation of the trade and nonagricultural residential residual is given for 1900, 1890, and 1880 in table 9.1.

**1860.** In order to make estimates for 1870 it was necessary first to deal with 1850 and 1860. We will therefore discuss the earlier years first. Once again we began by establishing the total value of real estate, and then obtained the value of residential and trade real estate as a residual. For 1860 there are two sources of the required aggregate value, since the census gives real estate values based both on tax appraisals and on owner valuations (US Census Office 1866, 294–95). As part of the population census, marshals asked each person the value of his or her real property. Each marshal was also to report the value of real and personal property returned in his district on the tax duplicate. He was then to sum up the values of real and personal property and mark up the sum, so that it reflected true value (US Census Office 1860).

Unfortunately for us, the marshals were not asked to estimate the true value of real property separately. However, limits on this value are readily established. The lower limit consists of the tax return itself, and rests on the assumption that only personal property was undervalued for tax purposes. The lower limit (tax appraisal) estimate is $6,973 million.

TABLE 9.2  **Value of trade and nonagricultural residential real estate, measured in current prices, 1860, in millions of dollars**

| | | |
|---|---|---|
| 1 | Total real estate, per owner estimates | $10,930 |
| 2 | Less agricultural real estate | 6,645 |
| 3 | Less 75 percent of manufacturing real estate | 366 |
| 4 | Less 75 percent of mining real estate | 62 |
| 5 | Less 10 percent of certain utilities real estate | 20 |
| 6 | Trade and nonagricultural residential real estate (line 1 minus the sum of lines 2, 3, 4, and 5) | 3,837 |

Sources: Line 1: US Census Office 1866, 319. Line 2: This is the census of agriculture figure underlying the work in chapter 7, above. See, e.g., US Bureau of the Census 1949, series E-3. Line 3: 0.75 × (line 2 + line 4), table 8.9. Line 4: 0.75 × (line 44 + line 46), table 8.3. Line 5: A guess. Line 6: Line 1 – line 2 – line 3 – line 4 – line 5.

The upper limit rests on the assumption that only real property was undervalued for tax purposes, and is derived by subtracting the tax return of personal property from the marshals' estimates of the true value of real and personal property. The upper limit estimate is $11,048 million. An intermediate estimate may be formed based on the assumption that the two types of property were undervalued for tax purposes to the same degree. It is $9,323 million.[2]

The sum of the owner valuations of real property came to $10,930 million (see table 9.2). This figure falls within the limits established by the tax data, if just within them. However, the tax-based estimates include property owned by corporations, whereas the owner-based estimate does not (see below). At a guess, a quarter of the property of mining and manufacturing firms and perhaps 55 percent of railroad property needs to be added to the owner valuation before it can be properly compared with the tax-based estimate. These adjustments raise the owner-based figure to $11,465 million, placing it just outside the upper limit established by the tax data.[3] The two forms of evidence, therefore, yield somewhat different results, although they are not strikingly far apart.

We chose to use the owner-based figure, rather than any of the tax-based figures, for three reasons: (1) the owner-based figure involved less processing than did the tax-based estimates; (2) we think it is more likely to be accurate than is the sum of tax duplicate values, adjusted by census marshals; and (3) the agricultural property estimates, which form a large part of the total value of property and thus figure importantly in the derivation of the residential and trade residual, are also based chiefly on appraisals of property rendered by owners, and are therefore more likely to be consistent with the aggregate owner-based estimates than with tax appraisals. The "Instructions to the Marshals" imply that owner estimates involve only real property reported as owned by individuals (US Census Office 1860). Governmental property and property of charitable institutions was to be excluded, while corporate stock held by individuals was to be included in personal property. The census figure of the value of real property, therefore, excludes the value of governmental and charitable institutions, and most corporate assets. We assumed that all railroads and most other utilities were so excluded. We could not make this assumption for manufacturing and mining firms, which were often small-scale, one-owner ventures, but manufacturing and mining interests do not make up a large portion of total nonfarm assets. We assumed, arbitrarily, that 75 percent of manufacturing and mining real property was included in the owner-based appraisal of real property. We also assumed that 10 percent of the value of the property of utilities, other than railroads and canals, was so included. As can be seen from the relative magnitudes in table 9.2, these matters are not of great importance.[4]

**1850.** Table 9.3 contains all of the published census data on total real and personal property in 1850. Tax duplicate data were collected by the marshals and true value estimates were made, in exactly the way in which they were to be made in 1860. Owner valuations of real property were collected, but were never totaled and published. However, Lee Soltow (1975) has sampled the manuscript census, and his data can be used to derive an 1850 aggregate comparable to the sum of the owner valuations of 1860.

Following precisely the methods described in connection with the 1860 estimates above, we obtained the following estimates from the 1850 data.[5] The lower limit (tax appraisal) was $3,899 million and the upper limit, $4,941 million. This intermediate value, generated using the assumptions outlined above, was $4,574 million.

Soltow's (1975, 76–77) work provides us with estimates in 1850 and 1860 of the average value of real estate (owner valuation) owned by free

TABLE 9.3  **1850 census wealth data, based on tax appraisals, in millions of dollars**

| 1 | Assessed value of real estate | $3,899 |
|---|---|---|
| 2 | Total assessed valuation, real and personal estate | 6,025 |
| 3 | Total "true value," taxed real and personal estate | 7,067 |
| 4 | Difference between lines 3 and 2 | 1,042 |
| 5 | Ratio of line 4 to line 2 | 0.173 |

Source: De Bow 1854, 190.

males twenty years old or older. With this information, plus the number of free males twenty years old or older at each of the two dates,[6] we developed an extrapolator for the 1860 value of real property (owner valuations), an extrapolator that covers most of the value of real property. The procedure yields an estimate of the market value of real estate (owner valuations) in 1850 of $5.2 million, which lies above the upper limit of the value of real estate in 1850 set by use of the tax data (see above). Thus, the results are similar to those obtained for 1860, but the margin between the owner-based and tax-based estimates is greater in 1850 than in 1860.

We ran a check on these results. We assumed that the markup ratios for real and personal property were the same in each year, and that the marshals understated them by the same proportion in each year. The following formula, then, can be used to work out the correct markup ratio in 1850: 1850 true markup ratio / 1850 marshal's markup ratio = 1860 true markup ratio / 1860 marshal's markup ratio. The 1860 marshals' markup ratio is taken from note 2 to this chapter, the 1860 true ratio from table 9.4, and the 1850 marshals' markup ratio from table 9.3. The true 1850 ratio, then, is 0.3307, which yields an estimate for the value of total real estate of $5.2 billion ($5,188 million), exactly the value we obtained by the extrapolation on Soltow's data. (The tax-based estimate is more comprehensive than the owner-based estimate—see table 9.4—but the difference is slight.)

Table 9.5 contains the derivation of our nonagricultural residential and trade real estate estimate, based on the adjusted tax-based estimate of total real property above. The figure obtained—$1,516 million—is very close to values that can be derived from Goldsmith's (1952) work.[7] Since

TABLE 9.4  **1860 ratio of appraised to true value of taxable real estate, in millions of dollars**

| | | |
|---|---|---|
| 1 | 1860 owners' estimate, total real estate | $10,930 |
| 2 | Add 25% of manufacturing real estate | 122 |
| 3 | Add 25% of mining real estate | 21 |
| 4 | Add 55% of railway real estate | 392 |
| 5 | Estimate of 1860 taxable real estate | 11,465 |
| 6 | Tax appraisal total, before markup | 6,973 |
| 7 | Correct amount of markup | 4,492 |
| 8 | Ratio of line 7 to line 6 | 0.6442 |

Sources: Line 1: table 9.2, line 1. Line 2: 0.25 × (line 2 + line 4, 1860, table 8.8). Line 3: 0.25 × (line 44 and 46, 1860, table 8.3). Line 4: 0.55 × current value of land and improvements, table 10.9. Line 5: line 1 + line 2 + line 3 + line 4. Line 6: see text (note 2) regarding tax duplicates. Line 7: line 5 − line 6.

TABLE 9.5 **Value of trade and nonagricultural residential real estate, measured in current prices, 1850, in millions of dollars**

| | | |
|---|---|---|
| 1 | Total taxable real estate | $5,188 |
| 2 | Agricultural real estate | 3,272 |
| 3 | Taxable portion of railroad real estate | 83 |
| 4 | Manufacturing real estate | 272 |
| 5 | Mining real estate | 25 |
| 6 | Taxable portion of other utility property | 20 |
| 7 | Trade and nonagricultural residential real estate | 1,516 |

Sources: Line 1: see text. Line 2: De Bow 1854, 169; also given in US Bureau of the Census 1949, series E-3. Line 3: The railroad real property figure is a total of land and improvements from table 10.6. We estimated that 50 percent of the total rail assets were included in the tax appraisal. This estimate is based on our 1880 analysis, indicating that about 65 percent of all railroads were in the tax appraisal at that time. Of thirty-three states, seventeen clearly recorded appraisals on county tax books, while eight exempted most or all rail property from property taxes per se. Of the remaining eight, some taxed certain categories of rail property (e.g., all except roadbeds), or the methods of taxation were such that we cannot determine if appraisals were made. Using a rough probability estimate for the latter, we feel that about 65 percent of all rail property was valued for taxation in 1880. For 1850, the percentage was probably slightly lower, hence our 50 percent estimate. The source of data for our taxation study was Adams, Williams, and Oberly 1880. Line 4: line 2 + line 4, table 8.8. Line 5: mining improvements and mining land estimates, line 44 + line 46, table 8.3. Line 6: a guess. Line 7: line 1 – line 2 – line 3 – line 4 – line 5 – line 6.

Goldsmith's sources and methods are very different from ours, the check is reassuring.

**1870.** No separate estimate is available for the "true value" of real estate in 1870. As in 1850, only the tax assessments of real and personal property, separately, and the "true" value of the two, together, are given. We therefore had to develop a markup ratio for real estate in order to adjust the tax appraisals to their true value. Once again, we had Soltow's work as a test of our results.

The 1880 census gives no total "true value" for total *taxable* real estate, only an appraisal value. In order to get a markup ratio for 1880 to compare with earlier years, we had to develop a taxable real estate true value total from the various categories listed in the census.

The ratio computed in table 9.6 is comparable to the 1860 ratio given in table 9.5. The 1870 ratio should probably be closer to the 1880 ratio of 0.707 than to the 1860 ratio of 0.644. The difference between the two ratios is small, and as a first approximation we applied the 1880 markup ratio to the 1870 appraisal of all taxable real estate: $(1 + 0.707) \times$ $9,915 million = $16,925 million. Since the test using Soltow's data to form an extrapolator (see section 9.4.3 above) gives an extraordinarily close check ($16.9 billion), we chose to adopt this figure.

TABLE 9.6  **1880 appraised and true value of taxable real estate, in millions of dollars**

| I | True value of farms | $10,197 |
|---|---|---|
| 2 | True value of residential and business real estate | 9,881 |
| 3 | True value of railroad real estate (to extent taxed) | 1,568 |
| 4 | True value of mining real estate | 602 |
| 5 | Total true value of taxable real estate | 22,248 |
| 6 | Appraised value of taxable real estate | 13,037 |
| 7 | Line 5 less line 6 | 9,211 |
| 8 | Ratio of line 7 to line 6 (markup ratio) | 0.707 |

Sources: Lines 1, 2, and 6: US Census Office 1884a, 9, 11. Note that the value in line 2 is a census estimate.
Line 3: 0.65 × (line 6 + line 7, table 10.9) (see notes to table 9.5). Line 4: line 44 + line 46, table 8.3.
Line 5: line 1 + line 2 + line 3 + line 4.

TABLE 9.7  **Value of trade and nonagricultural residential real estate, current prices, 1870, in millions of dollars**

| I | Taxable real estate | $16,925 |
|---|---|---|
| 2 | Less agricultural real estate | 9,263 |
| 3 | Less mining real estate | 256 |
| 4 | Less manufacturing real estate | 1,072 |
| 5 | Less taxable portion of railroad real estate | 1,033 |
| 6 | Less taxable portion of other utilities real estate | 30 |
| 7 | Trade and nonagricultural residential real estate | 5,271 |

Sources: Line 1: See text. Line 2: US Census Office 1872, 81. (N.B.: US Bureau of the Census 1949, series E-3, in this instance is wrong. It apparently refers to Superintendent Walker's conversion of current value to "gold" value.) Line 3: line 44 + line 46, table 8.3. Line 4: line 2 + line 4, table 8.8. Line 5: This is 60 percent of our table 10.9 estimate. See notes to line 3, table 9.5. Line 6: a guess. Line 7: line 1 − line 2 − line 3 − line 4.

We next deducted the other categories of taxable real estate to get the non-agricultural residential and trade residual, $5,270 million (see table 9.7).

**1840.** The 1840 census did not investigate the aggregate value of real property. We were forced to rely on other sources for our residential and trade real estate figure, but we had census data on property in trade that were useful in checking our result. Ezra Seaman (1852, 282) concluded that "the value of all dwelling houses in the United States in 1840, and the improvements around them, including yards, fences, outhouses, and trees, may be estimated at over a thousand million dollars." Assuming that this value includes farm barns, it can be compared with our 1850 estimate as in table 9.8.

A 27.3 percent increase in per capita residential wealth between 1840 and 1850 is indicated. This is not unreasonable. Tax appraisal data for Virginia and New York show per capita increases of 16.1 percent and 19.2 percent, respectively, for all taxable real property.[8] Because of the inclusion of agricultural land, all real property increases in value more slowly

TABLE 9.8  **Value of residential real estate, population, and the ratio of the former to the latter, 1840 and 1850**

|   |                                           | 1840     | 1850     |
|---|-------------------------------------------|----------|----------|
| 1 | Value of residences, etc., in millions    | $1,000   | $1,736   |
| 2 | Population, in millions                   | 17.1     | 23.3     |
| 3 | Residential value per person              | $58.50   | $74.50   |

Sources: Line 1: the 1840 estimate is from Seaman 1852, 282. The 1850 estimate is our estimate of nonagricultural residential real estate, plus our estimate of agricultural buildings (see tables 7.2 and 9.11). It was assumed that the yards underlying farm residences were of negligible value. Line 2: US Bureau of the Census 1960, series A 2. Line 3: line 1 ÷ line 2.

than residences, yards, and so on. Our data indicate that a per capita increase of 27.3 percent in the latter implies about a 19 percent increase in the former. Seaman's 1840 estimate therefore seems acceptable, and we assumed that it includes farm barns.

We next had to complete the estimate and divide it between agricultural and nonagricultural assets. We had all the necessary information to do this, except for the division of improvements between the two sectors. We obtained this information by extrapolation, on the basis of the results of a regression that relates changes in the ratio of agricultural buildings to trade and nonagricultural residential improvements, to changes in the ratio of agricultural workers to nonagricultural workers using national data for 1850, 1860, 1870, 1880, 1890, and 1900.[9] The regression provided the last piece of information necessary to complete the 1840 estimates.

The trade real estate estimate in table 9.9 is the result of our heroic use of a 1900 ratio for 1840. The 1840 census, unlike later censuses, lists the capital invested in the major categories of commerce. This information provides a very rough but interesting check on our trade/trade-and-residential ratio, and also on the level of our 1840 real estate estimate in general. The "commerce" capital figure in the 1840 census is $391 million. Our trade real estate estimate is equal to 50 percent of this value. The 1840 census "commerce" figure undoubtedly excludes many industrial categories that are included in our heterogeneous residual category called "trade," so that the true ratio of "trade" real estate to "trade" capital was probably less than 50 percent in 1840. The only other estimate of the ratio of trade real estate to trade capital is a 1922 figure of 39 percent by Kuznets.[10] The similarity between the 1840 and 1922 results is encouraging, but the early "trade" estimates must still be considered among the weakest in our series.

TABLE 9.9  **Value of trade and nonagricultural residential real estate, current prices, 1840, in millions of dollars**

| 1 | All residences, yards, etc. | $1,000 |
|---|---|---|
| 2 | Trade real estate | 195 |
| 3 | Residential and trade real estate | 1,195 |
| 4 | Agricultural buildings | 415 |
| 5 | Nonagricultural residential and trade improvements | 441 |
| 6 | Yards | 339 |
| 7 | Residential and trade real estate | 1,195 |

Sources:
Line 1: Seaman's estimate; see table 9.8.
Lines 2, 4, 5, and 6: The values were obtained by solving the following equations:
i. From our regression equation: line 4 = 0.942 × line 5; see section 9.4.
ii. From our nonagricultural residential and trade improvements-to-total real estate ratio:
Line 5 = 0.565 × (line 5 + line 6); see section 9.2,
iii. From our nonagricultural residential/residential and trade real estate ratio:
line 2 = 0.25 × (line 5 + line 6); see section 9.3.
iv. Line 2 = line 4 + line 5 + line 6 – line 1.
Line 3: line 1 + line 2.
Line 7: line 4 + line 5 + line 6.

## 9.5. Trade Equipment

Hardly any information on the value of trade equipment is available. We include this category only to make our total equipment figure comparable to our total improvements figure. Like Kuznets (1946, 214), we assumed that the ratio of trade equipment to trade real estate was 0.333 for the entire period. The only justification is approximate ratio applied to a small sample of Massachusetts nonmanufacturing corporations in 1920–21.

## 9.6. Summary for Nonfarm Residential and Trade Real Estate and Equipment

Table 9.10 provides estimates for the value of trade equipment. Table 9.11 summarizes the results for trade and nonresidential real estate.

## 9.7. Real Estate in Churches, Schools, and Government Buildings

This section details the estimation of the current-price and constant-price (1860) capital stock on a decadal basis from 1840 to 1900 for churches and schools, and government buildings (see table 9.12). For churches, we

TABLE 9.10 **Value of trade equipment, measured in current and 1860 prices, 1840–1900, in millions of dollars**

|   |   | 1840 | 1850 | 1860 | 1870 | 1880 | 1890 | 1900 |
|---|---|---|---|---|---|---|---|---|
| 1 | Value at current prices | 65 | 126 | 319 | 439 | 708 | 1,633 | 2,073 |
| 2 | Price index | 140 | 137 | 100 | 117 | 98 | 86 | 74 |
| 3 | Value at 1860 prices | 46 | 92 | 319 | 375 | 722 | 1,899 | 2,761 |

Sources: Line 1: 0.333 × line 5, table 9.11. Line 2: Brady's index of office furniture (Brady 1966, pp. 110, 111), extrapolated to 1869 on the price index of furniture and to 1899 on the price index of sewing machines (p. 109), adjusted to reflect the "0" years rather than the "9" years, per the adjustment factor for buildings, described in the notes to table 8.9, and extrapolated to 1840 on the mean of the indexes in lines 2 and 5 of table 8.9. Line 3: 100 × line 1 ÷ line 2.

TABLE 9.11 **Value of trade and nonagricultural residential real estate, measured in current and 1860 prices, 1840–1900, in millions of dollars**

|   |   | 1840 | 1850 | 1860 | 1870 | 1880 | 1890 | 1900 |
|---|---|---|---|---|---|---|---|---|
| 1 | Trade and nonagricultural residential real estate | 780 | 1,516 | 3,837 | 5,271 | 8,504 | 19,621 | 24,539 |
| 2 | Nonagricultural residential real estate | 585 | 1,137 | 2,878 | 3,953 | 6,378 | 14,716 | 18,404 |
| 3 | Nonagricultural residential improvements | 373 | 724 | 1,833 | 2,518 | 4,063 | 9,374 | 11,723 |
| 4 | Nonagricultural residential land | 212 | 413 | 1,045 | 1,435 | 2,315 | 5,342 | 6,681 |
| 5 | Trade real estate | 195 | 379 | 959 | 1,318 | 2,126 | 4,905 | 6,135 |
| 6 | Trade improvements | 68 | 133 | 336 | 461 | 744 | 1,717 | 2,147 |
| 7 | Trade land | 127 | 246 | 623 | 856 | 1,382 | 3,188 | 3,988 |
| 8 | Price index of houses and churches | 95 | 96 | 100 | 128 | 130 | 135 | 132 |
| 9 | Nonagricultural residential improvements, at 1860 prices | 393 | 754 | 1,833 | 1,967 | 3,125 | 6,944 | 8,881 |
| 10 | Price index of stores and factories | 105 | 106 | 100 | 95 | 114 | 91 | 89 |
| 11 | Trade improvements, at 1860 prices | 65 | 125 | 336 | 485 | 653 | 1,887 | 2,412 |

Sources: Line 1: See tables 9.1, 9.2, 9.5, 9.7, and 9.9. Line 2: line 1 × 0.75; see text. Line 3: line 2 × 0.637; see text. Line 4: line 2 × 0.363; see text. Line 5: line 1 × 0.25; see text. Line 6: line 5 × 0.35; see text. Line 7: line 5 × 0.65; see text. Line 8: table 7.2. Line 9: 100 × line 3 ÷ line 8. Line 10: table 8.9, line 2b. [Rhode: 95 in 1870 is not consistent with the source, which lists 90.] Line 11: 100 × line 6 ÷ line 10.

adopted Weiss's (1975, 150–52) current-price estimates, which he treats as net. For educational facilities, we adopted Weiss's (1969, 157–60) current price estimate, covering public and private sectors, schools and colleges. Again we assume the estimates are net. Weiss's deflation procedure suggests that he regards the data as expressed in market values or reproduction costs. The capital consists chiefly of buildings, but also includes some

TABLE 9.12  **Value of churches, schools, and government buildings, measured in current and 1860 prices, 1840–1900, in millions of dollars**

|   |   | 1840 | 1850 | 1860 | 1870 | 1880 | 1890 | 1900 |
|---|---|---|---|---|---|---|---|---|
| 1 | Price index | 95 | 96 | 100 | 128 | 130 | 135 | 132 |
| **Churches** | | | | | | | | |
| 2 | Value, at current prices | 50 | 87.4 | 171.4 | 354.5 | 520 | 679.4 | 1,040 |
| 3 | Value, at 1860 prices | 52.6 | 91.0 | 171.4 | 277 | 400 | 503.3 | 787 |
| **Schools** | | | | | | | | |
| 4 | Value, at current prices | 37 | 69 | 114 | 179 | 281 | 471 | 785 |
| 5 | Value, at 1860 prices | 39 | 72 | 114 | 140 | 216 | 349 | 595 |
| **Government buildings** | | | | | | | | |
| 6 | Value, at current prices | 8 | 10 | 16 | 22 | 46 | 92 | 124 |
| 7 | Value, at 1860 prices | 8 | 9 | 16 | 21 | 44 | 94 | 111 |

Sources: Line 1: Brady's adjusted price index of houses, churches, and schools, taken from table 7.2. Line 2: Weiss 1975, 151, dates these figures to 1839, 1849, etc., by which he designates the census year, which covered parts of two calendar years. We date the figures here by the date to which the wealth returns refer, June of 1840, 1850, etc. Line 3: 100 × line 2 ÷ line 1. Line 4: Weiss 1969, 158. Line 5: 100 × line 4 ÷ line 1. Lines 6 and 7: derived from data in Weiss 1969, table 49, column 3, and table 50, columns 3 and 4, in the manner described in the text. Weiss dates his estimates to 1839, 1849, etc., by which he apparently refers to the census year, a year incorporating parts of two calendar years (1839 and 1840, etc.). We have identified the estimates with the second calendar year contributing to the census year, 1840, 1850, etc.

land and equipment. Thus we deflated using the adjusted Brady index of houses, churches, and schools (see table 7.2).

Government investments in canals, river improvements, railroads, education, and inventories (including inventories of monetary metals) are treated in other sections of this volume. Here we are concerned exclusively with the value of governmental buildings, the land on which they stood, and the equipment they contained. We adopted Weiss's (1969, 150–56) series, to which we added his estimates of the value of marine hospitals (federal hospitals). Weiss provides figures on constant-price (1860) net capital stock, but reports only gross stocks in current prices. We extrapolated his 1860 net estimate on his gross series, to obtain net estimates in current prices for all years. We deflated his figures on the net value of marine hospitals by his implicit deflator for government buildings. While buildings were the principal element of capital covered by Weiss, small amounts of land and equipment also form part of his series. We did not attempt to disentangle these three elements of government property.

Estimates better devised to meet our current requirements could be made by rearranging the elements that make up the Weiss estimates, and by introducing the adjusted Brady deflators described in previous sections (Weiss used the unadjusted Brady series). But the necessary details are not available in Weiss's published work, and the improvements to be expected from the additional work would not be large, particularly in the context of the full array of our national capital stock estimates. Thus, we did not attempt to carry out these rearrangements and adjustments.

## 9.8. Conclusion

This chapter presents estimates of the capital stock in the nonfarm residences, the trade sector, churches and schools, and government buildings.

## CHAPTER TEN

# Transportation

## 10.1. Introduction

This chapter details the estimation of the current-price and constant-price (1860) capital stock on a decadal basis from 1840 to 1900 for the transportation sector. It covers, in turn, shipping, canals and river improvements, steam railroads, street railroads, Pullman and express cars, and pipelines.

## 10.2. Shipping

### 10.2.1. Current Value of Vessels

The censuses of 1880 and 1890 include statements of the value of vessels that seem reliable. The 1880 value of sailing vessels was established by an insurance expert; steam valuations were apparently obtained from steamboat owners (US Census Office 1883b, 718–19). In 1890 all valuations were "commercial valuations" estimated by owners (US Census Office 1895b, xii, 5). The fact that both steam and sailing values per ton show small increases between 1880 and 1890 is encouraging. All the appraisals appear to be in current market values.

We used the census data for 1880 and 1890 without modification. Our 1900 estimate is from Kuznets, who interpolated between 1890 and 1906 on the basis of tonnage figures (see table 10.1 and accompanying notes for details).

Gallman wrote the substance of this chapter. "We" and "our" refers to Gallman and Howle.

For 1870 and earlier, only official tonnage data are available. We first modified them to exclude ghost tonnage (US Bureau of the Census 1960, series Q-155, Q-161, Q-162, Q-178, Q-179). Then we extrapolated the 1880 valuations per ton, for each kind of vessel, back to 1840 on the basis of the adjusted Brady price index of ships and boats. Finally, we multiplied the tonnage figures by valuations per ton for each kind of vessel (steam, sail, and other) to yield total valuations (see table 10.1 and accompanying notes for details).[1]

Since the Brady index relates to the prices of vessels of constant size and quality, since price per ton was positively associated with size of vessel, and since the size of vessels was increasing, the current price series we computed is almost certainly biased upward, although probably only modestly—the bias being greater the earlier the date of the estimate.

### 10.2.2. Constant Value of Vessels

The current value of vessels was deflated by the Brady index.

### 10.2.3. Real Estate in Shipping

We were unable to develop an accurate estimate of the value of real estate in shipping. Rather than omit this component of capital entirely, we used a rough estimating procedure developed by Kuznets. We divided real estate between land and improvements according to our ratio for trade and nonfarm residential real estate. The improvement estimate was then deflated by Brady's adjusted price index for factories and stores (see table 10.1 for details).

## 10.3. Canals and River Improvements

### 10.3.1. Coverage

All canals and all river improvements, whether part of a canal system or not, are included. For convenience, we will henceforth use the term "canals" to include river improvements.

### 10.3.2. Derivation of Cost Estimates

We first estimated the cost of canal construction by decades. For the period 1815 through 1860, the most reliable source is an annual construction

TABLE 10.1  **Value of vessels and real estate in shipping, measured in current and 1860 prices, 1840–1900**

| | 1840 | 1850 | 1860 | 1870 | 1880 | 1890 | 1900 |
|---|---|---|---|---|---|---|---|
| Ghost tonnage deduction | 12% | 10% | 2.50% | — | — | — | — |
| **Steam vessels** | | | | | | | |
| Tons (in thousands) | 202 | 526 | 868 | 1,075 | — | — | — |
| Adjusted tonnage | 178 | 473 | 846 | 1,075 | — | — | — |
| Value per ton (in dollars) | 148 | 109 | 87 | 73 | 66 | — | — |
| Value, at current prices (in millions of dollars) | 26.3 | 51.6 | 73.6 | 78.5 | — | — | — |
| **Sailing vessels** | | | | | | | |
| Tons (in thousands) | 1,582 | 2,408 | 3,589 | 2,363 | — | — | — |
| Adjusted tonnage | 1,392 | 2,167 | 3,499 | 2,363 | — | — | — |
| Value per ton (in dollars) | 56 | 41 | 33 | 28 | 25 | — | — |
| Value, at current prices (in millions of dollars) | 78 | 88.8 | 115.5 | 66.2 | — | — | — |
| **Other vessels** | | | | | | | |
| Tons (in thousands) | 1,189 | 1,956 | 2,971 | 2,292 | — | — | — |
| Adjusted tonnage | 1,046 | 1,760 | 2,897 | 2,292 | — | — | — |
| Value per ton (in dollars) | 12.8 | 9.5 | 7.5 | 6.3 | 5.7 | — | — |
| Value, at current prices (in millions of dollars) | 13.4 | 16.7 | 21.7 | 14.4 | — | — | — |
| **All vessels** | | | | | | | |
| Tons (in thousands) | 2,973 | 4,890 | 7,428 | 5,730 | — | — | — |
| Adjusted tonnage | 2,616 | 4,401 | 7,242 | 5,730 | — | — | — |
| Value per ton (in dollars) | 44.9 | 36 | 29 | 27.6 | — | — | — |
| Value, at current prices (in millions of dollars) | 117.5 | 158.4 | 210 | 158.1 | 156 | 221 | 343 |
| **Price index** | 170 | 126 | 100 | 84 | 76 | 57 | 51 |
| Value, at 1860 prices (in millions of dollars) | 69.1 | 125.7 | 210 | 188.2 | 205 | 388 | 673 |
| **Real estate** | | | | | | | |
| **Improvements, at current prices (in millions of dollars)** | 20.4 | 27.6 | 36.5 | 27.5 | 27.1 | 38.5 | 59.7 |
| Price index | 107 | 108 | 100 | 90 | 114 | 91 | 89 |
| Real estate | | | | | | | |
| **Improvements, at 1860 prices (in millions of dollars)** | 19.1 | 25.6 | 36.5 | 30.6 | 23.8 | 42.3 | 67.1 |
| **Land, at current prices (in millions of dollars)** | 26.6 | 35.8 | 47.5 | 35.7 | 35.3 | 49.9 | 77.5 |

Sources:

Line 1: For all years, US Bureau of the Census 1960, 439, indicates that in 1841 official tonnage figures were reduced by about 12 percent to eliminate ghost tonnage. We accordingly reduced the 1840 unadjusted data by 12 percent. The next adjustment for ghost tonnage was made in 1855–58 and resulted in an 18 percent reduction of official tonnage figures. We prorated this by years, deducting 10 percent from the 1850 tonnage data. We also reduced our 1860 estimate on the assumption that undeducted ship losses accumulated at the same rate per year after 1858 as they did from 1841 to 1858. It was not necessary to adjust the tonnage figures for 1870 and later, since ghost tonnage represented a much smaller part of the total (1–3 percent).

Line 2: For all years, US Bureau of the Census 1960, series Q-155. Lines 3, 7, 11, and 15, for all years, lines 2, 6, 10, and 14 respectively, reduced by the percentage in line 1.

Lines 4, 8, and 12: For all years, the 1880 values were computed from US Census Office 1883b, 718–19). The price index in line 18 was used as an extrapolator to estimate values in 1840–70 from values in 1880.

Lines 5, 9, 13: For all years, adjusted tonnage multiplied by value per ton.

Line 6: For 1870, US Bureau of the Census 1960, series Q-161, hereafter Historical Statistics.

For 1840–60, certain vessels were included in the data that were not included in our 1880 value-per-ton figure. We reduced the Historical Statistics figure by 20 percent to account for this. The 20 percent estimate is somewhat arbitrary, since we know the tonnage of these vessels only after they were excluded from the sailing category. In the years from 1868 to 1875, the sailing category was smaller than it would have been if the pre-1869 classification had been used, by the following percentages:

1868  1869  1870  1871  1872  1873  1874  1875
20%   21%   25%   28%   30%   33%   32%   30%

US Bureau of the Census 1960, series Q-161 and Q-162. After 1875, the information for a comparison is not available. It can be seen that the data we have are insufficient to indicate a definite trend. Therefore, we reduced the 1840, 1850, and 1860 figures by 20 percent, the ratio computed from the 1868 data.

Line 10: Unfortunately, the 1960 Historical Statistics figures included only documented vessels. Many internal, non–passenger-carrying vessels were excluded. The "other ships" (canal boats and barges, series Q162) category in the 1960 Historical Statistics is therefore not nearly so broad as the ones in the 1880 or 1890 census. This miscellaneous category in 1880 made up 44 percent of total tonnage, and in 1890 it made up 57 percent. We assumed that this category made up 40 percent of total tonnage prior to 1880. Even though the tonnage is quite significant, the value is not, since this category has a low pre-ton value. See US Bureau of the Census 1960.

Line 14: For all years, line 2 + line 6 + line 10.

Line 16: For all years, line 17 ÷ line 15 (expressed in millions).

Line 17: For 1840–70, line 5 + line 9 + line 13. For 1880, US Census Office 1883b, 718–19. For 1890, US Census Office 1895b, xii, 5. For 1900, we accepted Kuznets's interpolation between 1890 and 1906, derived as follows: "The value of vessels is estimated as the product of the tonnage and the value per ton. Tonnage is interpolated between 1890 and 1906 (for 1890 given in [US Census Office 1897] and for 1906 in [US Bureau of the Census 1908] by tonnage of the total merchant marine [US Bureau of Navigation 1923]. Value per ton, computed for 1890 and 1906, is interpolated along a straight line. Value figures for 1890 and 1906 are from the sources cited for tonnage" (Kuznets 1946, 215).

Line 18: Brady 1966, 110–11, adjusted as follows. The Brady index numbers refer to the wrong years (see chapter 7, above). However, the evidence on lumber prices and the wage rates paid by shipbuilding firms suggest that the Brady indexes require no adjustment on this account, except for 1880 (1879). The Brady index of 1879 had to be raised by 5 percent to approximate a vessel's price index for 1880, an adjustment we made. See the Aldrich Report (US Senate 1893, 228 [white oak boards], 232 [yellow pine boards], 229 [white pine boards], and 238 [spruce boards]; Henry Hall 1884, 245–46; Joseph D. Weeks 1886, 499–500; US Bureau of the Census 1949, series L-9 and L-10. Brady reported price index numbers for census years 1834, 1844, and 1854, but not for 1839 or 1849. The 1834, 1844, and 1854 index numbers were found to be good proxies for index numbers for calendar years 1835, 1845, and 1855 (see above). We then interpolated between these values on data from the Weeks Report (Weeks 1886, 499), to obtain index numbers for 1840 and 1850 (calendar years).

Line 19: 100 × line 17 ÷ line 18.

Line 20: For all years, very little information is available on which to construct an estimate of real estate in shipping. Kuznets (1946, 211), used 1880 steamship figures to compute a ratio of the value of real estate to the value of vessels, a ratio he then used to estimate the value of real estate in shipping. We accepted Kuznets's ratio (0.40). We divided real estate between land (0.565) and improvements (0.435) according to ratios developed in Chapter 9.2, above.

Line 21: For all years, table 8.9, Line 5.

Line 22: For all years, 100 × line 20 ÷ line 21.

Line 23: For all years, same method as for line 20.

cost series done by H. Jerome Cranmer (1960, 547–64) and modified by
Harvey Segal (1961, 169–215). An alternate source for the period is US
Census Office (1883b), where cost and dates of construction are given for
each canal. The census estimates are slightly higher than the Cranmer-
Segal series, apparently because they include some maintenance costs and
noncanal assets. We therefore used the Cranmer-Segal estimates, with minor modifications (as indicated in table 10.2 and table 10.3) to include
river improvements and pre-1815 canal construction.

All of our cost figures for the 1860–1900 period are from the US Census Office (1883b, 753) and US Bureau of the Census (1929, 72–73). The
1860–80 census data omitted river improvements that were not part of a
canal system and canals constructed by the federal government. We modified the census data to include estimates of these items, as indicated in
tables 10.2 and 10.3.

Having determined the cost of canal construction by decades, we then
adjusted the data to exclude obsolete canals. When properly maintained,
canals do not wear out, but the development of the railroads made obsolescence an important factor. We deducted the cost of abandoned canals
from our decade cost totals from US Census Office 1883b and US Bureau
of the Census 1929. (The former source lists individual abandoned canals and dates of abandonment.) In addition, the value of an abandoned
canal can be considered to have been greatly impaired for a number of
years prior to abandonment, due to reduced traffic and inadequate maintenance. To compensate for this factor, we assumed that any canal abandoned during the ten years following a valuation date was of no value on
that date. For example, our 1870 canal estimate excludes the cost of all
canals abandoned before *1880*. This adjustment is the equivalent of our
depreciation adjustments of other wealth categories.

### 10.3.3. Division of Cost into Improvements, Equipment, and Land

We assumed that all construction costs were for improvements; land could
hardly have accounted for 1 percent of the total cost of canals. The principal component of equipment—and the only one we took into account—
was canal boats, which form part of our shipping series.

### 10.3.4. Derivation of Constant Cost Estimates

The cost basis estimates were deflated by decade of construction, as shown
in table 10.4. To obtain the construction dates of canals in operation at

TABLE 10.2 **Book value of canals, June 30, 1840, to June 30, 1900, in millions of dollars**

| | |
|---|---|
| Operating canals, 1840 | 112 |
| Less those abandoned, 1840–50[a] | −2 |
| | |
| Value of canals, 1840 | 110 |
| Add construction, 1840–50 | +44 |
| | |
| Operating canals, 1850 | 154 |
| Less those abandoned, 1850–60 | −3 |
| | |
| Value of canals, 1850 | 151 |
| Add construction, 1850–60 | +39 |
| | |
| Operating canals, 1860 | 190 |
| Less those abandoned, 1860–70 | −6 |
| | |
| Value of canals, 1860 | 184 |
| Add construction, 1860–70 | +9 |
| | |
| Operating canals, 1870 | 193 |
| Less those abandoned, 1870–80 | −25 |
| | |
| Value of canals, 1870 | 168 |
| Add construction, 1870–80 | +12 |
| | |
| Operating canals, 1880 | 180 |
| Less those abandoned, 1880–90 | −7 |
| | |
| Value of canals, 1880 | 173 |
| Add construction, 1880–90 | +11 |
| | |
| Operating canals, 1890 | 184 |
| Less those abandoned, 1890–1900 | −13 |
| | |
| Value of canals, 1890 | 171 |
| Add construction, 1890–1900 | +59 |
| | |
| Operating canals, 1900 | 230 |
| Less those abandoned, 1900–10 | −19 |
| | |
| Value of canals, 1900 | 211 |

[a]i.e. From June 30, 1840 through June 30, 1850

Sources:

Line 1: According to Cranmer's estimate, as modified by Segal (1961, 208–9), $107 million was invested in canal construction between 1815 and 1840. (We interpolated the June 31, 1840, figure from year-end figures for 1839 and 1840.) We added $5 million to this, as a rough allowance for canals constructed before 1815. The abandonment of canals prior to 1840 was negligible, so no adjustment on this account was necessary. See Goodrich's introduction to Segal 1961, 7, for a comment on abandonment. Lines 2, 6, 10, and 14: Estimated from data in US Census Office 1883b, we adjusted the census data upward by 5 percent to account for those abandoned canals with no valuation listed. Lines 18, 22, and 26: US Bureau of the Census 1929, 72–73. The 1890–1900 and 1900–1910 estimates were interpolated between 1889, 1906, and 1916. Lines 4 and 8: Segal 1961, 209, interpolated between year-end figures. To the Segal estimate we added the estimated cost of river improvements. See notes to lines 12 and 14. Lines 12 and 16: US Census Office 1883b listed the cost of construction of operating canals, and the dates of construction. From these data we estimated the decade totals. We added the cost of construction of US government-built canals and of river improvements that were not a part of canal systems, since neither was included in the census estimate. The costs of these categories were extrapolated from 1880, 1889, and 1906 on data found in U.S. Bureau of the Census 1908, 40. See table 10.3. Lines 20 and 24: US Bureau of the Census 1929, 72–73. The census lists the total cost of operating canals in 1880, 1889, and 1906. The cost of abandoned canals was also given for 1880–89, and 1889–1906. By subtracting the cost of operating canals in 1880 from the cost in 1889 and adding to the difference the cost of canals abandoned, we obtained the cost of canals constructed between 1880 and 1889. The same procedure was used for 1889–1906. The 1900 estimate was then interpolated between 1889 and 1906. We assumed that one-half of the total construction between 1889 and 1906 was carried out prior to 1900. We used only the incremental changes given in the census, not the census total cost figures, because we believe that the earlier canal cost totals are not accurate; see text. Lines 3, 5, 7, 9, 11, 13, 15, 17, 19, 21, 23, 25, and 27: Obtained from the other columns in this table by addition and subtraction as indicated.

TABLE 10.3 **Categories excluded from the Cranmer-Segal and tenth census estimates, 1840–1900, in millions of dollars**

|  | 1840 | 1850 | 1860 | 1870 | 1880 | 1889 | 1906 |
|---|---|---|---|---|---|---|---|
| US government canals | — | — | — | 4 | 8 | 21 | 27 |
| River improvements | — | 1 | 2 | 4 | 9 | 17 | 43 |
| Total | — | 1 | 2 | 8 | 17 | 38 | 70 |

Source: US Bureau of the Census 1908, 40.

each valuation date, we assumed that the canals abandoned earliest were the first to be constructed. Common labor is the major portion of construction cost. We therefore used Lebergott's common labor wage index as our price index. Since the wage index extends back only to 1832, we made a rough extrapolation to 1815, based on a comment by Segal regarding changes in canal construction costs during the 1815–44 period; see notes to table 10.2 for details.

## 10.4. Steam Railroads

### 10.4.1. Introduction

Two methods were available to us to make railroads asset estimates. The first, used by Kuznets (1946, 201–19), was to develop total capital estimates, break them down into their components using asset ratios (available for 1858 and 1880), and then apply appropriate price indexes to convert them to constant dollars. Instead, we used a procedure developed by Albert Fishlow (1965). The procedure allowed us to exploit more reliable evidence: evidence of the count of physical components of the capital stock. Indexes were developed that were adjusted for changes in resource content per unit of component. For example, a mile of track in 1850 might be considered to be the equivalent of 0.9 miles of track in 1900. Fishlow followed this procedure for track, locomotives, freight cars, and passenger cars. He then combined the indexes into an index of improvements and one of equipment, and used 1909 prices to convert them to constant dollars. Because we wanted our series in 1860 prices, we applied 1860 valuations to Fishlow's improvement and equipment series.[2] See table 10.5. The 1860 valuations were based on census data, but were modified because the census valuations did not represent the true value of the assets.

## 10.4.2. Value of 1860 Fixed Capital

The 1860 census lists $1,151.6 million as the cumulative cost of construction of railroads to that date (US Census Office 1866, 331). From what we know of railroad accounting methods of the period, we can be confident that no depreciation had been deducted. In addition, railroads typically paid for construction materials with stock; the result was that assets were set up on the books at valuations considerably above their cash prices. Fishlow's adjustment of the census cost of construction figure to exclude overvaluations, land purchases and non-railroad assets, and to include omitted railroads, reduced the census return from $1,151.6 to $990.7 million.[3] This figure is net of retirements, but gross of depreciation. It is also on a cost basis, which may represent a deviation from 1860 market prices. But before addressing these problems, we will show how we divided the total between improvements and equipment.

## 10.4.3. Value of Improvements and Equipment in 1860

Based on a sample of railroad balance sheets in 1858, we estimated that improvements made up 89.2 percent and equipment 10.8 percent of the total value of improvements and equipment. The sample from which we derived this estimate was weighted for size of railroad, to parallel the size distribution of the total population.[4] On this basis we divided Fishlow's total between its two major components (see table 10.6, panel A.)

Fishlow's (1965, 389) price indexes for railroad equipment and improvements indicate that there is no need to adjust the 1860 valuation from book to current value. Assuming a twenty-year life-span of equipment, and interpolating our equipment growth rate along the change in mileage (table 10.7), shows that the prices at which equipment was entered on the books averaged about 98 percent of average 1860 prices. The deviation of the book value of improvements from the 1860 price level was even smaller. We therefore used the estimates in table 10.6, panel A, as if they were in 1860 dollars—that is, as if they represented gross reproduction cost estimates.

Next, our equipment and improvements estimates had to be depreciated. Fishlow's equipment series is already properly depreciated, using a twenty- to twenty-five-year life, but we had to depreciate our 1860 value of equipment before we applied it to his series. Conveniently, we could use the ratio of undepreciated values to depreciated values for 1860 that

TABLE 10.4  **Value of canals and river improvements, measured in current and 1860 prices, 1840–1900, in millions of dollars**

| Date of valuation | Date of construction[a] | | | | | | | | | |
|---|---|---|---|---|---|---|---|---|---|---|
| | (1) | (2) | (3) | (4) | (5) | (6) | (7) | (8) | (9) | (10) |
| | Pre-1815 | 1815–35 | 1835–40 | 1840–50 | 1850–60 | 1860–70 | 1870–80 | 1880–90 | 1890–1900 | All |
| Price index (1860 = 100) | 73 | 73 | 91 | 91 | 91 | 131 | 126 | 127 | 136 | |
| **1840** | | | | | | | | | | |
| Cost valuation | 2 | 61 | 47 | | | | | | | 110 |
| Constant value | 3 | 84 | 52 | | | | | | | 139 |
| **1850** | | | | | | | | | | |
| Cost valuation | | 60 | 47 | 44 | | | | | | 151 |
| Constant value | | 82 | 52 | 48 | | | | | | 182 |
| **1860** | | | | | | | | | | |
| Cost valuation | | 54 | 47 | 44 | 39 | | | | | 184 |
| Constant value | | 74 | 52 | 48 | 43 | | | | | 217 |
| **1870** | | | | | | | | | | |
| Cost valuation | | 29 | 47 | 44 | 39 | 9 | | | | 168 |
| Constant value | | 40 | 52 | 48 | 43 | 7 | | | | 190 |

| | 1 | 2 | 3 | 4 | 5 | 6 | 7 | 8 | 9 |
|---|---|---|---|---|---|---|---|---|---|
| **1880** | | | | | | | | | |
| Cost valuation | 22 | 47 | 44 | 39 | 9 | 12 | | | 173 |
| Constant value | 30 | 52 | 48 | 43 | 7 | 10 | | | 190 |
| **1890** | | | | | | | | | |
| Cost valuation | 9 | 47 | 44 | 39 | 9 | 12 | 11 | | 171 |
| Constant value | 12 | 52 | 48 | 43 | 7 | 10 | 9 | | 181 |
| **1900** | | | | | | | | | |
| Cost valuation | 37 | | 44 | 39 | 9 | 12 | 11 | 59 | 211 |
| Constant value | 41 | | 48 | 43 | 7 | 10 | 9 | 43 | 201 |

ᵃThe dates refer to intervals extending from June 30 of the first date to June 30 of the second.

Sources:

Line 1: The price index is a common labor wage index for all years after 1834. For 1834–90, it is based on Lebergott's (1964, 298, 541) common labor daily earnings index. We shifted the Lebergott index to an 1860 base. The decade averages for 1850–60 and 1880–90 were obtained by averaging the wage index for the beginning and end of the decade, since annual data are not available. At least we know that this procedure is fairly reliable for 1880–90, since other wage indexes show a relatively constant increase from year to year during this period. Annual figures are available (Lebergott 1964, 298) for 1860–80, and the index numbers in this period are averages of the yearly indexes.

For 1890–1900, the Lebergott index was extrapolated on the index of lower skilled labor from US Bureau of the Census 1960, series D-602. Annual data were averaged to produce the decade indexes.

The pre-1835 index values are based on a statement by Segal (1961, 186): "We believe . . . that average construction cost rose sharply between the first (1815–34) and second (1834–44) canal cycles—perhaps by as much as thirty-three percent." David and Solar's (1977, 59) data suggest that the figure may have been more like 17 or 18 percent. We assumed a 25 percent increase.

Lines 2, 4, 6, 8, 10, 12, and 14: table 10.2. The pre-1840 values were broken down by construction cycle according to the Segal (1961, 208–9) annual construction index. Canals abandoned in the decade following each census date were treated as obsolete and of no value on the census date. See text.

Lines 3, 5, 7, 8, 11, 13, and 15: Lines 2, 4, 6, 8, 10, 12, and 14 respectively, divided by the price index and multiplied by 100.

TABLE 10.5  **Fishlow's railroad price indexes**

|      | Equipment | Improvement |
|------|-----------|-------------|
| 1840 | 79.3      | 99.8        |
| 1841 | 78.9      | 92.3        |
| 1842 | 76.2      | 90.2        |
| 1843 | 73.8      | 101.7       |
| 1844 | 75.5      | 99.0        |
| 1845 | 78.2      | 99.2        |
| 1846 | 83.3      | 110.9       |
| 1847 | 88.0      | 106.9       |
| 1848 | 86.5      | 99.3        |
| 1849 | 86.0      | 94.0        |
| 1850 | 84.3      | 88.2        |
| 1851 | 85.1      | 88.3        |
| 1852 | 87.1      | 89.0        |
| 1853 | 91.4      | 98.3        |
| 1854 | 96.7      | 108.0       |
| 1855 | 100.0     | 97.5        |
| 1856 | 100.1     | 106.5       |
| 1857 | 103.1     | 109.0       |
| 1858 | 106.3     | 104.0       |
| 1859 | 102.7     | 100.4       |
| 1860 | 100.0     | 100.0       |

Source: Correspondence with Albert Fishlow

is implicit in the Fishlow figures. We simply recomputed the 1860 value in Fishlow's series, but this time left out all adjustment for depreciation and retirements. In this way we determined that the depreciated value of equipment in 1858 was 65.3 percent of the new value, and we therefore multiplied the total cost of equipment, including retired equipment, by 0.653 to obtain the approximate depreciated value of equipment in 1860 (see table 10.6, panel B).

We could not follow the same procedure for depreciating improvements, because a useable estimate of depreciation is not implied in Fishlow's improvements index. Fishlow (1966c, 600) depreciated the long-lived railroad improvements (road bed), but assumed that the ratio of depreciated value to new value would remain about the same throughout the period for rails and ties. This assumption is reasonable as far as the index is concerned, but to apply our 1860 values to the index we had to depreciate all assets.[5] Fishlow (1966c, 596) estimated the accumulated depreciation on long-lived improvements at 8.9 percent of the value of *all* improvements in 1858, and 13.8 percent in 1869. An interpolation yields 9.8 for

TABLE 10.6  **Value of railroad assets, 1860, in millions of dollars**

**Panel A. Gross book value of railroad assets, 1860**

| 1 | Improvements | 883.70 |
|---|---|---|
| 2 | Equipment | 107 |
| 3 | Improvements and equipment | 990.70 |

**Panel B. Depreciated value of railroad equipment (net reproduction cost), 1860**

| 1 | Book value of equipment, December 1860 | 107.00 |
|---|---|---|
| 2 | Retirements through 1860 | 8.90 |
| 3 | Undepreciated value of equipment | 115.9 |
| 4 | Ratio of depreciated to undepreciated value | 0.653 |
| 5 | Depreciated value of equipment | 75.7 |
| 6 | Line 5 extrapolated from December to June | 73.7 |

**Panel C. Depreciated value of railroad improvements (net reproduction cost), 1860**

| 1 | Book value of improvements, December 1860 | 883.7 |
|---|---|---|
| 2 | Less depreciation | 199.7 |
| 3 | Depreciated value of improvements | 684 |
| 4 | Line 3 extrapolated from December to June | 666.2 |

Sources: Panel A. See text.
Panel B. Line 1: panel A, line 2. Line 2: communication from Albert Fishlow. Line 3: line 1 + line 2. Line 4: See text. Line 5: line 3 × line 4. Line 6: Line 5 was extrapolated for six months according to the interpolated change in railroad mileage in US Bureau of the Census 1960, series Q-43.
Panel C. Line 1: panel A, line 1. Line 2: The depreciation adjustment of 0.226 × line 1; see text. Line 3: line 1 − line 2. Line 4: Line 3 was extrapolated for six months according to the interpolated change in railroad mileage in US Bureau of the Census 1960, series Q-43.

1860. For all practical purposes, retirements of these assets were nil as of that date. To the cumulated depreciation of long-lived improvements we added the depreciation of rails and ties to obtain an estimate of the total accumulated depreciation of improvements still in use in 1860. (Since this total excludes retired assets, there was no need to add retired improvements to our book value of improvements, as we did with equipment.)

If we assume a ten-year life of rails and ties and interpolate Fishlow's improvements index along the change in railroad mileage, we find the depreciated value of rails and ties in use in 1860 amounting to about 62 percent of their new value.[6] This is probably too high, since rerolled rails were extensively used for replacement purposes (Fishlow 1965, 130). We have not been able to determine how much this affected the total value of all rails, but we lowered our estimate of the ratio of depreciated to

TABLE 10.7  Value of railroad equipment, measured in 1860 prices, 1840–1900

| | (1) | (2) | (3) | (4) | (5) | (6) | (7) | (8) | (9) | (10) |
|---|---|---|---|---|---|---|---|---|---|---|
| | Value, at 1909 prices, in millions of dollars | Decade increase | Track mileage | Track mileage | Track mileage | Ratio of mileage increase | Equipment increases to census date | Value, at 1909 prices, in millions of dollars | Equipment index (1860 = 100). | Value, at 1860 prices, in millions of dollars |
| Dec. 1838 | 2.9 | | 1,879 | | | | | | | |
| June 1840 | | | 2,510 | | 631 | 0.144 | 1.2 | 4.1 | 0.062 | 4.57 |
| Dec. 1848 | 11.4 | 8.5 | 6,262 | | 4,383 | | | | | |
| June 1850 | | | 7,941 | | 1,679 | 0.0863 | 4.1 | 15.5 | 0.233 | 17.2 |
| Dec. 1858 | 59.2 | 47.8 | 25,713 | | 19,451 | | | | | |
| June 1860 | | | 28,170 | | 2,457 | 0.138 | 7.2 | 66.4 | 1.00 | 73.7 |
| Dec. 1869 | 111.7 | 52.5 | 43,512 | 46,844 | 17,799 | | | | | |
| June 1870 | | | 49,883 | | 3,039 | 0.0765 | 13.3 | 125 | 1.883 | 138.8 |
| Dec. 1879 | 286.1 | 174.4 | 86,556 | | 39,712 | | | | | |
| June 1880 | | | 89,909 | | 3,353 | 0.0449 | 14.4 | 300.5 | 4.526 | 333.6 |
| Dec. 1889 | 606.8 | 320.7 | 160,884 | 161,276 | 74,720 | | | | | |
| June 1890 | | | 163,597 | | 2,713 | 0.0891 | 12.7 | 619.5 | 9.33 | 687.6 |
| Dec. 1899 | 749.6 | 142.8 | 191,321 | | 30,437 | | | | | |
| June 1900 | | | 193,346 | | 2,025 | 0.0429 | 39 | 788.6 | 11.877 | 875.3 |
| Dec. 1909 | 1658.2 | 908.6 | 238,564 | | 47,243 | | | | | |

Sources: Column 1: Fishlow 1966c, 606; see text. Column 2: column 1 less the column 1 estimate ten years earlier (i.e., the 1848 entry in column 2 is the 1848 entry in column 1 less the 1838 entry in column 1). Columns 3 and 4: Three different mileage series (miles built, miles operated, miles owned) were pieced together. See US Bureau of the Census 1960, series Q-15, Q-43, Q-47. The June estimates were obtained by interpolation, down to 1890; the December estimates were obtained thereafter. Column 5: the increase in columns 3 or 4 between the index date and the census date, and between two index dates (i.e., the 1840 entry in column 3 is the increase in column 3 from 1838 to 1840, while the 1848 entry in column 3 from 1838 to 1848). Column 6: The increase in mileage in column 5 from December 1838 to June 1840 is this portion of the increase from December 1838 to December 1840. The same procedure was used for other years. Column 7: Column 6 × column 2 entry for the corresponding period (i.e., the 1840 entry in column 6 was multiplied by the 1848 entry in column 2 to yield the 1840 column 7 figure). Column 8: To the column 1 index was added the interpolated increase indicated in column 7. Column 9: Column 8 was divided by its own 1860 entry so that 1860 = 100. Column 10: The 1860 figure is from table 10.6 in panel B above. For other years, the 1860 entry was multiplied by the column 9 entry for each respective year (i.e., for the 1870 estimate, 73.7 × 1.883 = 125.4).

undepreciated value from 62 to 60 percent, as a rough allowance. This meant lowering the value of rails and ties by 40 percent, or, since rails and ties made up about 32 percent of all improvements, lowering the value of the latter by 40 percent × 32 percent = 12.8 percent. Adding this to Fishlow's 9.8 percent depreciation of long-lived improvements gives a total depreciation allowance of 22.6 percent.

### 10.4.4. Equipment and Improvements: Constant Value Series

The Fishlow equipment and improvements indexes could now be used to determine the 1860 dollar value of these assets in all other years. As already mentioned, the indexes represent weighted physical counts of assets that have been adjusted for changes in resource content (over time) per unit of asset. The application of 1860 valuations to the Fishlow indexes is shown in table 10.7 for equipment, and in table 10.8 for improvements. (The indexes had first to be interpolated along rail mileage to coincide with census years.) Table 10.9 summarizes the results.

TABLE 10.8 **Value of railroad improvements, measured in 1860 prices, 1840–1900**

| | (1) | (2) | (3) | (4) | (5) | (6) | (7) |
|---|---|---|---|---|---|---|---|
| | Value, at 1909 prices, in millions of dollars | Decade increase | Ratio of mileage increase | Improvements increases to census date | Value, at 1909 prices, in millions of dollars | Improvement index 1860 = 100 | Value, at 1860 prices, in millions of dollars |
| Dec. 1838 | 1,986 | | | | | | |
| June 1840 | | | 0.144 | 500 | 2,486 | 0.092 | 61.3 |
| Dec. 1848 | 5,458 | 3,472 | | | | | |
| June 1850 | | | 0.0863 | 1,676 | 7,134 | 0.264 | 175.9 |
| Dec. 1858 | 24,877 | 19,419 | | | | | |
| June 1860 | | | 0.138 | 2,159 | 27,036 | 1.000 | 666.2 |
| Dec. 1869 | 40,533 | 15,656 | | | | | |
| June 1870 | | | 0.0765 | 2,630 | 43,163 | 1.597 | 1063.9 |
| Dec. 1879 | 74,906 | 34,373 | | | | | |
| June 1880 | | | 0.0449 | 3,190 | 78,096 | 2.889 | 1924.7 |
| Dec. 1889 | 145,949 | 71,043 | | | | | |
| June 1890 | | | 0.0891 | 2,092 | 148,041 | 5.476 | 3648.1 |
| Dec. 1899 | 169,429 | 23,480 | | | | | |
| June 1900 | | | 0.0429 | 2,122 | 171,551 | 6.345 | 4227 |
| Dec. 1909 | 218,897 | 49,468 | | | | | |

Sources: Column 1: Fishlow 1966c, 596; see text. Column 2: See notes to table 10.7, column 2. Column 3: table 10.7, column 6. Columns 4, 5, 6 and 7: derived in the same manner as columns 7, 8, 9 and 10, respectively, in table 10.7. The 1860 figure in column 7 is from table 10.6, panel C.

TABLE 10.9 **Value of railroad capital and land, measured in current and 1860 prices, 1840–1900, in millions of dollars**

|  | 1840 | 1850 | 1860 | 1870 | 1880 | 1890 | 1900 |
|---|---|---|---|---|---|---|---|
| **Equipment** | | | | | | | |
| 1 Value, at 1860 prices | 4.57 | 17.2 | 73.7 | 138.8 | 333.6 | 687.6 | 875.3 |
| 2 Price index | 79.3 | 84.3 | 100 | 62 | 61 | 49 | 43 |
| 3 Value, at current prices | 3.62 | 14.5 | 73.7 | 86.1 | 203.5 | 336.9 | 376.4 |
| **Improvement** | | | | | | | |
| 4 Value, at 1860 prices | 61.3 | 175.9 | 666.2 | 1,063.9 | 1,924.7 | 3,648.1 | 4,227.0 |
| 5 Price index | 99.8 | 88.2 | 100 | 151.3 | 117.1 | 107.6 | 109 |
| 6 Value, at current prices | 61.2 | 155.1 | 666.2 | 1,609.7 | 2,253.8 | 3,925.4 | 4,607.4 |
| **Land** | | | | | | | |
| 7 Value, at current prices | 4.3 | 10.9 | 46.6 | 112.7 | 157.8 | 274.8 | 322.5 |

Sources:

Line 1: Table 10.7, column 10.

Lines 2 and 5: 1840–60: Fishlow 1965, 389. 1870–1900: The equipment index is from Brady 1966, 111, adjusted per the notes to table 8.9. The improvements index was constructed following the procedures of Fishlow 1965, 387–90. We used the same wage rate series (weight of 6) as Fishlow (Lebergott 1960, 462). Unfortunately, Lebergott has no wage data for 1890 and 1900; we were obliged to substitute data for 1889 and 1899. For the building materials price index (weight 1) Fishlow used US Senate 1893; we substituted the Warren-Pearson index, which seems to have a slightly better structure and also covers the full period we required, which the Aldrich Report index does not. (See Fishlow's discussion of the Aldrich Report index, p. 390.) For the weights of the Warren-Pearson index, see Warren and Pearson 1932, 128. We constructed a chained rail price index (weight 3) from data in American Iron and Steel Association 1912, 86–89. The link between 1860 and 1870 was established on the basis of domestic iron rail prices (American Iron and Steel Association 1912, 87); the link between 1870 and subsequent years, on the basis of domestic steel rail prices (American Iron and Steel Association 1912, 89). Fishlow used imported rail prices in the antebellum period, since imports composed a large part of the rails used by American railroads. After the Civil War, domestic supply dominated the market.

Line 3: line 1 × line 2 ÷ 100. Line 5: table 10.8, column 7. Line 6: line 4 × line 5 ÷ 100. Line 7: A sample of railroad balance sheets taken from US Census Office 1883b, 60–131, indicates that land values amounted to percent of the value of improvements. Fishlow's (1965, 119) study shows that the percentage was about the same in the prewar period. Line 7 is therefore 7 percent of line 6.

## 10.5. Street Railways

### 10.5.1. Introduction

The value of street railways (gross book value) is listed in the censuses of 1860, 1890, and 1900 (Ulmer 1960, 159, 163). In addition, some data are available for 1870 and 1880 from US and state sources. Using these sources we developed undepreciated book value estimates, then depreciated and deflated to obtain our current and constant price series.

### 10.5.2. Undepreciated Book Values

**1880–90.** We used Kuznets's (1946, 201–2, 208–9, 213, 215) gross current price series, the estimates for 1890 and 1900, taken from the census, and the estimate for 1880, extrapolated on miles of track.

**1850–70.** Ulmer computed the total value of street railways for 1870, using the reports of the railroad commissions, but his sample covered only three states. He assumed that these three states contained the same portion of the total US street railways in 1870 as they did in 1890 (Ulmer 1946, 403, 413). We accepted Ulmer's estimate *for these three states*, but followed a different procedure in the construction of a national estimate.

The 1860 census gives the major city passenger railways and lists the cost of "roads, equipment, etc." as $14,862,840 (US Census Office 1866, 332). We do not know how reliable or complete the 1860 data are, how they were obtained, or even the concept of value involved, although we have assumed that it is gross book value. The implied growth rates of individual state roads after 1860 are plausible, however, and we therefore decided to accept the data in the absence of better evidence. Presumably the data were collected in the same way as other railroad data returned by the census.

The three states for which Ulmer has data (New York, Massachusetts, Pennsylvania) accounted for 93.2 percent of the total value of street railways in 1860, according to the census. Ulmer shows that in 1890 they contributed 48.7 percent of the total. We interpolated between 1860 and 1890, obtaining a value of 78.3 percent for 1870. We then divided Ulmer's data for the three states by 0.783 to get a figure of $45.57 million as the value of capital in 1870.

No primary data are available on which to base an estimate for 1850, but Willford King (1915, 257) published a figure of $4 million for that year. How King arrived at this result is unclear, but an exponential

TABLE 10.10  **Gross book value of capital of street railways, 1850–1900, in millions of dollars**

|   |                       | 1850 | 1860 | 1870 | 1880 | 1890 | 1900  |
|---|-----------------------|------|------|------|------|------|-------|
| 1 | Land                  | 0.5  | 1.8  | 5.4  | 15   | 41   | 157   |
| 2 | Improvements          | 2.8  | 10.4 | 31.9 | 104  | 288  | 1,131 |
| 3 | Equipment and animals | 0.7  | 2.7  | 8.3  | 19   | 60   | 288   |
| 4 | Total durable capital | 4    | 14.9 | 45.6 | 138  | 389  | 1,576 |

Sources:
1850: The total capital estimate is by Willford King (1915, 257). It agrees with the extrapolated growth rate indicated by our later figures. The total was divided among land, equipment, and improvements by the same procedure as that used for 1860.
1860: Total durable capital is from US Census Office 1866, 332. The value of equipment was obtained by using an 1890 ratio of equipment to total durable capital from US Census Office (1895a, 697) data on animal-drawn street railways. The remaining fixed capital was divided between land and improvements in accordance with Ulmer's (1960, 415) estimate that land made up 11.9 percent of total durable capital for animal-drawn roads.
1870: Total durable capital was estimated as described in the text, above. The total was divided among land, improvements, and equipment by the same procedure as that used for 1860.
1880, 1890, 1900: Kuznets's (1946) tables IV.1, line 9; IV.2, line 9; and IV.3, line 8.

TABLE 10.11 Net book values of street railway improvements, measured in current and 1860 prices, 1840–1900, in millions of dollars

| | | (1) | (2) | (3) | (4) | (5) | (6) | (7) | (8) |
|---|---|---|---|---|---|---|---|---|---|
| | | | | | | | | Improvements, depreciated | |
| | | 1840–50 | 1850–60 | 1860–70 | 1870–80 | 1880–90 | 1890–1900 | Cost basis | 1860 prices |
| 1 | Book value of improvements | 2.8 | 10.4 | 31.9 | 104 | 288 | 1,131 | | |
| 2 | increase | 2.8 | 7.6 | 21.5 | 72 | 184 | 843 | | |
| 3 | retirements | | | | 2.8 | 7.6 | 21.5 | | |
| 4 | Gross capital formation | 2.8 | 7.6 | 21.5 | 75 | 192 | 865 | | |
| 5 | Depreciated value on evaluation date | 1850 | 2.4 | | | | | | 2.4 | 2.9 |
| 6 | 1860 | 1.5 | 6.6 | | | | | 8.1 | 8.6 |
| 7 | 1870 | 0.6 | 4.1 | 18.6 | | | | 23.3 | 19.8 |
| 8 | 1880 | | 1.5 | 11.5 | 65 | | | 78 | 59.2 |
| 9 | 1890 | | | 4.3 | 40.1 | 166 | | 210.3 | 180.9 |
| 10 | 1900 | | | | 15 | 102 | 750 | 867 | 794 |
| 11 | Price index | Decade | 94 | 94.4 | 125.7 | 134.2 | 112.4 | 108.3 | |

Sources:

Columns 1–6. Line 1: table 10.10, book value at the end of the decade designated. Line 2: line 1, less line 1 entry for previous date. Line 3: A 30-year life span was assumed. Line 4: line 2 + line 3.

Lines 5–10: The gross capital formation for each decade was depreciated 3.33 percent per year. We assumed that the average age of capital formed during each decade was four years at the end of the decade. This assumption is approximately correct for the growth rate indicated. Line 11: table 10.9, column 6, means of terminal-year values, approximating decade averages.

Column 7: for all years, the totals of Cols. 1–6.

Column 8: Columns 1–6 were each divided by the relevant price index (line 11) and then multiplied by 100; the lines were then totaled for each valuation date.

TABLE 10.12  Net book value of street railway equipment, measured in current and 1860 prices, 1840–1900, in millions of dollars

| | | | (1) | (2) | (3) | (4) | (5) | (6) | (7) | (8) |
|---|---|---|---|---|---|---|---|---|---|---|
| | | | | | | | | | Equipment, depreciated | |
| | | | 1840–50 | 1850–60 | 1860–70 | 1870–80 | 1880–90 | 1890–1900 | Cost basis | 1860 prices |
| 1 | Book value of equipment | | 0.7 | 2.7 | 8.3 | 19 | 60 | 288 | | |
| 2 | increase | | 0.7 | 2.0 | 5.6 | 11 | 41 | 228 | | |
| 3 | retirements | | | | 0.7 | 2 | 6.3 | 13 | | |
| 4 | Gross capital formation | | 0.7 | 2.0 | 6.3 | 13 | 47 | 241 | | |
| 5 | Depreciated value | 1850 | 0.6 | 1.6 | | | | | 0.6 | 0.7 |
| 6 | on evaluation date | 1860 | 0.5 | 0.6 | 5.0 | | | | 0.8 | 2 |
| 7 | | 1870 | | | 1.9 | 10 | | | 5.6 | 6.8 |
| 8 | | 1880 | | | | 4 | 38 | | 11.9 | 18.6 |
| 9 | | 1890 | | | | | 14 | 193 | 42 | 76 |
| 10 | | 1900 | | | | | | 46 | 207 | 445 |
| 11 | Price index | Decade | 81.8 | 92.2 | 81 | 61.5 | 55 | 46 | | |

Sources: See notes to table 10.11. Here the life of equipment was assumed to be twenty years, and the average age of capital formed during each decade was assumed as four years. The price index is from table 10.9, the means of terminal year values (column 3) approximating decade averages.

extrapolation of our later estimates yields a value of slightly less than $5 million for 1850, so we accepted the King estimate.

The total asset figures for 1850, 1860, and 1870 were divided among land, improvements, and equipment according to 1870 and 1890 ratios. The notes to table 10.10 give further details.

### 10.5.3. Depreciation and Deflation

Depreciation and deflation of the book values are shown in tables 10.11 and 10.12; their derivation is explained in the notes.

## 10.6. Pullman and Express Cars

The value of equipment in this category is available for 1900 and 1904, but not for earlier years. We adjusted the 1900 figure and extrapolated it according to our general railway equipment category. US Bureau of the Census (1907, 22) gives a value of $98.8 million for Pullman and private cars in 1900. We assumed that the 1900 value given by the census is similar to the railroad valuation, since "the value of Pullman and Private cars was ascertained in connection with the estimates of the value of railroads" (US Bureau of the Census 1907, 23). In order to obtain an approximation to net reproduction cost, we reduced the stated valuation by the same proportion that our railroad estimate lies below the census returns for railroads (US Bureau of the Census 1907, 36). The adjusted 1900 Pullman and express valuation was then extrapolated along our current value general railroad equipment series. This seems to be appropriate because the ratio of Pullman

TABLE 10.13  **Value of Pullman and express cars, net reproduction cost, measured in current and 1860 prices, 1870–1900, in millions of dollars**

|   |   | **1870** | **1880** | **1890** | **1900** |
|---|---|---|---|---|---|
| 1 | Value, at current prices | 13.3 | 31 | 52 | 58 |
| 2 | Price index | 62 | 61 | 49 | 43 |
| 3 | Value, at 1860 prices | 21.5 | 551 | 106 | 135 |

Sources: Line 1, 1870–90, extrapolated from 1900 by the change in the current value of railroad equipment, table 10.9, line 4. 1900: The census estimate was $98.8 million. We reduced this by the ratio of our railroad asset valuation to the census valuation. 98.8 × 5307 ÷ 9036 = 58.0. See text and lines 4, 7, and 8 of table 10.9.
Line 2: see line 3 of table 10.9. Line 3: 100 × line 1 ÷ line 2.

TABLE 10.14  **Value of capital and land in pipelines, measured in current and 1860 prices, 1880–1900, in millions of dollars**

| | | Investment flows | | | Capital stocks | | |
|---|---|---|---|---|---|---|---|
| | | 1870–79 | 1880–89 | 1890–99 | 1880 | 1890 | 1900 |
| 1 | Net investment in improvements, book value | 10 | 32 | 99 | 10 | 42 | 141 |
| 2 | Price index (1860 = 100) | 126 | 127 | 136 | | | |
| 3 | Net investment in improvements, 1860 prices | 7.9 | 25 | 73 | 7.9 | 33 | 106 |
| 4 | Net investment in equipment, book value | 1 | 1 | 7 | 1 | 2 | 8 |
| 5 | Price index (1860 = 100) | 90.5 | 54 | 30 | | | |
| 6 | Net investment in equipment, 1860 prices | 1.1 | 1.9 | 23.3 | 1.1 | 3 | 25.2 |
| 7 | Value of land, at current prices | | | | 0.5 | 2 | 8 |

Sources: Line 1: Kuznets 1946, table IV, 2, line 17. We assumed that no improvements had been retired before 1900. Line 2: Table 10.3, line 1. Each index number represents an average price level for the indicated decade. Line 3: In columns 1–3, 100 × line 1 ÷ line 2. In columns 4–6, these are stock estimates, derived by cumulating the flows in columns 1–3. Line 4: Kuznets 1946, table IV, 3, line 16. We assumed that the equipment acquired in the period 1870 through 1879 was retired in the period 1890 through 1899. Line 5: Table 8.9, line 2, the means of the indexes for 1870 and 1880, 1880 and 1890, 1890 and 1900, respectively. These means were taken to represent the average price levels during the decades of the 1870s, 1880s, and 1890s respectively. Line 6: In columns 1–3, 100 × line 4 ÷ line 5. In columns 4–6, these are stock estimates, derived by cumulating the flows in columns 1–3. We assumed that the equipment acquired in the period 1870 through 1879 was retired in the period 1890 through 1899. Line 7: Kuznets 1946, table IV, 1, line 17.

and private car values to railroad asset values (census figures) remained constant from 1900 to 1904. Table 10.13 presents the summary estimates.

## 10.7. Pipelines

We adopted Kuznets's (1946) current price estimates (tables IV-1 and IV-2), which are in book values, presumably net, and deflated them, using price indexes assembled for the deflation of manufacturing and canal aggregates (described above). See the notes to table 10.14 for details.

## 10.8. Conclusion

This chapter details the estimation of the capital stock in the transportation sector (exclusive of the value of roads).

# Communication and Electric Utilities

## 11.1. Introduction

This chapter details the estimation of the current-price and constant-price (1860) capital stock on a decadal basis from 1840 to 1900 for communication and electric utilities. These include, in turn, telegraphs, telephones, and electric light and power. These estimates involve the use of perpetual inventory methods, and confront the problems of dealing with new goods.

## 11.2. Telegraph

### 11.2.1. Introduction

The early book value figures for the telegraph are unreliable. The frequent mergers before 1870 often caused book values to reflect acquisition cost, not construction cost. To make matters worse, in the 1860s Western Union declared a 100 percent stock dividend, and set it up on the books by doubling the value of "franchise and equipment" (Thompson 1947, 409).[1] In addition, no clear distinction was made between tangible and intangible assets.

Fortunately, there are sufficient data to construct a constant value series based on physical inventories. Estimates of the cost of constructing telegraph lines and equipping offices are available for 1860 and 1866.[2] With this information, and the physical count of miles of poles, miles of

The substance of this chapter was written by Gallman. "We" and "our" refers to Gallman and Howle.

wire, and the number of offices, estimates for 1850 through 1900 can be developed.[3]

## 11.2.2. Improvements

First, an index of resource content was developed. In 1866, W. Dennison, postmaster general, estimated that the construction of telegraph lines covering the principal mail routes (22,741 miles) would cost, for improvements alone:[4]

| one-wire line | $150 per mile |
| three-wire line | $300 per mile |
| six-wire line | $580 per mile |

Presumably these figures are for a quality of telegraph line superior to what then existed, but we can use them to develop an equation relating cost to miles of poles (pole line) and miles of wire.

$$I = K(P + 1.3w)$$

I = cost of improvements per mile

K = a dollar value to be developed from 1860 cost data

P = miles of poles

w = miles of wire (one to six per mile)[5]

Using K = $65, this equation fits the Dennison estimates fairly well:

| Dennison estimates | Equation |
| --- | --- |
| one-wire $150 | $65(1+1.3) = $150 |
| three-wire $300 | $65(1+3.9) = $319 |
| six-wire $580 | $65(1+7.8) = $572 |

Second, we developed estimates of K, expressed in 1860 prices, for each census year. George Prescott estimated that in 1860 the construction

TABLE 11.1 **K value based on 1902 book values, in millions of dollars**

| 1 | 1902 improvements and equipment | 162 |
|---|---|---|
| 2 | Less 10% (a minimum deduction for equipment and intangibles) | 16 |
| 3 | Maximum book value of improvements | 146 |
| 4 | Price index | 118 |
| 5 | Maximum book value in 1860 dollars | 124 |
| 6 | $124 = K(.238 + 1.3 \times 1.318)$ | |
| 7 | $K = 64$ | |

Sources: Line 1: US Bureau of the Census 1915, 159. Book values are not depreciated. Line 2: a guess; see text. Line 3: line 1 - line 2. Line 4: The life of telegraph improvements was slightly over ten years in 1900. The price index (table 11.8, line 6) shows a gradual decline from 126 in 1880 to 118 in 1890 and 115 in 1900. Since we are dealing with book values, 118 is approximately correct. Line 5: 100 × line 3 ÷ line 4. Line 6: value of improvements from line 5; miles of line and miles of wire from US Bureau of the Census 1915, 159. Line 7: solution to line 6.

cost for a line of the quality then existing was $61.80 per mile (US Senate 1865/66, 4). He went on to emphasize the inferior construction of these lines. It is likely that his estimate was for a one-wire line, because this was the most common kind in 1860. The Prescott estimate indicates a value of $K = \$27$: $\$27(1+1.3) = \$62.00$.

A joint letter from the presidents of the three leading telegraph companies estimated that a good quality line of six wires would cost $665 or slightly more in 1866, for improvements only (US Senate 1865/66, 12). This is roughly confirmed by Dennison's estimate of $580 (US Senate 1865/66, 1). Deflating the $665 estimate by our price index yields an 1860 cost of $354 (see table 11.6, line 6.) We may therefore say that the 1866 cost of a "good quality" six-wire line was $354, expressed in 1860 prices, implying a value of K of a little more than $40;[6] that is, $40.2(1 + 7.8) = \$354$.

Prescott also stated that the quality of telegraph construction had already shown considerable improvement from 1860 to 1866, so we might safely assume that by the terminal date of our series, 1900, the quality and resource content of lines would justify a K value at least as high as $40 (US Senate 1865/66, 5).

We can attempt to justify this by using book values that are available for 1902 (see table 11.1). Even in 1902 it is likely that the value of "construction and equipment" included intangibles, such as patent rights and goodwill resulting from mergers. We may therefore consider the K value based on the 1902 "construction and equipment" figure to be an upper bound.

Our assumption was that the K value might have increased from $27 in 1860 to $40 in 1900 as a result of the use of more resources for better quality construction. The K value obtained from 1902 book values

TABLE 11.2  **Values for K and m, 1850–1900**

|   | 1850 | 1860 | 1866 | 1870 | 1880 | 1890 | 1900 |
|---|------|------|------|------|------|------|------|
| K | $24 | $27 | $29 | $30 | $34 | $37 | $40 |
| m | 45 | 49 | 53 | 55 | 62 | 68 | 73 |

Sources: See text for sources of 1860 and 1900 values. All others are based on straight-line interpolation and extrapolations. It is assumed that m moves with K.

TABLE 11.3  **Value of telegraph improvements, 1860 prices, 1840–1900, in millions of dollars**

|   |   | 1850 | 1860 | 1870 | 1880 | 1890 | 1900 |
|---|---|------|------|------|------|------|------|
| 1 | K | 24 | 27 | 30 | 34 | 37 | 40 |
| 2 | Miles of wires | 12,000 | 60,000 | 150,000 | 291,000 | 849,000 | 1,166,000 |
| 3 | Miles of poles | 8,600 | 35,000 | 72,000 | 111,000 | 225,000 | 236,000 |
| 4 | Value of improvements | 0.58 | 3.05 | 8.01 | 16.64 | 49.16 | 70.07 |

Sources:
Line 1: For all years, table 11.2.
    Line 2, 1850: Thompson 1947, 241–42. 1860: Prescott estimated that there were more than 50,000 miles of wire in 1859 (US Senate 1865/66, 4). 1870: The ratio of the miles of wire owned by Western Union to the miles of wire owned by the rest of the industry was interpolated between 1866 and 1880. The 1870 ratio was then divided into the miles of wire owned by Western Union in 1870. 1866: Based on the capitalization figures on pp. 21 and 22 of document 49 and the Western Union mileage figure after consolidation (Thompson 1947, 426), with a rough allowance for the fact that Western Union was heavily overcapitalized (Thompson 1947, 414, 424). The capitalization of Western Union after consolidation was $41 million (Thompson 1947, 426), which is 80 percent of the capitalization of all telegraph companies in 1866 (US Senate 1965/66, 21–22). But document 49 omits seven companies for lack of data, and innumerable local companies. Also, Western Union capital figures are inflated. With allowance for these factors, Western Union is likely to have had nearer 70 than 80 percent of total capital. Rounding yields a figure of about 105,000 miles of wire in 1866, of which Western Union had 76,000. Our estimate is 105,000 miles in 1866, of which Western Union (after consolidation) had 76,000. Prescott gives a figure of over 150,000 miles, but he attributes more than 110,000 to Western Union and American, which, after consolidation with United States, had only 76,000, as mentioned above (US Senate 1965/66, 4). 1866, 1870, and 1880: Western Union data are from US Bureau of the Census 1960, series R-44; 1880 industry data are from US Census Office 1883b, 784. 1890 and 1900: Same procedure as 1870, with the ratio interpolated between 1880 and 1902. The ratio was in fact .80 in 1880 and in 1902. Western Union data are from US Bureau of the Census 1960, series R-44; industry data from US Census Office 1883b and US Bureau of the Census 1906, 159.
    Line 3, 1850–1900: The ratio of miles of poles to miles of wire is available for the industry for 1850 (0.72)] in US Census Office 1853a, 113, for 1880 (0.381), and for 1900 (0.202). It is also available for Western Union in 1866 (0.494) and 1880 (0.367) (Thompson 1947, 426). We interpolated between the industry-wide ratios for 1880 and 1900 to obtain the 1890 figure (0.265), adjusting this ratio downward so as to assure that the estimated miles of poles in 1890 were less than the actual miles in 1900. We extrapolated from 1880 to 1866 on Western Union data, interpolated to 1870 (0.48) from 1866 and 1880, and interpolated to 1860 (0.59) between 1866 and 1850.
    Line 4: For all years, lines 1, 2, and 3 are applied to the formula $I = K(P + 1.3w)$, where I = Improvements, P = miles of poles, and w = miles of wire.

(undepreciated), converted to 1860 prices, is $64. In view of what we know about telegraph book values, such a disparity does not seem unreasonable.

    We next interpolated the K values ($27 and $40) between 1860 and 1900, and extrapolated to 1850 (see table 11.2). This assumes a relatively constant increase in resource use over the period. On this basis we estimated telegraph improvements, in 1860 dollars, for all years (see table 11.3).

### 11.2.3. Equipment

Telegraph equipment during this period accounted for a small fraction of the value of capital. In 1866, for example, the presidents of the three major telegraph companies said that they had an investment of $760,000 in "office equipment."[7] Assuming that one-third of the equipment was purchased at prewar prices, this would be the equivalent of roughly $565,000 in 1860 dollars—only about one-tenth of our computed investment in improvements (interpolated on miles of wire).[8]

We also have an estimate, from the same source, of the cost of equipping an office in 1866, according to the number of wires in the line served by the office (US Senate 1865/66, 13):

one-wire line $150          six-wire line $350

The following formula fits these data:

$$E = mn(1.1 + 0.4w/P)$$

E = total undepreciated value of equipment

m = a dollar multiplier to be determined

n = number of offices

w = miles of wire

P = miles of poles.

For the 1866 per office cost data just quoted, an m value of $100 would be indicated, or $53 when deflated to 1860 dollars. We can compare this with the estimate we previously cited of the cost of office equipment of the three main telegraph companies: Setting $565,000 = 5,700 m (1.1 + 0.4 × 100,000/51,000), yields m = $53.[9]

We do not know how the value of m changed over time. Later office equipment was probably more complex than that existing in the 1860s. For lack of better information, we allowed m to change over time in proportion to the change in K, the improvements multiplier, as indicated in table 11.2.

The only remaining task was to estimate the number of offices in existence. To do this, we interpolated and extrapolated a ratio of the number of offices per mile of poles from 1880 (0.113) and 1902 (0.115) data for the

TABLE 11.4 **Background information for calculation of value of telegraph equipment, 1860 prices, 1840–1900, in millions of dollars**

| | 1850 | 1860 | 1870 | 1880 | 1890 | 1900 |
|---|---|---|---|---|---|---|
| 1 Multiple (m) | $45 | 49 | 55 | 62 | 68 | 73 |
| 2 Miles of poles | 8,600 | 35,000 | 72,000 | 111,000 | 225,000 | 236,000 |
| 3 Offices per mile of poles | 0.110 | 0.111 | 0.112 | 0.113 | 0.114 | 0.115 |
| 4 Number of offices (n) | 946 | 3,885 | 8,064 | 12,543 | 25,650 | 27,140 |
| 5 Wire/poles | 1.4 | 1.7 | 2.08 | 2.62 | 3.77 | 4.94 |
| 6 Equipment | 0.07 | 1.34 | 0.86 | 1.67 | 4.55 | 6.09 |

Sources: Line 1: See text, above. Line 2: table 11.3. Line 3: See text, above. Line 4: line 2 × line 3. Line 5: table 11.3, line 2 ÷ line 3. Line 6: from line 1, 4, and 5 according to the formula E = mn(1.1 + 0.4w/P).

industry to derive the following estimates: 1850, 0.110; 1860, 0.111; 1870, 0.112; 1890, 0.114; and 1900, 0.115. The 1880 ratio is from the US Census Office (1883b). The 1902 data are from the US Bureau of the Census (1906). The ratios for all other years were interpolated or extrapolated.

We then estimated the value of equipment, in 1860 dollars, for all years (see table 11.4).

## 11.2.4. Depreciation

The depreciation of telegraph assets is somewhat complicated because we have not developed an annual capital stock series. To develop a depreciated series, we first converted our stock estimates to estimates of the average total output of telegraph assets during each decade. Centering each estimate on the midyear of the decade, and assuming a constant rate of increase in the gross output of telegraph assets between decade mid-years, we developed an estimate of the average age of telegraph equipment. From this estimate, a ratio of depreciated to undepreciated assets values was developed.

The life of telegraph improvements and equipment was taken to be ten years.[10] Investment gross of replacement (hereafter, "gross investment") in year (t) is equal to investment net of replacements (hereafter, "net investment") in year (t) plus gross investment in year (t-10), investment being expressed in constant prices:

$$g_{(t)} = n_{(t)} + g_{(t-10)} = n_{(t)} + n_{(1-10)} + \ldots tn_{(t-10m)}$$

where (t-10m) is in the first decade of significant telegraph asset production.

We next determined the average net investment in the telegraph in each decade and centered it on the mid-year of the decade:

$$n_t = 0.1(s_{t+5} - s_{t-5})$$

where s is our undepreciated stock figure.

We now had a means of estimating the average gross investment per annum for each decade, and we centered this figure on the mid-year of the decade. We interpolated changes in investment along a straight line from one decade's mid-year to the next. Thus we could divide the investment within the decade into two parts. Part A corresponds to the level at the beginning of the 10-year period, continued throughout the decade; it is $10 \times g_{t-10}$. The average age of equipment produced at the constant rate represented by Part A is obviously five years. This corresponds to a ratio between depreciated and undepreciated value of 0.5, assuming straight-line depreciation. Part B represents a straight-line increase in investment during the decade; it is $(10 \times g_t - g_{t-10})/2$. The average age of equipment corresponding to part B is 3.33 years, and the ratio of depreciated to undepreciated value is 0.667 for this portion of the stock.

TABLE 11.5  **Depreciation of telegraph assets, 1860 Prices, 1840–1900, in millions of dollars**

| | (1) | (2) | (3) | (4) | (5) | (6) | (7) |
|---|---|---|---|---|---|---|---|
| | Undepreciated Stock (s) | Change in s | Net Investment (n) | Gross Investment (g) | Ratio (s0/s) | Depreciated improvement | Depreciated equipment |
| 1840 | 0 | | | | | | |
| 1845 | | | 0.07 | 0.07 | 0.67 | | |
| 1850 | 0.7 | 0.7 | | | (0.65) | 0.4 | 0.05 |
| 1855 | | | 0.27 | 0.34 | 0.63 | | |
| 1860 | 3.4 | 2.7 | | | (0.62) | 1.9 | 0.21 |
| 1865 | | | 0.55 | 0.89 | 0.6 | | |
| 1870 | 8.9 | 5.5 | | | (0.60) | 4.8 | 0.51 |
| 1875 | | | 0.94 | 1.83 | 0.59 | | |
| 1880 | 18.3 | 9.4 | | | (0.60) | 9.9 | 1 |
| 1885 | | | 3.54 | 5.37 | 0.61 | | |
| 1890 | 53.7 | 35.4 | | | (0.58) | 28.5 | 2.6 |
| 1895 | | | 2.25 | 7.62 | 0.55 | | |
| 1900 | 76.2 | 22.5 | | | (0.55) | 38.5 | 3.3 |

Sources: Column 1: The undepreciated stock of capital equals line 4, table 11.3 + line 6, table 11.4. Column 2: From column 1, $\Delta s = s_t - s_{t-10}$. Column 3: From column 2, $n = 0.1 \Delta s + 5$. Column 4: From column 3, $g_t = n_t + n_{t-10} + tn_{t-10}m$. See text, equation 2. Column 5: From column 4, $s_0/s = (0.667 g_t - 0.167 g_{t-10})/g_t$. See text, equation 5. The figures in parentheses are interpolations. Column 6: column 5 × line 4, table 11.3. Column 7: column 5 × line 6, table 11.4.

TABLE 11.6  **Price indexes of telegraph assets, 1850–1900, 1860 base**

|   |                    | 1850 | 1860 | 1866 | 1870 | 1880 | 1890 | 1900 |
|---|--------------------|------|------|------|------|------|------|------|
| 1 | Pine logs          | 94   | 100  | 200  | 125  | 150  | 150  | 150  |
| 2 | Iron wire          | 98   | 100  | 190  | 127  | 95   | 64   | 60   |
| 3 | Building trades     | 82   | 100  | 170  | 186  | 143  | 173  | 182  |
| 4 | Wet cell batteries  | 140  | 100  | —    | 120  | 74   | 57   | 40   |
| 5 | Electric apparatus  | 138  | 100  | —    | 100  | 88   | 78   | 69   |
| 6 | Improvement index   | 92   | 100  | 188  | 144  | 126  | 118  | 115  |
| 7 | Equipment Index     | 122  | 100  | 187  | 133  | 100  | 100  | 96   |

Sources:
Line 1: The 1860–1900 index is from the *Aldrich Report* (US Senate 1893, 47). This index seemed the most appropriate to reflect changes in the price of telegraph poles. The index was extrapolated to 1850 and to 1900 according to changes in the building materials index in US Bureau of the Census 1960, series E-8 and E-21.
Line 2, 1860–1900: *Aldrich Report* (US Senate 1893, 40) extrapolated to 1850 and 1900 according to changes in the metal and metal products index in US Bureau of the Census 1960, series E-7 and E-20. In the early 1900s both copper and iron lines were being used. Although it is not known to what extent copper had replaced iron by 1900, the price index of sheet copper (copper wire index not available; US Senate 1893, 40) did not deviate greatly from that of iron wire. Line 3: 1860–90: US Bureau of the Census 1960, series D-577. This index was extrapolated to 1900 by US Bureau of the Census 1960, series D-623, and to 1850 by an index of common labor (Lebergott 1964, 541). The building trades index seemed more appropriate than the other available wage indexes because it follows the skilled labor index (Lebergott 1964, 90) closely for the years of overlap. It also corresponds closely to the illuminating gas wages index, the only utility index that is available for the period.
Line 4: Brady's index, received by correspondence. The 1854 figure was used for 1850. Line 5: Brady's index, received by correspondence, unadjusted, extrapolated from 1860 to 1850 along changes in Brady's machine shop products index (table 8.9, line 2). Line 6: A weighted average of lines 1, 2, and 3. US Census Office 1883b furnishes a very detailed list of Canadian Telegraph assets. The total cost of poles and that of wire were about equal. The US telegraph industry had about the same ratio of miles of wire to poles in 1866 as the Canadian industry had in 1880. Considering the price fluctuations in these two items, we assumed that they were of about equal value in the United States in 1870. We weighted the change in relative importance of these two items according to the change in the average number of wires per line. The weighting of labor is a rough estimate. Line 6 was thus obtained by weighting lines 1, 2, and 3, respectively, as follows:

|  1850  |  1860  |  1866  |  1870  |  1880  |  1890  |  1900  |
|--------|--------|--------|--------|--------|--------|--------|
| 40, 30, 30 | 40, 30, 30 | 35, 35, 30 | 35, 35, 30 | 30, 30, 30 | 25, 45, 30 | 20, 50, 30 |

Line 7: No detailed account of the components of telegraph equipment was found. To obtain the equipment index, we arbitrarily weighted lines 3, 4, and 5, respectively, as follows:

|  1850  |  1860  |  1870  |  1880  |  1890  |  1900  |
|--------|--------|--------|--------|--------|--------|
| 30, 35, 35 | 30, 35, 35 | 30, 35, 35 | 30, 35, 35 | 30, 30, 40 | 30, 25, 45 |

To obtain the 1866 value, it was necessary to interpolate between 1860 and 1870 according to changes in the Warren-Pearson metal and metal products index (US Bureau of the Census 1960, series E-7).

The depreciated value/undepreciated value ratio therefore corresponds to:

$$(0.5\, g_{t-10} + 0.667 g_t - 0.667 g_{t-10})/g_t = (0.667 g_t - 0.167 g_{t-10})/g_t$$

This is subject to the restriction that investment must have first begun at (t-10) or earlier.

We next determined the depreciated/undepreciated value ratio and the depreciated value of telegraph assets for the 1850–1900 period (see table 11.5).

## 11.2.5. Current Value Estimate

Our price indexes were constructed as indicated in table 11.6. The constant-price series was multiplied by the price index to obtain the current-price series in table 11.7.

It is interesting to compare our estimates with the only other evaluations of telegraph assets that are not based on book values. These estimates, for 1872 and 1880, are found in US Census Office (1883b). They are based on an 1869 report of the president of Western Union. The 1869 data were extended to 1872 and 1880 by considering the change in miles of wire and miles of line during the period. It appears, however, that no adjustment was made for price changes. The series was intended to represent the cost of the assets, not depreciated values. Table 11.8 presents a comparison of our undepreciated estimates with US Census Office (1883b) evaluations.

TABLE 11.7  **Telegraph assets converted to current dollars, 1850–1900, in millions of dollars**

|   |                              | 1850 | 1860 | 1870 | 1880 | 1890 | 1900 |
|---|------------------------------|------|------|------|------|------|------|
|   | Improvement                  |      |      |      |      |      |      |
| 1 | Value, at 1860 prices        | 0.4  | 1.9  | 4.8  | 9.9  | 28.5 | 38.5 |
| 2 | Price index                  | 92   | 100  | 144  | 126  | 118  | 115  |
| 3 | Value, at current prices     | 0.4  | 1.9  | 6.9  | 12.5 | 33.6 | 44.3 |
|   | Equipment                    |      |      |      |      |      |      |
| 4 | Value, at 1860 prices        | 0.05 | 0.21 | 0.51 | 1.0  | 2.6  | 3.3  |
| 5 | Price index                  | 122  | 100  | 133  | 100  | 100  | 96   |
| 6 | Value, at current prices     | 0.06 | 0.21 | 0.68 | 1.0  | 2.6  | 3.2  |

Sources: Line 1, 4: table 11.5, above. Lines 2, 5: table 11.6, below. Line 3: line 1 × line 2 ÷ 100. Line 6: line 4 × line 5 ÷ 100.

TABLE 11.8  **Comparison of Gallman-Howle and US Census asset evaluations, in millions of current dollars**

|        | (1)                              | (2)          |
|--------|----------------------------------|--------------|
| Year   | **Gallman-Howle** (undepreciated) | **Tenth census** |
| 1870   | 12.7                             | —            |
| 1872   | 14.6                             | 11.9         |
| 1880   | 22.6                             | 18.7         |
| 1890   | 62.6                             | —            |
| 1900   | 86.4                             | —            |

Sources: Column 1: Table 11.3, line 4, and table 11.4, line 6 were each inflated by the appropriate price index, table 11.6. The improvements and equipment were then totaled together. The 1872 figure was interpolated between 1870 and 1880 along miles of Western Union wire. Column 2: US Census Office 1883b, 846–49.

## 11.3. Telephones

### 11.3.1. Current Value Series

We accepted Ulmer's (1960) estimates, which were constructed by inflating constant price cumulations of net investment flows.[11] Ulmer's figures refer to 1 January of each year; we interpolated between them to produce approximations to 1 June estimates. The only available breakdown into capital components is in a Federal Trade Commission report that established a breakdown for 1922 (Federal Trade Commission 1926, 30). We adjusted these figures, as explained in the notes to table 11.9. The results appear in table 11.10.

### 11.3.2. Deflation

We then deflated the telephone series by using our telegraph improvements and equipment indexes from table 11.6. Although telephones did not exist commercially before 1880, our price index extends back to 1860.

TABLE 11.9  **Telephone asset ratios, 1880–1922**

|   |              | 1880 | 1890 | 1900 | 1922 |
|---|--------------|------|------|------|------|
| 1 | Land         | 0.04 | 0.04 | 0.04 | 0.03 |
| 2 | Improvements | 0.48 | 0.46 | 0.44 | 0.40 |
| 3 | Equipment    | 0.48 | 0.50 | 0.52 | 0.57 |
| 4 | Fixed assets | 1.00 | 1.00 | 1.00 | 1.00 |

Sources: 1922 ratios were taken from data in Federal Trade Commission 1926. The 1880 ratios were roughly estimated by considering the 1922 ratios and the change in the nature of telephone assets between 1880 and 1922. The ratios were interpolated between 1880 and 1922.

TABLE 11.10  **Value of telephone assets, measured in current prices, 1880–1900, in millions of dollars**

|   |             | 1880 | 1890 | 1900  |
|---|-------------|------|------|-------|
| 1 | Land        | 0.3  | 1.4  | 8.2   |
| 2 | Improvement | 3.2  | 16.7 | 90.5  |
| 3 | Equipment   | 3.2  | 18.1 | 107.0 |
| 4 | Total       | 6.6  | 36.2 | 205.7 |

Sources: Lines 1, 2, and 3 obtained by multiplying Ulmer's (1960, table E-1) adjusted improvement and equipment total (line 4; see text for adjustment) by the ratios in table 11.9.

TABLE 11.11  **Value of telephone improvements and equipment, current and 1860 prices,**
**1880–1900, in millions of dollars**

|   |   | 1880 | 1890 | 1900 |
|---|---|------|------|------|
|   | **Improvements** | | | |
| 1 | Value, at current prices | 3.2 | 16.7 | 90.5 |
| 2 | Price index (1860 = 100) | 126 | 118 | 115 |
| 3 | Value, at 1860 prices | 2.5 | 14.2 | 78.7 |
|   | **Equipment** | | | |
| 4 | Value, at current prices | 3.2 | 18.1 | 107 |
| 5 | Price index (1860 = 100) | 100 | 100 | 96 |
| 6 | Value, at 1860 prices | 3.2 | 18.1 | 111.5 |

Sources: Line 1: table 11.10, line 2. Line 2: table 11.6, line 6. Line 3: 100 × line 1 ÷ line 2. Line 4: table 11.10, line 3.
Line 5: table 11.6, line 7. Line 6: 100 × line 4 ÷ line 5.

TABLE 11.12.  **Value of electric light and power assets, measured current and 1890**
**prices, 1890–1900, in millions of dollars**

|   |   | 1890 | 1900 |
|---|---|------|------|
|   | **Current prices** | | |
| 1 | Land | 2 | 13 |
| 2 | Improvements and equipment | 41 | 251 |
| 3 | Total | 43 | 264 |
|   | **1890 prices** | | |
| 4 | Improvements and equipment | 41 | 235 |

Sources: Line 1: Land made up about 5 percent of total fixed assets; see Ulmer 1960, table D-3.
Line 2: Ulmer's (1960, table D-1, column 1) estimate, interpolated between adjacent first of year
figures. Line 3: line 1 + line 2. Line 4: Ulmer's (1960, table D-1, column 2) constant value series
interpolated between adjacent first of year figures and adjusted to an 1890 base.

Therefore, for the sake of consistency with our other categories, we have
stated our telephone assets in 1860 dollars (see table 11.11). Readers will
notice that two sets of price indexes figure in the estimates: ours and Ulmer's. We run the risk, therefore, of having our constant price series determined in part by irrelevant differences between deflators. Comparison
of the changes described between the three census years by the two sets
of deflators suggests that the risk is not a great one.

## 11.4. Electric Light and Power

We used Ulmer's (1960, 293–363) estimates, which were made by cumulating net investment flows, in constant prices, and then inflating them.

The constant-price estimates are on an 1890 base, not an 1860 base. See table 11.12 for details.

## 11.5. Conclusion

This chapter details the procedures to estimate the capital stock in the communications and electric utilities sectors.

## CHAPTER TWELVE

# Inventories

## 12.1. Introduction

This chapter details estimates for inventory holdings of physical goods and of monetary metals (and changes in related claims on foreigners). The final section combines inventory data from other chapters (for example, adding the value of farm animals from chapter 7 on agriculture) and places overall series and its components into a more general context.

## 12.2. Physical Goods

This section details estimates for inventories of physical goods, other than monetary metals (which are treated below). Inventories of farm and range animals were included in the agricultural capital stock. Here we are concerned with all other inventories—specifically of mined, manufactured, and agricultural products, and of imports. In principle, animals held off farms and ranges should also be included, but we had insufficient data to prepare the estimates.[1]

In estimating the value of the remaining inventories, we followed the example of Kuznets (1946, 202, 228), taking one-half of the value of output of mining, manufacturing and agriculture and one-half of the value of imports to represent inventories.[2]

Gallman wrote sections 12.1 to 12.6; Rhode made minor revisions for clarity and wrote section 12.7.

TABLE 12.1  **Value of inventories of imported goods, measured current and 1860 prices, 1840–1900, in millions of dollars**

|   |   | 1840 | 1850 | 1860 | 1870 | 1880 | 1890 | 1900 |
|---|---|------|------|------|------|------|------|------|
| **Current dollars** | | | | | | | | |
| 1 | Value of imports, exclusive of duties | 100 | 180 | 368 | 449 | 681 | 845 | 858 |
| 2 | Duties | 15 | 40 | 53 | 192 | 183 | 227 | 229 |
| 3 | Value of imports, inclusive of duties | 115 | 220 | 421 | 641 | 864 | 1,072 | 1,087 |
| 4 | Inventories of imported goods | 58 | 110 | 211 | 321 | 432 | 536 | 544 |
| 5 | Price index (1860 = 100) | 92.1 | 90.3 | 100 | 145 | 108 | 88.6 | 82.4 |
| **1860 dollars** | | | | | | | | |
| 6 | Value of imports, exclusive of duties | 109 | 199 | 368 | 310 | 631 | 954 | 1,041 |
| 7 | Inventories of imported goods | 62 | 114 | 211 | 177 | 361 | 546 | 595 |

Sources: Line 1: North and Simon 1960, 577, 605, 643. Line 2: US Bureau of the Census 1960, series U-18. Line 3: line 1 + line 2. Line 4: For justification of this procedure, see text. Line 5: US Bureau of the Census 1960, series U-34 (1880, 1890, 1900), linked with series E-1 (1870), and series E-70 (1840, 1850, 1860). The first and third are import average value and price index series (see text). In the table, index numbers are rounded to the level at which the underlying series are rounded. Lines 6: 100 × line 1 ÷ line 5. Line 7: 1860 value of imports inclusive of duties as a ratio of the value of imports exclusive of duties. Line 8: line 7 × 0.5. Line 9: line 6 × line 8.

## 12.3. Imports

We took the value of imports from North and Simon (1960, 577, 605, 643), and adjusted the series to incorporate the value of duties, the latter taken from US Bureau of the Census 1960, series U-18.[3] The deflator was formed by linking together the average unit value of imports (series U-34, 1880, 1890, 1900), the Warren-Pearson all commodities index (series E-1, 1870), and the Bezanson price index of goods imported into Philadelphia (series E-70, 1840, 1850, 1860) from US Bureau of the Census 1960. The series exclusive of duties was deflated and then used as an extrapolator for the 1860 value of imports plus duties. Table 12.1 shows the results.

## 12.4. Agriculture

The agricultural output series is Gallman's gross income series, adjusted to include feed and seed allowances of corn, oats, and hay, and to exclude various items that either did not figure importantly in inventories or are

TABLE 12.2 **Value of inventories of agricultural products, measured in current and 1860 prices, 1840–1900, in millions of dollars**

|   |   | 1840 | 1850 | 1860 | 1870 | 1880 | 1890 | 1900 |
|---|---|---|---|---|---|---|---|---|
| 1 | Value of inventories in census-year prices | 388 | 489 | 889 | 1,368 | 1,425 | 1,555 | 1,840 |
| 2 | Price adjustment factor | 0.861 | 1.068 | 0.969 | 0.933 | 1.053 | 1.029 | 1.049 |
| 3 | Line 1 expressed in calendar-year prices (line 1 × 2) | 334 | 522 | 861 | 1,276 | 1,501 | 1,600 | 1,930 |
| 4 | Line 1 expressed in prices of 1879 | 417 | 542 | 792 | 917 | 1,426 | 1,953 | 2,268 |
| 5 | Line 3 ÷ line 4, 1860 |  |  | 1.0871 |  |  |  |  |
| 6 | Line 1 expressed in 1860 prices (line 4 × line 5) | 453 | 589 | 861 | 997 | 1,550 | 2,123 | 2,466 |

Sources: See text.

covered elsewhere.[4] The prices underlying the Gallman series are census year prices. Accordingly, the valuation base of the Gallman series was shifted to the calendar year, by means of the Warren-Pearson and BLS farm products price indexes reported in US Bureau of the Census 1960, series E-2 and E-15. Since Gallman's constant price series is based on 1879, it was necessary to shift the base to 1860. This was done without reweighting the index. Table 12.2 displays the agricultural inventory estimates.

## 12.5. Mining and Manufacturing

The mining and manufacturing inventory estimates were based on Gallman's value-added estimates. Once again, the valuation base was shifted from the census to the calendar year by means of the price indexes of Warren-Pearson and BLS.[5] The mining series was deflated by Gallman's price index, shifted to the base 1860. The manufacturing series, 1840–80, was deflated by the Gallman price index of manufacturing output, shifted

TABLE 12.3 **Value of inventories of mined products, measured in current and 1860 prices, 1840–1900, in millions of dollars**

| | | 1840 | 1850 | 1860 | 1870 | 1880 | 1890 | 1900 |
|---|---|---|---|---|---|---|---|---|
| 1 | Value of inventories in census-year prices | 5.2 | 9.8 | 19.7 | 72.3 | 88.8 | 164 | 270.7 |
| 2 | Price adjustment factor | 0.925 | 1.01 | 1.026 | 0.893 | 1.07 | 1.007 | 1.058 |
| 3 | Line 1 expressed in calendar-year prices (line 1 × 2) | 4.8 | 9.9 | 20.2 | 64.6 | 95 | 165.1 | 286.4 |
| 4 | Line 1 expressed in 1879 prices | 4.2 | 10.1 | 19 | 40.7 | 88.8 | 200.9 | 319.7 |
| 5 | Line 3 ÷ line 4, 1860 | | | 1.063 | | | | |
| 6 | Line 1 expressed in prices of 1860 (line 4 × line 5) | 4.5 | 10.7 | 20.2 | 43.3 | 94.4 | 213.6 | 339.8 |

Sources: Lines 1 and 4, value added × 0.58 (which yields a value roughly equal to value of output × 0.50). See Gallman 1956, 218.
Lines 2, 3, 5, 6, see text.

to the base 1860, without reweighting, and extrapolated to 1890 and 1900 on the Warren-Pearson "all commodities" index, which tracks the Gallman index very closely (Gallman 1956, 279). Table 12.3 details the inventory estimates for mined products; table 12.4 does the same for manufactured products. Table 12.5 then brings together the inventory estimates for all physical goods, including imports, agricultural products, mined products, and manufactured products. Metals held for monetary purposes are treated immediately below.

## 12.6. Monetary Metals and the Net International Position

This section consists of two components: the stock of monetary metals owned by Americans (including American governments), and the net international position of the United States (foreign debts held by Americans, minus American debts held by foreigners). The former we have taken chiefly from Hepburn and the 1929 *Annual Report* of the director of the Mint (see the notes to table 12.6). Unfortunately, neither of these

TABLE 12.4 **Value of inventories of manufactured products, current and 1860 prices, 1840–1900, in millions of dollars**

| | | 1840 | 1850 | 1860 | 1870 | 1880 | 1890 | 1900 |
|---|---|---|---|---|---|---|---|---|
| 1 | Value added by manufacturing, census-year prices | 250 | 447 | 815 | 1,631 | 1,962 | 3,727 | 5,044 |
| 2 | Adjustment factor | 1.124 | 1.124 | 1.126 | 1.238 | 1.359 | 1.142 | 1.19 |
| 3 | Value of inventories in census-year prices (line 1 × line 2) | 281 | 502.4 | 917.7 | 2,019.20 | 2,666.40 | 4,256.20 | 6,002.40 |
| 4 | Price adjustment factor | 0.918 | 1.012 | 0.989 | 0.944 | 1.053 | 1.006 | 1.036 |
| 5 | Line 4 in calendar prices (line 3 × line 4) | 258 | 508 | 908 | 1,906 | 2,808 | 4,282 | 6,218 |
| 6 | Price index, base 1879, census years | 109.7 | 85.6 | 95.7 | 140.8 | 100 | 86 | 85.8 |
| 7 | Line 3, expressed in 1879 prices (100 × line 3 ÷ line 6) | 256.2 | 586.9 | 958.9 | 1,434.10 | 2,666.40 | 4,949.10 | 6,995.80 |
| 8 | Line 5 ÷ line 7, 1880 | | | | | 0.947 | | |
| 9 | Line 5 expressed in 1860 prices (line 7 × line 8) | 243 | 556 | 908 | 1,358 | 2,525 | 4,687 | 6,625 |

Sources: Line 1: Gallman 1960, 56. The 1840 figure has been corrected here per Gallman 1966, 47. Line 2: 0.5 × value of product ÷ value added; derived from Gallman 1956, 38–39, 41. Lines 3–9: For sources and justification of the procedures, see text. We assumed that the same ratio held for 1840 and 1850.

TABLE 12.5 **Value of all inventories of physical goods, measured in current and 1860 prices, in millions of dollars**

|   |                           | 1840 | 1850  | 1860  | 1870  | 1880  | 1890  | 1900   |
|---|---------------------------|------|-------|-------|-------|-------|-------|--------|
| 1 | Value, at current prices  | 655  | 1,150 | 2,000 | 3,568 | 4,836 | 6,583 | 8,978  |
| 2 | Implicit price index      | 87   | 91    | 100   | 139   | 107   | 87    | 90     |
| 3 | Value, at 1860 prices     | 763  | 1,270 | 2,000 | 2,575 | 4,530 | 7,570 | 10,026 |

Sources:
Line 1: Sums of table 12.1, line 4; table 12.2, line 3; table 12.3, line 3; and table 12.4, line 5.
Line 2: 100 × line 1 ÷ line 3.
Line 3: Sums of table 12.1, line 9; table 12.2, line 6; table 12.3, line 6; and table 12.4, line 9.

TABLE 12.6 **Value of net US international assets, measured in current and 1860 prices, 1840–1900, in millions of dollars**

|   |                                        | 1840  | 1850  | 1860  | 1870   | 1880   | 1890   | 1900   |
|---|----------------------------------------|-------|-------|-------|--------|--------|--------|--------|
| 1 | Stock of monetary metals               | 83    | 154   | 253   | 217    | 500    | 1,159  | 1,682  |
| 2 | Net international position              | −261  | −217  | −377  | −1,252 | −1,584 | −2,894 | −2,501 |
| 3 | International assets, current prices    | −178  | −63   | −124  | −1,035 | −1,084 | −1,735 | −819   |
| 4 | Price index (base:1860)                | 102   | 90    | 100   | 145    | 108    | 88     | 88     |
| 5 | Deflated stock of monetary metals      | 81    | 171   | 253   | 150    | 463    | 1,317  | 1,911  |
| 6 | Deflated international position         | −256  | −241  | −377  | −863   | −1,467 | −3,289 | −2,842 |
| 7 | Net international assets, 1860 prices   | −175  | −70   | −124  | −713   | −1,004 | −1,972 | −931   |

Sources:
Line 1: 1840–60: Hepburn 1915, 160 ("Specie in the U.S."), 177 ("estimated specie in the U.S."). 1870: US Director of the Mint (1929, 106) figure for June 30, 1873, plus Hepburn's (1915) estimates of the value of net specie exports, fiscal years 1873, 1872, 1871, minus the value of the US gold production, 1871, 1872, 1873, the latter estimated as the product of gold output from US Bureau of the Census 1960, series M-246, and $20.67 times 1 plus the gold premium (Hepburn 1915, 226, means of highs and lows). We made no allowance for silver production on the grounds that during the period, silver was not being used significantly for monetary purposes in the United States. We were unable to make allowance for gold flowing into the arts, because we could find no basis for estimating the value of this flow. 1880–1900: US Director of the Mint 1929, 106. Line 2: US Bureau of the Census 1960, series U-207. Line 3: line 1 + line 2. Line 4: US Bureau of the Census 1960, series E-1, extrapolated to 1900 on series E-13. Line 5: 100 × line 1 ÷ line 4. Line 6: 100 × line 2 ÷ line 4. Line 7: line 5 ÷ line 6.

sources provides any clear indication of the bases for the figures. While the series of the director of the Mint might be supposed to rest on official evidence, the title of the table uses the term "estimates" to describe the series. Furthermore, the director's *Report* (1929, 106 and 110) includes two contradictory tables relating to gold stocks, and never references the contradiction; we used the series on p. 106.

The estimates of the director of the Mint appear to be dated 30 June, which is close to the date of the capital series (1 June). Hepburn does not indicate the day within the year to which his estimates relate, but one may suppose that the end of the federal fiscal year was intended. During the period in question, the federal fiscal year ended within three months of 1 June.

The net international position of the United States was taken from US Bureau of the Census 1960, series U-207, which was based on the very careful work of North and Simon (1960).

It is by no means clear how such series should be deflated, and one can even make a case that they should not figure in a constant price capital series. However, if they are to be deflated, presumably some general price index should be used, such as the GNP or capital stock deflator.[6] In the case of the net position of the United States, one could even argue that the appropriate procedure would be to deflate claims on the United States by a US deflator, and US claims on foreigners by a weighted average of the general price indexes of the countries on which Americans had claims. The one deflated aggregate would then be subtracted from the other, after due allowance for any change in the relevant rates of exchange.

Our view is that such complex procedures are unwarranted, given the nature of the interpretive issues surrounding the concepts. We chose the simplest procedure available, deflating with the Warren-Pearson and BLS. all-commodities price indexes, shifted to the base 1860 without re-weighting (see notes to table 12.6).

## 12.7. Placing the Inventory Data in Context

Tables 12.7 and 12.8 compile data on the distribution of inventories from 1840 to 1900. They include the value of farm animals from chapter 7 on agriculture. The tables allow us (1) to calculate a total value of inventories; (2) to derive the shares of inventories comprised by agricultural products, manufactured products, mined products, and others; and (3) to form the ratio of the inventory stock to GNP.

TABLE 12.7 **Values and shares of inventories, current and 1860 prices, 1840–1900, in millions of dollars**

| | | 1840 | 1850 | 1860 | 1870 | 1880 | 1890 | 1900 |
|---|---|---|---|---|---|---|---|---|
| | **Value at current prices** | | | | | | | |
| 1 | Total inventories | 1,100 | 1,737 | 3,074 | 5,234 | 6,680 | 9,299 | 12,046 |
| 2 | Animals | 445 | 587 | 1,074 | 1,666 | 1,844 | 2,716 | 3,068 |
| 3 | All products | 655 | 1,150 | 2,000 | 3,568 | 4,836 | 6,583 | 8,978 |
| 4 | Agricultural products | 334 | 552 | 861 | 1,276 | 1,501 | 1,600 | 1,930 |
| 5 | Mined products | 5 | 10 | 20 | 65 | 95 | 165 | 286 |
| 6 | Manufactured products | 258 | 508 | 908 | 1,906 | 2,808 | 4,282 | 6,218 |
| 7 | Other products | 58 | 80 | 211 | 321 | 432 | 536 | 544 |
| | **Value at 1860 prices** | | | | | | | |
| 8 | Total inventories | 1,439 | 2,061 | 3,074 | 3,686 | 6,075 | 9,625 | 12,246 |
| 9 | Animals | 676 | 791 | 1,074 | 1,111 | 1,545 | 2,055 | 2,220 |
| 10 | All products | 763 | 1,270 | 2,000 | 2,575 | 4,350 | 7,570 | 10,026 |
| 11 | Agricultural products | 453 | 589 | 861 | 997 | 1,550 | 2.123 | 2,466 |
| 12 | Mined products | 5 | 11 | 20 | 43 | 94 | 214 | 340 |
| 13 | Manufactured products | 243 | 556 | 908 | 1,358 | 2,525 | 4,687 | 6,625 |
| 14 | Other products (Above excludes monetary metals) | 62 | 114 | 211 | 177 | 361 | 546 | 595 |
| 15 | Current prices | 83 | 154 | 253 | 217 | 500 | 1,159 | 1,682 |
| 16 | 1860 prices | 81 | 171 | 253 | 159 | 463 | 1,317 | 1,991 |

Sources: Line 1: line 2 + line 3. Lines 2 and 9: table 7.3. Lines 3 and 10: table 12.5. Lines 4 and 11: table 12.2. Lines 5 and 12: table 12.3. Lines 6 and 13: table 12.4. Line 7: line 3 – line 4 – line 5 – line 6; other products are principally imports. Line 8: line 9 + line 10. Line 14: line 10 – line 11 – line 12 – line 13; other products are principally imports. Lines 15 and 16: table 12.6.

TABLE 12.8 **Shares of inventories, current and 1860 prices, 1840–1900**

| | | 1840 | 1850 | 1860 | 1870 | 1880 | 1890 | 1900 |
|---|---|---|---|---|---|---|---|---|
| | **Agricultural share** | | | | | | | |
| 1 | Current prices | 0.71 | 0.66 | 0.63 | 0.56 | 0.5 | 0.46 | 0.41 |
| 2 | 1860 prices | 0.78 | 0.67 | 0.63 | 0.57 | 0.51 | 0.43 | 0.38 |
| | **Manufacturing share** | | | | | | | |
| 3 | Current prices | 0.23 | 0.29 | 0.3 | 0.36 | 0.42 | 0.46 | 0.52 |
| 4 | 1860 prices | 0.17 | 0.27 | 0.3 | 0.37 | 0.42 | 0.49 | 0.54 |
| | **Mining and other share** | | | | | | | |
| 5 | Current prices | 0.06 | 0.05 | 0.08 | 0.07 | 0.08 | 0.08 | 0.06 |
| 6 | 1860 prices | 0.05 | 0.06 | 0.08 | 0.06 | 0.07 | 0.08 | 0.05 |
| | **Inventories/GNP** | | | | | | | |
| 7 | Current prices | 0.63 | 0.66 | 0.73 | NA | 0.69 | 0.74 | 0.74 |
| 8 | 1860 prices | 0.89 | 0.73 | 0.73 | 0.66 | 0.70 | 0.74 | 0.70 |

Sources: Line 1: from table 12.7, (line 2 + line 4) ÷ line 1. Line 2: from table 12.7, (line 9 + line 11) ÷ line 8. Line 3: table 12.7, line 6 ÷ line 1. Line 4: table 12.7, line 13 ÷ line 8. Line 5: from table 12.7, (line 5 + line 7) ÷ line 1. Line 6: from table 12.7, (line 12 + line 14) ÷ line 8. Line 7: from table 12.7, line 1 ÷ GNP in current prices in Gallman 2000, 7. Line 8: table 12.7, line 8 ÷ GNP in 1860 prices in Gallman 2000, 7.

The data shows that the share of agricultural products in inventories fell from about three-quarters of the total in 1840 to about four-tenths in 1900. The share of manufactured products in inventories climbed from less than one-quarter of the total in 1840 to over one-half in 1900. In current-price terms, the ratio of inventories to GNP rose between 1840 and 1900; in the constant-price terms, the ratio fell. These ratios differ somewhat from those reported in Gallman (1986) table 4.7, column 3. The difference is likely due to the use of a different GNP series in the denominator. The overall trends, however, are similar.

## CHAPTER THIRTEEN

# Consumer Durables

## 13.1. Introduction

Gallman believed that while his capital stock estimates provided a valuable picture of American wealth, they were incomplete. Among the important gaps were the exclusion of financial assets and that diverse body of skills and talents subsumed under the title "human capital."[1] His study focused on tangible capital, and largely excluded intangibles such as intellectual property rights and goodwill. Gallman considered measuring the stocks and flows of all these forms of capital beyond the scope of his study. This chapter presents information on the one step that Gallman did take to fill in the picture by introducing his estimates of the stocks of consumer durables.

Gallman argued that because the value of residential structures was already included in the capital stock, it was sensible to add up the value of long-lasting goods that heated, furnished, and decorated these buildings. Following Simon Kuznets (1938, 6), he defined durables as goods "that without marked change and retaining their essential physical identity, are ordinarily employed in their ultimate use over a long period," conventionally a period of three years or more. Such goods are valued principally for the flow of services they provided. By way of contrast, perishable goods such as food and fuel were consumed in less than six months, and semi-durable goods such as clothing were consumed over a period between six months and three years. Consumer durables differed from producer durables primarily on the basis of ownership—by the household, as

Gallman drafted the core sections, 13.4 and 13.5. Rhode wrote the introductory sections, 13.1, 13.2, and 13.3; and the concluding sections, 13.6 and 13.7.

opposed to the business firm—and on the scale of operations involved. Many pieces of capital equipment, such as sewing machines, initially were producer durables used in shops and factories. Once these durables could be made smaller and less expensive, they were sold to consumers and used within the household.

The chapter has the following form. Section 13.2 uses Gallman's flow data to document the rising share of consumer durables in expenditure over time, and to raise questions about when consumer durables became important in the American economy. Section 13.3 calls attention to Gallman's favorite example of a nineteenth-century consumer durable, the cast-iron stove. Section 13.4 provides Gallman's detailed description of his estimating procedures. Section 13.5 compares Gallman's estimates of the aggregate stock of consumer durables over the 1774–1900 period with his numbers for the aggregate capital stock. Section 13.6 concludes the chapter.

## 13.2. The Secular Rise of Consumer Durables Spending

A commonplace in economic history is to associate the rise of spending on long-lasting consumer products with the "consumer durables revolution" of the early twentieth century.[2] Automobiles and electric appliances are given pride of place. Based on his annual flow data, Gallman tended to view the rise of durables spending as part of a longer-term process, as one involving more continuity than change. Gallman's view differed from the scholars who focused on the 1920s and 1930s primarily because he was taking a much longer perspective.

Gallman and Howle (1971, 33) wrote, "The pre–Civil War durables may have differed from those in use today, but they did perform essentially the same kinds of functions." They reported that the share of durables in consumption (measured either in current or constant price terms) doubled from 5 percent in the 1839–58 period to 10 percent in the 1919–38 period. It then remained constant through the 1939–53 period.

Indeed, Gallman's annual product data indicate that the rise in the durables' share of GNP over the 1840–90 period exceeded what occurred later.[3] Figure 13.1, panel A, graphs the annual series on the share of consumer durables in consumption and GNP, all measured by constant price series, from the 1830s to the 1950s using Gallman's and Kuznets's data. The Gallman series are from chapter 5; the Kuznets (1961b) data are his constant (1929) price variant III series from his T-Tables. (Using Kuznets's variant I series would create no significant differences.) The

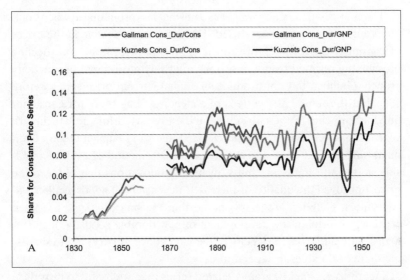

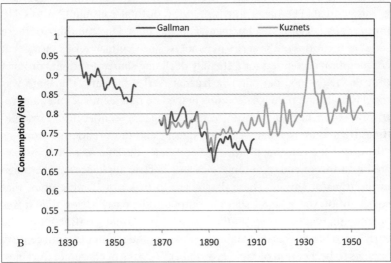

FIGURE 13.1  (a) Consumer durables share of consumption and annual product; (b) consumption as a share of annual product. Sources: See text.

series in figure 13.1, panel A, display sharp increases in the 1840s and 1850s and again in the late 1880s and early 1890s.[4] Notably, the volatility of the consumer durables shares over the 1920–50 period appears much greater than in Gallman's estimates. The importance of this category of spending for business cycle fluctuations might have changed.

The changes in the shares appear somewhat less pronounced when Gall-man's current price series are used. This reflects the decline in the prices of consumer durables relative to the aggregate price level. This decline presumably resulted from the sector's relatively more rapid productivity growth. Gallman did not produce an annual current price series before 1860, but the same basic pattern of a steadily rising share for consumer durables appears in the current value data reported for the benchmark years 1839, 1844, 1849, 1854, and 1859 in table 5 of Gallman (1966). Gall-man's share-based approach embraced the interaction of both demand-side shifts and supply-side shifts, including innovations that reduced the price, improved the quality, or increased the variety of goods available to consumers. Gallman (1972, 58) noted that "technical change has been especially fruitful in the development of new durable goods," which (to-gether with an income elasticity of demand above unitary) led to the ris-ing share of durables in expenditures.

Figure 13.1, panel B, graphs related series that are useful to introduce in this context. The panel shows the ratio of total consumption to GNP for the constant-price Gallman and Kuznets data. One can think of these series as the ratios of the series in panel A. The Gallman series shows that consumption accounted for a steadily declining share of national product over the 1839–1909 period. The Kuznets series indicates the share was roughly constant, perhaps declining in the late nineteenth century and re-covering over the mid-twentieth century. The nineteenth century is some-times treated as "the age of the producer" and the twentieth century as "the era of the consumer," with the consumer durable revolution associ-ated with the spread of automobiles and electric appliances as the hinge in the transformation. These data serve to make the simple point that consumption was a larger share of output in the early period than it was anytime thereafter, except in the throes of the Great Contraction of the early 1930s.[5] In figures that Gallman provides, the mid-nineteenth century appears to be a period of rapid growth in the stocks of consumer durables. What was happening during this crucial period?

## 13.3. Exemplar of Nineteenth-Century Consumer Durables: Cast-Iron Stoves

Gallman's favorite example of a mid-nineteenth-century consumer du-rable was the cast-iron stove. He believed that the innovation deserved far wider notice than it has received. In his *Cambridge Economic History of the United States*, volume 2, chapter 1, Gallman (2000, 33) wrote, "In the antebellum years the production and sale of stoves increased dramatically. Stoves vastly improved the quality of heating of homes and cooking." Stoves were not the most important consumer durable; timepieces and furniture dwarfed stoves in total volume. Nor were they the fastest-growing; timepieces and musical instruments outpaced stoves. And if price declines indicate innovation in production, stoves did not experience the most rapid advance in the period where data are available (see Nordhaus 1996 for the phenomenal declines in the price of lighting).

Yet when he was teaching and writing about nineteenth-century America, Gallman often highlighted the cast-iron stove. This was in part due to his interest in its effects on architecture and construction. As Virginia and Lee McAlester (1984, 28) argue, the cast-iron stoves and their venting systems "were far easier to install than massive fireplaces and thus permitted the wider use of larger—and less regular—house plans. Compound plans, in particular, now became more common."

Several other scholars have shared Gallman's appreciation of the cast-iron stove. Ruth Schwartz Cowan (1997, 197) called the cast-iron stove "the first do-it-yourself consumer durable, the first mass-produced appliance intended for use in people's homes."[6] Kathleen Smallzried (1956, 93–94) stated (italics in the original): "It can be said without exaggeration that *the cast-iron range created the first major revolution in cooking since the discovery of fire.*" Sigfried Giedion (1948, 528) opined that in the nineteenth century, "the cast-iron stove and range were identified with America much as the automobile was later."

The first stoves developed in Europe dated to the end of the fifteenth century. The first model invented and used in North America is typically credited to Benjamin Franklin. In 1744, Franklin built his famous free-standing stove, but it proved to be inefficient, smoky, and of limited popularity. Predating Franklin's efforts, several Pennsylvanians produced jamb (five-plate) stoves of German design that were set against the wall in front of the fireplace. Six-plate stoves, which were essentially cubic metal boxes with plates on each side, appeared on the market in the late eighteenth century and were much cheaper than Franklin's model. Ten-plate stoves represented an enlargement of the six-plate model; some contained internal ovens, making them the prototypes of the cook stove. The early nineteenth century stove remained "a fire hazard and, besides, the plates had to be replaced frequently" (Brady 1964, 176–77).

Only after stove makers began in the 1830s to use cast iron instead of sheet iron plates did households adopt stoves in place of the traditional fireplaces (McAlester 1984, 52). Over the antebellum period, American stove makers solved a number of technical problems—how to design fireboxes and grates to sustain fires with less care; how to ease disposal of ash and clinkers (unburned coal or charcoal); how to allow for a steady draft of air and prevent smoke from being released indoors; how to spread heat evenly, especially around the oven; and how to capture heat for hot water, vent coal gas, and make the coal feed itself automatically into the fire. They learned how to create better, more evenly heated ovens and ranges for cooking. And they developed better materials and casting techniques to reduce production costs and increase product durability.

Stoves evolved from simple utilitarian fireboxes designed to provide heat for general use into a diverse range of specialized and often highly ornate household appliances. Dorothy Brady (1964, 148) observed, "The Victorian preferences for ornamentation found their outlet mainly in goods manufactured for the use of the consumer. Factory production began with simple and mainly functional models, but decoration and variety were introduced fairly quickly wherever ornament did not appear to interfere with use. By 1850, a large proportion of the patent applications for stoves (48 out of 54 in 1849) pertained to ornamental moldings, carvings, forms and figures; and by 1890, the Aldrich Committee found no way to give a simple functional description of a cook stove."

The initial takeoff in the diffusion process for stoves is typically dated to the 1830s. Production rose from 25,000 in 1830, 100,000 in 1840, and 375,000 in 1850 to one million in 1860 and 2.1 million in 1870 (Dwyer, 1968, 361). Based on these figures, Stanley Lebergott (1984, 71) conjectured that less than 1 percent of American families had cast-iron stoves in the period before 1830, whereas two-thirds did by 1860. Gallman's figures of the stocks of "stoves, ranges, and fireless cookers" in table 13.3 rise in rough parallel with these data on production flows, although Gallman's numbers show a decline between 1870 and 1880.

Perhaps the greatest importance of the stoves was to economize on fuel. According to a detailed study reported in the 1830 *Transactions of the American Philosophical Society*, stoves could save between 50 and 90 percent of the firewood that a fireplace required to heat a room to a given temperature (Bull 1830). Stoves could be placed so as to warm a space more evenly; and with the proper layout of stovepipes, far less of the heat went "up in smoke." The commonly-cited statistic is that 80 percent of the heat generated in a fireplace escaped up the chimney (Reynolds and Pierson 1942, 3).

One factor slowing the adoption of stoves was the purported love of Americans for large open fires. In his classic *The Great Forest*, Richard G. Lillard (1947, 85) proclaimed, "All cabin dwellers gloried in the warmth of their fireplaces, exploiting their world of surplus trees where a poor man, even a plantation slave, could burn bigger fires than most noblemen in Europe. . . ." He added: "If the fire was too hot, he left the doors open, but fire he would have, if only to brighten up the dark end of the house." In the areas of the new nation where "trees were weeds," Americans could indulge in their love of open fires at low cost.

Another offsetting factor was that the wood used in stoves typically had to be split and "bucked up" into smaller pieces. Fireplaces could hold logs of two feet or more, whereas most stoves required lengths of sixteen inches or less. It took roughly twice the labor to cut the standard four-foot logs to stove lengths as was needed to produce fuel for fireplaces.[7] In *Energy in the American Economy*, Sam Schurr and Bruce Netschert (1960, 50) attribute the relatively slow transition from the fireplace to the country stove in the United States to "the simple fact that to chop fuel wood small enough for use in stoves would have required a substantial amount of human labor. Energy in the form of fuel wood was abundant, but manpower was scarce. It made no sense to waste man-hours in order to economize in the use of a seeming unlimited natural resource. Man's labor was the most valuable resource of all."[8] But by their own numbers, "the same quantity of wood, burned in a well-constructed wood stove, would supply about four times as much heat as when used in an open fireplace." Even with the need for bucking and splitting, it did not require four times as much labor to produce wood that fit into the stove rather than the fireplace.

The use of the cast-iron stoves facilitated the use of coal in heating homes. In the early 1800s, innovators developed grates allowing the combustion of coal without the forced draft that was used in furnaces and forges. Coal had several advantages over wood in urban settings. It had more fuel value per unit of weight and volume. Hence, coal required less space to store, was easier to transport, and was generally cheaper per BTU than wood in cities. Among the coals, anthracite was preferred for domestic uses. It produced less smoke and ash than either bituminous coal or wood. The map on fuel use in the 1880 census clearly indicates that the use of coal as a domestic fuel was concentrated in urban areas, and that wood burning predominated throughout rural America (Sargent 1884, 489). Lebergott (1976, 276) estimated that in 1880, 98 percent of farm households heated with wood, whereas 16 percent of urban households did. In total, 65 percent of US households burned wood in that year, whereas 35 percent burned coal.[9] Coal could be burned in fireplaces, as was relatively common in Europe. But the mineral fuel gave off dangerous and corrosive gases during combustion. In the Victorian era, many households used equipment similar to iron stoves built into the fireplace to control these gases.

These features of stoves had important consequences of industrializing and urbanizing America. Lebergott (1984, 71) observed, "As cities grew and the trees around them were cut down for firewood, the price of wood rose steadily." He argues that this created "irresistible" cost incentives to adopt the cast-iron stoves. Brady (1972, 71) noted, "Fuel was a costly element in the city workers' budget, especially when inefficient fireplaces were the only means for heating and cooking. The search for more efficient cooking and heating equipment suitable for the dwellings in the growing cities of the eighteenth and nineteenth centuries led to many innovations in the design of stoves. . . . The diffusion of stoves made its contribution to low-cost housing simply by eliminating the masonry in the fireplace."[10] The adoption of the cast-iron stove occurred just when America was moving into the Great Lakes region—what became known in the twentieth century as the "Snow Belt."

Gallman (1966, 64) was acutely aware of the role of firewood production in the early American economy. One of his three main improvements to Kuznets's annual national product was to include the value of firewood production (see chapter 5). According to Gallman's constant 1860 price series, firewood accounted for roughly 6.5 percent of all goods and services consumed circa 1839, several times the share spent on durables. By 1869 the firewood share in consumption had fallen to 3.0 percent, and by 1909 to only about 0.4 percent. The spread of cast-iron stoves thus had indirect effects on the allocation of consumer spending. Firewood was a perishable good, and hence by economizing on its use, the cast-iron stoves increased the share of consumer spending that could be devoted to nonperishables, including consumer durables.

In his draft outline for the *Cambridge* chapter, Gallman set the issues broadly: "Stress the importance of other elements than nutrition to human health and well-being—Elements promoted by growth (e.g. stoves— importance for quality of cooking and quality of home heating and for economy of both)—Talk about the innovation and diffusion of stoves, Talk about the innovation and diffusion of the balloon frame—effect on cost and quality of housing, etc."[11] Given his interest in architecture and construction, it is easy to see why Gallman was intrigued by the potential complementarity of cast-iron stoves and balloon-frame housing. (For the importance of balloon-frame construction of housing, see the discussion of structures in chapter 4). The cast-iron stove was only one example of the increasing importance of consumer durables during the "long" nineteenth century. Far greater detail on a comprehensive set of durables—including pianos, sewing machines, timepieces, furniture, and tombstones—may be found below. Gallman's estimates of household capital goods will now be presented in his own words.

## 13.4. Decadal Estimates of Consumer Durables, 1840–1900

This section details the estimation of consumer durables on a decadal basis from 1840 to 1900. The estimates for 1850, 1860, 1890, and 1900 were made by cumulating annual flows of the output of consumers' durables, expressed in 1860 prices and appropriately adjusted for capital consumption. These cumulations were then inflated to produce current price figures; see table 13.1.

The annual output series do not extend uninterruptedly for enough years to permit estimates of the stock of consumer durables for 1840, 1870, and 1880 to be made on the basis of cumulations of output flows alone. The cumulations for the years available (1834–39 for 1840; 1855–59, 1869, and half of 1870, taken together, for 1870; 1869–79 for 1880) were assembled, and the patterns of accumulation embodied in the estimates for the other benchmark years (1850, 1860, 1890, 1900) were used as means for blowing up the partial cumulations to achieve comprehensive estimates for 1840, 1870, and 1880 (see the notes to table 13.1).

The antebellum annual output flows refer to census years; for example, the estimate for 1839 refers to the flow across the period 1 June 1839 through 31 May 1840. These data were employed without adjustment. The postbellum series is a calendar-year series; it was converted into a form more suitable for present purposes by the calculation of two-year moving averages.

The system of capital consumption employed was straight-line. The reciprocal of the average life expectation of consumers' durables was computed (see below), and the value of each annual investment flow was reduced

TABLE 13.1 **Value of consumers' durables, measured in current and 1860 prices, 1840–1900, in millions of dollars**

**Panel A: 1840–70**

| | Value of output | | | | |
|---|---|---|---|---|---|
| Census years | 1860 prices | Remaining in | | | |
| | | 1840 | 1850 | 1860 | 1870 |
| 1834 | 25.5 | 17.9 | 2.6 | | |
| 1835 | 30.7 | 23.3 | 4.9 | | |
| 1836 | 28.8 | 23.6 | 6.3 | | |
| 1837 | 34.4 | 30.3 | 9.6 | | |
| 1838 | 36.7 | 34.5 | 12.5 | | |
| 1839 | 31.1 | 31.1 | 12.4 | | |
| 1840 | 29.0 | | 13.3 | | |
| 1841 | 36.2 | | 18.8 | | |
| 1842 | 40.0 | | 23.2 | | |
| 1843 | 41.8 | | 26.8 | 1.7 | |
| 1844 | 51.9 | | 36.3 | 5.2 | |
| 1845 | 60.2 | | 45.8 | 9.6 | |
| 1846 | 68.4 | | 56.1 | 15.0 | |
| 1847 | 82.9 | | 73.0 | 23.2 | |
| 1848 | 90.3 | | 84.9 | 30.7 | |
| 1849 | 96.6 | | 96.6 | 38.6 | |
| 1850 | 108.5 | | | 49.9 | |
| 1851 | 127.8 | | | 56.2 | |
| 1852 | 156.6 | | | 79.9 | |
| 1853 | 162.0 | | | 94.0 | |
| 1854 | 162.3 | | | 105.5 | |
| 1855 | 177.0 | | | 127.4 | 3.5 |
| 1856 | 187.0 | | | 147.7 | 16.8 |
| 1857 | 184.2 | | | 158.4 | 29.5 |
| 1858 | 197.5 | | | 183.7 | 45.4 |
| 1859 | 200.4 | | | 200.4 | 60.1 |
| 1869 (calendar) | 349 | | | | 338.5 |
| 1870 (1/2 calendar year output) | 165 | | | | 165 |
| 1. Totals, six most recent years | | 160.7 | 392.7 | 923.1 | |
| 2. Total value of consumers' durables at 1860 prices | | (231) | 524.1 | 1,327.10 | (2190.8) |
| 3. Ratio of lines 2 to 1 | | (1.4377) | 1.3346 | 1.4377 | |
| 4. Price index | | 115.6 | 113.3 | 100 | 114.2 |
| 5. Total value of consumers' durables at current prices (Line 2 × line 4 ÷ 100) | | 267 | 593.8 | 1,327.10 | 2,501.90 |

TABLE 13.1 *(continued)*

**Panel A: 1840–70**

| Census years | Value of output 1860 prices | Remaining in | | | |
|---|---|---|---|---|---|
| | | 1840 | 1850 | 1860 | 1870 |
| 6. Total of first 5 years & last 1-1/2 | | | 157.6 | 338.6 | 658.8 |
| 7. Ratio of lines 2 and 6 | | 3.3255 | 3.9194 | (3.3255) | |

**Panel B: 1870–1900**

| | Value of output, 1860 prices | | Remaining in | | |
|---|---|---|---|---|---|
| | Calendar years | Census years | 1880 | 1890 | 1900 |
| 1869 | 349 | 339.5 | 101.9 | | |
| 1870 | 330 | 227.5 | 121.2 | | |
| 1871 | 325 | 375.0 | 16.05 | | |
| 1872 | 425 | 433.5 | 221.1 | | |
| 1873 | 442 | 415.5 | 241.0 | | |
| 1874 | 389 | 419.5 | 272.7 | | |
| 1875 | 450 | 448.5 | 322.9 | 9.0 | |
| 1876 | 447 | 466.5 | 368.5 | 42.0 | |
| 1877 | 486 | 480.0 | 412.8 | 76.8 | |
| 1884 | 474 | 512.0 | 476.2 | 117.8 | |
| 1879 | 550 | 572.5 | 572.5 | 171.8 | |
| 1880 | 595 | 634.0 | | 234.6 | |
| 1881 | 673 | 705.0 | | 310.2 | |
| 1882 | 737 | 744.5 | | 379.7 | |
| 1883 | 752 | 755.0 | | 437.9 | |
| 1884 | 758 | 812.5 | | 528.1 | |
| 1885 | 867 | 932.5 | | 671.4 | 18.7 |
| 1886 | 998 | 1,037.5 | | 819.6 | 93.4 |
| 1887 | 1,077 | 1,084.5 | | 932.7 | 173.5 |
| 1888 | 1,092 | 1,090.0 | | 1,013.7 | 250.7 |
| 1889 | 1,088 | 1,125.0 | | 1,125.0 | 337.5 |
| 1890 | 1,162 | 1,172.5 | | | 433.8 |
| 1891 | 1,183 | 1,218.0 | | | 535.9 |
| 1892 | 1,253 | 1,183.5 | | | 603.6 |
| 1893 | 1,114 | 1,051.0 | | | 609.6 |
| 1894 | 988 | 1,097.0 | | | 713.1 |
| 1895 | 1,206 | 1,196.5 | | | 861.5 |
| 1896 | 1,187 | 1,228.5 | | | 970.5 |
| 1897 | 1,270 | 1,250.0 | | | 1,075.0 |
| 1898 | 1,230 | 1,316.5 | | | 1,224.3 |
| 1899 | 1,403 | 1,369.0 | | | 1,369.0 |
| 1900 | 1,335 | | | | |

*continues*

TABLE 13.1 (*continued*)

**Panel B: 1870–1900**

| | Value of output, 1860 prices | | Remaining in | | |
|---|---|---|---|---|---|
| | Calendar years | Census years | 1880 | 1890 | 1900 |
| 1. Totals, 11 most recent years | | | 3,275.8 | 6,624.7 | 8,733.8 |
| 2. Total value of consumers' durables at 1860 prices | | | (3439.6) | (6870.3) | (9270.1) |
| 3. Ratio of lines 2 and 1 | | | (1.05) | 1.0371 | 1.0614 |
| 4. Price index | | | 87.3 | 68.2 | 62.5 |
| 5. Total value of consumers' durables at current prices (line 2 × line 4 ÷ 100) | | | 3,002.8 | 4,685.5 | 5,793.8 |

Sources:

Panels A and B, column 1: The estimation of this series is described in Gallman (1966). Panel B, column 2: Two-year moving averages of data in column 1, dated to the earlier of the two years (i.e., the mean of 1869 and 1870 is dated to 1869 and stands for census year 1869). Panel A, columns 2–5, and panel B, columns 3–5: These columns contain the depreciated flows of column 1 (panel A) and 2 (panel B). For example, the average life expectation of durables produced in census year 1834 was probably about 16.7 years (see table 13.2, 1840). The reciprocal of 16.7 is .06; i.e., the appropriate depreciation rate is 6 percent. By June 1 of 1840, goods produced in census year 1834 (i.e., between June 1, 1834, and May 31, 1835) were five years old, and had therefore lost 30 per cent of their original value. Thirty percent of $25.5 million (panel A, column 1) is $7.65 million, leaving $17.85 million (rounded to 17.9) left on June 1 of 1840, the figure appearing in the column headed "1840." For the years 1834 through 1850, a depreciation rate of 6 percent was employed; thereafter, a rate of 7 percent (see table 13.2).

Lines 1–3 in panels A and B and lines 6 and 7 in panel A are devoted to the estimation of the value of consumers' durables, in 1860 prices, at census dates, 1840–1900. For the years 1850, 1860, 1890, and 1900, the estimates were made simply by summing up the depreciated annual flows. For the years 1840, 1870, and 1880, it was necessary to blow up incomplete flows. The blow-up ratios (rows 3 and 7) were taken from evidence for years for which complete information was available. The estimate for 1840 was based on evidence for 1860 (i.e., the bracketed ratio in row 3 for 1840 was taken from 1860), rather than an average of the experience reflected in the 1860 and 1850 data, because the circumstances of the period during which the stock was being accumulated are more nearly similar for 1840 and 1860 than is the case for 1840 and 1850. Like reasoning led to the application to the 1870 data of a blow-up ratio drawn from the 1850 data. The blow-up ratio for 1880 is a rough average of experience in 1860 (1.043), 1890 (1.037), and 1900 (1.061). Clearly, hard data figure more importantly in the estimate for 1880 (95 percent) than in the estimates for 1840 (70 percent) and 1870 (30 percent). The figure for 1880 seems quite secure; the figures for the other two years seem much less so. Line 4 in each panel contains price index numbers, derived in table 13.3. Line 5 lists the current price estimates, calculated by multiplying the constant price estimates by the price index numbers, divided by 100.

by this fraction for each year following the investment. Thus, if consumers' durables lasted, on average, 16.7 years, the depreciation rate would be 6 percent. An investment of $100 in year t would become a capital stock of $94 in year t + 1 ($100 minus $6), and $88 ($94 minus $6), in year t + 2, and so forth.[12]

TABLE 13.2  **Mean life expectancy of new consumers' durables, 1850–90**

|  | Life expectancy | | | |
|---|---|---|---|---|
|  | **20 years** | **12 years** | **10 years** | **Totals** |
| **Real value of output, in millions of dollars** | | | | |
| 1840 | 13.6 | 1.4 | 5.8 | 20.8 |
| 1850 | 27.7 | 5.3 | 20.4 | 53.4 |
| 1860 | 50.3 | 17.2 | 47.9 | 115.4 |
| 1870 | 93.1 | 23.7 | 75.5 | 192.3 |
| 1880 | 148.0 | 27.0 | 166.2 | 341.2 |
| 1890 | 259.1 | 57.5 | 339.7 | 656.3 |
| 1900 | 324.1 | 97.9 | 464.4 | 886.4 |
| **Shares in output** | | | | |
| 1840 | 0.654 | 0.067 | 0.279 | 1.000 |
| 1850 | 0.519 | 0.099 | 0.382 | 1.000 |
| 1860 | 0.436 | 0.149 | 0.415 | 1.000 |
| 1870 | 0.484 | 0.123 | 0.393 | 1.000 |
| 1880 | 0.433 | 0.079 | 0.487 | 1.000 |
| 1890 | 0.395 | 0.088 | 0.517 | 1.000 |
| 1900 | 0.366 | 0.11 | 0.524 | 1.000 |

| **Life expectancies × shares** | | | | **Mean life expectancy** | **Depreciation rate** |
|---|---|---|---|---|---|
| 1840 | 13.08 | 0.80 | 2.79 | 16.67 | 6.0 |
| 1850 | 10.38 | 1.19 | 3.82 | 15.39 | 6.5 |
| 1860 | 8.72 | 1.79 | 4.15 | 14.66 | 6.8 |
| 1870 | 9.68 | 1.48 | 3.93 | 15.09 | 6.6 |
| 1880 | 8.66 | 0.95 | 4.87 | 14.48 | 6.9 |
| 1890 | 7.90 | 1.06 | 5.17 | 14.13 | 7.1 |
| 1900 | 7.32 | 1.32 | 5.24 | 13.88 | 7.1 |

Sources:
The data in the first panel, which distributes outputs among classes of goods having different degrees of durability, are drawn from table 13.3. Specifically, the first column is (table 13.3, line A.4.b. + A.5.x.) ÷ A.5.z.; the second column is table 13.3, line B.6.y.; the third column is (table 13.3, line C.14.b., + C.15.x.) ÷ line C.15.y. The second panel was computed from data in the first panel by dividing the total for each year through the entries recorded for the three classes of goods. The third panel was calculated by multiplying the share of each class of goods in total output for each year (taken from the second panel) by the life expectancy of new goods of this type (table heading). The sum across each row in the panel yields the average life expectancy of goods produced in that year. The depreciation rates are the reciprocals of the life expectancy estimates.

Table 13.2 presents estimates of the mean life expectations of new consumer durables and the associated depreciation rate. The life expectations of different classes of new durables were taken from Goldsmith, except for carriages. (Goldsmith does not treat carriages; here they are given a life expectation of twenty years, the same as furniture.) The classes were combined to produce average life expectations for durables of all types in the following way. Production of the various types of durables for benchmark years was drawn from the work of Shaw and Gallman, which is based on the census. These output flows were then deflated by means of Dorothy Brady's price index numbers, and used to compute the average expectation of life of the durables produced at each census date. These figures are consistent with depreciation rates of about 7 per cent after 1850, and about 6 per cent for 1850 and earlier years.

Brady's weighted index numbers were used to inflate the constant price benchmark stock estimates. The price index weights were established in the following way. The fraction of total constant price output accounted for by each class of property—classes being defined in terms of durability— was established by deflating the benchmark output estimates. Given the flow of real output of each type of property, together with the durability of each type of property, it was then possible to estimate the structure of the stock of durables (i.e., the distribution of the stock among classes defined in terms of life expectation) in each benchmark year. Table 13.3 presents, in detail, the consumer durable price estimates for the 1840–1900 period.

TABLE 13.3 **Consumers' durables price indexes, 1840–1900**

|     |                                                    | 1840 | 1850 | 1860 | 1870 | 1880 | 1890 | 1900  |
|-----|----------------------------------------------------|------|------|------|------|------|------|-------|
| **A.** | **Consumers' durables with 20-year lives**       |      |      |      |      |      |      |       |
| 1a  | New furniture                                      |      |      |      |      |      |      |       |
| 1b  | Household furniture Value, at current prices (mil. $) | 6.5 | 16.6 | 22 | 58.4 | 66.3 | 95.2 | 106.7 |
| 1c  | Price index: furniture: tables, chairs and bedsteads | — | 111 | 100 | 108 | 79 | 70 | — |
| 1d  | Value, at 1860 prices (mil. $)                     | — | 15 | 22 | 54.1 | 83.9 | 136 | — |
| 2a  | Carriages and wagons                               |      |      |      |      |      |      |       |
| 2b  | Value, at current prices (mil. $)                  | 6.1 | 8.1 | 19.6 | 36.1 | 36 | 56 | 55.6 |
| 2c  | Price index: Carriages, buggies, and wagons        | — | 91 | 100 | 148 | 89 | 76 | 77 |
| 2d  | Value, at 1860 prices (mil. $)                     | — | 8.9 | 19.6 | 24.4 | 40.4 | 73.7 | 72.2 |
| 3a  | Musical instruments                                |      |      |      |      |      |      |       |
| 3b  | Value, at current prices (mil. $)                  | 0.7 | 1.9 | 5.1 | 10.1 | 14.1 | 26.9 | 34.2 |
| 3c  | Price index: pianos and reed organs                | — | 96 | 99 | 112 | 95 | 92 | 82 |
| 3d  | Value, at 1860 prices (mil. $)                     | — | 2 | 5.2 | 9 | 14.8 | 29.2 | 41.7 |
| 4a  | Tombstones                                         |      |      |      |      |      |      |       |
| 4b  | Value, at current prices (mil. $)                  | 0.8 | 1.8 | 3.5 | 6.6 | 7.5 | 15.2 | 20.3 |
| 4c  | Price index (none)                                 |      |      |      |      |      |      |       |

TABLE 13.3 *(continued)*

| | | 1840 | 1850 | 1860 | 1870 | 1880 | 1890 | 1900 |
|---|---|---|---|---|---|---|---|---|
| 5x | Total value, at current prices (mil $), rows 1b, 2b and 3b | 13.3 | 26.6 | 46.7 | 104.6 | 116.4 | 178.1 | 196.5 |
| 5y | Total value, at 1860 prices (mil. $) | 12.8 | 25.9 | 46.8 | 87.5 | 139.1 | 238.9 | 293.7 |
| 5z | Price index (103.6) | — | 102.7 | 100 | 119.5 | 83.7 | 74.6 | 66.9 |
| **B.** | **Consumers' durables with 12-year lives** | | | | | | | |
| 1a | Household appliances | | | | | | | |
| 1b | Refrigerators Value, at current prices (mil. $) | — | — | 0.2 | 0.6 | 1.7 | 4.5 | 5.3 |
| 1c | Price index: refrigerators | — | — | 100 | 105 | 73 | 65 | — |
| 1d | Value, at 1860 prices (mil. $) | — | — | 0.2 | 0.6 | 2.3 | 6.9 | — |
| 2a | Stoves, ranges, and fireless cookers | | | | | | | |
| 2b | Value, at current prices (mil. $) | 1.6 | 6.1 | 14.1 | 15.3 | 11.5 | 24.2 | 39.2 |
| 2c | Price index: stoves | 117 | 116 | 100 | 146 | 114 | 71 | 68 |
| 2d | Value, at 1860 prices (mil. $) | 1.4 | 5.3 | 14.1 | 10.5 | 10.1 | 34.1 | 57.6 |
| 3a | Sewing machines, household | | | | | | | |
| 3b | Value, at current prices (mil. $) | — | — | 2.8 | 9.2 | 8.7 | 8.1 | 11.5 |
| 3c | Price index: sewing machines | — | — | 100 | 83 | 66 | 62 | 53 |
| 3d | Value, at 1860 prices (mil. $) | — | — | 2.8 | 11.1 | 13.2 | 13.1 | 21.7 |
| 4a | Washing machines and clothes dryers | | | | | | | |
| 4b | Value, at current prices (mil. $) | — | — | 0.1 | 1.4 | 1.2 | 2.5 | 3.7 |
| 4c | Price index: washing machines | — | — | 100 | 92 | 83 | 73 | — |
| 4d | Value, at 1860 prices (mil. $) | — | — | 0.1 | 1.5 | 1.4 | 3.4 | — |
| 5a | Elect. household appliances and supplies | | | | | | | |
| 5b | Value, at current prices (mil. $) | — | — | — | — | — | — | 1.9 |
| 6x | Total value,, at current prices (mil. $), rows 1b,2b,3b,4b | 1.6 | 6.1 | 17.2 | 26.5 | 23.1 | 39.3 | 59.7 |
| 6y | Total value, at 1860 prices (mil. $) | 1.4 | 5.3 | 17.2 | 23.7 | 27 | 57.5 | 97.9 |
| 6z | Price index | 117 | 116 | 100 | 111.8 | 85.6 | 68.3 | 61 |

*continues*

TABLE 13.3 (*continued*)

| | | 1840 | 1850 | 1860 | 1870 | 1880 | 1890 | 1900 |
|---|---|---|---|---|---|---|---|---|
| C. | **Consumers' durables with 10-year lives** | | | | | | | |
| 1a | House furnishings | | | | | | | |
| 1b | Floor coverings Value, at current prices (mil. $) | 1.6 | 5.5 | 9.7 | 22.1 | 30.3 | 44 | 47 |
| 1c | Price index: rugs | 241 | 139 | 100 | 189 | 91 | 78 | 71 |
| 1d | Value, at 1860 prices (mil. $) | 0.7 | 4 | 9.7 | 11.7 | 33.3 | 56.4 | 66.2 |
| 2a | Blankets: all-wool woven, cotton warp woven, and cotton mixed woven | | | | | | | |
| 2b | Value, at current prices (mil. $) | 0.6 | 0.7 | 1.3 | 5.1 | 5.5 | 7.2 | 5.2 |
| 2c | Price index: blankets | 145 | 111 | 106 | 95 | 71 | 59 | 62 |
| 2d | Value, at 1860 prices (mil. $) | 0.4 | 0.6 | 1.2 | 5.4 | 7.7 | 12.2 | 8.4 |
| 3a | Lamps and chimneys | | | | | | | |
| 3b | Value, at current prices (mil. $) | — | 0.6 | 1.2 | 2.4 | 4.3 | 6 | 10.9 |
| 3c | Price index: lamps | — | 154 | 96 | 88 | 50 | 65 | 50 |
| 3d | Value, at 1860 prices (mil. $) | — | 0.4 | 1.3 | 2.7 | 8.6 | 9.2 | 21.8 |
| 4a | Mattresses and string beds NES. | | | | | | | |
| 4b | Value, at current prices (mil. $) | — | — | 0.4 | — | 5 | 15 | 17.6 |
| 4c | Price index: mattresses and springs | — | — | 100 | — | 65 | 43 | 53 |
| 4d | Value, at 1860 prices (mil. $) | — | — | 0.4 | — | 7.7 | 34.9 | 33.2 |
| 5a | Mirrors, framed and unframed | | | | | | | |
| 5b | Value, at current prices (mil. $) | — | — | — | 0.3 | 0.2 | 3.4 | 4.6 |
| 5c | Price index: looking glasses | — | — | — | 120 | 133 | 100 | (77) |
| 5d | Value, at 1860 prices (mil. $) | — | — | — | 0.3 | 0.2 | 3.4 | 6.0 |
| 6a | Feather pillows and beds; other misc. | | | | | | | |
| 6b | Value, at current prices (mil. $) | — | 0.8 | 2.1 | 6.5 | 10.4 | 19.7 | 22.9 |
| 7q | Total value, at current prices (mil. $), rows 1b,2b,3b,4b,5b | 2.2 | 6.8 | 12.6 | 29.9 | 45.3 | 75.6 | 85.3 |
| 7r | Total value, at 1860 prices (mil. $) | 1.1 | 5 | 12.6 | 20.1 | 57.1 | 116.1 | 135.6 |
| 7w | Price index | 200 | 136 | 100 | 148.8 | 79.3 | 65.1 | 62.9 |
| 8a | China, tableware | | | | | | | |

TABLE 13.3 *(continued)*

|  |  | 1840 | 1850 | 1860 | 1870 | 1880 | 1890 | 1900 |
|---|---|---|---|---|---|---|---|---|
| 8b | Razors and table cutlery Value, at current prices (mil. $) | 1 | 1.6 | 1.9 | 4.3 | 4.5 | 4.3 | 5.8 |
| 8c | Price index: cutlery | — | — | 100 | 115 | 116 | 71 | 66 |
| 8d | Value, at 1860 prices (mil. $) | — | — | 1.9 | 3.7 | 3.8 | 6.1 | 8.8 |
| 9a | China, earthenware, etc. | | | | | | | |
| 9b | Value, at current prices (mil. $) | 0.7 | 1 | 1.9 | 4 | 4.6 | 9.9 | 14.1 |
| 9c | Price index: china, earthenware | 140 | — | 100 | 112 | 89 | 70 | — |
| 9d | Value, at 1860 prices (mil. $) | 0.5 | — | 1.9 | 3.6 | 5.2 | 14.1 | — |
| 10a | Wooden Goods NES | | | | | | | |
| 10b | Value, at current prices (mil. $) | 0.8 | 1.1 | 2.2 | 5.5 | 5.6 | 3.8 | 3.8 |
| 10c | Price index: woodenware | — | 132 | 108 | 129 | 86 | 76 | 72 |
| 10d | Value, at 1860 prices (mil. $) | — | 0.8 | 2 | 4.3 | 6.5 | 5 | 5.3 |
| 11a | Blown tumblers, etc. | | | | | | | |
| 11b | Value, at current prices (mil. $) | 0.6 | 1 | 3.8 | 3.7 | 4.7 | 9.1 | 13.6 |
| 11c | Price index: glassware | 147 | — | 100 | 84 | 47 | 37 | |
| 11d | Value, at 1860 prices (mil. $) | 0.4 | — | 3.8 | 4.4 | 10 | 24.6 | |
| 12a | All other utensils | | | | | | | |
| 12b | Value, at current prices (mil. $) | — | 0.1 | 0.2 | 1 | 0.9 | 1.4 | 6.4 |
| 13q | Total value, at current prices (mil. $) rows 8b,9b,10b,11b | 3.1 | 4.7 | 9.8 | 17.5 | 19.4 | 27.1 | 37.3 |
| 13r | Total value, at 1860 prices (mil. $) | 2.1 | 3.8 | 9.6 | 16 | 25.6 | 49.8 | 73.6 |
| 13w | Price index | -147.4 | 102.1 | 109.4 | 75.8 | 54.4 | 50.7 | 124.8 |
| 14a | Jewelry, etc. | | | | | | | |
| 14b | Clocks; watches and watch movements; other jewelry; books; luggage; motor vehicles; motorcycles and bicycles; pleasure craft Value, at current prices (mil. $) | 4.3 | 15.2 | 25.9 | 51.7 | 65.3 | 107.6 | 168.3 |
| 15x | Total value, at current prices (mil. $) rows 7a,13a | 5.3 | 11.5 | 22.4 | 47.4 | 64.7 | 102.7 | 122.6 |
| 15y | Total value, at 1860 prices (mil. $) | 3.2 | 8.8 | 22.2 | 36.1 | 82.7 | 165.9 | 209.2 |
| 15z | Price index | 165.6 | 130.7 | 100.9 | 131.3 | 78.2 | 61.9 | 58.6 |

*continues*

TABLE 13.3 (*continued*)

| | | 1840 | 1850 | 1860 | 1870 | 1880 | 1890 | 1900 |
|---|---|---|---|---|---|---|---|---|
| **D.** | **Consumers' durables with 5-year lives** | | | | | | | |
| 1a | Ophthalamic and orthopedic products; eyeglasses; artificial limbs | | | | | | | |
| 1b | Value, at current prices (mil. $) | | | 0.1 | 0.4 | 0.7 | 2.3 | 4.8 |
| **E.** | **Weighted average price indexes of consumers' durables stocks** | | | | | | | |
| 1 | Weights | | | | | | | |
| a | 20-year life | 0.702 | 0.572 | 0.515 | 0.544 | 0.501 | 0.456 | 0.433 |
| b | 12-year life | 0.058 | 0.089 | 0.128 | 0.109 | 0.07 | 0.079 | 0.093 |
| c | 10-year life | 0.24 | 0.339 | 0.357 | 0.347 | 0.429 | 0.465 | 0.474 |
| 2 | Indexes × weights | | | | | | | |
| a | 20-year life | 72.7 | 58.7 | 51.5 | 65 | 42 | 34 | 29 |
| b | 12-year life | 6.8 | 10.3 | 12.8 | 12.2 | 6 | 5.4 | 5.7 |
| c | 10-year life | 39.7 | 44.3 | 36 | 45.6 | 33.6 | 28.8 | 27.8 |
| d | Totals: weighted indexes, unadjusted | 119.2 | 113.3 | 100.3 | 122.8 | 81.6 | 68.2 | 62.5 |
| e | Adjusted to the dates of the consumers' durables stock estimates | 115.6 | 113.3 | 100 | 114.2 | 87.3 | 68.2 | 62.5 |

Note:

(mil. $) = in millions of dollars

Sources:

Sections A through D: Lines whose enumerations end in "a" describe the consumers' durables that fall within each durability class, according to Goldsmith (1951, 23). In lines whose enumerations end in "b," the descriptive material and the estimates are from Shaw and Gallman. The Shaw data cover the years 1870–1900 (census years 1869–99), and the Gallman data cover the years 1840–60 (census years 1839–1859). The Gallman data are from worksheets underlying Gallman's numbers in Gallman 1966; the Shaw data come from Shaw 1947, 118–24. Shaw's estimates have been slightly modified to enhance the comparability of the antebellum and postbellum estimates. In lines whose enumerations end in "c," the descriptive material and estimates are from Brady 1966. Lines whose enumerations end in "q" or "x" contain sums of the lines specified.

Lines whose enumerations end in "r" or "y" contain sums of constant price data, comparable with the sums in lines ending in "q" or "x," with the following exceptions. Line A.5.y., 1840 and 1900, were calculated by deflating line A.5.x., 1840 and 1900, by indexes in Line A.5.z. Lines B.6.y., 1900, C.13.w., 1840 and 1850, were computed in a like manner. Lines whose enumerations end in "w" or "z" contain the indexes implicit in the appropriate lines "q" and "r" or "x" and "y," with the exceptions of line A.5.z., 1840 and 1900 (extrapolated on line B.6.z.); line B.6.z., 1900 (extrapolated from 1890 on a weighted index of lines C.2.c. and 3.c.); and line C.13.z., 1840 and 1850 (extrapolated in a like manner).

   Section E: (1.) Based chiefly on table 13.2. For the years 1850–1900, the price index numbers of the three durability classes were weighted in the following way. The price index for property that had life expectancies of ten or twelve years when new received the weight given in the first panel of table 13.2, while the index for the property with a life expectancy of twenty years received a weight equal to the sum of the entry in table 13.2 for the given year, and half of the entry for the preceding census year. For example, the weights accorded the three types of durables in 1850 were as follows: ten-year life, $20.4 million; twelve-year life, $5.3 million; twenty-year life, $27.7 million plus ($13.6 million/2), or $34.5 million. For 1840 the same scheme was followed, except that in the absence of a figure for census 1830, the price index number for property with an expected life of twenty years was given a weight equal to one and one-quarter times the 1840 real value of output of goods with an expected life of twenty years. The weighting scheme is intended to take into account the fact that durable goods stay in the stock longer than those of lesser durability. (2.a.–c.) The weights of E.1. multiplied by the indexes in lines A.5.z., B.6.z., and C.15.z. (2.d.) The sums of Lines E.2.a.–c., which compose the weighted price indexes. (2.e.) The indexes in line E.2.d. do not correspond exactly with the dates of the consumers' durables estimates. Line E.2.e. contains indexes adjusted to the proper year. The adjustment device is described in the notes to table 8.9, above.

## 13.5. Estimates for Years before 1840

The section details the estimates of consumer durables before 1840.

**1774.** According to Jones (1980, 90), the stock of consumers' durables, other than apparel, ("equipment, furniture, other," in Jones's words) was worth 6,370,000 pounds in 1774. Jones's concept appears to be identical with the one underlying the consumers' durables estimates for 1840–1900, to be discussed below. Shifting from pounds to dollars by means of Jones's exchange rate ($4.15, p. 10) yields a dollar estimate of $26,435,500 for consumers' durables in 1774.

Table 13.4 presents a price index for 1809, assembled from the work of Dorothy Brady (1966, 107) and Anne Bezanson (US Bureau of the Census 1960, series E-76, E-78, and E-82), appropriately weighted. The value of consumers' durables in 1774, expressed in prices of 1860, then, is $26,435,500 divided by 1.39, or $19,018,345.

TABLE 13.4 **Price index for 1809**

| Panel A | | | Price | Base | Weight |
|---|---|---|---|---|---|
| 1 | a | Furniture (tables, chairs, bedsteads) | 289 | 1860 | 0.57 |
| 1 | b | Carriages, buggies, wagons | 234 | 1860 | 0.35 |
| 1 | c | Pianos, reed organs | 153 | 1860 | 0.08 |
| 1 | d | Weighted average, 1a–1c | 258 | 1860 | [0.70] |
| 2 | | Stoves | 154 | 1860 | [0.06] |
| 3 | a | Rugs | 301 | 1860 | 0.36 |
| 3 | b | Blankets | 197 | 1860 | 0.04 |
| 3 | c | Lamps | 180 | 1860 | 0.04 |
| 3 | d | Cutlery | 250 | 1860 | 0.07 |
| 3 | e | China, earthware | 172 | 1860 | 0.07 |
| 3 | d | Woodenware | 194 | 1860 | 0.07 |
| 3 | g | Glassware | 256 | 1860 | 0.14 |
| 3 | h | Clocks | 517 | 1860 | 0.04 |
| 3 | i | Books | 267 | 1860 | 0.16 |
| 3 | j | Weighted average, 3a–3i | 266 | 1860 | [0.24] |
| 4 | | Weighted average, 1d, 2, 3j. | 254 | 1860 | |
| **Panel B** | | | | | |
| 5 | | Lumber products | 79.4 | 1809 | |
| 6 | | Industrial consumption goods | 61.3 | 1809 | |
| 7 | | Weighted average | 74 | 1809 | |
| **Panel C** | | | | | |
| 8 | | Bezanson's 1774 index shifted to 1784 | 73.9 | | |
| 9 | | Line 7 × line 8 ÷ 100 | 54.7 | | |
| 10 | | Line 4 × line 9 ÷ 100 | | | |
| | | 1774 consumers' durables price | 139 | 1860 | |

Source: See text.

The original Jones estimate of the value of consumers' durables, in prices of 1774, has all the strength of Jones's figures, in general, which is considerable strength. The deflator for 1809 rests on good evidence that relates to the important components of the stock of consumers' durables, and the weighting system is at least relevant to mid-nineteenth century circumstances. There is no strong reason to believe that it misrepresents the conditions of 1809. It will be obvious to the reader that the extension of the index number to 1784 is less secure, while the further extension to 1774 is even less so. Nonetheless, the deflator is not without merit and the ultimate results seem plausible, as will appear.

**1799, 1805, 1815.** There are no strong bases for estimating the value of the stocks of consumers' durables in 1799, 1805, or 1815, and to accept weak estimates just for the sake of completeness does not seem very sensible. Goldsmith has figures for 1805, derived from Blodget, but they are very heavily processed, involving some important guesses, and the final results place the relative importance of consumers' durables (i.e., their importance relative to the rest of the capital stock) so far out of line with the figures for 1774 and for 1840 through 1900 that they seem clearly unacceptable. This gap, then, is left unfilled.

## 13.6. Gallman's Estimates of the Stock of Consumer Durables

Table 13.5 displays Gallman's estimates of the aggregate *stock* of consumer durables from 1774 to 1900 (lines 1 and 2). To provide context, the table also included his estimated figures for the domestic capital stock, excluding consumer durables (lines 4 and 5).[13] Finally, the table has relevant price indexes for consumer durables (line 3) and domestic capital (line 6). Their ratio, displayed in line 9, shows that the price of consumer durables fell much faster than the price of domestic capital over most of this period. As the data displayed in line 8 reveal, the ratio of the stock of consumer durables to domestic capital in constant 1860 prices rose almost continuously over the 1774–1900 period. The ratio quadrupled from 4 percent in 1774, just before American independence, to nearly 16 percent at the beginning of the twentieth century. Given the discussion in the preceding section, it should not be surprising that most of this increase occurred between 1840 and 1870.

The ratio of consumer durable to domestic capital, measured in current prices, fluctuated more widely. This ratio fell from 1774 to 1840,

TABLE 13-5 **Value of the stocks of consumers' durables, 1774–1900, in millions of dollars**

| | 1774 | 1840 | 1850 | 1860 | 1870 | 1880 | 1890 | 1900 |
|---|---|---|---|---|---|---|---|---|
| **Consumer durables** | | | | | | | | |
| 1 Value, at current prices | 26 | 267 | 594 | 1,327 | 2,502 | 3,003 | 4,686 | 5,794 |
| 2 Value, at 1860 prices | 19 | 231 | 524 | 1,327 | 2,191 | 3,440 | 6,870 | 9,270 |
| 3 Price index | 139 | 116 | 113 | 100 | 114 | 87 | 68 | 63 |
| **Domestic capital** | | | | | | | | |
| 4 Value, at current prices | 284 | 4,069 | 6,334 | 12,394 | 18,831 | 24,752 | 40,715 | 53,784 |
| 5 Value, at 1860 prices | 481 | 4,828 | 7,091 | 12,395 | 15,204 | 22,907 | 42,349 | 59,313 |
| 6 Price index | 59 | 84.3 | 89.3 | 100 | 123.9 | 108.1 | 96.1 | 90.7 |
| **Ratio of consumers' durables to domestic capital** | | | | | | | | |
| 7 Value, at current prices | 0.092 | 0.066 | 0.094 | 0.107 | 0.133 | 0.121 | 0.115 | 0.108 |
| 8 Value, at 1860 prices | 0.04 | 0.048 | 0.074 | 0.107 | 0.144 | 0.15 | 0.162 | 0.156 |
| 9 Relative price (line 3 ÷ line 6) | 235.4 | 137.6 | 126.5 | 100 | 92 | 80.5 | 70.7 | 69.5 |

Note: Domestic capital excludes consumers' durables.
Source: See text.

rebounded and rose until 1870, and then again declined. It is possible that the 1840 current price figure is too low.[14] By Gallman's estimate, consumer durable prices fell between 1774 and 1840 during a period when other prices (capital and the CPI) were rising.

## 13.7 Conclusion

This chapter has opened a window into Gallman's stock data on consumer durables. It has offered his arguments regarding the quantitative and qualitative importance of these goods in the "long" nineteenth century, before the "consumer durables revolution" of the early twentieth century.

## CHAPTER FOURTEEN

# Wealth in the Colonial and Early National Periods

## 14.1. Introduction

The materials from which wealth and capital estimates may be made for the late eighteenth and early nineteenth centuries are moderately rich, and the various series overlap sufficiently so that useful consistency tests can be conducted. We begin by identifying the principal estimates.

## 14.2. Principal Aggregate and Component Wealth Estimates

The aggregate estimates that have the firmest empirical basis are those prepared by Alice Hanson Jones (1978, 1980) for the year 1774. These estimates are based on a sample of probate records, adjusted to allow for nonprobate wealth and weighted so as to reflect wealth holdings by the living population. Jones provides considerable detail: fifteen components of wealth are distinguished. Two divisions that would have proved helpful were apparently not made: those between the value of slaves and of indentured servants, and between the value of land and improvements thereon. The estimating procedures were exceptionally careful. Perhaps the weakest element in the procedures—the estimation of nonprobate wealth—is relatively unimportant, so far as the estimation of aggregate wealth is concerned. Nonprobate wealth accounts for less than one-fifth of total wealth (Jones 1980, 39–40, 129, 349–51).

Gallman wrote this chapter. Rhode made minor revisions for clarity and consistency.

Jones (1980, 10) also provides a dollar/pound exchange rate, which "may be thought of as the number of dollars at 1774 prices which a pound sterling would have bought if the American dollar had then existed with the same gold content as the one of 1792."

The most extensive comprehensive estimates are those prepared by Samuel Blodget (1810).[1] Blodget made detailed estimates (eleven components are distinguished) for 1805 and then extended the aggregate series (called "value of all real and personal property in the US") to 1774, 1784, and the 1790–1809 period. The 1774 and 1784 values are expressed in dollars, presumably the same kind of dollars as those appearing in the Jones exchange rate for 1774. Blodget also provides for the same years fifty additional relevant series (some estimates are missing for the early years), of which the most useful for present purposes are the number of slaves; the number of persons to each square mile; the number of dwelling houses inhabited; the acreage of improved land (divided into three types; acres of unimproved land can be inferred from other information); the average price per acre of cultivated land; the same for land in its natural state; the number of horses; the number of horned cattle; the capital stock of toll bridge companies, turnpikes, canals, insurance companies, and banks; the public debt; the tonnage of merchant vessels; the value of merchandise imports; the average price of labor per day; the average price of wheat per bushel; and the amount of metallic money and banknotes in circulation. The 1805 estimates were worked over by Raymond Goldsmith (1952, 315–16), who made some adjustments and developed further details.

The federal government levied direct taxes in 1798, 1813, and 1815. The act of 1798 called for the enumeration of slaves over twelve years of age and under fifty, and for the enumeration and valuation of "every dwelling house, which, with the outhouses, appurtenant thereto, and the land, whereon the same were erected, not exceeding two acres," was worth more than one hundred dollars (Pitkin 1835, 309).[2] Houses worth one hundred dollars or less were apparently to be enumerated, but not valued. The returns were incomplete, but Lee Soltow (1987, 181–85) has estimated the total number and value of all houses, as well as the number and value of each of the two components, rural and urban houses. "Value" seems to have been intended to mean market value. Soltow refers to the valuation date as 1798; Pitkin refers to it as 1799. Since the law was passed in July of 1798, and since the appraisal apparatus must have been quite elaborate, it seems reasonable to suppose that assessments were not begun until 1799. In what follows—particularly having to do with deflation—this interpretation is adopted. However, when Soltow's estimation procedures are under discussion, Soltow's view that the assessment year was 1798 is necessarily accepted.

In 1813 a second direct tax was levied, this one based "on the value of all lands and lots of ground, with their improvements, dwelling houses and slaves" (Pitkin 1816, 329).[3] Pitkin's account of the assessment process is not clear. Apparently, the secretary of the treasury offered two systems by which the burden of the tax could be distributed among the counties of each state. (The burden was distributed among states on the basis of population, as the Constitution required.) Where states had property taxes, state assessments would serve; otherwise, the value of property in each county could be established by extrapolation from 1799 on the basis of population. But Pitkin also says that assessments were to be made within the sixty days following 1 February 1814, and that appraisals were to be made "at the rate each of them was worth in money," which suggests that a separate assessment was made, beyond the systems of valuation previously described. In any case, seven states assumed the burden of the tax, and for none of these states was an assessment returned. The 1813 returns, therefore, are far from complete.

In 1815 a new tax was levied and appraisals were to be made for all states, even those that assumed the burden. The 1814 appraisals were to be acceptable unless property values had changed in the meantime; in only one case (Maryland) was the precise 1814 valuation repeated, but in nine other cases the 1814 and 1815 values are so close that, given the major change in prices between the two years, it seems likely that 1814 prices dominate the valuations for these states as well. It is also clear that the assessments did not represent a simple extrapolation of the 1799 values on population (see table 14.1).

As Pitkin (1816, 333) noted, "The quotas of each state were not again apportioned among the several counties, in this tax, as in the former, but the valuations through each state are to be equalized by the principal assessors, and the tax is to be laid and collected on the assessments thus equalized" (Pitkin 1816, 333). Although some states returned the value of all types of property together in one aggregate, Pitkin worked out a division of the totals between the value of slaves and the value of real property.

There are a number of annual series describing elements of the wealth stock or providing part of the means for estimating elements of the wealth

TABLE 14.1  **Comparison of 1799 and 1815 assessments**

| | Percentage increase of | | | | | |
| | assessments | | | population | | Per capita rate of increase |
| | Current prices | Constant prices | | | | |
| | 1799–1815 | 1799–1815 | | 1800–10 | 1800–20 | |
| N.H. | 67% | 42% | * | 17% | 33% | 0.80% |
| Mass. and Me. | 68 | 45 | * | 22 | 43 | 0.5 |
| R.I. | 89 | 60 | * | 11 | 20 | 2 |
| Conn. | 83 | 55 | * | 4 | 10 | 2.3 |
| Vt. | 94 | 64 | * | 41 | 53 | 0.7 |
| N.Y. | 168 | 127 | * | 63 | 133 | 0.9 |
| N.J. | 163 | 86 | | 16 | 31 | 2.6 |
| Pa. | 239 | 141 | | 34 | 74 | 2.8 |
| Del. | 116 | 83 | * | 13 | 13 | 3.1 |
| Md. | 229 | 178 | * | 11 | 19 | 5.7 |
| Va. and W.Va. | 133 | 65 | | 11 | 21 | 2.2 |
| N.C. | 67 | 42 | * | 16 | 34 | 0.8 |
| S.C. | 326 | 202 | | 20 | 45 | 5.3 |
| Ga. | 161 | 85 | | 55 | 110 | 0.1 |
| Ky. | 212 | 122 | | 84 | 155 | 0.1 |
| Tenn. | 295 | 235 | * | 148 | 300 | 0.2 |

Sources:
Column 1: Pitkin (1835, 313). Column 2: computed from Pitkin's (1816, 313) data, deflated by Adams's (1975, 311) Philadelphia construction cost index as reported in column 7. The starred rates are based on data deflated by an 1814 index number; the unstarred items are based on data deflated by an 1815 index number (see text). Columns 3 and 4: US Bureau of the Census 1960, series A-124–29, 131–33, 149–50, 152–56, and 159–60. Column 5: based on data underlying column 2 and estimated rates of population growth, 1799–1815, based on data underlying columns 3 and 4. The rates in the last column for Maryland and South Carolina seem implausibly high, but whether this means that the estimates for 1799 are too low, that the estimates for 1815 are too high, or that the deflator is inappropriate is by no means clear.

stock. Notable are figures of the value of net claims of Americans on foreigners (negative throughout this period), which cover the years 1789 onward but can also be extended to 1774; estimates of the value of imports (important in the derivation of the value of inventories); and the tonnage of the merchant marine.[4]

Finally, the work of Towne and Rasmussen (1960) and Poulson (1975) provides evidence for 1800 (Towne and Rasmussen) and 1810 (Towne and Rasmussen, Poulson) on the value of output of agricultural, mined (1810 only), and manufactured (1810 only) goods, which proves useful for purposes of testing and for assembling estimates of the value of inventories.

## 14.3. Evaluation of Estimates

### 14.3.1. Consistency Tests

This section performs tests of the consistency of the estimates against related data.

**1774.** According to Jones (1980, 90, 122, 128), the value of the total physical wealth of the colonies in 1774 (i.e., including slaves and servants, and excluding financial assets and liabilities) was £109,590,000. Multiplying by Jones's (1980, 10) dollar/pound exchange rate of $4.15 yields a total value of $454,715,500, compared with Blodget's estimate for the same year of $600,000,000.

Blodget's (1810, 68, 196) concept, however, is more comprehensive than Jones's. It is supposed to cover "all real and personal property in the U.S." Blodget (1810, 196) shows exactly what is included in this aggregate in his detailed breakdown for 1805. The following items are clearly not included in Jones's total: (1) public buildings, etc.; (2) specie; (3) bank stock, insurance stock and all other incorporated funds; and (4) turnpike, canal, and toll bridge stock.

Blodget gives the value of specie for 1774—$4 million—but does not provide data with respect to the other categories. Assuming that they were of about the same importance, relative to the total value of real and personal property, in 1774 as in 1805 (possibly too large an estimate), they must have amounted to about $11 million in 1774. Thus, Blodget's value should be reduced by about $15 million, to make it more nearly comparable with Jones's: $600 million minus $15 million equals $585 million.

Another deduction is also surely called for, however. Blodget's (1810, 196) total land estimates are based on the assumption that the United States contained 640 million acres before the Louisiana Purchase, while the correct figure is 526 million acres; see the 1783 entry for "treaty with Great Britain" in US Bureau of the Census 1960, series J-4. Deducting the extra 114 million acres from Blodget's total, valuing this land at Blodget's price for acres of land "in their natural state" yields the following result: $585 minus $40 million equals $545 million.

It is likely, however, that a further deduction is required. Jones (1980, 354) points out that Blodget's land figure is "of the same order of magnitude" as hers, but somewhat lower. Now in order to get Blodget's value of land figure for 1774, we are obliged to do a little estimating. The value for "improved land including pastures" is easily obtained, since Blodget

(1810, 60) gives both the number of these acres and their average price. But Blodget, in his 1805 estimate, refers to two other types of land: "acres adjoining the cultivated lands" and "the residue of all lands in the United States." The former can be obtained for 1774 only by extrapolation on the value of "improved land"—on the whole, not a bad procedure. The latter can be computed by subtracting the number of acres of "improved land" plus the number of acres of "adjoining" land from the total number of acres in the United States, and then multiplying by Blodget's (1810, 60) price for acres "in their natural state." Following through with these calculations—and employing the proper total of acres of land in the United States, rather than Blodget's figure—yields a total value of land in 1774 of $318 million. Since this value exceeds Jones's (1980, 10, 90) estimate of the value of real estate in 1774 (£60,221 times $4.15), $249.9 million, it could not be the value Jones had in mind when she said that Blodget's estimate was of the same order of magnitude as hers, but lower.

By way of experiment, one could drop Blodget's residual category, since this land is less likely to have been owned by private persons and therefore less likely to be incorporated in the holdings of the people Jones sampled. Such a deduction reduces "Blodget's" estimate of the value of land in 1774 (i.e., Blodget's estimate, adjusted as described above) to $169 million, a figure more likely to have been regarded by Jones as similar to but lower than hers.[5] Subtracting the value of the residual land from Blodget's overall total reduces the latter to $545 million minus $149 million equals $396 million, a value closer to Jones's figure of $455 million. The match would be even closer were we to adjust Blodget's land estimate (improved land plus adjoining land) to bring it into conformity with Jones's probable estimate.

The totals are still not perfectly comparable, however, since Jones's estimate includes the value of indentured servants, while Blodget's apparently does not. Data in Jones (1980, 115, 353) suggest that servants accounted for about 22 percent of the value of slaves and servants.

Thus: £21,463,000 times 0.22 equals £4,722,000; £4,722,000 times $4.15 equals $19,597,000. Deducting the value of servants reduces Jones's estimate to: $455 million minus $20 million equals $435 million. The adjusted Jones and Blodget figures, then, are within 10 percent of each other.

There are two other respects in which the work of Jones and Blodget can be compared. Jones (1980, 39) estimates that there were 480,932 slaves in the colonies in 1774; Blodget (1810, 59) puts the figure at around 500,000. Jones (1980, 354) says that Blodget's estimates of the number of horses and horned cattle are similar to hers, but lower.

On the whole, then, Jones's and Blodget's work appears to be consistent. The importance of the point is not simply that consistency strengthens our belief in these two estimates, but that there is now a better reason than before to believe that Blodget's work with respect to the early nineteenth century can be profitably compared with Jones's for the late eighteenth—that is, that the two were dealing with roughly the same aggregate conceptually (with the exceptions previously discussed), and that, in the one year of overlap, they obtained roughly the same results.

**1798/99, 1805, 1813/15.** The existing data and estimates for the last year or two of the eighteenth century and the early years of the nineteenth also permit a number of consistency tests to be run.

(1) Blodget's (1810, 60) estimate of acres under crops in 1800 is consistent with the Towne and Rasmussen (1960, 294–99, 303, 305) statements of crop outputs and with yield estimates for 1791, based on the returns of crop reporters (Blodget 1810, 97–98). The relationships among Blodget's estimates of the stock of horned cattle (p. 60), the number slaughtered (p. 90), and the Towne and Rasmussen (1960) figures of the amounts of beef and pork produced are also altogether plausible. See Gallman (1972, 197–200, 204).

(2) Based chiefly on Blodget's figures, Goldsmith (1952, 315) estimates that farm residences and service buildings were worth $210 million in 1805, while nonfarm residences and other buildings (exclusive of mills and public buildings) ran $120 million. According to Lee Soltow (1987, 182)—working with data assembled by the assessors of the direct tax of 1798—rural dwellings of free persons appraised under that law were worth $95.6 million, and urban dwellings were worth $55.7 million (numbers of houses multiplied by mean values). Soltow (1987, 181) tells us that these values were about 85 percent of market value, while according to Adams (1975, 311, col. 7), construction costs were about 1.084 times as high in 1799 as in 1805. Adding $1 million to the 1799 rural value to account for slave dwellings (a guess), adjusting upward by 17.6 percent to allow for undervaluation, and deflating on the base 1805 on the basis of prices of new residences yields the following estimates. In 1799, rural property was worth $105 million, and urban property $60 million; in 1805, farm property was worth $210 million, and nonfarm property $120 million. The proportions between rural and urban, farm and nonfarm property values are virtually identical, which is moderately encouraging, even though rural and urban, farm and nonfarm are not identical breakdowns.

The 1805 values may be more comprehensive than those for 1799, since they include barns, sheds, warehouses, and other structures, while the 1799 values include only dwelling houses and "the out houses, appurtenant thereto" (Pitkin 1835, 309). On the other hand, the 1799 figures include the value of the land on which the dwellings were located (up to two acres), while the 1805 data probably refer only to structures (Goldsmith 1952, 315). Goldsmith (1952, 319) suggests that land may have accounted for about one-sixth of the value of dwellings and the land on which they stood in 1850. This figure is close to the value one would obtain if one were to assume that land accounted for 36.3 percent of the value of urban residential real estate (see the treatment of nonfarm residences, 1840–1900, above) and that rural residential land bore a price equal to the one assigned to cultivated land by Blodget (1810, 60). (Assuming one acre per rural plot, the ratio of the value of land to the total value of land and structures is 14.9 percent; two acres, 16.5 percent.) Allowing one acre per rural dwelling, the following figures were computed: rural, $102 million; urban, $39 million. The calculations were conducted in current prices, and then the estimated values of structures were deflated.

The value of nonresidential structures in 1805 is unlikely to have amounted to more than three-tenths of the total value of residential and nonresidential structures.[6] Adjusting on this basis gives the following: farm dwellings, $147 million; and nonfarm dwellings, $84 million.

In per capita terms, the adjusted estimates are thus: 1799, $27; 1805, $37.

The computed increase over this period, which is an increase in real terms, seems very large, suggesting that the two sets of estimates may be inconsistent. Where does the inconsistency arise? There are two possibilities: each estimate either depends upon (Blodget-Goldsmith) or implies (Soltow) an estimate of the number of families. The inconsistency between the two estimates—if, indeed, there is one—could have arisen because of problems with the estimates of the numbers of families, or because of differences with respect to the estimation of the value of dwellings per family. Let us consider each possibility.

Blodget sets the number of families in 1805 at about 1 million, a figure Goldsmith raises to 1.1 million. The bases for this adjustment are Goldsmith's derivation of average free family size (5.73) by interpolation between the census figures for 1790 and 1850, and his apparent assumption that enslaved families were, on average, the same size as free families (Goldsmith 1952, 315). Assuming that there were about 5.2 million free persons in 1805 (Blodget 1810, 58), which is likely, then we may infer (with Goldsmith) that there were about 908,000 free families in 1805 (5.2 million divided by 5.73). According to Soltow (1987, 183) there were 715,000 free families in 1798. Assuming that there were between 4.1 and 4.2 million free persons in that year (Blodget 1810, 58; the second digit of Blodget's figure for 1798 is clearly a misprint, a "9" appearing where a "1" was surely intended), then Soltow also seems to have assumed an average free family size of about 5.7 or 5.8. The difference between Blodget-Goldsmith and Soltow, with respect to the per capita values, then, lies not in their views of average family size, but in their estimation of the value of dwellings per family.[7]

(3) Another way to check the estimates is to draw comparisons between Jones and Soltow. To do so requires a long chain of reasoning and estimation, as follows:

(a) Convert Jones's (1980, 90) real estate estimate from pounds into dollars: £60,221,000 times $4.15 per pound equals $249,917,150.

(b) In 1799, dwellings accounted for 24 percent of the value of land and dwellings, according to Soltow (1987). Other structures could not have amounted to more than 35 percent of the value of all structures.[8] Assuming that both conditions also held in 1774, then dwellings must have come to no more than 21 percent of the value of real estate, or about $52 million.

(c) Assuming that land under dwellings represented about 15 percent of the value of dwellings (see above, 1799), then dwelling structures in 1774 must have been worth about $45 million.

(d) Shifting Adams's variant B construction price index to the base 1805, and extending it to the years before 1785 on the index described in the notes to table 14.2 yields a construction price index of 79 in 1774. The value of dwellings in 1774, in prices of 1805, then comes to $57 million.

(e) Dividing by the total population in 1774, 2.3 million (Jones 1980, 37), yields $25. This is the per capita value of dwellings in 1774, expressed in prices of 1805. It compares with the 1799 value derived, above, from Soltow's manipulation of the direct tax data, of $27, again in 1805 prices. These are not wildly implausible results, but they come at the end of a long chain of reasoning and estimating. What seems plausible will also depend upon one's preconceived notions of the probable course of development between 1774 and 1799—notions that are likely to differ somewhat from one analyst to the next. Given the nature of the test, the results are modestly encouraging.

(4) A final test can be conducted through the direct tax returns for 1813–15. According to Pitkin (1835, 40), the value of houses, lands, and

TABLE 14.2 **Value of structures, measured in current and 1860 prices, 1774–1815, in millions of dollars**

| | | 1774 | 1799 | 1805 | 1815 |
|---|---|---|---|---|---|
| **A. Value, current prices** | | | | | |
| 1 | Farm dwellings | | | 147 | |
| 2 | Rural dwellings | | 110 | | |
| 3 | Nonfarm dwellings | | 84 | | |
| 4 | Urban dwellings | | 42 | | |
| 5 | All dwellings | 45 | 152 | 231 | 457 |
| 6 | Farm structures | | | 210 | |
| 7 | Rural Structures | | 157 | | |
| 8 | Nonfarm structures | | 142 | | |
| 9 | Urban structures | | 70 | | |
| 10 | All structures | 67 | 227 | 352 | 697 |
| **B. Price index** | | 80 | 110 | 101 | 155 |
| **C. Value, 1860 prices** | | | | | |
| 1 | Farm dwellings | | | 146 | |
| 2 | Rural dwellings | | 100 | | |
| 3 | Nonfarm dwellings | | 83 | | |
| 4 | Urban dwellings | | 38 | | |
| 5 | All dwellings | 56 | 138 | 229 | 295 |
| 6 | Farm structures | | | 208 | |
| 7 | Rural structures | | 141 | | |
| 8 | Nonfarm structures | | 141 | | |
| 9 | Urban structures | | 64 | | |
| 10 | All structures | 84 | 206 | 349 | 450 |

Sources:

Line A1: Goldsmith 1952, 315, "farm residences and service buildings" × 0.7, to remove the service buildings. The estimate of 0.7 is a guess, based on the belief that farm service buildings probably accounted for a smaller proportion of the value of farm buildings than nonfarm service buildings did of nonfarm buildings. In 1840 and 1850, the share of the former in the latter was a little less than four-tenths. At a guess, then, farm service buildings may have accounted for three-tenths of the value of farm buildings, while farm residences may have accounted for the remaining seven-tenths.

Line A2: Soltow's (1987) estimate of the value of rural dwellings was increased by $1 million to account for slave dwellings. The new total was divided by 0.85 to allow for undervaluation, per Soltow. The value of land under rural dwellings was estimated on the assumption that rural dwellings occupied, on average, one acre of land each, and that the value of land under rural houses equaled the value per acre of cultivated land, according to Blodget (1810, 60). No allowance was made for the value of land under slave dwellings. The value of land under rural dwellings, thus computed, was subtracted from the estimate of the value of dwellings to obtain the value of dwelling structures, exclusive of land.

Line A3: Goldsmith 1952, 315, "non-farm residences and other buildings" × 0.7, the ratio of nonfarm dwellings to all nonfarm structures (exclusive of public buildings, which are not incorporated in his "other buildings").

Line A4: Derived from Soltow 1987, 182, for number of urban houses times the average value, divided by 0.85 (to adjust for undervaluation) on the assumption that urban residential structures accounted for 63.7 percent of the value of urban residential structures plus land, the same fraction employed in the estimation of the value of nonfarm residential structures in the year 1840.

Line A5, 1774: The value of real estate, according to Jones (1980, 90), converted to dollars, per Jones's exchange rate (p. 10), multiplied by 0.21 to yield the value of dwellings (see text), with the result multiplied by 0.85 to remove the value of land (15 percent of the value of dwellings). 1799: line A2 + line A4. 1805: line A1 + line A3. 1815: Pitkin 1835, 313, value of houses and lands, adjusted to an 1815 valuation. The valuation adjustment was made on the basis of Adams's (1975) construction cost index, variant B. The following states were supposed to have returned 1814 valuations (compare Pitkin 1816, 329–30, with Pitkin 1835, 313): New Hampshire, Massachusetts, Vermont, Rhode Island, Connecticut, Delaware, Maryland, New York, North Carolina, and Tennessee. The adjusted figure was then multiplied by 0.24 to obtain the value of dwellings alone, and by 1.06 to include dwellings worth $100 or less (see Soltow 1987). This total was increased by $3 million to account for slave dwellings; the result was divided by 0.85 to allow for underenumeration—the same allowance as Soltow (1987) claims is required for 1799—and then multiplied by 0.85 to obtain the value of structures, exclusive of the land on which they were built.

slaves "as revised and equalized, by the principal assessors, in 1814 and 1815" came to $1,902 million, exclusive of property in Louisiana, the returns for which were incomplete. Pitkin estimated that the value of land and houses alone amounted to $1,631 million. Assuming that the value of dwellings represented the same share as in 1799 of the value of land and dwellings together (0.24, according to Soltow), then the value of dwellings was $391 million. Adjusting for the value of slave dwellings, for the value of houses worth $100 or less, for the undervaluation of property, and to remove the value of the land on which houses stood—in each case following the procedures described above for 1799—results in an estimate of the value of free and slave dwellings (structures only) of $409 million. Weighting the Adams price index numbers by the proportions of the total value of land and structures assessed in the two years 1814 and 1815 yields a price index number of 1.407, on the base 1805. The real value of structures in 1815, then, was about $291 million.

The 1815 estimate—$35 in per capita terms—may be compared to estimates for 1774, $25; 1799, $27; and 1805, $37. All values are expressed in prices of 1805. There is no way of determining with absolute certainty that these figures are or are not consistent, one with the other, making proper allowance for historical changes in material circumstances. If in fact firm conclusions of this type could be made, there would be no need to put together a capital stock series: the information sought through the series would already be known. It does seem highly unlikely that the real value

---

Sources: (*continued*)

Line A6: Goldsmith 1952, 315.

Line A7: line A2 ÷ 0.7. See the notes for line A1, above.

Line A8: Goldsmith 1952, 315; nonfarm residences and other buildings plus mills plus public buildings, the last reduced from a value of $20 million to $17 million to eliminate Washington city lots, naval and military stores, arms, ammunition, frigates, dock yards and timber, all of which are included in Blodget's figure which Goldsmith identifies with public buildings. Blodget (1810, 60) puts a value of $1.5 million on the Washington lots and says that the Navy had twenty vessels in 1804. If they averaged 200 tons each, they were probably worth about $0.1 million in 1805. How much the inventories of military supplies and the naval dockyards were worth is by no means clear, but Blodget (1810, 66) sets a figure of $1,709,189 on expenditures for the army, navy, and contingencies, which at least establishes an order of magnitude. At a guess, then, the items that should be deducted from the Blodget-Goldsmith total to get it down to a figure approximating the value of all public buildings is about $3 million.

Line A9: line A4 ÷ 0.6. See line A1.

Line A10, 1774: Line A5 ÷ 0.670, the same ratio as in 1799. 1815: line A5 ÷ 0.656, the ratio of the value of dwellings to the value of structures in 1805.

Line B, price index: The index for 1840 from table 7.2 extrapolated to 1785 on the Adams (1975) construction cost index, variant B, and extended to 1774 on the Bezanson price index (US Bureau of the Census 1960, series E-82) and a wage rate index, both shifted to the base 1785 and the two weighted equally. The wage rate index was constructed from the David-Solar (1977, 59) common wage rate index (this index is based on data for Massachusetts) and the Adams index of the wage rate of agricultural workers in Maryland, both shifted to the base 1785 without reweighting, and then combined with equal weights.

Lines C1–C10: The values in panel A deflated by the price index numbers in line B.

of dwellings per capita rose from $27 to as much as $37 between 1799 and 1805. It may be, then, that the estimate for 1799 is a little too low, and the one for 1805 too high. On the whole, the results are quite encouraging.

### 14.4.2. The Remaining Blodget Estimates

We have seen that Blodget's estimate for 1774 is consistent with Alice Jones's work for that year, while his figures for 1805 are readily squared with various independent sources of evidence. His estimate of the value of dwellings for that year may be high, but it seems not very far out of line. The question then arises as to the usefulness of the rest of his series, the estimates for 1784, 1790–1804, and 1806–1809. As will appear, a number of Blodget's series seem to be quite useful, but the overall estimates of the value of all property follow a course over time that is sufficiently peculiar as to call them into question. Specifically, the value of property per capita (using Blodget's population estimates) rises steadily and quite pronouncedly until 1796. Then it turns down—at first rather modestly and slowly, and then more dramatically. A similar pattern appears when the per capita values are deflated, except that the downturn occurs after 1793, while for the next ten years the figures rise and fall modestly, showing no clear trend. The pattern of rise and decline is made much more intense if one deletes from the series the principal elements other than the value of structures: the value of land, animal inventories, shipping, specie, slaves, and inventories. The residual (per capita, in real terms) rises quite dramatically to the early 1790s, and then falls equally dramatically. A possible cause of this development—and perhaps for the peculiar behavior of the aggregate series—may be found in the relationship between Blodget's estimates of the population and of dwellings (see note 7). Presumably, Blodget's figures with respect to dwellings tell us something about his view of the changing value of dwellings, the principal component of the value of structures. In fact, the number of dwellings, according to Blodget, increased faster than the population down to the early 1790s. The population and the number of dwellings then increased at about the same rate for almost a decade, and then, after the mid-1800s, population began to grow faster than the number of dwellings. There does not seem to be any good reason why these developments should have taken place, and while they are not pronounced enough to account fully for the peculiar behavior of the aggregate and residual series, they do appear to contribute to it. In any case, the movements described are sufficiently dubious so that one should probably place little confidence in the aggregate and residual series, apart from the two dates discussed in previous sections. Various component series, however, do seem useful, as will be seen in the subsequent sections.

## 14.4. The Capital Stock Estimates

### 14.4.1. Introduction

The general procedure followed was to build up comprehensive estimates at the benchmark years 1774 and 1805, based chiefly on the work of Jones, Blodget, and Goldsmith. For 1774 this meant extracting capital figures from the more comprehensive wealth estimates provided by Jones. Certain new estimates were also substituted for elements of the Jones and Blodget-Goldsmith estimates. The reason for the substitution was sometimes that the new estimate was deemed superior to the old; more often, the purpose was to link the early estimates with those for the years 1840 onward. For example, new estimates of inventories held in 1805 were substituted for the figures given by Blodget and Goldsmith, not in the secure belief that the new estimates were better, but because the estimating procedures adopted to make the new estimates were consistent with those used to assemble the inventory figures for 1840 onward. Comparisons between the 1805 and 1840–1900 estimates can thus be made with some confidence that the comparisons reveal real differences, rather than simply differences in estimating techniques.

Estimates were also built up for the years 1799 and 1815, based on the work of Soltow and Pitkin, as well as the series described in the previous paragraph. These sources are incomplete, so that comprehensive estimates for 1799 and 1815 had to be computed by blowing up the incomplete figures on the basis of relationships observed in 1805.

Finally, estimates of the value of agricultural land improvements (other than structures, which have already been discussed) were constructed on the basis of Blodget's estimates of the acreage of improved land (as adjusted) and the procedures employed to build similar estimates for the years 1840 to 1900, described above.

### 14.4.2. Structures

The chief estimating procedures have already been described in the sections above on testing. Details are contained in the notes to table 14.2.

Briefly, the Goldsmith revisions of Blodget's estimates for 1805 were accepted, with one minor modification. The reader should recall that the tests suggest that these estimates are somewhat too high.

Estimates of the value of rural and urban dwellings in 1799 were derived from Soltow's work, in precisely the way described in the testing sections above. They were blown up to include other structures, on the basis of the relationships between the values of dwellings and other structures in 1805 and in later years, again in the manner described previously. These estimates are based on very firm data on dwellings, carefully developed by Soltow. The extension of the estimates to cover other structures rests on much shakier ground, however.

The Pitkin data for 1815 are less detailed than Soltow's—there is no breakdown between rural and urban property—and Pitkin's handling of them does not measure up to Soltow's management of the 1799 data. The 1815 figures are also short, since they do not cover Louisiana, and the procedures by which they were created are less clear and less certainly professional than is the case for 1799. Nonetheless, the tests suggest that they may not be bad. The components of the estimates that appear to have been valued on the basis of 1814 prices were shifted to an 1815 basis, and the value of dwellings was blown up to cover missing elements of the value of structures, on the basis of relationships that hold for 1805.

The 1774 figures were computed in precisely the way described in the testing section above. The underlying basis for these estimates is the very strong work of Jones (1978, 1980). Unfortunately, Jones does not provide a breakdown of her real estate estimate into the components, land and improvements. It was necessary, therefore, to work out estimating devices for drawing this distinction, and at this stage the opportunity for error to enter emerged. Nonetheless, the tests suggest that the final results are reasonably good.

The estimates for the years 1799, 1805, and 1815 were deflated by use of a price index number for 1840 (table 7.2), extrapolated to these dates on the Adams cost index of residential construction. The Adams index is a good index, but it has some deficiencies in the present context. First, it is a cost index, rather than the desired price index, as discussed in chapter 7. It does allow for shifts in the structure of costs in response to changes in relative prices, a feature that makes it more like a price index than a standard fixed weight cost index would be. As a proxy for a price index it has an important weakness: since it does not allow for productivity improvements, it overstates increases in prices and understates decreases in prices

TABLE 14.3 **Wage rates and construction costs, 1840 base**

|  |  | 1785 | 1799 | 1805 | 1815 | 1840 |
|---|---|---|---|---|---|---|
| **Wage rates** | | | | | | |
| 1 | Philadelphia construction labor | 97.6 | 106.4 | 90.0 | 160.0 | 100 |
| 2 | Maryland farm labor | 99.6 | 117.1 | 117.9 | 141.6 | 100 |
| 3 | Massachussetts common labor | 57.1 | 67.5 | 80.5 | 119.5 | 100 |
| **Construction materials prices** | | | | | | |
| 4 | Adams | 91.8 | 132.2 | 146.0 | 173.6 | 100 |
| 5 | Bezanson | 102.6 | 116.3 | 138.4 | 184.0 | 100 |
| 6 | Warren-Pearson | 55.4 | 78.5 | 89.2 | 116.9 | 100 |

Sources:
Lines 1 and 2: Adams 1975, 1986. Adams's (1968, 1982) farm wage rate series for Philadelphia and the Brandywine region match his construction series less closely, but the gaps in these series make drawing meaningful comparisons difficult. Line 3: David and Solar 1977. Line 4: The Adams materials price index was derived from table A-1 in Adams 1975. Lines 5–6: The Warren-Pearson and Bezanson construction materials price indexes were taken from US Bureau of the Census 1960, series E-8 ("building materials") and E-76 ("lumber products and naval stores"). All indexes were shifted to the base 1840 without reweighting.

over time. Thus, a capital stock series deflated by it is likely to understate the true rate of change of the real capital stock.

The index also refers only to costs of commercial building projects— that is, projects built by people in the construction trades. Many structures during this period were likely to have been built by farmers from farm materials, a point also discussed in chapter 7. It does not appear that this represents an important problem during the period under consideration here, however. According to Adams's data, the wage rates of construction workers and farm workers moved similarly during these years (see table 14.3).

Construction cost indexes based on these two series (lines 1 and 2) and on a common materials cost series (line 4) would not be far different from each other; see Adams 1975, 1986. A further problem is that the index refers to Philadelphia alone, and there are indications that price movements in Philadelphia did not match those in other parts of the country. For example, wage series from Massachusetts (line 3) and a construction materials price index from New York exhibit patterns (line 6) quite different from those of the Adams series.

The Massachusetts common wage is based on David and Solar (1977); Rothenberg's (1988) Massachusetts farm wage rate series displays a very similar pattern. The Bezanson price index refers to Philadelphia, while the Warren-Pearson index refers to New York. The Adams series represents the materials prices that enter his Philadelphia cost index. The Philadelphia series—those of Adams and Bezanson—move fairly closely together, while the New York and Massachusetts series display a common pattern, but one far removed from the one exhibited by the Philadelphia series.

How important a matter is the disparity between the Massachusetts-New York series and the Philadelphia-Maryland series? A test was run by producing a construction cost index for Massachusetts-New York, based on the David-Solar wage series, the Warren-Pearson materials price index, and Adams's weighting scheme. (Unfortunately, there is no very good way to incorporate other geographic areas into the test.) The resulting series was combined with Adams's figures, and the new index thus produced was used to deflate the "all structures" figures for 1799, 1805, and 1815 in table 14.2.[9] The results were as follows: for 1799, the revised constant price figure was just under 24 percent larger than the figure in table 14.2; for 1805, a little more than 11 percent larger; and for 1815, less than 16 percent larger.

Despite these marked differences, the original estimates were left unchanged. There are two reasons for this decision. First, the construction cost index derived for Massachusetts–New York is markedly inferior to the Adams index, since it does not reflect the wage rates of skilled construction workers, and because the materials price index is not nearly so carefully weighted as is the Adams materials index. Second, we know that the best construction cost index is virtually certain to give a biased representation of construction prices; it is virtually certain to overstate price increases and understate price decreases. Leaving New York and New England unrepresented in the construction cost index apparently imparts a bias in the opposite direction, compensating in some measure for the cost index bias. Whether the compensation is too much, too little, or exactly the right amount one cannot say. But it seems highly probable that the Adams series alone gives a better representation of the course of *prices* than does the combined index.

Finally, it is likely that price *levels* of structures varied from state to state, while the relative importance (price weights) of the various states changed as time passed. How, if at all, did shifts in the weights to be appropriately attached to state price indexes affect the level of the true national price index? Must the Adams index be adjusted to take this matter into account?

A test was run making use of data in the 1840 census (US Census Office 1841, 91). The census requested information on the numbers of two types of houses constructed in the census year, those built of brick and

TABLE 14.4 **State fixed effects from the Regression**

| | |
|---|---|
| Maine | 0.955 |
| New Hampshire | 0.860 |
| Massachusetts | 1.932 |
| Rhode Island | 1.379 |
| Connecticut | 1.854 |
| Vermont | 0.679 |
| New York | 1.423 |
| New Jersey | 1.103 |
| Pennsylvania | 0.843 |
| Ohio | 1.034 |
| Indiana | 0.517 |
| Illinois | 0.887 |
| Michigan | 0.862 |
| Wisconsin | 0.619 |
| Iowa | 0.384 |
| North Carolina | 0.496 |
| South Carolina | 1.602 |
| Georgia | 0.657 |
| Florida | 1.142 |
| Alabama | 1.492 |
| Mississippi | 1.492 |
| Louisiana | 2.645 |
| Arkansas | 2.060 |
| District of Columbia | 0.490 |
| Delaware | 0.442 |
| Maryland | 0.764 |
| Virginia | 0.666 |
| Tennessee | 0.413 |
| Kentucky | 0.513 |
| Missouri | 0.735 |

Sources: See text.

stone and those built of wood, as well as the value of both types of houses taken together. The state data were used in a regression analysis to obtain intercept values and coefficients for each of the two types of houses. The intercept values and the coefficients were then employed to value the houses constructed in each state, and the figures thus obtained were divided through the census returns of the value of houses built to get an index number for each state.[10] The state index numbers, which appear in table 14.4, compare the value of houses constructed in the state with the value that would have obtained if construction costs had been at the level of the national average. Clearly, the index numbers reflect not only variations in building costs—which are required for the proposed analysis—but also differences in the average size and quality of new houses from state to state. Since cost, size, and quality are likely to have varied together—frontier

areas having lower building costs, smaller houses, and houses of lower quality than urban centers—the index numbers almost certainly exaggerate the
regional variations in building costs, a point to be borne in mind as the
analysis unfolds.

The individual state index numbers were then used to deflate the state
returns of the value of real estate in 1799, according to the direct tax (Pitkin 1835, 313). (These figures appear to provide the best available weights
for the index numbers.) The sum of the deflated returns was then divided
through the aggregate current price value of real estate in 1799, according
to the direct tax. The result is an index number of 0.932, which compares
with the 1840 index number of 1.000; that is, according to these calculations, the shifting weights among states tended to raise, very slightly, the
true price index of structures between 1799 and 1840. Indeed, the index
numbers almost certainly overstate the true impact of the redistribution
of the value of structures among states in this period, because the state
index numbers overstate (for reasons previously given) the true variation
in building costs among states. It appears, then, that it is unnecessary to
adjust the Adams cost index to take into account the effects of the shifting
value-of-structures weights among states. This is particularly the case in
view of the fact that the Adams index is a cost index and is likely, therefore, to exaggerate the extent to which the prices of buildings rose, or understate the extent to which they fell, during this period.

The index was extended from 1785 (the earliest date in the series) to
1774 on a general Philadelphia price index and a wage index designed to
capture wage changes in New England and the Middle Colonies. This is
the best series available, but clearly it is far weaker than the series for the
years 1799, 1805, and 1815—which, in turn, is weaker than the series for
the period 1840–1900.

### 14.4.3. Shipping

Blodget and Goldsmith provide an estimate of the value of ships in 1805;
Jones apparently combined ships with other items of "equipment of nonfarm business." Rather than adopt the former and attempt to disengage
the value of ships from the larger aggregate in the case of the latter, it
seemed preferable to produce fresh estimates (see table 14.5). The data
available to do so are reasonably good, and they permit establishing a clear
link with the shipping estimates for the years 1799, 1815, and 1840–1900.
The new estimate for 1805 ($68 million) is substantially higher than the

Blodget-Goldsmith figure ($40 million). The new estimate for 1774 is also apparently substantially higher than the comparable figure probably buried in Jones's aggregate; it runs $7 million, whereas Jones's estimate of the value of all "equipment of non-farm business" comes to less than $2 million. Why this should be so is by no means clear. The new estimate at least has the virtue that it has emerged from a process of estimation common to all of the shipping estimates, 1774–1900, in this series, so that observed changes in shipping values over time are at least not the product of shifts in estimating procedure. The estimating procedure is described in chapter 10, especially in the notes to table 10.1. The following notes describe the steps taken to derive the figures for 1774–1815. Steam vessels were of negligible importance. Therefore, these notes focus on sailing vessels.

The official series on the tonnage of sailing vessels extends back only to 1790, but Blodget (1810, 62), whose data closely follow the official series, provides a figure for 1774. The official series are inflated by the tonnage of vessels that had left the fleet. Periodically, this ghost tonnage was cleared from the records. Line 1 of table 10.1 exhibits the fruit of an effort to distribute the ghost tonnage among the years in which vessels actually left the fleet. If this procedure was successful, line B represents the true tonnage of the American fleet in each year.

The estimates were first valued in constant prices, using data from table 10.1. In all likelihood, these estimates somewhat overstate the true real values of vessels treated in table 14.5. The reason is that large vessels cost more per ton than did small ones, and vessel size increased over time. Thus, the 1860 prices applied to the tonnage series probably represent larger vessels—more valuable per ton—than the vessels represented in table 14.5. This in turn means that the rate of change described by the shipping series—say, from 1774 to 1860—probably understates the true growth rate of shipping. Current price estimates were assembled by inflating the constant price series. The price index (described in the notes to the table) leaves something to be desired, but it may capture the trend in prices adequately. It is less likely to describe accurately the year-to-year movements, which are probably less pronounced than the price series shows.

The weakest element of all consists of the value of real estate improvements associated with the shipping industry (docks, etc.). These estimates were made by extrapolation (in current prices) on the value of vessels. They were deflated by the series described in the notes to table 7.1. While these procedures are quite slapdash, the results are unlikely to be very markedly wrong, at least with respect to trend.

TABLE 14.5 **Value of vessels and real estate in shipping, measured in current and 1860 prices, 1774–1815, in millions of dollars**

| | 1774 | 1799 | 1805 | 1815 |
|---|---|---|---|---|
| A. Tonnage of vessels (in thousands of tons) | | | | |
| 1  Steam | — | — | — | 3 |
| 2  Sail | 198 | 919 | 1,091 | 1,261 |
| | | | | |
| B. Adjusted tonnage (000 tons) | | | | |
| Ghost tonnage deleted | 198 | 792 | 1,041 | 1,170 |
| | | | | |
| C. Value, at 1860 prices, in millions of dollars | | | | |
| 1  Steam | — | — | — | 0.3 |
| 2  Sail | 6.5 | 26.1 | 34.4 | 38.6 |
| | | | | |
| D. Price index (1860 = 100) | 105 | 161 | 197 | 279 |
| | | | | |
| E. Value, at current prices, in millions of dollars | | | | |
| 1  Steam | — | — | — | 0.8 |
| 2  Sail | 6.9 | 42.0 | 67.8 | 107.7 |
| | | | | |
| F. Value of real estate improvements, at 1860 prices, in millions of dollars | 1.5 | 6.6 | 11.7 | 12.1 |
| | | | | |
| G. Price index (1860 = 100) | 80 | 110 | 101 | 155 |
| | | | | |
| H. Value of real estate improvements, at current prices, in mil. dollars | 1.2 | 7.3 | 11.8 | 18.7 |

Sources:
Line A1: US Bureau of the Census 1960, series Q-155. Line A2: 1774 from Blodget 1810, 62; 1799–1815, US Bureau of the Census 1960), series Q-161 (hereafter *Historical Statistics*). Series Q161 includes canal boats and barges. The estimates for 1840–70 (see table 10.1) were adjusted to eliminate these vessels. No similar adjustment was made to the 1774–1815 data, on the ground that the tonnage of such vessels was negligible during this period. The official data refer to the stock as of December 31, and presumably the Blodget estimate for 1774 has a similar reference. The data in the table for 1799–1815 are in fact averages of data for two years, a device employed to approximate the vessel inventory as of July 1 (thus, for example, the data listed under the year 1799 are in fact averages of data for 1798 and 1799), and to place the shipping estimates on the same basis as the estimates for the rest of the capital stock. It was impossible to correct the 1774 estimate in the same way. The Blodget and *Historical Statistics* series are very similar, down to 1802, when suddenly Blodget gives a much larger value than does *Historical Statistics*. According to *Historical Statistics*, ghost tonnage of 197,000 tons was cleared in "1800–01." It seems more likely, however, that the clearance took place in 1802. Thus, the *Historical Statistics* figure for 1802 plus 197,000 comes to 1,089,000, which approximates Blodget's 1,003,000. It seems reasonable to suppose, then, that *Historical Statistics* and Blodget are largely consistent before 1802, and to accept Blodget's 1774 figure as a logical extension of the *Historical Statistics* series. It is well to remember, however, that Blodget offers no source for this figure.
    Line B: According to the US Bureau of the Census 1960, 439, the data in line A2 were periodically cleared of ghost tonnage; 1800–01, 197,000 tons; 1811, amount unknown, but inspection of the series suggests it was about 180,000 tons; 1818, 182,000 tons. The dating of the first clearing to 1800–1801 is certainly wrong (see the notes to Line A2, above). The proper date is 1802. Line B was computed by assuming that the 182,000 tons of ghost tonnage accumulated between 1811 and 1818 at a rate of 26,000 tons per year. Thus, to clear the series in line A2 requires that 78,000 tons be subtracted from the value for 1814 and 104,000 for the value for 1815, or a total of 91,000 from the "calendar" 1815 appearing in this table. The 180,000 tons accumulated between 1802 and 1811 were assumed to have built up at the rate of 20,000 per year, the adjustments being carried out in a manner analogous to that described above. The 197,000 tons added before 1802 were also assumed to have accumulated at a rate of 20,000 tons per year. The required adjustments will be evident.

## 14.4.4. International Sector

The procedures followed to develop the estimates in table 14.6 were similar to those described in chapter 12. The international sector contributes two elements to the capital stock: the stock of monetary metals owned by Americans and their governments, and the net international position of the United States (foreign debts held by Americans minus American debts held by foreigners). With respect to the first element Blodget (1810, 66), provides estimates for 1774, 1799, and 1805; Hepburn (1915) for 1815.

The net international position of the United States is available in *Historical Statistics* (based on the work of North and Simon) for the years back to 1789. Jones gives the aggregate debts and credits of Americans in 1774. Since each debt by an American to an American creates a credit of equal value, the difference between debts and credits in 1774 should measure the net international position of the American colonies at that date, exclusive of institutional claims. The value obtained is also plausible. According to Jacob Price (1980), pre-1776 colonial debt still owing to British creditors in 1790 (exclusive of interest) ran to £2.9 million, or about $12 million, at Jones's exchange rate. Price (1980, 8) goes on to state:

> These figures do not, however, represent the total prewar debt owed at the peak
> (about 1774). Some merchants and planters voluntarily settled with their British creditors in the 1780s, particularly those desirous of reestablishing credit
> in Great Britain. (Outside Virginia, others were obliged to settle when state

---

Sources: (*continued*)

Line C1: column 1 multiplied by price per ton of steam vessels in 1860, table 10.1, line 4. Line C2: column 5 multiplied by price per ton of sailing vessels in 1860, table 10.1, line 8. N.B.: Insofar as vessel designs, the distribution of vessels among types, and vessel sizes changed, line C2 misstates changes in the real value of vessels. In all likelihood, since price per ton increased with vessel size, and since the average sizes of vessels were increasing between this period and 1860, this series overstates the real value of vessels, 1774–1815, and understates the growth rate of the stock of vessels, expressed in constant prices (see the text and the notes to Table 10.1).

Line D: Price data are limited and are often contradictory. See, for example, Davis, Gallman, and Hutchins 1988, 393, and Brady 1966, 110–11. The results contained in line D are thus subject to doubt. As of 1791, according to Hutchins (1941, 202) quoting Tench Coxe, the "best double-decked ships, with live oak lower timber, and red cedar top timbers can be built and fitted for taking a cargo at $34 per ton," while in the early 1830s, the "best American ships rarely cost over $55 per ton." Brady (1966, 110) has an index number for 1834 of 189, on the base 1860. Thus, an appropriate price index number for 1791 might be 117 (34/55 × 189). A series of price index numbers for 1774, 1799, 1805, and 1815 was created by combining US Bureau of the Census 1960, series E-76 (Bezanson's Philadelphia price index for lumber and naval stores), extrapolated to 1774 on series E-81, with David and Solar's (1977, 59) common wage index, both shifted to the base 1860 without reweighting. This series was used to link the two index numbers previously obtained (1834: 189; 1791: 117) and to extend them to 1774.

Line H: extrapolated (simple splicing: 0.174) from 1840–1900 on line E2.

Line G: table 14.2.

Line F: 100 × line H ÷ line G.

TABLE 14.6  **Value of net US international assets, measured in current and 1860 prices, 1774–1815, in millions of dollars**

|   |   | 1774 | 1799 | 1805 | 1815 |
|---|---|------|------|------|------|
| 1 | Stock of monetary metals | 4 | 17 | 18 | 25 |
| 2 | Net international position of the United States | –26 | –81 | –75 | –80 |
| 3 | Line 1 plus line 2 | –22 | –64 | –57 | –55 |
| 4 | Price index (1860 = 100) | 82 | 135 | 152 | 183 |
| 5 | 100 × line 1 ÷ line 4 | 5 | 13 | 12 | 14 |
| 6 | 100 × line 2 ÷ line 4 | –32 | –60 | –49 | –44 |
| 7 | Line 5 plus line 6, net international position in 1860 prices | –27 | –47 | –37 | –30 |

Sources: Line 1: 1774, 1799, 1805, Blodget 1810, 66; 1815, Hepburn 1915, 129. Line 2: US Bureau of the Census 1960, series U-207. Line 4: US Bureau of the Census 1960, series E-1, shifted to the base 1860 without reweighting. Lines 3, 5, 6, and 7: See text.

courts—for example, those of Maryland in 1787—recognized the validity of prewar bonds and other specialties securing debts to British merchants.) More important, during the last year before the war (the twelve or so months ending September 1775), importations into the colonies were prohibited by Congress, though exports to Britain were permitted. At that time, we learn from a later writer, "the factors, whom the Glasgow merchants had established in America, by their prudent exertions, and the friendly terms on which they generally were with the planters [perhaps not all of them], had been enabled to make large remittances to their constituents, before matters were brought to the last extremity." According to the well-informed Bristol merchant Richard Champion, the amounts owing from America were reduced from £6 million in December 1774 to £2 million in December 1775.

At $4.15 to the pound, £6 million comes to just under $25 million, a close check with Jones's figure; see Price 1980, 8–11. The series were deflated by the Warren-Pearson all-commodities price index, shifted to the base 1860 without reweighting.

### 14.4.5. Animal Inventories

Table 14.7 presents figures for animal inventories. Blodget (1810, 60) has estimates of the number of horses and horned cattle, 1774, 1784, 1790–1809; figures apparently refer to mature animals on farms (see Gallman 1972, 204). These estimates were valued in 1860 prices and were used to

TABLE 14.7 **Value of animal inventories, measured in current and 1860 prices, 1774–1840**

| | 1774 | 1799 | 1805 | 1809 | 1815 | 1840 |
|---|---|---|---|---|---|---|
| **Number of mature animals, in millions** | | | | | | |
| Horses | 0.4 | 1.03 | 1.2 | 1.4 | | 3.85 |
| Cattle | 0.85 | 2.35 | 2.95 | 3.66 | | 15.00 |
| **Value, at 1860 prices, in millions of dollars** | | | | | | |
| Horses | 22.5 | 58.0 | 67.5 | 78.8 | | 216.7 |
| Cattle | 15.9 | 44.0 | 55.2 | 68.5 | | 280.7 |
| Total | 38.4 | 102.0 | 122.7 | 147.3 | | 497.4 |
| All stocks | 52.2 | 138.6 | 166.7 | 200.2 | 241.2 | 676.0 |
| | | | | | | |
| **Price index (1860 = 100)** | 80.6 | 86.8 | 96.0 | | 146.8 | |
| | | | | | | |
| **Value at current prices, in millions of dollars** | | | | | | |
| All stocks | 42.1 | 120.3 | 160.0 | | 354.1 | |

Sources:

Lines 1 and 2, 1774–1809: Blodget 1810, 60. 1840: Census estimates are summarized in the 1950 US Census of Agriculture (US Bureau of the Census 1952, 361–63). Also in this census is a discussion of the coverage of each preceding census (pp. 364–68) and a comparison of the census figures with the estimates of the Bureau of Agricultural Economics (pp. 352–353). On the basis of this information, census estimates were adjusted to eliminate young animals. (The information regarding the age coverage of the census given in tables on pp. 352–53 of the 1950 census is at variance with the text comments on pp. 364–68. The text is correct.)

Line 3: line 1 × the 1860 prices of cattle ($18.71). Line 4: line 2 × the 1860 prices of horses ($56.29). These estimates are only crude approximations to the true prices of mature animals. They were derived from 1867 figures produced by the Bureau of Agricultural Economics (US Bureau of the Census 1960, 289–90), adjusted downward slightly to allow for the fact that the application of these prices to 1860 census data on the numbers of animals of all types generates a value slightly higher than the 1860 census return of the value of animals. Since the 1860 census returned some young animals, the derived prices are about 5 percent lower than the true prices of mature animals. For present purposes—to generate an extrapolating series—this disparity between the prices estimated and the prices sought is a matter of very modest importance.

Line 5: line 3 + line 4.

Line 6, 1774–1809: extrapolated from 1840 on line 5. 1815: extrapolated from 1809 on the assumption that the real value of the total stock grew at a rate of 3.167 percent per year between 1809 and 1815. The rate of change was computed on the basis of the Towne and Rasmussen (1960, 282) data on the value of output of the following animal products, expressed in prices of 1910–14: cattle and calves, hogs, sheep and lambs, and horses and mules. The weight accorded to the horses and mules, however, was increased so that in 1820 it equaled the weight given to cattle and calves (see the text). 1840, table 7.3.

Line 7: Price index numbers were first established for 1800 and 1810 in the following way. Index numbers on the base 1860 were computed from data in Towne and Rasmussen 1960, 283–86, for the prices of horses and mules, beef and veal, pork, and mutton and lamb. The first two index numbers were used to inflate (separately) the real value of horses and horned cattle in 1800 and the values shown in lines 3 and 4, above, for 1809. The other two indexes, weighted equally (see table 7.3), were combined and used to inflate the difference between lines 5 and 6, 1800 and 1809. (This procedure probably gives too great a weight to the proxies for the prices of swine and sheep, since part of the difference between lines 5 and 6 reflects the value of young horses, mules, and cattle. Since there was no good basis for adjusting to remove this problem, and since the index numbers were expected to be useful crude approximations at best, no adjustments were made.) The current price aggregate divided by the constant price aggregate (line 6) yielded implicit price indexes for 1800 and 1810 (1809 weights), 91.6 and 95.1. Index numbers for the other years—except 1774—were constructed by extrapolating the 1810 estimate (see below) on the basis of prices of beef and pork, taken from Cole 1938. Cole gives monthly prices. The ones chosen in this case were January prices at Philadelphia. In the case of beef, mess beef, 1799 and 1805; Philadelphia mess beef, 1810 and 1815. In the case of pork, Burlington, 1799; Burlington mess, 1805; mess, 1810; Philadelphia mess, 1815. Some effort was made to see whether these descriptive changes imply real changes in quality. The device used was to compare price change across a period of designation change with price changes observed for other types of beef or pork, for which there was no designation change. Conversions were derived on the basis of information supplied by Cole (1938, ix and x). The beef index was given a weight of 4; the pork index was given a weight of 1 (see table 7.3). Where gaps appeared, the index was interpolated on one of its components. Estimates were made for all the years 1798 through 1810, and the resulting index numbers vary little from year to year, with one exception. Stability is also the impression given by the indexes derived from Towne and Rasmussen (see above). Therefore it seemed reasonable to extrapolate the 1810 index number from Towne and Rasmussen, 95.1, on the series derived from Cole. The index numbers for 1800 were not used as bases for this extrapolation because the year 1800 is the year referred to above—the one in which the Cole-based index number is far out of line with the index numbers of the other years. It seems probable that 1800 was an unusual year, and that Towne and Rasmussen took that into account when they derived their price data for 1800. That is, it seems probable that the Towne and Rasmussen price data for 1800 should be understood to refer to trend-level figures for the turn of the century, and not to 1800 specifically. The price index number for 1774 was obtained by dividing the current price estimate for that year (based on Jones) by the constant price estimate (based on Blodget; see the text).

Line 8: line 6 × line 7 ÷ 100.

extrapolate the total value of all animal inventories (1860 prices) from 1840 to the years 1774, 1799, 1805, and 1809. The 1809 figure was extrapolated to 1815 on the assumption that the annual rate of growth of animal stocks between 1809 and 1815 was the same as the rate of growth of the real value of the products of cattle, hogs, sheep, horses and mules combined, according to Towne and Rasmussen (1960), between 1810 and 1820. For purposes of these computations, however, the horses and mules component of the Towne and Rasmussen series received the same weight as the cattle component, approximating the relationship of the value of the inventories of these animals in the years 1840 to 1860. The extrapolation rests on the assumption that in the years between 1809 and 1815 the value of the output of animal products changed at about the rate of the value of inventories, and that the annual rates of change of these variables were constant between 1809 and 1820. These assumptions are unlikely to yield a reliable estimate of the true real value of animal inventories in 1815, but they *are* likely to produce something approximating the trend level of the real value of animal inventories in that year, which is the best that can be hoped for.

Apart from the problems peculiar to the 1815 estimate, there are three major potential sources of error in this set of estimates. First, Blodget's estimates of the numbers of animals may be wrong, since there is no obvious, reliable, comprehensive source from which he could have drawn them (other than state property tax assessments). The figures for 1800, however, have survived a certain amount of testing (Gallman 1972, 204), which suggests that Blodget's evidence may be adequate to at least establish a trend level for the turn of the century. The reasonably close match between Blodget's overall estimate in 1774 and Jones's figure for that year (see above) also tends to increase one's confidence in Blodget's ability to establish accurate wealth estimates, and Jones (1980, 354), as we have seen, has reported that Blodget's estimates of the number of horses and horned cattle in 1774 are consistent—if a little too low—with the results she obtained from her sample. Since Jones's data include all animals while Blodget's apparently cover only mature animals, it should not be a surprise that the Blodget figures are lower than those of Jones.

Second, it is possible that the quantitative relationships between the extrapolating series and the series being extrapolated changed between 1774 and 1840. That would constitute a more serious worry if the extrapolator accounted for a small fraction of the full series, or if the relationship was unstable. In fact, the extrapolator accounts for about three-quarters of the full series, and the relationship is quite stable in the years 1840–1870 (see Gallman 1972, 204). The proportions run thus: 73.6 percent for 1840, 74.4 percent for 1850, 72.8 percent for 1860, and 76.3 percent for 1870. They rise in subsequent years, going from about 80 percent in 1880 to 90 percent in 1900.

Finally, the process of deflation rests on the assumption that a horse is a horse and a cow is a cow. If in fact the types of animals represented in the stock changed importantly over time—particularly, if the quality of animals in the stock changed—then this procedure would not be warranted. But while there can be little doubt that the types of animals did shift and there may have been quality improvements in some elements of the stock, it is doubtful that these sources of error are important.[11] To the extent that these factors produce errors in the estimates, the errors probably lead to *overestimates* of the real value of animal stocks in the early years. Rates of growth computed from series in which the estimates for the early years are too large will necessarily be biased in a *downward* direction.

The constant price series was inflated to produce current price estimates. First, comprehensive benchmark price index numbers were established for 1800, 1810, 1820, and 1860 on the basis of data in Towne and Rasmussen. It should be said that the prices for cattle, swine, and sheep were derived from prices of meat products, and therefore represent imperfectly the prices of the animals for which they are proxies. The benchmark estimates, in turn, were interpolated (to 1805 and 1815) and extrapolated (to 1799) on more limited animal products price series (pork, beef) taken from A. H. Cole. These series seem to tell the same story, with respect to price movements in the early nineteenth century, as do the Towne and Rasmussen data. However, the Cole data lack information on the prices of horses and mules, and thus seem inadequate bases for extrapolating the price index back to 1774. Since Jones has pointed out that her data on animal inventories are consistent with Blodget's, it seemed the better part of wisdom to accept Jones's estimate of the value of animal inventories (current prices) and convert it from pounds sterling to dollars. The price index for 1774, then, is the index implicit in the constant price series, derived from Blodget's data, and the current price series, derived from Jones's work.

### 14.4.6. Inventories

**1799–1815.** For these years, the procedures to develop the series in table 14.8 are similar to those employed to estimate the value of inventories for the

TABLE 14.8 **Value of inventories, measured in current and 1860 prices, 1774–1815, in millions of dollars**

| | | 1774 | 1799 | 1805 | 1815 |
|---|---|---|---|---|---|
| 1 | Value of imports, excluding duties, at current prices | 17 | 81 | 126 | 85 |
| 2 | Duties | 15 | 24 | 38 | |
| 3 | Value of imports, including duties | 17 | 96 | 150 | 123 |
| 4 | Value of inventories of imports (line 3 × 0.5) | 9 | 48 | 75 | 62 |
| 5 | Price index (1860 = 100) | 85 | 167 | 153 | 220 |
| 6 | Value of imports, excluding duties, at 1860 prices (100 × line 1 ÷ line 5) | 20 | 49 | 82 | 39 |
| 7 | Value of imports, including duties, as a ratio of the value of imports excluding duties, 1860: 1.144 | | | | |
| 8 | Line 7 × 0.5 = 0.572 | | | | |
| 9 | Inventories of imported goods, at 1860 prices (line 6 × line 8) | 11 | 28 | 47 | 22 |
| | **Agricultural products** | | | | |
| 10 | Inventories, at current prices | 20 | 125 | 175 | 251 |
| 11 | Price index (1860 = 100) | 61 | 95 | 111 | 119 |
| 12 | Inventories, at 1860 prices | 33 | 131 | 157 | 211 |
| | **Mined and manufactured products** | | | | |
| 13 | Inventories, at current prices | 10 | 67 | 86 | 130 |
| 14 | Price index (1860 = 100) | 65 | 120 | 119 | 158 |
| 15 | Inventories, at 1860 prices | 15 | 56 | 72 | 82 |
| | **Totals** | | | | |
| 16 | Inventories, at current prices | 39 | 240 | 336 | 443 |
| 17 | Inventories, at 1860 prices | 59 | 215 | 276 | 315 |

Sources: See text.

years 1840 to 1900 (see chapter 12). The following notes refer to the estimates for these years. The year 1774 is a special case, and is dealt with separately at the end.

**Imports.** The value of merchandise imports was taken from North (1960, 600). The years are fiscal years, ending 30 September, and the values were established at the ports of embarkation. Ideally, the values would refer to calendar years and include shipping costs, but given the nature of the estimates to be derived from them, these deviations from the ideal are of modest importance. See North's account for a description of other weaknesses of the data.

Pitkin's (1835, 333–34) statements of duties were added to the value of imports. Before 1815 they include "tonnage, passports, clearances, light money etc.," which appear to have accounted for about one-twentieth of the total of duties plus the other items.

The series, exclusive of duties, was deflated and then used as an extrapolator for the 1860 value of imports plus duties to create a constant price series. The deflator (shifted to the base 1860 without reweighting) consisted of the Bezanson index of prices of goods imported into Philadelphia (US Bureau of the Census 1975, series E-99). The index numbers refer to calendar years, so that they do not exactly match the years to which the import data refer. No effort was made to adjust for this inconsistency, which on the whole is a matter of modest importance.

The value of inventories of imports was assumed to be equal to one-half the value of imports, including duties.

**Agriculture.** Benchmark estimates were prepared from the data of Towne and Rasmussen (1960) for the years 1800, 1810, and 1820. (As indicated previously, the Towne and Rasmussen estimates of crops and animal products are consistent, in 1800, with various pieces of evidence supplied by Blodget.) The procedure was as follows. Various items (the value of inventory changes of livestock, chickens and eggs, other poultry, dairy products, truck crops and fruits, and "miscellaneous") were deducted from the Towne and Rasmussen estimates of the value of farm output. The seed and feed allowances for corn, oats, and hay were added back in (see chapter 12 for justifications of these additions and subtractions). The constant price data were then shifted to the price base 1860 by the two components, livestock products and crops, but without reweighting within these broad classes. The constant price data were then interpolated to the years 1805 and 1815 and extrapolated to the year 1799, on the assumptions that the annual rate of change remained constant between 1799 and 1810 and between 1810 and 1820. These assumptions are unlikely to mirror reality very exactly, but are perhaps adequate for the purpose of obtaining approximations to trend level values. The implicit price index numbers were extrapolated to 1799 and interpolated to 1805 and 1815 on the Bezanson agricultural price index (US Bureau of the Census 1975, series E-100).

**Mining and Manufacturing.** Estimates were derived for the year 1810 by extrapolating the 1840 and 1850 figures (tables 12.3 and 12.4) on Poulson's (1975) current and constant price estimates of the value of output of mined products (less gold) and value added by manufacturing. The constant price series was then carried to the years 1799, 1805, and 1815 on the assumption that mining and manufacturing accounted for the same share of inventories (0.26) in these years as in 1810. Once again, this appears to be the best way to get approximations of trend values. The implicit price index for 1810 was extrapolated to the other years on the Bezanson price index of industrial goods in US Bureau of the Census 1975, series E-101.

**1774.** The value of imports was computed by extrapolating the Shepherd and Walton estimate for 1772 (US Bureau of the Census 1975, series Z-287, New England, Middle Colonies, Upper South, Lower South) to 1774 (on the sum of US Bureau of the Census 1975, series Z-214 and Z-228) and then converting to "dollars" by means of the Jones (1980, 10) exchange rate of $4.15. No adjustment could be made for duties. The alternative procedure of extrapolating the value of imports from 1790 on the Blodget series produces a much lower value: $9–10 million, as compared with $17 million. Shepherd and Walton appear to be the better source.

Jones (1980) has an estimate of the value of crop inventories, which implies about the same per capita value, in real terms, as the estimates for 1799–1815, a plausible result. The crop estimate, expressed in dollars, was blown up to include the rest of the inventories of agricultural goods, on the assumption that these elements composed the same share as in 1799 of the total value of inventories of agricultural goods.

Jones (1980) has an estimate of the value of business inventories, which presumably includes imported goods and domestically produced goods. Subtracting the estimate of the value of inventories of imports, described above, from the Jones figure of the value of business inventories, expressed in dollar values, should yield the value of inventories of nonagricultural, domestically produced goods, most of which would be mined and manufactured goods. Unfortunately, however, the procedure more than exhausts the Jones business inventories, and therefore a new estimate of the value of mined and manufactured goods in inventory had to be made. The estimate was based on the assumption that the share of mined and manufactured goods in the real value of inventories was the same in 1774 as it was in 1799, a technique that may overstate the value of these inventories in 1774. It is also true that relying exclusively on Jones would result in a substantially lower (almost 50 percent lower) estimate of the value of all inventories, and perhaps a more accurate estimate. The virtue of the estimate adopted is that it was constructed by means of evidence and estimating procedures similar to those used to produce the estimates for the years 1799 to 1900, and is therefore more likely to be comparable with these figures than would an estimate employing only the data supplied by Jones. This is an important virtue; the estimates assembled in this study are intended to form time series, and thus they should be comparable above all else. The price indexes described above, in the section dealing with 1799–1815, were extended to 1784 and then carried to 1774 on the Bezanson general price index for Philadelphia in US Bureau of the Census 1975, series E-111.

### 14.4.7. Equipment

Table 14.9 provides estimates of the value of equipment. They are derived as follows.

**1799–1815.** Goldsmith (1952), basing his work on Blodget's data, estimated that agricultural implements amounted in value to $32 million in 1805. The estimate is not particularly strong, but there is little choice but to accept it if complete estimates are to be prepared. As to other equipment, Goldsmith has no suggestions. Extrapolating the value of equipment in mining, manufacturing, and trade from 1840 to 1810 on Poulson's (1975) estimates (current prices) of value added in mining and manufacturing, and then carrying the figure to 1805 on the assumption that the rate of change was unaltered between 1805 and 1840 yields a figure of roughly the same value as Goldsmith's agricultural implements figure. At a guess, then, equipment of all types amounted to about $65 million in 1805. This estimate was extrapolated to 1799 and 1815 on the value of inventories of all kinds and the value of shipping. Structures were left out of the extrapolator because the estimate of the value of structures in 1805 is suspect. A deflator was constructed by extrapolating the weighted average price index number of agricultural, manufacturing and trade equipment in 1840 to 1799, 1805, and 1815 on the Warren-Pearson price index of metals and metal products (US Bureau of the Census 1975, series E-58)— the best option, but by no means a good one, in view of the fact that most equipment was made of wood. Unfortunately, however, there is no wood price index that is likely to be superior.

**1774.** Jones's (1980, 90) estimates of the value of the equipment of "farm and household" and "equipment of nonfarm business" were converted to

TABLE 14.9 **Value of equipment, measured in current and 1860 prices, 1774–1815, in millions of dollars**

|   |                           | 1774 | 1799 | 1805 | 1815 |
|---|---------------------------|------|------|------|------|
| 1 | Value, at current prices  | 15   | 46   | 65   | 88   |
| 2 | Price index               | 161  | 225  | 224  | 289  |
| 3 | Value, at 1860 prices     | 9    | 20   | 29   | 30   |

Sources: See text.

dollars and accepted. Household equipment refers not to furniture, bed-
ding, or eating and cooking equipment, but rather to tools employed in
producing goods that at a later date were to be produced chiefly in shops
and mills—that is, artisan's tools. It would be helpful to be able to distinguish between farm and household equipment—especially in view of the
fact that household equipment of this type is excluded from the capital
stock estimates—but that proved impossible. The estimate was deflated
by the index described above for 1799, carried to 1774 on the Bezanson
general price index for Philadelphia (US Bureau of the Census 1975,
series E-111).

## 14.4.8. Other Improvements to Farmland

The estimating procedures are described in full in chapter 7, which deals
with the 1840–1900 period. These notes describe procedures peculiar to
the 1774–1815 period. The bases for estimating the value of fences, irrigation works, and drainage works are very slender. These improvements
have therefore been omitted. Table 14.10 summarizes the main results;
table 14.11 provides the details to back up the main results.

TABLE 14.10  **Value of agricultural land improvements (clearing and breaking), measured in
current and 1860 prices, 1774–1815, in millions of dollars**

|   |   | 1774 | 1799 | 1805 | 1815 |
|---|---|------|------|------|------|
| 1 | Improved land, from Blodget, millions of acres | 20.86 | 36.30 | 39.40 | — |
| 2 | Line 1, adjusted | 15.88 | 28.05 | 30.58 | — |
| 3 | Man-months of labor clearing improved land | 14.77 | 26.09 | 28.44 | 32.84 |
| 4 | 1860 monthly wage rate (weighted averages of regional rates) | $18.24 | $18.37 | $18.49 | $18.60 |
| 5 | Value of clearing, at 1860 prices, in millions of dollars (line 3 × line 4) | 269.40 | 479.27 | 525.86 | 610.82 |
| 6 | Current monthly wage rate | $7.68 | $14.57 | $13.39 | $12.21 |
| 7 | Value of clearing, at current prices. in millions of dollars (line 3 × line 6) | 113.40 | 380.13 | 380.81 | 401.00 |
| 8 | Value added per cleared acre (line 7 ÷ line 2) | 7.14 | 13.55 | 12.45 | — |

Sources:
Line 1: Blodget (1810, 60. Line 2: line 1 adjusted to make the figures comparable to those underlying the estimates
for 1840–1900; see text. Line 3, 1774–1805: line 2 × 0.93; 1815: 1805 extrapolated to 1815 on the assumption that
the annual rate of change in 1805–15, was the same as the annual rate of change in 1799–1805. See text. Line 4:
Regional estimates of labor consumed in land clearing and breaking (see text) were weighted with 1860 regional
wage rates (see table 7.6), to produce average annual constant price wage rate estimates for the years 1774, 1800,
and 1809. The wage rate with 1800 weights was applied to the data in line 3 for 1799; the mean of the wage rates
with 1800 and 1809 weights was applied to the 1805 data; the wage rate with 1809 weights was applied to the 1815
data. Line 5: line 3 × line 4. Line 6: See table 14.11. Line 7: line 3 × line 6. Line 8: line 7 ÷ line 2.

| | 1774 | 1800 | 1809 | 1815 | 1818 |
|---|---|---|---|---|---|
| **I. Improved land, in millions of acres** | | | | | |
| New England | 3.20 | 5.28 | 5.40 | | |
| Middle Atlantic | 3.24 | 5.77 | 7.07 | | |
| East North Central | | 0.23 | 1.06 | | |
| West North Central | | | 0.07 | | |
| South Atlantic | 9.44 | 15.95 | 15.9 | | |
| East South Central | | 1.23 | 2.22 | | |
| West South Central | | | 0.22 | | |
| Totals: Blodget's Adjusted | 15.88 | 28.45 | 31.94 | | |
| Weighted regional estimates | 13.52 | 29.70 | 39.00 | | |
| **II. Labor consumed in clearing and breaking land, in millions of man-months** | | | | | |
| **(I., above, divided by 0.93)** | | | | | |
| New England | 2.98 | 4.91 | 5.02 | | |
| Middle Atlantic | 3.01 | 5.37 | 6.58 | | |
| East North Central | | 0.21 | 0.99 | | |
| West North Central | | | 0.07 | | |
| South Atlantic | 8.78 | 14.83 | 14.79 | | |
| East South Central | | 1.14 | 2.06 | | |
| West South Central | | | 0.2 | | |
| Total | 14.77 | 26.46 | 29.71 | | |
| **III. Value of land clearing and breaking, at 1860 prices, in millions of dollars** | | | | | |
| New England | 65.86 | 108.5 | 110.9 | | |
| Middle Atlantic | 57.58 | 102.7 | 125.9 | | |
| East North Central | | 4.3 | 20.5 | | |
| West North Central | | | 1.4 | | |
| South Atlantic | 145.92 | 246.5 | 245.8 | | |
| East South Central | | 24.0 | 43.5 | | |
| West South Central | | | 4.7 | | |
| Totals | 269.36 | 486.1 | 552.6 | | |
| **IV. Average 1860 wage rates, various weights** | | | | | |
| **(III, totals, divided by II, totals)** | $18.24 | $18.37 | $18.60 | | |

**V. Regional wage rates, adjusted for the value of board**

| | 1800 | 1818 |
|---|---|---|
| New England | $18.89 | $17.85 |
| Middle Atlantic | 15.59 | 14.73 |
| East North Central | 14.07 | 13.29 |
| West North Central | | 15.23 |
| South Atlantic | 12.86 | 12.15 |
| East South Central | 13.56 | 15.54 |

**VI. Value of land clearing and breaking, at current prices, (II, 1800 and 1809, times V, 1800 and 1818), in millions of dollars**

| | 1800 | 1818 |
|---|---|---|
| New England | 92.75 | 89.61 |
| Middle Atlantic | 83.72 | 96.92 |
| East North Central | 2.95 | 3.16 |
| West North Central | | 1.07 |

*continues*

TABLE 14.11 *(continued)*

|  | 1774 | 1800 | 1809 | 1815 | 1818 |
|---|---|---|---|---|---|
| **VI. Value of land clearing and breaking, at current prices, (II, 1800 and 1809, times V, 1800 and 1818), in millions of dollars** | | | | | |
| South Atlantic |  | 190.71 |  |  | 179.7 |
| East South Central |  | 15.46 |  |  | 32.01 |
| Totals |  | 385.59 |  |  | 412.47 |
| | | | | | |
| **VII. Average wage rates (VI divided by II)** |  | $14.57 |  |  | $13.88 |

**VIII. Indexes of Adams's farm wage rate series, Base 1818 = 100**

|  | 1774 | 1800 | 1809 | 1815 | 1818 |
|---|---|---|---|---|---|
| 1. Brandywine | — | — | 100[b] | 90 | 100 |
| 2. Philadelphia | — | — | 94.1[b] | 96.1 | 100 |
| 3. Maryland | 55.3 | — | 96.0[b] | 80 | 100 |

**IX. Estimated wage rates, including the value of board**

|  | 1774 | 1800 | 1809 | 1815 | 1818 |
|---|---|---|---|---|---|
|  | $7.68 | 14.57[a] | 13.39[b] | 12.21 | 13.88 |

Sources: See text.

Notes: [a]1799 rather than 1800; [b]1805 rather than 1809. Adjustments to Blodget's improved acres: The 1800 number in table 14.11, line 1 is slightly (0.4 million acres) higher than the 1799 number in table 14.10, line 2. Weighted regional estimates: estimates based on 1840 per capita rates and regions distribution of population in 1774, 1800, and 1809. Estimated average wage rates for 1800 and 1818 (1809 weights) were carried to 1774, 1799, 1805, and 1815 on Adams's (1968, 1982, 1986) farm wage rates for the Brandywine, Philadelphia, and Maryland. The 1800 and 1818 data were taken from Lebergott (1964, 257, 539) and adjusted upward by 50 percent to incorporate the value of board (see chapter 7). It should be said that Adams finds that board in the Brandywine region was relatively more valuable than this, equal to between 53 percent (1801) and 94 percent (1804) of the straight wage in this period. It seemed safer to adhere to Lebergott's correction and to use it systematically, rather than to rely on the evidence of the Brandywine alone to describe circumstances in the nation at large. Lebergott (1964) does not give regional data for 1800. Regional estimates were constructed on the basis of Lebergott's average US estimates for 1800 and 1818, and the percentage deviation in 1818 of the regional wage rates from the average US rate. In Section VIII, 1815 is calculated as 1818 × 0.88 (which is the mean of indexes for Philadelphia and Maryland); 1805 is calculated as 1818 × 0.965 (which is the mean of Brandywine, Philadelphia, and Maryland); 1799 is 1800; and 1774 is 1818 × 0.553.

Blodget's estimates of the acreage of improved land—"acres in tillage," "meadows and fallow ground," and other improved lands "including pastures"—were accepted subject to one revision: half of the land in the last category was treated as improved, and the other half as unimproved. The purpose of this adjustment is to bring Blodget's totals into conformity with the standards of the censuses of 1850 to 1900, and thus to make them comparable to the estimates for the 1840–1900 period in chapter 7 (see Gallman 1972, 202, note 13).

Virtually all the land improved in the period treated in this section had previously been forest. According to Primack (see chapter 7), techniques for clearing forestland did not change before 1860. Labor embodied in the clearing of an acre of cleared land was therefore assumed to be the same in 1774–1815 as in 1840–60: approximately 0.93 months per acre (see tables 7.4 and 7.5).

Blodget has no estimate of the acreage of cleared land in 1815. It was therefore necessary to extrapolate the labor embodied in cleared land from 1805 to 1815. The assumption was made that the annual rate of change of the labor content of cleared land was the same between 1805 and 1815 as between 1799 and 1805. The estimate is probably adequate, if viewed as a trend-level estimate.

For purposes of valuation, it was necessary to divide Blodget's improved land estimates (as adjusted) among geographic regions. This was accomplished by applying the 1840 regional rates of improved land per capita to regional population estimates for 1774 (Jones 1980, 37), 1800, and 1810 (US Bureau of the Census 1960, series A-123 to A-180), and then distributing the adjusted improved land estimates among regions on the basis of these figures. The data for 1800 were used to distribute the 1799 and 1805 totals, while the data for 1810 were used for the 1815 total. The aggregate results appear in table 14.11. Blodget (1810) does not provide sufficient details with regard to the land supply in 1809 to permit the adjustment of his improved land estimate for that year to be carried out in the same way as the adjustments for the 1774 and 1800 estimates. Instead, the ratio of the adjusted estimates to the unadjusted estimates (0.78) for 1774 through 1805 was applied to Blodget's 1809 estimate of the acreage of improved land, to obtain the adjusted figure for that year.

Constant price estimates were made by applying Lebergott's (1964) regional wage rates (adjusted for the value of board—see chapter 7) to the relevant regional totals of the labor content of cleared land. The 1815 current price estimate was made by weighting Lebergott's 1818 regional wage rates (adjusted for board) with 1809 labor weights (i.e., the labor content of cleared land), and then carrying the average wage rate so computed from 1818 to 1815 on Adams's farm wage rate series (see table 14.11). Similarly, Lebergott's 1818 regional data and 1800 national average estimate were used to derive regional figures for 1800. These data were then weighted by the regional figures on the labor content of cleared land to produce an appropriately weighted average wage rate for 1800, which was then carried to 1774, 1799, and 1805 on Adams's series.

Two sets of consistency tests can be made. According to Jones (1980, 10, 90), the value of real estate in 1774 came to about $250 million. The value imparted to land by clearing it (table 14.10, $113 million) and building structures (table 14.3, $67 million) amounted to $180 million, leaving

$70 million to be accounted for by the value of fencing, drainage and irrigation works, privately owned roads, and the value of the land itself. In 1840, fencing, drainage and irrigation works were equal in value to about 29.2 percent of the value of clearing. If this relationship applied also to 1774, then the value of the land itself and the value of privately-owned roads amounted to only $37 million ($70 million minus 29.2 percent of $113 million). If Jones's real estate estimate refers to all the land in what was to become the United States, 526 million acres, then the land itself plus the value of privately-owned roads came to seven cents an acre. If on the other hand we assume that Jones's real estate figure covers only the land that Blodget refers to as "cultivated" and "adjoining"—which the previous consistency tests (see section 14.3.1, 1774) suggested was the case—then the value of the land itself plus the value of privately-owned roads comes to about 36.6 cents per acre. This is close to Blodget's estimate of the value of land in its natural state in 1774, 35 cents per acre (for qualifications, see the discussion in chapter 7.)

The results of the second test are less satisfactory. According to table 14.10, line 8, the average value added to land by clearing was in $7.14 per acre in 1774, $13.55 in 1799, and $12.45 in 1805. Blodget's (1810, 60) estimates of the average value of cultivated land per acre in these years are much lower: $2.50, $5.50, and $6.25 respectively. Blodget's figures refer to market prices, while the data in table 14.10 are gross reproduction cost estimates; but the same considerations apply to the test against the Jones data, described above.

The clear suggestion is that Blodget's estimates of the average price of cultivated land are inconsistent with the land clearing data and perhaps the Jones data as well (which qualifies the results of the consistency test described in the introductory parts of this section). It seems probable that Blodget's figures are just too low, though the possibility that the clearing estimates are too high cannot be entirely excluded. For example, it may have been more common to leave stumps in the ground when clearing land in the seventeenth, eighteenth, and early nineteenth centuries than became usual later on (see chapter 7). Thus the estimating procedure employed may be more appropriate to the years 1840 to 1900 than to the years 1774 to 1815. It is also possible, of course, that the wage rates employed in the estimation are unrepresentative and too high. The success of the test with the Jones data leads one to suppose that the Blodget estimates are more likely to be wrong than are the clearing estimates or the wage rates. But one's satisfaction with the test against the Jones data is qualified by the fact that the Blodget estimates play a role, however peripheral, in this test (see the introductory parts of this section for the consistency tests between the Blodget and Jones estimates). Clearly, the tests are less than conclusive, though the check against the Jones data is moderately reassuring.

## 14.5. Conclusion

This chapter summarizes Gallman's capital stock estimates for the period from 1774 to 1815.

## CHAPTER FIFTEEN

# Wrapping Up

In the early 1950s, when Robert Gallman was a graduate student training under Simon Kuznets at the University of Pennsylvania, capital accumulation was at the center of economists' understanding of the process of economic growth. The countries with high and rising incomes were those that were wealthy and that saved a larger share of their income. Some economists during this period, most notably Walt Rostow (1960), held that a substantial increase in a country's saving rate was a necessary precondition for its "takeoff" into modern economic growth. Neither Gallman nor Kuznets subscribed to this view.

But Gallman would not accept today's orthodoxy either. New Growth theorists Charles Jones and Paul Romer (2010, 226) write: "Ideas, institutions, population, and human capital are now at the center of growth theory. Physical capital has been pushed to the periphery." The view that the accumulation of physical capital is not important for long-run growth is based on several lines of thinking. Most macro-growth economists focus on balanced growth paths that fit Nicholas Kaldor's (1961) so-called stylized facts. In addition, growth theories, such as Solow's neoclassical model, yield predictions where changes in the saving rate affect the short-run dynamics but not the economy's long-run growth rate. Under the assumptions of decreasing returns to capital in production and of capital consumption (depreciation) proportional to the capital stock, a Solow economy with capital accumulation but no technical change settles down to zero-growth equilibrium.

Anecdotal evidence is put into play. Advanced market-based economies (such as Germany and Japan) can see their capital stocks devastated

Rhode wrote this chapter.

during war, and then experience growth miracles in the aftermath. Less advanced economies can receive capital inflows as result of foreign aid but enjoy no lasting beneficial effects for development. And planned economies (such as the Soviet Union) can massively shift resources from consumption to investment without creating the conditions for long-run growth.[1]

Growth accounting exercises, which were popularized by Moses Abramovitz (1956), Robert Solow (1957), John Kendrick (1961), and Edward Denison (1962), also deemphasized the role of capital accumulation relative to technological change. In the horserace between invention and thrift, invention wins. But as Abramovitz (1989) noted, while the residual in growth accounting exercises may be labeled as "total factor productivity" or TFP, it is more properly called a "measure of our ignorance." Abramovitz thought it meant we did not sufficiently understand the nature of the investment process.[2]

Gallman's career was devoted in large part to enhancing our understanding of that process. He sought to document the growth of the American capital stock, to relate these stocks to investment flows using the national product accounts, and (in work with Lance Davis) to determine how these investment flows were financed. Gallman's research showed that the rate of capital formation soared and the capital-to-output ratio doubled over the "long" nineteenth century. The capital-to-output ratio increased across a broad spectrum of economic activities, and real interest rates declined; these changes were signs that an increasing saving rate, rather than technologically induced shifts in investment demand, was the important driver. Gallman also found that the price of capital generally fell relative to other goods, and that capital consumption also rose as a share of gross product (see also Kuznets 1961).

In Gallman's view, capital accumulation clearly mattered for nineteenth-century America. It mattered for the creation of vast acreages of farm land as part of the process of territorial expansion, for the development of its sprawling transportation infrastructure and burgeoning cities, for the adoption of new technologies embodied in physical capital, and for the catching-up growth to attain the economy's potential, following the losses from the greatest war fought on American soil. The growth process slowed down, at least temporarily, when crises damaged the financial system's capacity to facilitate investment (most notably in the 1890s, 1930s, and in recent years). Growth accelerated in the postbellum period when market developments and policy changes enhanced the ability of financial intermediaries to better connect savers who had a surplus to lend, and investors with profit opportunities to justify borrowing. Over the long nineteenth century, as Gallman often noted, America's capital stock grew enormously—faster than output, faster than its population, faster than its labor force, and faster than its land base. As his application of growth accounting exercises for the nineteenth century indicates, capital formation was a strong driver of the accelerated growth over the period from 1840 to 1900. He was, of course, aware that historical periods differed.

To understand capital formation and its relationship to economic growth, Gallman needed better measures of both income and capital. He needed to build national product accounts and capital stock series. These data are essential for understanding not only when economic growth occurred, but also how and why. This volume caps the lifetime of effort that Gallman dedicated to constructing a consistent and detailed record of American economic growth over the long nineteenth century.

# Notes

## Chapter One

1. He was interested in the reproducible physical capital stock excluding financial assets and raw land. In Gallman's conceptual framework, raw land was nonreproducible and was a part of wealth, but not of the capital stock. The only financial assets that Gallman considered were stocks of monetary metals, and net claims on foreigners. These were parts of "national wealth," though not "domestic wealth." Gallman focused on the tangible capital stock and did not include the value of intellectual property or human capital. He did enumerate consumer durables, long-lasting goods owned by households.

2. As an example, his library contained Peterson 1971. See also "Letter to W. Erwin Diewert," proposing a paper for the fiftieth anniversary meeting of the Conference on Research on Income and Wealth, Gallman papers.

3. According to Gallman, the two first met around 1960 after Davis offered a trenchant analysis, delivered in his characteristic rapid-fire fashion, of John F. Kennedy's election prospects. Gallman, a Democrat in the era of Eisenhower, liked what he heard.

4. Gallman, NSF Proposal, 19 August 1981, p. 3, Gallman papers.

5. Although Gallman treated enslaved African-Americans as people and not property in calculating the US capital stock, he also noted how slaves differed from wage labor. See Anderson and Gallman 1977.

6. The Brady indexes, which were constructed largely from prices in northeastern cities, were akin to GDP deflators in that they were based on currently produced goods.

7. Chain-linked price indexes vary the price weights over time using information on quantities or shares. Double-deflation of value added used different price indexes to deflate the input and output bundles. See David 1962.

8. "Chapter 2: Problems of Concept and Measurement: The Capital Stock," p. 4 in Gallman's papers. Gallman (1972, 47–50) discusses index numbers in more conventional terms.

9. He did take pains to recenter the Brady price indexes to conform to the census dates.

10. "Reswitching" occurs if the ordering of two production techniques in terms of the capital-to-labor ratio changes as the rate-of-profit-to-wage ratio changes. One technique may be more capital-intensive than the other at a high rate-of-profit-to-wage ratio, and less capital-intensive at a low ratio.

11. Together with William Parker, he was among the first economic historians to assemble and analyze a microsample from the manuscript census—the Parker-Gallman sample of individual agricultural operations in cotton-producing counties from the 1860 census. Samples for rice and sugar followed.

12. A joint paper by Gallman and Howle on the capital stock was presented at the February 1965 meetings of the Purdue University Seminar on the Application of Economic Theory and Quantitative Techniques to the Problems of Economic History. Gallman's return to the capital project can be dated to a 1981 NSF grant, which noted the possibility of linking to the work of Alice Hanson Jones for 1774.

13. As an example, when calculating the gross capital formation rate over a decade, he sums the ten years of gross investment flows and divides by the ten years of GNP. He does not take the ten-year average of the yearly rate. Given the nature of his data and the way he adds components available at different frequency, this choice is sensible. It can lead to different results for cyclical variables or cases where the numerator and denominator are correlated. As another example, when calculating annual growth rates between decadal benchmarks, Gallman uses annual compounding rather than continuous compounding.

14. The growth rate of NNP was slowing (as capital consumption comprised a rising share of output); the growth rate of GNP per capita was rising.

15. The inclusion of inventory changes leads the series reported in table 1.3 to differ from Gallman's widely reproduced series. See the discussion in section 8 of chapter 5.

16. This discussion relates to the capital stocks. The picture for gross investment flows was different. (The depreciation rate for equipment was much higher than for structures.) As Gallman (1966, 15) noted in his analysis of the changing composition of gross domestic capital formation over the 1834–1908 period, the "share of construction fell from about 80 per cent to less than 50 per cent, while the share of manufactured producer durables rose from about 20 per cent to over 50 per cent." This discussion related to conventionally defined investment flows, excluding land breaking and clearing.

17. Gallman (1986) quotes a share of 38.4 percent, based on a concept consistent with the 1900 number quoted in the text. The concept includes land clearing and breaking, fencing, and investments for irrigation and drainage. Gallman 1992, table 2.8, has somewhat lower shares. This is based on a concept including land clearing and breaking, but excluding fencing, irrigation, and drainage.

18. His work on the levels and growth rates of income almost always included international comparisons. Incorporating the role of capital formation in such cross-country comparisons was an unfinished task (Davis and Gallman 2001).

## Chapter Two

1. Gallman, NSF proposal, 19 August 1981, p. 28, Gallman papers.

2. Net international assets include stocks of monetary metals and net claims on foreigners. Note that domestic capital = national capital – net international assets. During the 1850–1900 period, net international assets were negative, so domestic capital was larger than national capital.

3. For the period before 1840, Gallman says, "The bases for estimating the value of fences, irrigation works, and drainage works are very slender. These improvements have been, therefore, omitted." Gallman papers.

4. Gallman's own labeling sometimes creates confusion. Gallman (1992) properly defines his series in panel B of table 2.8. But Gallman (2000) reproduces the numbers in panels C and D in table 13 and states that the data include fencing. They do not.

5. Carter, et al. 2006, series Bb 213, reports the value of slave stocks in current prices as \$1.286 billion in 1850 and \$3.059 billion in 1860. According to Gallman (1986), table 4.A.1, the current value of national wealth, excluding slaves, was \$7.89 billion in 1850 and \$16.39 billion in 1860. If one adds the value of slaves to that of land and capital, slaves comprise 14.1 percent of the total in 1850 and 15.7 percent in 1860.

6. As detailed in chapter 9, Gallman allocated the value of nonagricultural residential real estate according to a fixed ratio—0.638 to structures and 0.362 to land—across the 1840–1900 period.

7. These are current-price series, which differ from the constant-price series discussed in chapter 1.

8. See Gallman and Howle 1972, 32; and Davis and Gallman 1973, 457, for ratios based on prior series.

9. Substitution and sectoral shifts were of roughly equal importance. Measured in 1860 prices, the share of equipment in the sum of equipment and structures climbed from 16.2 percent in 1840 to 40.1 percent in 1900, a change of 23.9 percentage points. If one conducts a shift-share analysis, fixes the equipment ratios at their 1900 values, and allows the sectoral shares to change, one finds that the aggregate equipment share rises by 12.9 percentage points between 1840 and 1900. Sectoral shifts account for slightly more than one-half (53.7 percent) of the change.

## Chapter Three

1. The following discussion was developed with fixed capital chiefly in mind, although it can also be made to apply to inventories and international claims, with exceptions: there is no clear correspondence between "acquisition cost" and any single system of inventory accounting. For present purposes, that is not an important matter. All inventories treated herein are valued at market prices. So far as

international claims are concerned, there is no good counterpart of reproduction cost, other than market price.

2. A fourth method—not relevant to the series of this chapter, and therefore left undiscussed here—measures capital in terms of its current capacity to produce output. The problems of defining capacity and of measuring it in a meaningful way are ably discussed in Denison 1957, and Ruggles 1961.

3. Whether loss of value due to obsolescence should figure in capital consumption has been hotly debated; see Denison 1957 and Ruggles 1961. As a practical matter, it almost always does. We take no final stand on the theoretical issue, though the case of those who accept obsolescence as a factor in capital consumption seems the stronger of the two. Similar arguments apply to casualty losses.

4. This analysis ignores the problems posed by taxes and subsidies, problems of modest dimensions throughout most of the nineteenth century.

5. This is particularly true with respect to the manufacturing sector, which was experiencing extraordinarily high rates of growth.

6. That is, the fit for 1840 is almost as good as the fit for 1850 or 1860; the fit for 1870 is at least as good as the fit for 1880, 1890, or 1900.

7. Following Kuznets (1946), Gallman and Howle (1965) report a separate set of estimates—distinct from the agricultural estimates—of irrigation improvements, which they treated as part of the capital stock.

8. Rhode adds: This index in Davis et al. (1972, 34) was based in 1840. It ran 1840 (100), 1850 (181), 1860 (357), 1870 (512), 1880 (785), 1890 (1559), 1900 (2343). It matches the series reported in table 3.3. The 1840 = 100 series is slightly more precise and is used to compute the annual growth rates.

Davis and Gallman (1973, 457) report that, using the 1860 constant price series, the ratio of depreciable capital to annual output in 1860 was 1.6. The capital estimates were based on the original Gallman-Howle series and the output on Gallman (1966). Output in 1859 value at 1860 prices was $4.10 billion, making the depreciable capital stock estimate $6.56 billion, with bounds of 0.205 billion on either side due to rounding error. Depreciable capital, which Gallman also calls fixed reproducible capital, includes improvements and equipment but excludes inventories. The variant B estimate depreciable national capital stock for 1860 is $6.07 billion, which is below the lower bound for the original series.

9. Goldsmith and Kuznets apparently include farmland improvements, other than structures, with land rather than with capital.

10. The analysis uses the dating scheme relevant to the capital stock series (1840, 1850, etc.). Notice that the GNP series is dated to years different from these, the disparity being particularly wide in the case of the first post–Civil War date. See the notes to table 3.5.

11. If the measure of capital employed here had included inventories, this result might have been different.

12. The indirect effects, through changing supply and demand conditions for capital goods, constitute another matter. The rapid expansion in the stock

of machinery and equipment, for example—a development that, we have seen, played a role in the rise of the overall capital-to-output ratio—was related to the revolutionary growth of the industrial sector (mining, manufacturing, hand trades).

13. See Davis and Gallman 1973 for an effort to work through an analysis of this type in quantitative terms, making use of the original Gallman-Howle capital stock estimates.

14. Notice that the postbellum pattern of change differs between the estimates based on the stock and flow data. In the former series, the net proportion peaks in the 1880s; in the latter, the net proportion is higher in both the 1870s and 1890s than in the 1880s.

15. The Goldsmith (1982) series differ from the Goldsmith series discussed in the previous sections. The latter consisted chiefly of census-style estimates, whereas the twentieth-century series were built up by perpetual inventory procedures. Goldsmith (1982) provides a statement of the valuation system followed in assembling the series. The Goldsmith series excludes net claims on foreigners.

16. These results were worked out from Goldsmith et al. 1963, 2, 72–73, which is the source of the 1900 data in Goldsmith 1982.

17. It is well known that the deflation base selected can affect the rate of change of a real capital stock series, earlier bases typically producing higher rates of growth than late ones. It is therefore fortunate, for present purposes, that the deflation bases of the two series being considered here occupy similar relative temporal positions. Thus, the Goldsmith series is deflated on the base 1929, twenty-eight years from the first year in the series and fifty-one years from the last; the Gallman series, on 1860, twenty years from the first year in that series and forty years from the last.

## Chapter Four

1. Should the value of slaves be counted as part of the value of the capital stock? If we are interested, say, in the savings and investment behavior of planters, then the answer is surely yes. This chapter is not concerned with that topic. It is concerned with the measurement of long-term economic growth. Slaves are regarded as part of the labor force. They are also treated as part of population, for purposes of computing per capita levels of the capital stock.

While this chapter will present no estimates of the value of human capital, the general pattern of change in this variable before 1860 is quite clear. Both the fraction of the population of children attending school and the length of the school year increased as time passed, as did the fraction of the work force holding semi-skilled and skilled jobs. The rate of increase of human capital is therefore almost certain to have risen as time passed. See Fishlow 1966a, 1966b; and Uselding 1971.

2. The value of consumer durables is also sometimes incorporated in capital stock estimates, but it appears in only one table in this chapter, because

appropriate figures are only intermittently available. The loss is not great. The value of consumer durables was small, compared with the rest of the capital stock, through most of the period considered in this chapter, and the rate of change of the capital stock is approximately the same, regardless of whether durables are treated as capital.

3. The calculations also assume that the treatment of stumps was the same at all dates: specifically, that one-third of the stumps were removed immediately, and that the rest were left in the land to rot away on their own. It may be that an even smaller share of the stumps was taken out in the earlier years, but allowing for the removal of no stumps would not bring the current estimates and Blodget's very much closer together.

The matter of stumps is tricky. What is the reproduction labor cost of ten acres of stumpless cleared land that was formerly under trees? Is it the full labor cost of clearing the land and removing all the stumps? Or is it the labor cost of cutting down the trees, removing the one-third of the stumps that were originally removed, and then plowing the land? The estimates assume the latter, but clearly one could make a case for other options.

4. A word should be said about the land series, although there is inadequate space to go through the estimating procedures and tests. The 1850–1900 data come from the census, with some adjustments. The adjustments depend in part on the work of Primack (1962). The 1840 figures are weaker. They come from Seaman (1852), again adjusted and distributed, partly on the basis of the work of Primack. The figures for 1774 through 1805 are from Blodget 1806, adjusted in various ways. The 1815 figure is a rough extrapolation from 1805. For a discussion of these matters, see Gallman 1972.

5. One should not infer much about productivity changes from the relative movements of price and cost indexes between 1836 and 1844, however. Between these two dates lay a very sharp contraction. At least part of the decline in prices reflected falling profits, not rising productivity. It is also likely that workers discounted standard wage rates in order to hold their jobs.

6. For example, "Although many authorities assert that balloon frame construction had 'almost completely replaced the hewn frame for domestic construction by the time of the Civil War' . . . in North Carolina field surveys demonstrate the prevalence of heavy mortised-and-tenoned house frames until the Civil War" (Bishir et al. 1990, 457). An architect whose book was published in 1855 writes: "There is no doubt that if the subject received closer attention, a better mode of framing than that generally employed, could be suggested. Timbers are often unnecessarily heavy, but are afterwards so weakened by the mode of framing which is in vogue, and which compels the cutting of mortices and tenons and insertion of one timber into another, that the frame is less substantial than if constructed of lighter stuff differently put together. It is difficult to persuade carpenters of this" (Wheeler 1855, 407). The implication of the last statement is important. The

building industry was a conservative, locally organized industry. The architect goes on: "The *New York Tribune* of January 18, 1855, reported a meeting of the American Institute Farmers' Club, and contained amongst other items some remarks from one of the members upon a novel mode of constructing cheap wooden dwellings" (408). The "novel method" was the balloon frame.

The extent to which innovations had diffused is relevant because it would have determined the degree to which prices responded to innovations. Prices would have been potentially affected only in localities in which the new framing system had begun to diffuse; and even there, prices need not have fallen immediately if competition among builders was not severe. If builders commonly used cost plus pricing, of course, prices would have fallen immediately in areas where the balloon frame was put in use.

There is a question as to whether Brady's prices refer to average practice or best practice. The estimates are based on the assumption that they refer to average practice. If this assumption is wrong, and if builders followed cost plus pricing practices, then the Brady price index numbers exaggerate the true decline in average prices. The course of average relative prices of residences after 1849 suggests that the ambiguity with respect to the meaning of the price indexes is unimportant for these years.

7. The two indexes should ideally be weighted by the state distribution of the real value of houses in the capital stock. These in fact are the weights used for 1799, but the weights for 1840 are the real values of houses built in the census year.

8. The capital and income (Weiss) data permit a check on an inference advanced by Davis and Gallman (1978, 2), who estimated that the net investment rate averaged between 6.2 percent and 7.0 percent in the period 1805–40. The rates of growth and capital-to-output ratios in or underlying table 4.7 are consistent with net investment rates (relative to GDP) of between 5 percent and 6.5 percent. The Davis and Gallman figures were computed as a share of NNP, however. If the data in and underlying table 4.7 are adjusted to make them conform more nearly to the concepts that Davis and Gallman were employing, the implied investment rates become roughly 5.9 percent and 7.2 percent, reasonably close to the Davis-Gallman figures.

9. The estimate is based on Jones (1980, 30) and Weiss (1992). According to Jones, there were 53,056 indentured servants in 1774 and 480,932 slaves. All indentured servants were in the work force; following Weiss's judgment for 1800, slaves aged ten and older probably amounted to 65 percent of the population of slaves, and nine-tenths of these people were in the work force. According to Jones, there were 396,158 free adult males, of whom, if we follow Weiss's treatment for the nineteenth century, 87.2 percent were in the work force. The rest of the population—1,034,456—consisted of youths and children, by Jones's account. Assuming that half were males (a safe guess) and that they were distributed among the age groups as was the white population of 1800, then there were about

55,000 males who were ten to fourteen years old, of whom 22.1 percent were in the work force (following Weiss's judgment for 1800), and there were 53,815 who were fifteen to twenty years old, of whom (again following Weiss) 87.2 percent worked. Adding free females ten years old and older (497,973, with a participation rate of 7.5 percent, per Weiss), brings the total labor force to 776,241. A check on the total, assuming an overall participation rate of 32.5 percent (typical of the early decades of the nineteenth century, according to Weiss), yields a figure of 765,039, which is close enough.

10. First in principle, but not in fact. The quality adjustments were worked out first.

11. Gallman 966, 35, variant I. The estimates are available in constant prices only. Current price estimates were made by assuming that the ratio of improvements to farm value added was the same in current and constant prices. The average value of improvements for 1834–43 was taken to correspond to the value of improvements in census year 1839, and so forth. The ratio of the value of improvements to the value of farm value added in 1859 was estimated on the basis of the ratio of improvements, 1849–58, and farm value added 1854. A similar procedure was followed to obtain the ratio for census year 1869.

## Chapter Five

1. Parts of these data have been published in Carter et al. (2006), series Ca 192–207 (for 1869–1909) and Ca 219–32 (for 1834–1859).

2. "Notes for the File on National Accounts," p. 5, Gallman papers. This note was not dated, but internal evidence suggests that Gallman composed it in 1996 and 1997 while working on Davis and Gallman 2001.

3. Gallman (2000, 8) generally believed that as decadal averages the "estimates for the latter years are more reliable than those for the earlier years."

4. Tables A-2 and A-3 in Gallman 1966 provide current-value estimates, broken down by major spending category, for the years 1839, 1844, 1849, 1854, and 1859.

5. Gallman revised his postbellum manufactured producer durable series between the preparation of the volume 30 paper for publication and June 1965. The June 1967 spreadsheets note that manufactured producer durables "may be slightly different from the series underlying Vol. 30." During the 1990s, Gallman was apparently unable to locate the exact spreadsheets used in the volume 30 tables. In a 21 January 1994 letter to Richard Sutch, Gallman recounted having "a dim recollection of making minor changes of this cost (of manufacturing durables) after the Vol. 30 paper was in press." Similarly, on 15 August 1995, Gallman wrote to Benjamin Friedman, "The series I am sending you differ slightly, but only slightly—from those that figure in the Volume 30 paper."

As Gallman's notes for 13 March 1985 indicate, manufactured producers' durables series from the June 1965 worksheet "misses consistently—clearly modestly different series." While spreadsheets exist that perform some of the interpolations used in the new series, none fully document the changes. It is likely that they were the result of Gallman's creation of new benchmarks using better price series. One extant set of spreadsheets in the manufacturer's producer durable files contains the notes "price data . . . found after conference paper series completed." Gallman papers.

6. Mimeo June 1965, Gallman papers.

7. Material sent to Robert Margo, 7 February 1996, Gallman papers.

8. Letter from Robert E. Gallman to Benjamin Friedman, 15 August 1995, Gallman papers.

9. "Notes for the File on National Accounts," p. 5. The 1860-value inventory change estimates are from a spreadsheet labeled D-1 in the inventory estimation files; the current-value estimates from sheets labeled B-1. Gallman papers.

10. Handwritten spreadsheet, June 1967, Gallman papers.

11. See point 1.e: "There are no net national product estimates." in "Memo to Mike Butler, 20 May 1985," Gallman papers.

12. See above. Also, "Notes on Mat'ls taken to England," Gallman papers.

13. The errors were not offset by corresponding errors in the series on "all other construction." As a result, they carry through to Gallman's total construction, capital formation, and GNP estimates for these years. There is some evidence that Gallman found the movements of the railroad series suspicious, because there is a checkmark next to the numbers. As noted below, Gallman produced in 1994 a new set of railroad construction estimates that avoid these problems entirely.

14. In addition to minor typos, there was an inconsistency in the current-price inventory estimates for livestock over the 1869–79 period. Gallman employed the *Historical Statistics* (1975) values for farm animals, K 564–73. These series use gold rather than greenback values, though that is not explicitly noted in the source. This was made more consistent by converting the livestock values into greenbacks using prices from the USDA, *Annual Reports*, 1869–78.

15. Shaw (1947) provided annual estimates of commodity production after 1889 and single-year estimates for 1869 and 1879. Kuznets (1946) then interpolated between the 1869, 1879, and 1889 benchmarks using annual series for available components; see his *National Product*, pp. 90–117, for details. See also Simon Kuznets, "Annual Estimates, 1869–1953, T-Tables 1–15 (technical tables underlying series in *Supplement to Summary Volume of Capital and Financing*)," New York, NBER, c. 1961. http://www.nber.org/data-appendix/c1454/appendix.pdf.

16. To deflate the value of production of perishables, semiperishables, consumer durables, and manufactured producers' durables, Gallman used detailed information on commodity flows from Shaw and his own volume 24 piece and on prices from Brady to create benchmark estimates for 1869, 1879, 1889, and 1899 using 1860 prices. He then employed the yearly variations in the corresponding Kuznets constant 1929-price annual series to interpolate between the benchmarks. The 1900–1909 figures were simply extrapolated on the basis of the Kuznets series.

Simon Kuznets published his series on national product and its subcomponents only as five-year moving averages.

17. Gallman (1966, 37) estimated service flows differently in the antebellum and postbellum periods. For the 1869–1909 period he followed the procedure of Kuznets, using budget studies to derive the ratio of consumer expenditures on services relative to commodities and then multiplying the commodity flow series by this ratio. For the antebellum period, Gallman built up service flows primarily from capital stock estimates, particularly on the value of housing.

18. In a world with high compound growth rates, the use of straight-line interpolation also introduces biases in the timing of the expansion. The direction of the bias depends on whether the interpolator series grows faster or slower than the benchmark series.

19. For these reasons, Gallman was generally opposed to work using his annual national product series to compare the volatility of nineteenth and twentieth century business cycles. But he also took strong issue with claims that his procedures to estimate noncommodity production over the 1839–59 period were "flawed" and generated excessively volatile series. In his view, any bias in volatility due to his construction procedure was likely to be weak or to work in opposite direction from what is usually suggested. The antebellum series were not constructed using the Kuznets ratio method to estimate service flows, but rather using the growth of housing stocks, which was far smoother. Note services accounted for about 24 percent of Gallman's real-value estimate of national product (excluding changes in inventories) over the 1834–59 period. In addition, the estimates for firewood production, which accounted for about 6 percent of national product, relied on straight-line interpolation. One offsetting force was the interpolation using net imports, which tended to "oscillate fairly widely" over the 1834–42 period (Gallman 1966, 64). But, as p. 71 notes, he "attempted to dilute the effect of these oscillations by bringing the leather series into the interpolator." Clearly, the volatility displayed in the annual series was the product of explicit, conscious data collection and assembly choices.

20. See especially table 8 in Davis and Gallman (1973, 456–57) which was based on a 1966 version of Robert E. Gallman and Edward S. Howle, "The Structure of U.S. Wealth in the Nineteenth Century" in Gallman papers.

21. Mimeo with pen note "Corrected Copy, Oct. 28, 1963," Gallman papers.

22. "Chapter 3: Appendix U.S. Estimates of National Product" in Davis and Gallman 2001, 342–44. Also see "Notes for the File on National Accounts," Gallman papers. Gallman is presumably referring to Kuznets's T-tables. Kuznets (1961a, 546) observed that "the series available as annual interpolators were most frequently the more sensitive indexes and would yield annual series exaggerating the short-term changes." His annual gross product estimates "would not be acceptable measures of the amplitude of short-term changes" and, therefore, "are not shown."

23. The contrast between the antebellum and postbellum periods is largely the result of using benchmarks every five years in the early period and every ten years in the later period. It also helps that few of the postbellum benchmark years coincided with peaks or troughs of the business cycle.

24. There is internal evidence in Gallman's files that he and his research assistants made such comparisons themselves. "Gallman vs. Berry" file, Gallman papers.

25. "Notes for the File on National Accounts" pp. 7–8, Gallman papers.

26. Gallman created no current-value estimates for the 1834–59 period that can be considered "finished work," so no implicit price deflators exist for the antebellum period.

27. The rate was likely even lower before the 1830s than afterward (Davis and Gallman 1994).

28. Memo to Mike Butler, 20 May 1985, Gallman papers.

29. "Measurement of U.S. Nineteenth Century National Product," Gallman papers. Butler and Gallman's attempt to remove the $6.4 million spent on the Pennsylvania Mainline railroad between 1829 and 1845 yielded the revisions to the 1834–45 series, shown in the far right columns of table 5.1. The revisions changed real GNP by more than the rounding error only in 1834 and 1838. "Note on the Adjustment of Canal Construction Estimates," Gallman papers.

30. Sutch to Gallman, 26 September and 19 November 1993; Gallman to Sutch, 14 and 21 January 1994.

31. *Railway Age* 128, no. 1, 7 January 1950, p, 246. This series is also available at the NBER macrohistory website and is quite similar to the railroad construction series reported in *Poor's Manual* from 1880 on.

32. Based on series Q-329, -321, and -287 from *Historical Statistics, Bicentennial Edition* (1975). The Q-329 series had an unexplained gap between 1879 and 1893. Gallman instead interpolated using the changes in the Q-321 and -287 series, the number of railroad miles operated. The correlation with the *Railway Age* series is close but not exact. Using his improved capital stock estimates, Gallman created a revised series on railroad construction investment over the 1870–1909 period. He allocated his decadal estimates of real gross investments in railways over the years based on the miles of track constructed annually (or on the changes in railroad miles operated). Letter to Sutch, 14 January 1994, and spreadsheet dated 27 January 1996, Gallman papers.

33. Letter to Diane Lindstrom, 10 June 1988, Gallman papers. The common practice of presenting real GNP, nominal GNP, and the implicit price deflator as separate columns in tables misstates their interdependence. Obviously any two aggregate series yield the third, but the procedures used to construct the aggregates typically involve combinations of all three. That is, for some components, price indes and quantities are multiplied to derive values; for others, quantities are estimated from values divided by a price series; and for still others, implicit prices

are derived from values divided by quantities. This implies that decisions about the price concepts must be made in the process of generating the real product series.

34. The procedure used to derive the antebellum service flows appears as follows. Gallman had estimates for the 1869 value of services in 1860 prices and three extrapolating series: (a) the value of churches (available in 1870 and 1860), (b) the value of tax receipts of state and local governments (running back to 1849), and (c) the value of residential housing (with existing estimates available back to 1850 and Gallman's extrapolation to 1840). Gallman first converted all of the extrapolators into 1860 dollars, and then used all three to estimate the 1859 benchmark from the 1869 value. Then he used real values of (b) and (c) to derive the 1849 benchmark, and finally (c) alone to calculate the 1839 benchmarks. To interpolate between the 1839, 1849, and 1859 levels, Gallman employed Gottlieb's estimates of the stock of residential housing (which must be a fairly smooth series); and to extrapolate back of 1839, he used his lumber series. See Gallman 1966, 57–60, 63–64.

35. Inclusion of ΔINV in the numerator and denominator of the series in column 1 of table 1.3 created the differences for Gallman's widely reproduced series on conventional gross investment (GI) to GNP (in constant prices) reported in table 3 of Gallman (1966, 11). Call the series in table 1.3, $x = GI/GNP$, and the series in Gallman 1966, $y = (GI - \Delta INV)/(GNP - \Delta INV)$. One can relate the two series using the ratio $z = \Delta INV/GI$, reported in column 6 in table 2.10. Writing all the ratios in decimal terms, one can show that $x = y/(1 - z + zy)$.

36. Recall structures that depreciate more slowly than equipment. Davis and Gallman (1973, 438), for example, assume "a longevity of 50 years for structures and 15 years for equipment. . . ."

## Chapter Six

1. In the period after the Civil War, the series depend importantly on Simon Kuznets's (1961b) work sheets. See chapter 5.

2. As Lance Davis has pointed out, a second version of net reproduction cost values each piece of capital at the price required to replace it in a given year (or in the base year, in the case of constant-price estimates with an equally productive piece of capital). How "equally productive" should be defined is not clear, nor are the uses to which such a series could be put. One leading solution to the definition problem would turn the capital stock into a simple transformation of national income. See the exchanges between Edward F. Denison (1957, 233–54) and Simon Kuznets (1957, 273–84).

3. The question addressed to farmers and householders appears to have referred to market value, or possibly to net reproduction cost.

4. All the estimates computed were of gross stocks. I also made calculations with net stocks (straight-line depreciation) for 1869. The resulting ratio was 0.93, the same as the ratio of the gross estimates for that year.

5. Based on Davis and Gallman 1978, p. 23, table 7, col. B(r), and p. 26, table 9, col. 5, and sources underlying these tables.

6. Kuznets (1946, 116–17); inferred from the notes to col. 1, lines 1–10 and col. 4, lines 3–9, of the table. See also p. 197, where the content of capital consumption is defined.

7. See also Goldsmith 1956, vol. 3, table W-7, pp. 32–38.

8. R. Winfrey, *Statistical Analysis of Industrial Property Retirements*, as reported in Young and Musgrave 1980.

9. Where it was possible to identify census-style capital produced from farm materials (e.g., certain types of fences, the value of land clearing), it was deleted from the estimates used in the consistency tests described in this section. But the census did not distinguish buildings by the types of materials from which they were built.

10. The Goldin and Lewis figure is the Civil War loss, discounted back to 1861. I probably should have used the undiscounted figure (about $200 million higher), but in view of the roughness of the calculations, I decided that this would represent an unjustified refinement.

11. In principle, a separate calculation of net losses should be made for each of the five primary series underlying table 6.5, instead of the two sets of estimates made here. Such a refinement would be unlikely to alter table 6.5 very far.


## Chapter Seven

1. Primack (1962, 33–45) offers a criticism of Tostlebe's work.

2. Materials prices were measured by the Warren-Pearson building materials price index from US Bureau of the Census (1949), series L-10; labor costs, by Donald Adams's Philadelphia series (1975, 809–10), linked with US Bureau of the Census (1949), series D-110 and D-111, all series shifted to the base 1860 without reweighting. The labor and materials indexes were combined on the assumption that the shares of labor (60 percent) and materials (40 percent) in current price value of output were constant, an assumption supported by evidence in Adams (1975). We assumed that antebellum census-year price indexes could be approximated by averaging calendar year prices; e.g., census year 1849 = the mean of calendar years 1849 and 1850. Adams's variant B construction cost index would have served as well for the antebellum period, but we preferred to build an index with a common materials price component for both the antebellum and the postbellum periods.

3. The relevant data are gathered in US Bureau of the Census (1975), series K564-573). See also US Department of Agriculture, *Agriculture Statistics* (1936-). Farms include ranches. For discussions of the problems posed by range animals, see US Census Office (1872, 73; 1883a, xv; 1902, cxliii–cxlvi). The USDA data appear to include range animals.

4. See also table 7.3. We established the relationship between June 1 and January 1 values on the basis of average relationships for the years 1920 and 1921.

5. The labor time needed to prepare farm materials for use in fencing—e.g., rail-splitting—was included by Primack and by us in the total labor required to build fences.

6. Gallman (1956) suggests other revisions to the census data, none of which could be carried through in the construction of our estimates of improvements. (None of them is of great importance for present purposes.)

7. For Rhode's comments on the 1840 estimates, see this chapter's epilogue.

8. In the case of Illinois, there appears to be something wrong with Primack's estimates of grassland improved in the 1890s and perhaps the 1880s. We therefore reversed the procedure described above, estimating acres of forest improved and taking grassland improved as a residual.

9. Primack's figures differ slightly from one table to the next, almost certainly due to rounding errors (except for a typographical error in table 20, by which the total rods of fencing for 1890 and 1900 are reversed). The 1880 figure for rods of fencing per acre in text table 23 is given as 3.6, but should apparently be 4.0.

10. We assumed that woven wire (probably unimportant before 1900, in any case) and plain wire fences called for the same amounts of labor and materials per rod.

11. Earl W. Hayter (1929, 191) says that production ran 400,000 to 600,000 miles of single-strand wire between 1880 and 1884, about 150,000 tons in 1888, and about 157,000 tons in 1895. Hayter implies that a ton of wire ran to five to six miles in length. We converted his ton estimates into miles at 5.5 miles per ton, assumed 330 rods per mile, and then created the following production estimates (in million rods): 1880, 132.0; 1881, 148.5; 1882, 165.0; 1883, 181.5; 1884, 198.0; 1885, 216.6; 1886, 235.1; 1887, 253.7; 1888, 272.3; 1889, 274.1; 1890, 275.9; 1891, 277.7; 1892, 279.5; 1893, 281.3; 1894, 283.1; 1895, 284.9; 1896, 286.8; 1897, 288.6; 1898, 290.4; 1899, 292.2.

12. Man-months of labor required to produce one rod of fencing: worm, 0.01538 all years; post and rail, 0.01307 all years; hedge, 0.01423 all years; stone, 0.07693 all years; board, 0.007693 all years; wire 0.003461 1840–70; 0.003077 1880–90; 0.002308, 1900.

13. See US Department of Agriculture 1871. Compare the tables on pp. 508–9. Since there were unlikely to have been fewer than four rails per fence (see p. 497), an average of four to five rods of fencing per rod of fence implies that often (but not always; perhaps half the time), farm materials were used for posts, which is probably what was in fact practice.

14. We estimated the July prices for pine in 1840 and 1850 from the annual average price and data on pine boards in US Senate 1893, 229.

15. Regional averages were produced by weighting the state cost data with 1870 fencing totals (since we had no data on fencing by type, by state). The regional average costs of each type of fencing were then weighted by the regional distribution of that type of fencing in 1870, per Primack, to produce weighted national average cost figures by type of fence.

16. The value of farms was taken from the census. It also appears in the various volumes of *Historical Statistics* (e.g., US Bureau of the Census 1960, series K-4).

However, the 1949 edition carries the census estimate of the gold value of farm property in 1870, in place of the current value.

17. We took data on the value of buildings from Primack 1962, 174–75). With respect to fencing, we computed the average value per acre for the United States, and then adjusted this figure upward according to the ratio of the value of farm buildings per acre in the four states, divided by the value of farm buildings per acre in the United States, on the grounds that states well-endowed with farm buildings—as these four were—would also be likely to be well-endowed with fences.

## Chapter Eight

1. Statements to this effect are found in several places in the censuses. See, for example, the quotation in section 8.2.4, above, regarding a similar question posed to mine owners.

## Chapter Nine

1. The 1890 census may have included some utility property in the real property returns for a few states, but it is impossible to determine how much. Insofar as the manufacturing and mining estimates deviate from market value, the residuals in tables 9.1 are in error, but we do not believe that this is a serious source of error. For evidence that the census was attempting to obtain market values, and that the attempt was well planned, see US Bureau of the Census 1907, 4-6; US Census Office 1895c, 7; US Census Office 1884a, 100–11.

2. The tax duplicates showed that real property was $6,973 million, personal property $5,112 million, and total property $12,085 million. The marshals estimated the true value of real and personal property together at $16,160 million, a mark-up on assessed value of 33.7 percent. See US Census Office 1866, 294–95.

3. Taking the owner estimate of the value of real estate ($10,930) plus 0.25 × the sum of lines 2 and 4 for 1860 table 8.8 ($122) plus 0.25 × the sum of lines 44 and 46 for 1860 table 8.3 ($21) plus 0.55 × the current value of land and improvements, table 10.9 ($392) yields $11,465 million.

4. Railroads, however, had sizable real estate holdings, and our assumption that railroads were of corporate form and hence excluded is crucial. It is also reasonable.

5. For the method and the data, see the estimation procedures for 1860 and table 9.3.

6. US Bureau of the Census 1960, series A-75, A-84, "white," divided by two. Free nonwhites—not very numerous—were left out of the calculations.

7. Goldsmith (1952, 317) estimated the value of nonfarm residences at $800 million, and appears to have believed that the value of "factory, office, store and

miscellaneous business buildings" (p. 320) probably ran about one-third below the figure given by Willford King ($563 million), or at about $376 million. Deducting the value of improvements in mining and manufacturing (tables 8.3 and 8.8, above) from the latter figure yields an approximation to the value of "trade" improvements, roughly $300 million. As to the value of nonfarm residential and trade land, Goldsmith's position is a little unclear. On page 318 he says that land accounted for about one-third of the value of real estate, which implies that nonfarm residential and trade land was worth $550 million ([800 + 300] × 0.5). But in table V (p. 317), he lists all nonfarm land at $400 million. Yet another possibility is that his statement "Approximately one-third of the value of non-farm real estate represented the value of non-agricultural land" was in error, and that he intended to say that the ratio of the value of land to the value of improvements was as one is to three (p. 259), in which case the required figure should be: (800 + 30) × 0.333 = $366 million. Goldsmith's estimates, then, imply that the value of nonfarm residential and trade real estate in 1850 amounted to $1,466 million, $1,500 million, or $1,650 million. The figures bracket our estimate, and the one that most probably represents Goldsmith's views—the second—is virtually identical to ours.

8. The Virginia appraisal data (1838 and 1852) are from Seaman 1852, 616; the New York figures are from the *Auditor's Report*, 1834–36 and 1852, from De Bow 1854. Data were extrapolated from 1835, 1838, and 1852 to 1840 and 1850 on population series. US Bureau of the Census 1960, 12–13.

9. We used the decadal national-level gainful worker series in US Bureau of the Census 1960, Series D-57 and D-58, for reasons given in Gallman 1975, 35–39, 49–51. The data had to be adjusted after 1870 to compensate for a change in the classification method. We multiplied the estimates for 1880–1900 by the ratio (1.0653 = 6850/6430) of the first 1870 figure (the one comparable to the data for earlier years) to the second 1870 figure (the one comparable to the data for later years). The estimates of all gainful workers and agricultural gainful workers were so adjusted. The number of nonagricultural workers in each year was taken as a residual. [Rhode: My best attempts to replicate the regression, including creating the relevant data series, yielded an estimate of the ratio of 0.930, rather than 0.941 as Gallman reports. The discrepancy speaks to the error bounds associated with all the numbers reported. There are several possible sources, including differences in rounding or statistical software. In this case the difference is neither economically nor statistically significant.]

10. This ratio is implicit in Kuznets's estimates. See table IV-2, line 4; table IV-3, line 4; and the notes to line 4.


**Chapter Ten**


1. The official system of measuring vessels changed in 1865, with problematic consequences for total tonnage (US Bureau of the Census 1960, 439). Professor Brady's price index numbers apparently do not recognize the change. Her price

index numbers for the antebellum period refer to old style tons; her index numbers for the postwar years refer to new style tons. Since we used Brady's work to develop both our current and our constant price series, we were able to make use of the official tonnage series, unadjusted for changes in measurement. See the notes to table 10.1.

2. Since we necessarily used the aggregate equipment index produced by Fishlow, the relative levels of the equipment index numbers in the various years reflect relative equipment prices in 1909, not 1860.

3. Data supplied by Fishlow in correspondence.

4. The sample contains date for fifty-eight railroads and was taken from Stow 1859. Fishlow (1965, 351, table 48) has developed an asset breakdown for 1851–60 with percentages almost identical to ours: 88.5 and 11.5 percent (1965, 351, table 48). We counted as improvements graduation, masonry and bridging; superstructure; buildings and machinery; and engineering.

5. The assumption would probably not affect the rate of increase in improvements indicated by Fishlow's index. In the late 1900s railroad growth slowed considerably, causing the capital in rails and ties to become older; but the increasing life of these assets is a counterbalancing influence.

6. The life of ties was seven to eight years, while the life of rails varied greatly with the use they received (Fishlow 1965, 380).

## Chapter Eleven

1. The balance sheet data in US Census Office 1883b, 783, indicate that the dividend was recorded in this way.

2. The estimates of several experts, including a joint estimate by the presidents of the three largest telegraph companies, are found in Senate Executive Document 49, 39th Congress, 1st Session, (US Senate 1865/66), henceforth called "Document 49."

3. Physical data are available from a variety of sources. See notes to tables.

4. Dennison provided his estimates to a Senate select committee formed to consider incorporating a national telegraph company as part of the Postal Service (US Senate 1865/66, 1). Presumably Dennison based his judgments on the advice of experts. The written testimony of two experts (US Senate 1865/66, 2, 5) contains very much higher figures. But both of these men had in mind the construction of the "most permanent" lines, "far superior . . . to the lines which have been constructed by private companies. . . ." The postmaster general apparently was thinking in terms of a less exalted standard.

5. "Miles of poles" refers to the distance covered by a line. "Miles of wire" refers to the amount of wire used in a line. Thus, a six-wire line between two towns 200 miles apart would consist of 200 miles of poles and 1,200 miles of wire.

6. This implies a cost per mile for a good quality one-wire line of $92, or $30 more than Prescott's estimate of the cost of construction in 1860. But Prescott

goes on to say that the 1860 cost would have been $150 per mile, if the lines had been built "as they should be" (US Senate 1865/66, 4). Presumably what we have here are figures of (1) historical cost ($61.80), (2) the cost that would have been incurred had the lines been built in 1860 to a "good" standard ($92), and (3) the cost that would have been incurred if the lines had been built to an "excellent" standard ($150).

7. US Senate 1865/66, 27. The Western Union and US companies owned $360,000 in office fittings; the American Company owned $400,000.

8. See price index, table 11.6, line 7. This assumes that one-third of the stock was bought at 1860 prices (index of 100), that prices increased at 11 percent each year from 1860 to 1866, and that the average prices at which equipment was purchased during the years 1861 to 1866 were the prices of 1864 (index 151.8).

9. Sources as follows: "E" from text above (these three companies made up perhaps 90 percent of the industry), "n" from table 11.4 interpolated to 1866, and "w" and "p" from table 11.3, interpolated to 1866.

10. The presidents of the three leading telegraph companies stated in 1865 that telegraph lines lasted ten years (US Senate 1865/66, 2–3, 13). According to Ulmer (1960, 380), telephone assets lasted ten years circa 1880.

11. Ulmer (1960, 368, tables E-3 and E-4) made use of *Report on the Investigation of the Telephone Industry in the United States* (Federal Communications Commission 1939, exhibit 1360-A).

## Chapter Twelve

1. The omission does not appear to be very serious. In 1860, assistant census marshals estimated the number of such animals; see US Census Office 1864, cix, 192. Their value (horses, asses and mules, cattle, sheep, and swine), priced at the same prices we used for agricultural animals, comes to 10.6 percent of our estimate of the value of animals on farms and ranges. In 1900, the census again collected data on the numbers "kept in enclosures." Whether the qualification has any significance we do not know. In any case, their value comes to 6.7 percent of our estimate of the value of animals on farms and ranges in 1900. Some part of this group consisted of work animals in mining, manufacturing, transportation, and other sectors, all or most of which are included in our estimates of the value of equipment in these sectors. Another part comprised consumer durables: carriage horses, and milk cows kept by nonfarm families. Thus it is probable that very few animals were improperly omitted from our capital stock estimates.

2. Secular changes in inventory investments merit more investigation. Field (1987) posits that large-scale enterprise, or modern business enterprise in Chandler's parlance, represented a capital-saving innovation that reduced the inventory-to-output or inventory-to-sales ratios. Abramovitz (1950) is the name most closely

associated with the study of inventory movement, but his analysis focuses on business cycle fluctuations.

3. The series on duties is not altogether consistent with the North and Simon import series. It is also gross of drawbacks, and probably lags behind actual imports. But it is the best series available for present purposes.

4. See Gallman (1960, 44–53). The items omitted were the value of home manufacturing, farm improvements, market garden products (assumed equal to $50 million in 1890 and 1900, in prices of 1879; and $50 million in 1890, in current prices), grapes, dairy products, chickens and eggs, and orchard fruits. The antebellum value of the output of corn, oats, and hay was approximated by dividing the gross incomes from these crops (Gallman 1960, 46–47) by the ratios in Gallman 1960, table A-3, 52. For the postbellum years the values were derived from Strauss and Bean 1940, 39 (corn, crop year farm value; crop year production times 1879 crop year price), 43 (oats, crop year farm value; crop year production times 1879 crop year price), and 59 (production of all hay and hay prices).

5. "Fuel and lighting" for mining (series E-6, E-19) and "all commodities" for manufacturing (series E-1, E-13) in US Bureau of the Census 1960.

6. See Raymond W. Goldsmith and Robert E. Lipsey 1963, 159–60, which argues, in an analogous case, that deflation should yield the purchasing power of the item of wealth, in base year prices. Notice, however, that this involves a change in the conceptual basis for deflation that we have adopted with respect to the other components of the capital stock. That is, up to this point, all of our deflations have been asset-specific, and they have had the purpose of producing capital stock series that reflect the changing volume and quality of specific assets, not the purchasing power of the liquidated value of these assets.

## Chapter Thirteen

1. Gallman (1977) stressed the importance of additions to American stocks of human capital from immigration. Gallman (2000, 29) compared estimates from Fishlow (1966b) of the opportunity cost of schoolchildren's time to his own estimates of GNP. This component of the investment in human capital equaled 0.5 percent of GNP in 1860, 0.7 percent in 1880, and 1.2 percent in 1900. The opportunity cost of time "came to roughly 40 percent of total school costs, direct costs plus opportunity costs."

2. For the debate over the consumer durables revolution in the 1920s, see Vatter 1967, Juster 1966, and Olney 1991. For a related recent contribution, see Greenwood, Seshadri, and Yorkoglu (2005).

3. The emphasis on the shares of consumer durables spending in GDP and total consumption differs from the definition of the consumer durable revolution presented elsewhere. For example, Olney (1991, 2) defines "the existence of a

Consumer Durables Revolution as the existence of shifts in the demand for durable goods. . . ." This definition is intended to capture, in an observational testable form, Vatter's claim that the 1920s witnessed a structural shift in consumers' tastes in favor of durables. In her empirical analysis, Olney found that consumers did indeed display greater responsiveness (in terms of income- and price-elasticity parameters) in their durables purchase decisions during the 1920s than during the previous (1902–19) period. These parameter shifts, linked in the book's narrative to changes in the availability of consumer credit and the volume of adverting, implies in Olney's view that a consumer durable revolution did occur in the 1920s. Given data availability, conducting such a demand-side analysis for the nineteenth-century American economy is problematic. The shares approach has the advantage of embracing supply-side shifts, such as innovations reducing their relative prices or increasing the variety of products available to consumers, that increase the importance of consumer durable goods in the economy.

4. The boom in the late Eighties and early Nineties has received little scholarly attention. It coincides with the bicycling craze following the invention of the "safety" bicycle. But the surge must have included a much wider range of durables.

5. The historical literature on "the birth of the consumer society" is large, complex, and global in scope. For a point of entry, see Trentmann 2012.

6. Cowan (1997) argued that the stove, like many other household innovations, created "more work for mother." The stove saved the male labor devoted to supplying firewood, but increased the female work load in cleaning and polishing the stove. Brewer (2000) presents a learned discussion of the cultural aspects of the spread of the cast-iron stove and oven.

7. US Department of Agriculture 1921, 33, indicates that stove-size cordwood was 43 percent more expensive than ordinary cordwood.

8. Schurr and Netschert (1960, 50) also attribute the slow diffusion to "the high cost of manufactured equipment and the transportation difficulties prevailing around the middle of the nineteenth century."

9. Lebergott (1976, 276) further documented the shift toward fossil fuel over the late nineteenth and early twentieth centuries. In 1908, 63 percent of US households used coal, 1 percent petroleum, and 36 percent used wood.

10. According to Adams (1975, 797), masonry was a major expense, accounting for about one-third of the cost of building American homes over the 1785–1830 period.

11. Gallman, March 1996 notes, Gallman papers.

12. This is not a perfectly accurate way of handling the problem (it would be better to distinguish flows of durables of different life expectations), but it is a good approximation, and certainly adequate for present purposes. No effort was made to allow for differences in the actual lifespans of durables of a given type, a matter of small importance in the present context.

13. Goldsmith (1952, 306) provides alternative estimates. He places the value of consumer durables, in billions of current dollars, at 0.3 in 1850, 2.4 in 1880, 4.5 in

1890, and 6.0 in 1900. The consumer durable share of the combined capital stock changed from 7.2 percent in 1850 to 9.8 percent in 1900.

14. Thomas Weiss is to be thanked for raising this issue. The 1774 current price figures taken from Alice Jones appear more reliable than the 1840 or 1870 values, which were obtained by cumulating annual flows. As Gallman notes, "Clearly, hard data figure more importantly in the estimate for 1880 (95%) than in the estimates for 1840 (70%) and 1870 (30%). The figure for 1880 seems quite secure; the figures for [1840 and 1870] . . . much less so."

## Chapter Fourteen

1. Blodget's 1806 and 1810 editions of *Economica* appear to be identical, except that the later edition extends his estimates to 1809.

2. Pitkin (1835, 310–14) reports the results of the laws of 1798, 1813, and 1815. See also Pitkin 1816, 325–34, and Seybert 1818, 50, 504, 506.

3. While this description sounds more inclusive than the one that established the tax base for 1799, Seybert and Pitkin treat the appraisals under the 1798, 1813, and 1815 laws as though they covered the same property, and Pitkin (1835, 313) refers to the data he drew from the 1814 and 1815 tax records as "the valuations of houses, lands, and slaves."

4. See North (1960, 600) for estimates of the value of imports and net claims. Jones (1980) estimated the financial credits and debits of Americans in 1774. Since each American debt to an American produces an exactly offsetting credit, Jones's net balance (negative) must measure the net position of the American colonies in 1774—exclusive, of course, of the net balance attributable to institutions such as governments and corporations. The North net claims estimates were modified slightly when they were prepared for publication in *Historical Statistics*, to make them conceptually closer to the twentieth-century series, with which they link. (See US Bureau of the Census 1975, p. 858, for a discussion of the North series, and pp. 742–44 and 750, for data on shipping.) The US Bureau of the Census (1975) series on imports also differ from the North series, because the former includes the value of specie, while the latter does not. The unadjusted North series on the value of imports is the better one for present purposes, and it was therefore employed.

5. According to Seybert (1818, 504), land was appraised by the officials of the 1798 direct tax assessment at about 77 percent of the value of land and dwellings, taken together; Soltow puts the ratio at 76 percent. Adding in nonresidential property might reduce the fraction of the value of real estate accounted for by land nearer to two-thirds, while adding in the land under structures (see below) would probably raise it to closer to three-quarters. Notice that the ratio between "Blodget's" land estimate and Jones's real estate estimate, implied by the text calculations, is 68 percent, which suggests that the reconstructed Blodget figure may

very well be the value Jones had in mind. That is, if land accounted for about 75 percent of the value of real estate in 1774, then Jones's characterization of Blodget's land estimate for 1774—similar to but lower than hers—fits the reconstructed Blodget figure very well. Is it possible that Jones, when she referred to Blodget's land estimate, had in mind his figure for improved land alone? It is true that only the improved land estimate appears on the page in Blodget, cited by Jones. But the value of this land comes to only $52 million, which seems to be much too low to be characterized as being of "the same order of magnitude" as Jones's estimate.

6. This is roughly the share of nonresidential structures (exclusive of public buildings) in the total value of all nonfarm structures in 1840 and 1850. In principle, mills, in addition to public buildings, should also have been dropped from the numerator of this ratio, but there is no readily defensible way to estimate the value of mills and remove them from the numerator.

7. The careful reader of Blodget and Soltow may be led to a different conclusion, since Soltow claims that there were only 577,000 dwellings of free persons in 1798, while Blodget (1810, 58) puts the total of all dwellings of free persons and slaves at 1,010,000 in that year. It is likely that the two are using the term differently: by Soltow to refer to houses, and by Blodget to refer to family dwellings, of which any house may have more than one. But it is true that Blodget's 1798 estimate of "dwelling houses inhabited" (p.58), if it be taken to be equivalent to "families," implies a larger number of free families than Soltow recognizes. Thus, if we deduct 147,000 from Blodget's "dwellings" total, to allow for slave families (838,000 slaves, per Blodget 1810, 58, divided by a family size of 5.7), we arrive at an estimate of 863,000 dwellings inhabited by free families—136,000 more families than Soltow allows for. It seems clear that Soltow and Blodget differ in their view of typical family size in 1798; but that appears not to be the case with respect to Soltow 1798 and Blodget-Goldsmith 1805. Blodget's estimates of dwellings (and thus families) in the 1790s are rather peculiar, as will be seen. While the valuation base of the direct tax seems to have been 1799, Soltow attaches the date 1798 to his estimates.

8. The estimate—or perhaps "guess" is the better word—was previously advanced that no more than three-tenths of the value of structures, exclusive of mills and public buildings, consisted of nonresidential buildings in 1805. Adding mills and public buildings to the totals raises this share to 35 percent.

9. The Massachusetts–New York index was supposed to represent New England and New York; the Adams index, Pennsylvania, Delaware, and Maryland. According to Pitkin, the value of real estate in these two areas was about equal in 1799. The two indexes were therefore weighted equally.

10. The regression equation is $Y = 170,570 + 2,734x + 301z$ where $Y$ = the total value of dwellings; $x$ = brick and stone dwellings; and $z$ = wooden dwellings. While the range of these index numbers is very wide indeed, and there are some implausible figures, on the whole the pattern that emerges is reasonable. That is, it

captures what seem to be probable cost-quality-size differences among the states. Notice that if the index numbers for Massachusetts–New York and Pennsylvania, discussed in the text, capture differential price trends in these two regions, then the disparity between the levels of prices in these two regions was very much smaller in 1799 than in 1840.

11. There was much experimentation with new types of animals, but there seems to have been no widespread adoption of improved breeds before the mid-1840s or 1850s; and even then, most farmers must have been using stock that was not blooded, even to the slightest degree. Indeed, for parts of the period between 1774 and 1860, and for important segments of the United States, the quality of animals, on average, was probably deteriorating rather than improving. Failure to allow in the estimating procedure for changes in the average quality of animals between 1774 and 1840, or 1850, or even 1860, is unlikely to amount to a major source of error, however. See Gray 1941, ch. 35; Bidwell and Falconer 1973, ch.12, 13, 17, 33–38; Bogue 1963, ch. 5 and 6; and Bonner 1964, ch. 9. [Rhode suggests reading Olmstead and Rhode 2008. The introduction of Merin sheep in the 1800s represented an early adoption of improved stock.]

## Chapter Fifteen

1. See Weil 2009, 75, which treats capital accumulation as one part of the growth process but not the main driver. The argument about Germany and Japan is not altogether convincing, because the rate of capital formation helps determines the speed of recovery from the wartime destruction.

2. One needs a measure of the capital stock to perform the growth accounting exercise to calculate TPF.

# References

Abramovitz, Moses. 1950. *Inventories and Business Cycles, with Special Reference to Manufacturer's Inventories*. New York: National Bureau of Economic Research.

———. 1956. "Resource and Output Trends in the United States since 1870." *American Economic Review* 46(2): 5–23.

———. 1989. *Thinking about Growth and Other Essays on Economic Growth and Welfare*. New York: Cambridge University Press.

Abramovitz, Moses, and Paul David. 1973a. "Economic Growth in America: Historical Realities and Neoclassical Parables." *De Economist* 121:251–72.

———. 1973b. "Reinterpreting Economic Growth: Parables and Realities." *American Economic Review* 63(2): 428–39.

Adams, C. F., Jr., W. B. Williams, and J. H. Oberly. 1880. *Taxation of Railroads and Railroad Securities*. New York: Railroad Gazette.

Adams, Donald R., Jr. 1968. "Wage Rates in the Early National Period: Philadelphia, 1785–1830." *Journal of Economic History* 28(3): 404–26.

———. 1975. "Residential Construction Industry in the Early Nineteenth Century." *Journal of Economic History* 35(4): 794–816.

———. 1982. "The Standard of Living during American Industrialization: Evidence from the Brandywine Region, 1800–1860." *Journal of Economic History* 42(4): 903–17.

———. 1986. "Prices and Wages in Maryland, 1750–1850." *Journal of Economic History* 46(3): 625–45.

American Iron and Steel Association. 1912. *Statistics of the American and Foreign Iron Trades: Part I of the Annual Report for 1911*. Philadelphia: American Iron and Steel Association.

Anderson, Ralph V., and Robert E. Gallman. 1977. "Slaves as Fixed Capital: Slave Labor and Southern Economic Development." *Journal of American History* 64(1): 24–46.

Balke, Nathan S., and Robert J. Gordon. 1989. "The Estimation of Prewar Gross National Product: Methodology and New Evidence." *Journal of Political Economy* 97(1): 38–92.

Barger, Harold. 1955. *Distribution's Place in the American Economy since 1869.* Princeton, NJ: Princeton University Press.

Bateman, Fred, and Thomas Weiss. 1981. *A Deplorable Scarcity: The Failure of Industrialization in the Slave Economy.* Chapel Hill: University of North Carolina Press.

Berry, Thomas Senior. 1978. *Revised Annual Estimates of American Gross National Product: Preliminary Annual Estimates of Four Major Components of Demands, 1789–1889. Bostwick Paper No. 3.* Richmond, VA: Bostwick Press.

———. 1988. *Production and Population since 1789: Revised GNP Series in Constant Dollars. Bostwick Paper No. 6.* Richmond, VA: Bostwick Press.

Bidwell, Percy W., and John I. Falconer. 1973. *History of Agriculture in the Northern United States, 1620–1860.* Clifton, NJ: Augustus M. Kelley, reprint edition.

Bishir, Catherine W., Charlotte V. Brown, Carl R. Lounsbury, and Ernest H. Wood III. 1990. *Architects and Builders in North Carolina: A History of the Practice of Building.* Chapel Hill: University of North Carolina Press.

Blodget, Samuel. 1806. *Economica: A Statistical Manual for the United States of America.* Washington: printed by the author.

———. 1810. *Economica: A Statistical Manual for the United States of America, with Additions to the Beginning of the Year 1810.* Washington: printed by the author.

Bogue, Allan G. 1963. *From Prairie to Corn Belt.* Chicago: University of Chicago Press.

Bonner, James C. 1964. *History of Georgia Agriculture, 1732–1860.* Athens: University of Georgia Press.

Brady, Dorothy S. 1964. "Relative Prices in the Nineteenth Century." *Journal of Economic History* 24(2): 145–203.

———. 1966. "Price Deflators for Final Product." In *Output, Employment, and Productivity in the United States after 1800. Studies in Income and Wealth. Vol. 30,* edited by Dorothy S. Brady, 91–115. New York: Columbia University Press.

———. 1972. "Consumption and the Style of Life." In *American Economic Growth: An Economist's History of the United States,* edited by Lance E. Davis et al., 61–89. New York: Harper and Row.

Brewer, Priscilla J. 2000. *From Fireplace to Cookstove: Technology and the Domestic Ideal in America.* Syracuse, NY: Syracuse University Press.

Bull, Marcus. 1830. "Experiments to Determine the Comparative Quantities of Heat." *Transactions of the American Philosophical Society, Held at Philadelphia for Promoting Useful Knowledge* 3:1–64.

Carr, Edward H. 1961. *What Is History?* London: Macmillan.

Carter, Susan, et al., eds. 2006. *Historical Statistics of the United States, Millennial Edition.* New York: Cambridge University Press.

Cole, A. H. 1938. *Wholesale Commodity Prices in the United States, 1700–1860.* Cambridge, MA: Harvard University Press.

Cowan, Ruth Schwartz. 1997. *A Social History of American Technology*. New York: Oxford University Press.

Coyle, Diane. 2014. *GDP: A Brief but Affectionate History*. Princeton, NJ: Princeton University Press.

Cranmer, H. Jerome. 1960. "Canal Investment, 1815–1860." In *Trends in the American Economy in the Nineteenth Century: Studies in Income and Wealth*, Vol. 24, edited by William N. Parker, 547–64. Princeton, NJ: Princeton University Press.

Creamer, Daniel, Sergei Dobrovolsky, and Israel Borenstein. 1960. *Capital in Manufacturing and Mining: Its Formation and Financing*. Princeton, NJ: Princeton University Press.

Danhof, Clarence. 1944. "The Fencing Problem in the Eighteen-Fifties." *Agricultural History* 18(4): 168–86.

David, Paul A. 1962. "The Deflation of Value Added." *Review of Economics and Statistics* 44(2): 148–55.

David, Paul A., and Peter Solar. 1977. "A Bicentenary Contribution to the History of the Cost of Living in America." *Research in Economic History* 2:1–80.

Davis, Joseph H. 2004. "An Annual Index of U.S. Industrial Production, 1790–1915." *Quarterly Journal of Economics* 119(4): 1177-1215.

Davis, Lance E., and Robert E. Gallman. 1973. "The Share of Saving and Investment in Gross National Product during the 19th Century, United States of America." In *Fourth International Conference of Economic History, Bloomington, 1968*, edited by F. C. Lane, 437–66. Paris: Mouton.

———. 1978. "Capital Formation in the United States during the Nineteenth Century." In *Cambridge Economic History of Europe, Vol. VII: The Industrial Economies, Capital, Labour, and Enterprise. Part 2, The United States, Japan, and Russia*, edited by Peter Mathias and M. M. Postan, 1–69. New York: Cambridge University Press.

———. 1994. "Savings, Investment, and Economic Growth: The United States in the 19th Century." In *Capitalism in Context*, edited by John James and Mark Thomas, 202–29. Chicago: University of Chicago Press.

———. 2001. *Evolving Financial Markets and International Capital Flows*. New York: Cambridge University Press.

Davis, Lance E., Robert E. Gallman, and Teresa D. Hutchins. 1987. "The Structure of the Capital Stock on Economic Growth and Decline: The New Bedford Whaling Fleet in the Nineteenth Century." In *Quantity and Quiddity: Essays in U.S. Economic History*, edited by Peter Kilby, 336–98. Middletown, CT: Wesleyan University Press.

———. 1988. "The Decline of U.S. Whaling: Was the Stock of Whales Running Out?" *Business History Review* 62(4): 569–95.

Davis, Lance E., et al. 1972. *American Economic Growth: An Economist's History of the United States*. New York: Harper and Row.

De Bow, J. D. B. 1854. *Statistical View of the United States, Being a Compendium of the Seventh Census*. Washington: Beverly Tucker, Senate Printer.

Deane, Phyllis, and W. A. Cole. 1962. *British Economic Growth, 1688–1959: Trends and Structure*. Cambridge: Cambridge University Press.

Denison, Edward F. 1957. "Theoretical Aspects of Quality Change, Capital Consumption, and Net Capital Formation" In *Problems of Capital Formation: Concepts, Measurement, and Controlling Factors. Studies in Income and Wealth. Vol. 19*, edited by Franco Modigliani. 215–84, Princeton, NJ: Princeton University Press.

———. 1962. *The Sources of Economic Growth in the United States and the Alternatives before Us*. New York: Committee on Economic Development.

Douglas, Paul. 1934. *The Theory of Wages*. New York: MacMillan.

Dwyer, Jeremiah. 1968. "Stoves and Heating Apparatus." In *One Hundred Years of American Commerce. Vol. II*, edited by Chauncey M. Depew, 357–62. New York: Greenwood, orig. 1895.

Easterlin, Richard. 1960. "Interregional Differences on Per Capita Income, Population, and Total Income, 1840–1950." In *Trends in the American Economy in the Nineteenth Century. Studies in Income and Wealth. Vol. 24*, edited by William N. Parker, 73–140. Princeton, NJ: Princeton University Press.

Engerman, Stanley L., and Robert E. Gallman. 1983. "U.S. Economic Growth, 1783–1860." *Research in Economic History* 9:1–46.

Federal Communications Commission. 1939. *Report on the Investigation of the Telephone Industry in the United States*. Washington: Government Printing Office.

Federal Trade Commission. 1926. *National Wealth and Income. 69th Congress, 1st Sess., Senate Document 126*. Washington: Government Printing Office.

Field, Alexander J. 1987. "Modern Business Enterprise as a Capital-Saving Innovation." *Journal of Economic History* 47(2): 473–85.

———. 2009. "US Economic Growth in the Gilded Age." *Journal of Macroeconomics* 31(1): 173–90.

Fishlow, Albert. 1965. *American Railroads and the Transformation of the Antebellum Economy*. Cambridge, MA: Harvard University Press.

———. 1966a. "The American Common School Revival: Fact or Fancy?" In *Industrialization in Two Systems*, edited by Henry Rosovsky, 40–67. New York: Wiley.

———. 1966b. "Levels of Nineteenth Century American Investment in Education." *Journal of Economic History* 26(4): 418–36.

———. 1966c. "Productivity and Technological Change in the Railroad Sector, 1840–1910." In *Output, Employment, and Productivity in the United States after 1899: Studies in Income and Wealth, Vol. 30*, edited by Dorothy S. Brady, 583–646. New York: National Bureau of Economic Research.

Fogel, Robert W. 1999. "Catching Up with the Economy." *American Economic Review* 89(1): 1–21.

Fogel, Robert W., and Stanley L. Engerman. 1974. *Time on the Cross: The Economics of American Negro Slavery, Vol. 1*. Boston: Little, Brown.

———. 1977. "Explaining the Relative Efficiency of Slave Agriculture in the Antebellum South." *American Economic Review* 67(3): 275–96.

Friedman, Milton, and Anna J. Schwartz. 1982. *Monetary Trends in the United States and the United Kingdom: Their Relation to Income, Prices, and Interest Rates, 1867–1975*. Chicago: University of Chicago Press.

Gallman, Robert E. 1956. "Value Added by Agriculture, Mining and Manufacturing, 1840–1880." PhD diss., University of Pennsylvania.

———. 1960. "Commodity Output, 1839–1899." In *Trends in the American Economy in the Nineteenth Century: Studies in Income and Wealth, Vol. 24*, edited by William N. Parker, 13–67. Princeton, NJ: Princeton University Press.

———. 1961. "Estimates of American National Product Made before the Civil War." In *Essays in the Quantitative Study of Economic Growth, Presented to Simon Kuznets on the Occasion of his Sixtieth Birthday*. Special issue, *Economic Development and Cultural Change* 9(3): 392–412.

———. 1963. "A Note of the Patent Office Estimates, 1841–1848." *Journal of Economic History* 23(2): 185–95.

———. 1965. "The Social Distribution of Wealth in the United States of America." In *Third International Conference of Economic History*, 313–24. Paris: Mouton.

———. 1966. "Gross National Product in the United States, 1834–1909." In *Output, Employment, and Productivity in the United States after 1899: Studies in Income and Wealth, Vol. 30*, edited by Dorothy S. Brady, 3–76. New York: Columbia University Press.

———. 1971. "The Statistical Approach: Fundamental Concepts as Applied to History." In *Approaches to American Economic History*, edited by George Rogers Taylor and Lucius F. Ellsworth, 63–86. Charlottesville, VA: University Press of Virginia.

———. 1972a. "Changes in Total U.S. Agricultural Factor Productivity in the Nineteenth Century." *Agricultural History* 46(1): 191–209.

———. 1972b. "The Pace and Pattern of American Economic Growth." In *American Economic Growth: An Economist's History of the United States*, edited by Lance E. Davis et al., 15–60. New York: Harper and Row.

———. 1975. "The Agricultural Sector and the Pace of Economic Growth: U.S. Experience in the Nineteenth Century." In *Essays in Nineteenth Century Economic History*, edited by David C. Klingaman and Richard K. Vedder, 35–76. Athens: Ohio University Press.

———. 1977. "Human Capital in the First 80 Years of the Republic: How Much Did America Owe the Rest of the World?" *American Economic Review* 67(1): 27–31.

———. 1978a. "Comments on 'Investment Strategy in Private Enterprise and the Role of the State Sector, 19th–20th Centuries.'" In *Proceedings of the Sixth International Congress on Economic History*. Copenhagen: Daniels Society for Economic and Social History.

———. 1978b. "Did We Eat Better in 1850?" *Wilson Quarterly* 2(2): 190.

———. 1978c. "Professor Pessen and the 'Egalitarian Myth.'" *Social Science History* 2(2): 194–207.

———. 1980. "Economic Growth." In *Encyclopedia of American Economic History, Vol. I*, edited by Glenn Porter, 133–50. New York: Scribner.

———. 1981. "The 'Egalitarian Myth,' Once Again." *Social Science History* 5(2): 223–34.

———. 1986. "The United States Capital Stock in the Nineteenth Century." In *Long-Term Factors in American Economic Growth: Studies in Income and Wealth, Vol. 51*, edited by Stanley L. Engerman and Robert E. Gallman, 165–213. Chicago: University of Chicago Press.

———. 1987. "Investment Flows and Capital Stocks: U.S. Experience in the Nineteenth Century." In *Quantity and Quiddity: Essays in U.S. Economic History*, edited by Peter Kilby, 214–54. Middletown, CT: Wesleyan University Press.

———. 1992. "American Economic Growth before the Civil War: The Testimony of the Capital Stock Estimates." In *American Economic Growth and Standards of Living before the Civil War*, edited by Robert E. Gallman and John Joseph Wallis, 79–115. Chicago: University of Chicago Press.

———. 1999. "Can We Build National Accounts for the Colonial Period of American History?" *William and Mary Quarterly* 56(1): 23–30.

———. 2000. "Economic Growth and Structural Change in the Long Nineteenth Century." In *Cambridge Economic History of the United States, Vol. II: The Long Nineteenth Century*, edited by Stanley L. Engerman and Robert E. Gallman, 1–56. New York: Cambridge University Press.

Gallman, Robert E., and Edward S. Howle. 1971. "Trends in the Structure of the American Economy since 1840." In *The Reinterpretation of American Economic History*, edited by Robert W. Fogel and Stanley L. Engerman, 25–37. New York: Harper and Row.

———. No date. "Fixed Reproducible Capital in the United States, 1840–1900," mimeographed.

Gallman, Robert E., and Thomas Weiss. 1969. "The Service Industries in the Nineteenth Century." In *Production and Productivity in the Service Industries: Studies in Income and Wealth, Vol. 34*, edited by Victor R. Fuchs, 287–381. New York: Columbia University Press.

Gallman, Robert E., D. E. Swan, J. D. Foust. 1966. "Efficiency and Farm Interdependence in an Agricultural Export Region: Size and Scope of the Matched Sample." Working paper, University of North Carolina.

Giedion, Siegfried. 1948. *Mechanization Takes Command: A Contribution to Anonymous History*. Oxford: Oxford University Press.

Giffen, Robert. 1889. *Growth of Capital*. London: George Bell.

Goldin, Claudia. 1990. *Understanding the Gender Gap: An Economic History of American Women*. New York: Oxford University Press.

Goldin, Claudia, and Frank Lewis. 1975. "The Economic Cost of the American Civil War: Estimates and Implications." *Journal of Economic History* 25(2): 299–308.

Goldin, Claudia, and Robert A. Margo. 1989. "Wages, Prices, and Labor Markets before the Civil War." NBER Working Paper no. 3198. Cambridge, MA: National Bureau of Economic Research.

Goldsmith, Raymond W. 1950. "Measuring National Wealth in a System of Social Accounting." In *Conference on Research in Income and Wealth: Studies in Income and Wealth, Vol. 12*. New York: National Bureau of Economic Research.

———. 1951. "A Perpetual Inventory of National Wealth." In *Conference on Research in Income and Wealth: Studies in Income and Wealth. Vol. 14*. New York: National Bureau of Economic Research.

———. 1952. "The Growth of Reproducible Wealth of the United States of America from 1805 to 1950." In *International Association for Research in Income and Wealth. Income and Wealth of the United States: Trends and Structure, Income and Wealth Series II*. 244–325. London: Bowes and Bowes.

———. 1956. *A Study of Saving in the United States, Vol. 3*. New York: National Bureau of Economic Research.

———. 1982. *The National Balance Sheet of the United States, 1953–1980*. Chicago: University of Chicago Press.

———. 1985. *Comparative National Balance Sheets: A Study of Twenty Countries, 1688–1978*. Chicago: University of Chicago Press.

Goldsmith, Raymond W., and Robert E. Lipsey. 1963. *Studies in the National Balance Sheet of the United States, Vol. I*. Princeton, NJ: Princeton University Press.

Goldsmith, Raymond W., Robert E. Lipsey, and Morris Mendelson. 1963. *Studies in the National Balance Sheet of the United States, Vol. 2*. New York: National Bureau of Economic Research.

Gray, Lewis C. 1941. *History of Agriculture in the Southern United States to 1860, Vol. II*. New York: Peter Smith.

Grebler, Leo, David M. Blank, and Louis Winnick. 1956. *Capital Formation in Residential Real Estate: Trends and Prospects*. Princeton, NJ: Princeton University Press.

Greenwood, Jeremy, Ananth Seshadri, and Mehmet Yorkoglu. 2005. "Engines of Liberation." *Review of Economic Studies* 72:109–33.

Hall, Henry. 1884. "Report on the Shipbuilding Industry of the United States." Tenth Census of the United States, 1880, Vol. VIII. Washington: Government Printing Office.

Hayter, Earl W. 1939. "Barbed Wire Fencing: A Prairie Invention." *Agricultural History* 13(4): 191–207.

Hepburn, A. Barton. 1915. *A History of Currency in the United States*. New York: Macmillan.

Hoenack, Stephen A. 1964. "Appendix I: Part B Historical Censuses and Estimates of Wealth in the United States." In *Measuring the Nation's Wealth:*

*Studies in Income and Wealth, Vol. 29*, edited by John W. Kendrick, 177–218. Washington: Government Printing Office.

Homer, Sidney. 1963. *A History of Interest Rates*. New Brunswick, NJ: Rutgers University Press.

Humphrey, H. N. 1916. "Cost of Fencing Farms in the North Central States." *USDA Bulletin*, no. 321. Washington: Government Printing Office.

Hutchins, John B. 1941. *American Maritime Industries and Public Policy, 1789–1914*. New York: Russell.

Jones, Alice Hanson. 1978. *American Colonial Wealth: Documents and Methods*. 3 Vols., Second Edition. New York: Arno Press.

———. 1980. *Wealth of a Nation to Be*. New York: Columbia University Press.

Jones, Charles I., and Paul M. Romer. 2010. "The New Kaldor Facts: Ideas, Institutions, Population, and Human Capital." *American Economic Journal: Macroeconomics* 2(1): 224–45.

Juster, F. Thomas. 1966. *Household Capital Formation and Financing, 1897–1962*. New York: National Bureau of Economic Research.

Kaldor, Nicholas. 1961. "Capital Accumulation and Economic Growth." In *The Theory of Capital*, edited by L.A. Lutz and D. C. Hague, 177–222. New York: St. Martin's Press.

Keller, Edward A. 1939. *A Study of the Physical Assets, Sometimes Called Wealth, of the United States, 1922–1933*. Notre Dame, IN: Bureau of Economic Research, University of Notre Dame.

Kendrick, John W. 1961. *Productivity Trends in the United States*. New York: National Bureau of Economic Research.

———. 1964. *Measuring the Nation's Wealth: Studies in Income and Wealth, Vol. 29*. Joint Committee Print, 88th Congress, 2nd Sess. Washington: Government Printing Office.

King, Willford Isbell. 1915. *The Wealth and Income of the People of the United States*. New York: Macmillan.

Kuznets, Simon. 1938. "On the Measurement of National Wealth." In *Conference on Research in Income and Wealth: Studies in Income and Wealth*. Vol. 2: 3–61. New York: National Bureau of Economic Research.

———. 1938. *Commodity Flow and Capital Formation*. Vol. I, Publications of the National Bureau of Economic Research, Inc. no. 34. New York: National Bureau of Economic Research.

———. 1946. *National Product since 1869*. New York: National Bureau of Economic Research.

———. 1957. "Comment on Denison." In *Problems of Capital Formation: Concepts, Measurement, and Controlling Factors. Studies in Income and Wealth. Vol. 19*, edited by Franco Modigliani, 271–79. Princeton, NJ: Princeton University Press.

———. 1961a. *Capital in the American Economy: Its Formation and Financing*. Princeton, NJ: Princeton University Press.

———. 1961b. "Annual Estimates, 1869–1953, T-Tables 1–15 (Technical Tables Underlying Series in Supplement to Summary Volume of Capital and Financing)." New York: National Bureau of Economic Research. http://www.nber .org/data-appendix/c1454/appendix.pdf.

Lebergott, Stanley. 1960. "Wage Trends, 1800–1900." In *Trends in the American Economy in the Nineteenth Century: Studies in Income and Wealth, Vol. 24*, edited by William N. Parker, 449–98. Princeton, NJ: Princeton University Press.

———. 1964. *Manpower in Economic Growth*. New York: McGraw-Hill.

———. 1976. *The American Economy: Income, Wealth, and Want*. Princeton, NJ: Princeton University Press.

———. 1984. *The Americans: An Economic Report*. New York: W. W. Norton.

———. 1985. "The Demand for Land: The United States, 1820–1860." *Journal of Economic History* 65(2): 181–212.

———. 1993. *Pursuing Happiness: American Consumers in the Twentieth Century*. Princeton, NJ: Princeton University Press.

———. 1996. *Consumer Expenditures: New Measures and Old Motives*. Princeton, NJ: Princeton University Press.

Lillard, Richard Gordon. 1947. *The Great Forest*. New York: Alfred A. Knopf.

Lindert, Peter H. 1988. "Long-Run Trends in American Farmland Values." Agricultural History Center working paper no. 45, University of California, Davis. Available at http://gpih.ucdavis.edu/files/Lindert.pdf.

Margo, Robert A. 1992. "Wages and Prices in the Antebellum Period: A Survey and New Evidence." In *American Economic Growth and Standards of Living before the Civil War*, edited by Robert E. Gallman and John Joseph Wallis, 172–210. Chicago: University of Chicago Press.

Martin, Robert F. 1939. *National Income in the United States, 1799–1938*. National Industrial Conference Board Study no. 241. New York: National Industrial Conference Board.

McAlester, Virginia and Lee. 1984. *A Field Guide to American Houses*. New York: Alfred A Knopf.

New York State. 1834–52. Auditor's report.

Nordhaus, William D. 1996. "Do Real Output and Real Wage Measures Capture Reality? The History of Lighting Suggests Not." In *The Economics of New Goods*, edited by Robert J. Gordon and Timothy F. Bresnahan, 27–70. Chicago: University of Chicago Press.

North, Douglass. 1960. "The United States Balance of Payments, 1790–1860." In *Trends in the American Economy in the Nineteenth Century: Studies in Income and Wealth. Vol. 24*, edited by William N. Parker, 573–628. Princeton. NJ: Princeton University Press.

Olmstead, Alan L., and Paul W. Rhode. 2008. *Creating Abundance: Biological Innovation and American Agricultural Development*. New York: Cambridge University Press, 2008.

Olney, Martha. 1991. *Buy Now, Pay Later: Advertising, Credit, and Consumer Durables in the 1920s*. Chapel Hill: University of North Carolina.

Parker, William N., ed. 1960. *Trends in the American Economy in the Nineteenth Century: Studies in Income and Wealth, Vol. 24*. Princeton, NJ: Princeton University Press.

Pessen, Edward. 1977. "Equality and Opportunity in America, 1800–1940." *Wilson Quarterly* 1 (5): 136–42.

Peterson, Charles E., ed. 1971. *The Rules of Work of the Carpenters' Company of the City and County of Philadelphia*. Princeton, NJ: Pyne Press.

Piketty, Thomas. 2014. *Capital in the Twenty-First Century*. Translated by Arthur Goldhammner. Cambridge, MA: Harvard University Press.

Piketty, Thomas, and Gabriel Zucman. 2014. "Capital Is Back: Wealth-Income Ratio in Rich Countries, 1700–2100." *Quarterly Journal of Economics* 129(3): 1255–1310, and online appendix.

Philipsen, Dirk. 2015. *The Little Big Number: How GDP Came to Rule the World and What to Do about It*. Princeton, NJ: Princeton University Press.

Pitkin, Timothy. 1816. *Statistical View of the Commerce of the United States*. Hartford, CT: Charles Hosmer.

———. 1835. *A Statistical View of the Commerce of the United States of America*. New Haven, CT: Durrie and Peck.

Poulson, Barry Warren. 1975. *Value Added in Manufacturing, Mining, and Agriculture in the American Economy from 1809 to 1839*. New York: Arno Press.

Price, Jacob. 1980. *Capital and Credit in British Overseas Trade: The View from the Chesapeake, 1700–1776*. Cambridge. MA: Harvard University Press.

Primack, Martin L. 1962. "Farm Formed Capital in American Agriculture, 1850 to 1910." PhD diss., University of North Carolina.

*Railway Age*. 1950. 128, no. 1 (7 January): 246.

Ransom, Roger, and Richard Sutch. 1975. "The Impact of the Civil War and Emancipation on Southern Agriculture." *Explorations in Economic History* 12(1): 1–28.

Reynolds, R. V., and Albert H. Pierson. 1942. "Fuel Wood Used in the United States, 1630–1930." USDA circular no. 641. Washington: Government Printing Office.

Romer, Christina D. 1989. "The Prewar Business Cycle Reconsidered: New Estimates of Gross National Product, 1869–1908." *Journal of Political Economy* 97(1): 1–37.

Rostow, Walt. 1960. *The Stages of Economic Growth: A Non-Communist Manifesto*. Cambridge: Cambridge University Press.

Rothenberg, Winifred. 1988. "The Emergence of Farm Labor Markets and the Transformation of the Rural Economy: Massachusetts, 1750–1855." *Journal of Economic History* 48(3): 537–66.

Ruggles, Richard, and Nancy Ruggles. 1961. "Concepts of Real Capital Stocks and Services." In *Conference on Research in Income and Wealth. Output, Input, and Productivity Measurement: Studies in Income and Wealth. Vol. 25.* 387–412. Princeton, NJ: Princeton University Press.

Sargent, C. S. 1884. *Tenth Census of the United States, 1880: Vol. 9. The Forests of North America (Exclusive of Mexico).* Washington: Government Printing Office.

Schaefer, Donald F. 1967. "A Quantitative Description and Analysis of the Growth of the Pennsylvania Anthracite Coal Industry, 1820 to 1865." PhD diss., University of North Carolina.

Schurr, Sam H., and Bruce C. Netschert. 1960. *Energy in the American Economy, 1850–1975: An Economic Study of Its History and Prospects.* Baltimore: Johns Hopkins University Press for Resources for the Future.

Seaman, Ezra C. 1852. *Essays on the Progress of Nations.* New York: Scribner.

Segal, Harvey. 1961. "Cycles in Canal Construction." In *Canals and American Economic Development,* edited by Carter Goodrich, 169–215. New York: Columbia University Press.

Seybert, Adam. 1818. *Statistical Annals.* Philadelphia: Thomas Dobson.

Shaw, William Howard. 1947. *Value of Commodity Output since 1869.* New York: National Bureau of Economic Research.

Simon, Matthew. 1960. "The United States Balance of Payments, 1861–1900." In *Trends in the American Economy in the Nineteenth Century: Studies in Income and Wealth. Vol. 24,* edited by William N. Parker, 629–711. New York: National Bureau of Economic Research.

Smallzried, Kathleen Ann. *The Everlasting Pleasure: Influences on America's Kitchens, Cooks and Cookery, from 1565 to the Year 2000.* New York: Appleton-Century-Crofts, 1956.

Smith, Walter B. 1963. "Wage Rates on the Erie Canal." *Journal of Economic History* 23(2): 298–311.

Sokoloff, Kenneth L. "Invention, Innovation, and Manufacturing Productivity Growth in the Antebellum Northeast." In *American Economic Growth and Standards of Living before the Civil War,* edited by Robert E. Gallman and John Joseph Wallis, 345–78. Chicago: University of Chicago Press.

Solow, Robert M. 1957. "Technical Change and the Aggregate Production Function." *Review of Economics and Statistics* 39(3): 312–20.

Soltow, Lee. 1975. *Men and Wealth in the United States, 1850–1870.* New Haven: Yale University Press.

———. 1984. "Wealth Inequality in the United States in 1798 and 1860." *Review of Economics and Statistics* 66(3): 444–51.

———. 1987. "The Distribution of Income in the United States in 1798: Estimates Based on the Federal Housing Inventory." *Review of Economics and Statistics* 69(1): 181–85.

Steckel, Richard H. 1992. "Statute and Living Standards in the United States." In *American Economic Growth and Standards of Living before the Civil War,* edited by Robert E. Gallman and John Joseph Wallis, 265–308. Chicago: University of Chicago Press.

Stow, F. H. 1859. *Capitalist Guide and Railway Annual for 1859*. New York: Samuel T. Callahan.

Strauss, Frederick, and Louis H. Bean. 1940. "Gross Income and Indices of Farm Production and Prices in the United States, 1869–1937." *USDA Technical Bulletin* no. 703. Washington: Government Printing Office.

Thompson, Robert L. 1947. *Wiring a Continent*. Princeton, NJ: Princeton University Press.

Tostlebe, Alvin S. 1957. *Capital in Agriculture: Its Formation and Financing since 1870*. Princeton, NJ: Princeton University Press.

Towne, Marvin W., and Wayne D. Rasmussen. 1960. "Farm Gross Product and Gross Investment in the Nineteenth Century." In *Trends in the American Economy in the Nineteenth Century: Studies in Income and Wealth, Vol. 24*, edited by William N. Parker, 255–312. New York: National Bureau of Economic Research.

Trentmann, Frank. 2012. Introduction to *The Oxford Handbook of the History of Consumption*, edited by Frank Trentmann, 1–25. New York: Oxford University Press.

Tucker, George. 1843. *Progress of the United States in Population and Wealth in Fifty Years: As Exhibited by the Decennial Census*. New York: Hunt's Merchant Magazine.

US Bureau of the Census. 1902. *Twelfth Census of the United States. Vol. V. Agriculture, Part I. Farms, Live Stock, and Animal Products*. Washington: Government Printing Office.

———. 1906. *Special Report: Telephones and Telegraphs, 1902*. Washington: Government Printing Office.

———. 1907. *Wealth, Debt, and Taxation*. Washington: Government Printing Office.

———. 1908. *Census of Transportation by Water*. Washington: Government Printing Office.

———. 1913. *Thirteenth Census of the United States. Vol. XI. Mines and Quarries, 1909*. Washington: Government Printing Office.

———. 1929. *Transportation by Water, 1916*. Washington: Government Printing Office.

———. 1949. *Historical Statistics of the United States, 1789 to 1945: A Supplement to the Statistical Abstract of the United States*. Washington: Government Printing Office.

———. 1952. *US Census of Agriculture: 1950, Vol. II: General Report, Statistics by Subjects*. Washington: Government Printing Office.

———. 1960. *Historical Statistics of the United States, Colonial Times to 1957*. Washington: Government Printing Office.

————. 1975. *Historical Statistics of the United States, Bicentennial Edition*. Washington: Government Printing Office.

US Bureau of Navigation. 1923. *Annual Report*. Washington: Government Printing Office.

US Census Office————. 1841. *Compendium of the Enumeration of the Inhabitants and Statistics of the United States as Obtained at the Department of State, from the Returns of the Sixth Census*. Washington: Blair and Rives.

————. 1853a. *Abstract of the Seventh Census*. Washington: Government Printing Office.

————. 1853b. *Seventh Census of the United States, 1850*. Washington: Robert Armstrong, Public Printer.

————. 1860. *Instructions to US Marshals*. Washington: Government Printing Office.

————. 1864. *Eighth Census of the United States: Agriculture of the United States in 1860*. Washington: Government Printing Office.

————. 1866. *Statistics of the United States (including Mortality, Property, etc.) in 1860*. Washington: Government Printing Office.

————. 1872. *Ninth Census of the United States. Vol. 3. The Statistics of the Wealth and Industry of the United States*. Washington. Government Printing Office.

————. 1883a. *Tenth Census of the United States, 1880. Vol. III. Report of the Products of Agriculture*. Washington: Government Printing Office.

————. 1883b. *Tenth Census of the United States, 1880. Vol. IV. Report on the Agencies of Transportation*. Washington: Government Printing Office.

————. 1884a. *Tenth Census of the United States, 1880. Vol. VII. Report on Valuation, Taxation, and Public Indebtedness in the United States*. Washington: Government Printing Office.

————. 1884b. *Tenth Census of the United States, 1880. Vol. X. Productivity, Technology, and Uses of Petroleum and Its Products*. Washington: Government Printing Office.

————. 1884c. *Valuation, Taxation, and Public Indebtedness in the United States, as Returned at the Tenth Census*. Washington. Government Printing Office.

————. 1885. *Tenth Census of the United States, 1880. Vol. XIII. Statistics and Technology of the Precious Metals*. Washington: Government Printing Office.

————. 1886. *Tenth Census of the United States. Vol. 15. Report on the Mining Industries of the United States*. Washington: Government Printing Office.

————. 1892a. *Eleventh Census of the United States. Vol. 7. Mineral Industries*. Washington: Government Printing Office.

————. 1892b. *Eleventh Census of the United States. Vol. 6. Manufacturing Industries. Part I. Totals for States and Industries*. Washington. Government Printing Office.

————. 1892c. *Report on Mineral Industries in the United States at the Eleventh Census, 1890*. Washington: Government Printing Office.

———. 1895a. *Report on Transportation Business in the United States at the Eleventh Census, 1890. Vol. 14. Part I. Transportation by Land.* Washington: Government Printing Office.

———. 1895b. *Report on Transportation Business in the United States at the Eleventh Census, 1890. Vol. 14. Part II. Transportation by Water.* Washington: Government Printing Office.

———. 1895c. *Report on Wealth, Debt, and Taxation at the Eleventh Census, 1890. Part II. Valuation and Taxation.* Washington: Government Printing Office.

———. 1897. *Census Compendium, 1890. Part 3.* Washington: Government Printing Office.

———. 1902. *Twelfth Census of the United States. Vol. V. Agriculture. Part I.* Washington: Government Printing Office.

US Department of Agriculture. 1871. *Report of the Commissioner of Agriculture 1871.* Washington, DC: Government Printing Office.

———. 1924. *Bureau of Agricultural Economics, Atlas of American Agriculture. Part I. Section E.* Washington, DC: Government Printing Office.

———. 1925. *Yearbook of Agriculture, 1924.* Washington, DC: Government Printing Office.

———. 1936–. *Agriculture Statistics.* Washington, DC: Government Printing Office.

———. *Monthly Crop Reporter.* Washington, DC: Government Printing Office.

US Department of State. 1841. *Compendium of the Inhabitants and Statistics of the United States as Obtained at the Department State from the Returns of the Sixth Census.* Washington: Blair and Rives.

US Director of the Mint. 1929. *Annual Report of the Director of the Mint for the Fiscal Year Ended in June 30, 1929.* Washington: Government Printing Office.

US Senate. 1865/66. Senate Executive Document 49. 39th Congress, 1st Session. Washington: Government Printing Office.

———. 1893. *Wholesale Prices, Wages and Transportation Report of the Senate Committee on Finance. 52nd Congress, 2nd Session, Senate Report 1394. Vol. 3, Part 2.* Washington: Government Printing Office.

Ulmer, Melville J. 1960. *Capital in Transportation, Communications, and Public Utilities: Its Formation and Financing.* Princeton, NJ: Princeton University Press.

Uselding, Paul. 1971. "Conjectural Estimates of Gross Human Capital Inflows to the American Economy, 1790–1860." *Explorations in Economic History* 9(1): 49–62.

Usher, Dan. 1980. Introduction to *The Measurement of Capital. Studies in Income and Wealth, Vol. 45*, edited by Dan Usher. 1–22. Chicago: University of Chicago Press.

Vatter, Harold G. 1967. "Has There Been a Twentieth-Century Consumer Durables Revolution?" *Journal of Economic History* 27(1): 1–16.

Warren, George F., and Frank A. Pearson. 1932. Wholesale Prices for 213 Years, 1720 to 1932. Part I. Cornell University Agricultural Experiment Station Memoir 142. Ithaca, NY.

Weeks, Joseph D. 1886. "Statistics of Wages in Manufacturing Industries." Tenth Census, 1880, Vol. XX. Washington: Government Printing Office.

Weil, David N. 2009. *Economic Growth, 2nd ed.* Boston: Pearson.

Weiss, Thomas J. 1967. "The Service Sector in the United States, 1839–1899." PhD diss., University of North Carolina.

———. 1975. *The Service Sector in the United States, 1839 through 1899.* New York: Arno Press.

———. 1992. "U.S. Labor Force Estimates and Economic Growth, 1800–1860." In *American Economic Growth and Standards of Living before the Civil War*, edited by Robert E. Gallman and John Joseph Wallis. 19–75, Chicago: University of Chicago Press.

Wheeler, Gervase. 1855. *Homes for the People in Suburb and Country.* New York: Scribner.

Williamson, Jeffrey G. 1974. "Watersheds and Turning Points: Conjectures on the Long-term Impact of Civil War Financing." *Journal of Economic History* 34(3): 636–61.

Winfrey, R. 1935. "Statistical Analysis of Industrial Property Retirements." Iowa Engineering Experiment Station Bulletin 125. Ames, IA: Iowa Engineering Experiment Station.

Winnick, Louis. 1953. "Wealth Estimates for Residential Real Estate, 1890–1950." PhD diss., Columbia University.

Wright, Carroll D. 1900. *The History and Growth of the United States Census.* Washington: Government Printing Office.

Young, Allan H., and John C. Musgrave. 1980. "Estimation of Capital Stock in the United States." In *The Measurement of Capital. Studies in Income and Wealth. Vol. 45*, edited by Dan Usher. 23–82. Chicago: University of Chicago Press.

# Index